Red on Red

Red on Red

Native American Literary Separatism

Craig S. Womack

University of Minnesota Press
Minneapolis
London

All royalties earned from the sale of this book will be donated to the Muskogee Nation Language Preservation Program.

Published by the University of Minnesota Press
111 Third Avenue South, Suite 290
Minneapolis, MN 55401-2520
http://www.upress.umn.edu

Library of Congress Cataloging-in-Publication Data

Womack, Craig S.
   Red on red : Native American literary separatism / Craig S. Womack
     p.   cm.
   Includes index.
   ISBN 978-0-8166-3022-6 (hc). — ISBN 978-0-8166-3023-3 (pb).
     1. American literature — Indian authors — History and criticism.
   2. Group identity in literature.   3. Indians in literature.
   I. Title.
   PS153.I52W66   2000
   810.9'897 — dc21   99-38735

Printed in the United States of America on acid-free paper

The University of Minnesota is an equal-opportunity educator and employer.

11 10 09 08   10 9 8 7 6 5 4

Contents

Acknowledgments

Osage scholar Robert Warrior and Creek scholar Tsianina Lomawaima gave me excellent readings of the original manuscript submitted for this book. I am especially grateful for their willingness to look beyond the rough nature of the early draft and to speak on behalf of the book's potential. I would like to thank my great-aunt, Barbara Coachman, for stories, instruction, and limitless kindness. At the University of Oklahoma, Professor Geary Hobson has, without compromise, emphasized to me the importance of looking at Native literatures from Indian viewpoints, and I've learned from him both in and out of the classroom. Michael Manley deserves thanks for taking me out to the Indian Baptist Church in Weleetka that he attends, there near my dad's hometown, and for many hilarious stories during these trips, including the cockroach story. Helen Chalakee Burgess and her husband, Jim, graciously allowed me to camp with them at Tallahassee Grounds for Green Corn the year the dissertation form of the book was written, and I want to thank them for providing this place for me, and other friends, to come. Linda Alexander deserves a very special thanks for the Turtle story she told to me, contained in the pages of this book, and the many other stories she tells in the Creek community. She is the consummate Creek literary artist. The love and hard work of members of New Tallahassee stomp grounds inspire me ever onward. I'll never forget coming from my place under the arbors, back into camp, and finding Joy reading the manuscript of this book. She's been a supportive, careful reader and much more. My partner, Gerardo Tristan, had to live with me while I wrote this, not an easy task, and the book couldn't have been written without his loving presence. Finally, my mom and dad, Coy and Wilma Womack, are the two most generous people I know, and they have supported me through all this work.

INTRODUCTION

American Indian Literary Self-Determination

My purpose in writing *Red on Red* is to contribute, probably in a small way, toward opening up a dialogue among Creek people, specifically, and Native people, more generally, regarding what constitutes meaningful literary efforts. My attempts toward such a conversation, I hope, are more suggestive than prescriptive, more a working out of beginnings rather than endings, more gauged toward encouraging tribal people to talk about literature rather than dictating the terms of such a dialogue. My greatest wish is that tribes, and tribal members, will have an increasingly important role in evaluating tribal literatures. It goes without saying that I cannot speak for Creek people or anyone else; however, I do have the responsibility as a Creek-Cherokee critic to try to include Creek perspectives in my approaches to Native literature, especially given the wealth of Creek wisdom on the subject. This book arises out of the conviction that Native literature, and the criticism that surrounds it, needs to see more attention devoted to tribally specific concerns.

This study, unfortunately, does not include all Creek writers and artists. A number of people, such as Vincent Mendoza, Eddie Chuculate, Susanna Factor, Helen Chalakee Burgess, and others, deserve to be included. Jim Pepper's horn probably belongs in here somewhere. Creek author Thomas E. Moore, writing under the nom de plume William Harjo, continued his version of the Fus Fixico tradition in the 1930s for Oklahoma City and Tulsa newspapers in a regular Sunday feature entitled *Sour Sofke*. Stephanie Berryhill's wonderful series on original Creek allottees, in which she records the language of elders in all its beauty without trying to shape it into "proper" English, is superlative work that has been appearing as a regular installment in the *Muskogee Nation News*. Durango Mendoza's short story "Summer Water and Shirley" is a beautiful evocation of a Creek worldview that could be discussed in these pages.[1]

Earlier writers offer further possibilities for study: Charles Gibson, a journalist and contemporary of Alexander Posey, wrote comic caricatures in Red English,[2] and G. W. Grayson recounted his Civil War experience in a very interesting autobiography.[3] In the final analysis, limited by the demands of time and the strictures of publication in terms of length requirements, I made the trade-off between writing a "perfect" book and a book that actually appears in print.

Just as there are a number of realities that constitute Indian identity — rez, urban, full-blood, mixed-blood, language speakers, nonspeakers, gay, straight, and many other possibilities — there are also a number of legitimate approaches to analyzing Native literary production. Some of these, I will argue in this book, are more effective than others; nonetheless, *Red on Red* is merely a point on this spectrum, not the spectrum itself. I do not believe in a critical approach that preempts or cancels out all those that came before it. In fact, I will try to point out the ways in which tribal authors are influenced by those writers in their own tribes who preceded them. Although we are in dire need of examination of new ways to engage in the discipline rather than unquestioned acceptance of what we have inherited under the rubric Native studies, we have nevertheless been passed down an important intellectual tradition built not only on the last thirty years or so, in terms of the rise of Native studies programs in universities, but on past generations of Native writers and thinkers.

Indian people have authored a lot of books, a history that reaches back to the 1770s in terms of writing in English, and hundreds of years before contact in terms of Mayan and Aztec pictoglyphic alphabets in which were written the vast libraries of Mesoamerica. As rich as oral tradition is, we also have a vast, and vastly understudied, written tradition. *Red on Red* assumes that attention to this Native-authored written tradition should prove valuable toward formulating literary theory. We have a large group of authors available for study, including Samson Occum, David Cusick, William Apess, George Copway, Elias Boudinot, John Rollins Ridge, Peter Dooyentate Clark, Elias Johnson, Sarah Winnemucca, William Warren, Alice Callahan, Simon Pokagon, and E. Pauline Johnson, as a mere sampling of Native people writing before the turn of the century. This does not even include those writing for periodicals and newspapers, or the early-twentieth-century writers who are often overlooked, as well. These are some of our ancestral voices, the pioneers, those who came before us whose writings paved the way for what Native authors can do today. Nineteenth-century Indian resistance did not merely take the form of plains warriors on horseback; Indian people authored books that often argued for Indian rights and criticized land theft. In addition to publishing books, many of these authors engaged in other rhetorical acts such as national speaking tours lobbying for Native rights. Their life stories, as well as their literary ideas, provide a useful study of the evolution of Native thought that has led up to contemporary notions of sovereignty and literature. Not nearly enough of this intellectual history has been brought to bear on a study of contemporary Native writings. Most approaches to the "Native American Literary Renaissance" have proceeded as if the Indian discovered the novel, the short story, and the poem only yesterday.

Because of these factors, I do not bother much in this book with the skepticism of postmodernism in relation to history. It is way too premature for Native scholars to deconstruct history when we haven't yet constructed it. We need, for example, to recover the nineteenth century, especially in terms of understanding what Native writers were up to during that time and how their struggles have evolved toward what Indian writers can say in print today, as well as the foundational principles they provide for an indigenous criticism. Abenaki poet Cheryl Savageau, in a personal correspondence that she gave me permission to publish, said this:

> I never even encountered the word "essentialist" before coming to grad school, and then it was thrown at me like a dirty word, mostly because I wrote something about Native writers and the land in a paper.
> ... The same professor who labeled me "essentialist," said there was no truth, no history, just lots of people's viewpoints. I argued that some things actually did happen. That some versions of history are not just a point of view, but actual distortions and lies.
> It is just now, when we are starting to tell our stories that suddenly there is no truth. It's a big cop out as far as I'm concerned, a real political move by the mainstream to protect itself from the stories that Native people, African Americans, gay and lesbian folks ... are telling. If everybody's story is all of a sudden equally true, then there is no guilt, no

accountability, no need to change anything, no need for reparations, no arguments for sovereign nation status, and their positions of power are maintained.

...As I write this [statement about intellectuals who seem smart and have garnered a lot of power] I can hear my grandmother saying, "but smart and good aren't the same things." Such an essentialist, huh?

So, at least until we get our stories told, especially in terms of establishing a body of Native criticism in relation to nineteenth-century writings, postmodernism may have some limitations in regards to its applicability to Native scholarship. Encouragingly, things have started to change, and we see more and more Native scholars examining the nineteenth century and tracing developments in this century as well that lead up to the great outpouring of Indian literature we have seen recently. Osage writer Robert Warrior, I think, has provided us with incredibly important models in these regards, especially the way he traces out the intellectual underpinnings of the Indian movement through several decades this century in his work *Like a Hurricane: The Indian Movement from Alcatraz to Wounded Knee*. His work will influence many of us in the years to come.

I would like to think, then, that I have not written *Red on Red* in a rejectionist mode but that, to the contrary, I seek to examine these histories to search for those ideas, articulated by Indian people, that best serve a contemporary critical framework. More specifically, in terms of a Creek national literature, the process has been based on the assumption that it is valuable to look toward Creek authors and their works to understand Creek writing. My argument is not that this is the *only* way to understand Creek writing but an important one given that literatures bear some kind of relationship to communities, both writing communities and the community of the primary culture, from which they originate.

In arguing, then, that one viable approach is to examine Creek authors to understand Creek texts, or, more generally, Native authors to understand Native textual production, this study assumes that there *is* such a thing as a Native perspective and that seeking it out is a worthwhile endeavor. I do not subscribe, in other words, to the notion that a Native perspective is, at best, problematic, if not impossible. I feel that Native perspectives have to do with allowing Indian people to speak for themselves, that is to say, with prioritizing Native voices. Those voices may vary in quality, but they rise out of a historical reality wherein Native people have been excluded from discourse concerning their own cultures, and Indian people must be, ultimately will be, heard. Native viewpoints are important because, to quote Métis scholar and activist Howard Adams, the state, rather than Indians, controls "the mental means of production."[4] Adams goes on to say:

> Aboriginal consciousness cannot be a facade; it is an intrinsic or inner essence that lies somewhere between instinct and intuition, and it evolves from the humanness and spirituality of our collective, Aboriginal community. Without an indigenous consciousness, Indians, Métis, and Inuit peoples' only claim to Aboriginality is race and heritage. That is not enough to achieve true liberation. To accomplish self-determination, we need more than racial pride. We must have Aboriginal nationalism, an understanding of the state's capitalist ideology and its oppression, and, ultimately, a counter-consciousness.[5]

The idea of a Native consciousness interests me. The critics of Native literary nationalism have faulted Native specialists with a fundamental naïveté, claiming we argue that Native perspectives are pure, authoritative, uncontaminated by European influences. This misses the point. Native viewpoints are necessary because the "mental means of production" in regards to analyzing Indian cultures have been owned, almost exclusively, by non-Indians. Radical Native viewpoints, voices of difference rather than commonality, are called for to disrupt the powers of the literary status quo as well as the powers of the state — there is a link between thought and activism, surely. Such disruption does not come about by merely emphasizing that all things Native are, in reality, filtered through contact with Europe, that there is no "uncorrupted" Indian reality in this postcontact world we live in. This is an assimilationist ideology, a retreat into sameness and blending in.

To be sure, there is no one pure or authoritative act that constitutes Native literary criticism. We can only take such a notion so far, though. The postmodernists might laugh at claims of prioritizing insider status, questioning the very nature of what constitutes an insider and pointing out that no pure Creek, or Native, viewpoint exists, that Native and non-Native are constantly deconstructing each other. In terms of a reality check, however, we might remind ourselves that authenticity and insider and outsider status are, in fact, often discussed in Native communities, especially given the historical reality that outsiders have so often been the ones interpreting things Indian. Further, it seems foolhardy to me to abandon a search for the affirmation of a national literary identity simply to fall in line with the latest literary trend. The construction of such an identity reaffirms the real truth about our place in history — we are not mere victims but active agents in history, innovators of new ways, of Indian ways, of thinking and being and speaking and authoring in this world created by colonial contact.

Whatever we might say about the inherent problems concerning what constitutes an Indian viewpoint, we can still reasonably assert that such a viewpoint exists and has been silenced throughout U.S. history to the degree that it finally needs to be heard. Whatever one might argue about postmodern representation, there is the legal reality of tribal sovereignty, recognized by the U.S. Constitution and defined over the last 160 years by the Supreme Court, that affects the everyday lives of individuals and tribal nations and, therefore, has something to do with tribal literatures as well.

Take as an example earlier writers: let's say the novelists, autobiographers, and poets of the nineteenth century; as another group, the writers, such as Charles Eastman, Carlos Montezuma, and Gertrude Bonnin, associated with the Society of American Indians (SAI) in the early part of this century; then, finally, the Native novelists of the 1920s and 1930s. In many cases, these earlier writers were uncertain or hesitant about whether a Native voice, Native viewpoint, the narration of tribal life, or even a Native future was possible. In a short time, Native writing has come a long way toward legitimizing tribal experience as an appropriate subject for writing and, most importantly, toward assuming tribal life will continue in the future. The uncertainty of this earlier epoch seems a little like a first cousin to the ambiguity of this later postmodern criticism with its tendency to decenter everything, including the legitimacy of a Native perspective. This kind of criticism hearkens back to the earlier days of questioning whether a Native voice was even possible. No matter how slick the literary strategy that gets us there, this seems the wrong political move to me.

To take this one step further, the primary purpose of this study is not to argue for canonical inclusion or opening up Native literature to a broader audience. Efforts toward that end may be necessary for forming broader alliances, and others have taken up these issues in other books. This study takes a different tack. I say that tribal literatures are not some branch waiting to be grafted onto the main trunk. Tribal literatures are the *tree,* the oldest literatures in the Americas, the most American of American literatures. We *are* the canon. Native people have been on this continent at least thirty thousand years, and the stories tell us we have been here even longer than that, that we were set down by the Creator on this continent, that we originated here. For much of this time period, we have had literatures. Without Native American literature, *there is no American canon.* We should not allow ourselves, through the definitions we choose and the language we use, to ever assume we are outside the canon; we should not play along and confess to being a second-rate literature. Let Americanists struggle for *their* place in the canon. (Understand this is not an argument for inclusion — I am saying with all the bias I can muster that *our* American canon, the Native literary canon of the Americas, predates *their* American canon. I see them as two separate canons.)

Some Native American writers have made inclusionary arguments, claiming that they do not wish to be considered "just an Indian writer." My problem is with the word "just," and my question is, why not? When we use this kind of language, admitting lesser roles for ourselves, to what degree are we internalizing dominant culture racism? What's wrong with being an Indian writer? Why is that a diminished role among writers? Who made up these rules? Why should we want to adhere to them? Does a description of Faulkner as a Southern writer make him any less an important figure? Should his Nobel Prize be taken back because he was "just a Southern writer"? Just what is there to write about that is more important than Native authors testifying to surviving genocide and advocating sovereignty and survival? Here, I am endorsing Flannery O'Connor's well-known argument that the deeper an author delves into her own home country, the more universal and powerful her writing becomes.

The current state of Native literature is, at least partially, a colonized one. This colonization can be seen in many forms, but I'll mention a few examples from the academic end, since that is an arena I operate in frequently. One is the way Native literary specialists must present their work at Modern Language Association conferences (not a bad thing in and of itself); but as of yet, MLA has few, if any, ties to Indian communities. The degree to which such participation is voluntary for Native lit scholars is somewhat questionable, since he or she must go to MLA for job interviews and to present papers, or to other conferences equally removed from Indian communities, to remain credible in his or her department and to get tenure if the scholar works, or ever wants to work, in an English department. Of course, MLA has begun to open up spaces for building a body of interest in important underdeveloped areas of Native literary inquiry, such as panels on nineteenth-century Native authors, so again, the institution, as monolithic as it is, is not to be totally discredited.

Another example of the colonized state of Native literature might be the way in which teaching jobs in the field are often advertised as "ethnic literature" slots or housed in "ethnic literature" departments, calling for academics who have broad comparative backgrounds rather than training in tribally specific cultures. Often, the candidate soon discovers, even jobs advertised as Native lit positions are really minority lit jobs. Having experience with a specific tribe often discredits the applicants for these positions. Departments often look for someone to do multicultural literature rather than Native studies; teach an Amy Tan novel now and then, throw in a little Ralph Ellison, a native author once in a while, and string it all together with the same damn Bakhtin quotes we've all heard a million times, reducing literary studies to little more than an English department version of the melting pot. Everybody loses — this is demeaning and destructive to Asian American studies, African American studies, Native American studies, and other minority literatures, a system that makes it difficult to hire those with close ties to the subject matter they teach. Fortunately, this is not always the case — a number of English departments, and even some of the ethnic literature departments, have hired people for very solid Native lit jobs where the candidate teaches only Native literature and develops a core program of Indian literature courses within the department — but enough of the multicultural recruiting exists to cause concern.

Another example of colonialism related to teaching and hiring might be the number of search committees for slots in Native literature with no Native people on the committee. As difficult as that is to justify from an Indian viewpoint, I know I have sat in many a job interview facing that very situation, answering questions posed by people who did not even know what to ask. Or what about this — Native studies progams with few or sometimes even no Native faculty? What would we say about African American studies or Chicano studies programs that were run without African Americans or Chicanos? The appropriation of Native issues by non-Natives is still acceptable in Native studies in ways that have long been unacceptable in regards to other minorities. Native scholars have faced variants of these stories in a thousand different ways, so there is no use in belaboring the point here, other than to say that surely we need to work toward creating a better space for Native literary studies than what we have inherited. Perhaps we need some retrospection at this point—a time of self-scrutiny as to where Native literature has been, where it is going, and to what degree Indian people should control how it gets there.

Although her comments reference written histories, perhaps Anna Lee Walters's cogent remarks apply here as well:

> Scholars or authorities from academia, from outside tribal societies, do not necessarily know tribal people best. There is an inherent right of tribal people to interpret events and time in their worlds according to their own aesthetics and values, as a component of American history, even when this interpretation is different from that of mainstream history.[6]

I might add, *especially* when the interpretation is different from that of the mainstream.

Finally, as Native writers, our own resistance to forming a substantive body of critical discussion surrounding our own literature and our willingness to turn the task over to outsiders, to "those who write criticism," or "those who do theory," may indicate the degree to which we have internalized colonization. We have gone too long thinking that storytellers cannot also talk about stories, that fiction writers and poets do one thing and critics and academics quite another. When I am back home (that is, in Indian communities in Oklahoma), I am always amazed when I encounter individuals who are encyclopedic in their knowledge of their own tribe—they sort of put me in a state of awe. Though often having no formal connection to the academy, they have read every book on their tribe; they can recall family tribal histories with a breadth that is astounding; they have an amazing sense of place and culture. I often wonder why *these* people are not doing literary criticism and writing book reviews. Of course, I know some of the reasons why they are not; nonetheless, I lament this loss and wish some of these folks, the real Indian experts, could have a more prominent place in the development of our literary approaches.

I was reminded of these things at Tahlequah recently, at a Native writers' festival, after I heard what seemed like the umpteenth-million poem (read by writers whining about being mixed-bloods) about nice, kindly Indian grandmothers and was having difficulty recognizing any of the Indian women I have known in these highly tamed, docile old ladies. Surely, there are other areas of discourse we can give our attention to while paying the appropriate kind of respect to ancestral voices. My point is this: I was dismayed at just how little formal discussion there was among Indian writers concerning who controls Indian literature, what is the purpose of Indian literature, what constitutes Native literatures of excellence, how such criteria should be determined, what set of ethical issues surrounds being a Native writer, and what role should tribes play in the whole process. What happens, it seems to me, is that when we abandon such a discussion, we give away all our power to a group of outsiders who then determine our aesthetics *for* us, and this happens without even a fight!

A more subtle form of the colonization of Native literature may occur as an aftereffect of a phenomenon that has been overall very positive. Literary critics have attached a great deal of relevance to the "Native American literary renaissance," the great outpouring of texts authored by Native writers over the last thirty years, noting, among other things, that Native people have taken up the pen to speak rather than be spoken for. To quote Vine Deloria's polemic title, "We talk, you listen." Native literature is ahead of the game, compared to other areas of Native studies, in that one can teach courses on Native lit, and now even on Native literary criticism, assigning as texts, books authored exclusively by Native people. This is much harder to do in history or anthropology or other areas of inquiry (though not impossible, and it seems to me that the minimal requirement for a Native studies course should be that every classroom text is written by a Native author; otherwise, how can we possibly lay claim to presenting Native perspectives?).

To continue in regards to the "renaissance" and this great outpouring of Native-authored texts, one overwhelming theme of the authors writing Native creative literature is that the cultures of which they are writing have not vanished. These works seek creative and evocative ways to argue that Native cultures continue to survive and evolve. Perhaps, however, some further questions need to be asked about this renaissance, given that so much ground has been gained in the areas of fiction, especially in the forms of short stories, novels, and poetry. In addition to the many positive aspects of this burgeoning literature, does the frontier for fiction serve partially to deny Native peoples a place in the nonfictional world, in the arena where sovereignty, religious freedom, treaty rights, land claims, language retention, tribal education, and many other elements of culture continue to affect the daily destinies of tribes? Why haven't Native-written histories, or political analyses, for example, experienced a renaissance of the same magnitude?[7] Does the fictional work of the "renaissance" effectively present these Native social realities?

Overall, it seems to me, Native-written fictional stories about reconnection to Native culture enjoy a much wider popular appeal than nonfiction written by Indians concerning their tribe's land claims or politics. In terms of fiction itself, take as an example the glaring difference between the attention given to Leslie Silko's *Ceremony*, a novel about a warrior's reintegration into Laguna society, and the same author's *Almanac of the Dead*, a novel that posits that indigenous peoples throughout the Americas will take back their land. America loves Indian culture; America is much less enthusiastic about Indian land title.

Does the Native American literary renaissance, in addition to its many positive qualities, also play, in troubling ways, into the vanishing notion by allowing Native people to be fictional but not real? In this study, I will concentrate on the idea that Native literary aesthetics must be politicized and that autonomy, self-determination, and sovereignty serve as useful literary concepts. Further, I wish to suggest that literature has something to add to the arena of Native political struggle. The attempt, then, will be to break down oppositions between the world of literature and the very real struggles of American Indian communities, arguing for both an intrinsic and extrinsic relationship between the two. I will seek a literary criticism that emphasizes Native resistance movements against colonialism, confronts racism, discusses sovereignty and Native nationalism, seeks connections between literature and liberation struggles, and, finally, roots literature in land and culture. This criticism emphasizes unique Native worldviews and political realities, searches for differences as often as similarities, and attempts to find Native literature's place in Indian country, rather than Native literature's place in the canon.

What is called for, perhaps, is a kind of "Red Stick" literary criticism. I am referring to the group of traditionalist Creeks in 1813 to 1814 who, seeing their land invaded from all sides, with demands for land cessions increasing all the time, had to come up with a radically different way of dealing with a threat that hitherto had not existed. What they had to develop was a vision that was not simply reactionary but the application of tradition in radical new ways with attention given to analysis, criticism, and political reflection. This anticolonial movement, fueled by religion and myth, was both influenced by Shawnee ally Tecumseh's apocalyptic teachings and rooted in the Creek square grounds. In Joel Martin's book on the Red Sticks, entitled *Sacred Revolt,* the author says, "Not only did they react and rebel against colonialism — they also innovated on tradition and initiated new ways of life within the world created by contact."[8]

There is a difference here that is vital. In looking at Creek literature, I want to emphasize "innovat[ion] on tradition" and "initiat[ion of] new ways of life" rather than "the world created by contact." European contact is a given; toward the purpose of contributing something toward Native studies, however, I am more interested in what can be innovated and initiated by Native people in analyzing their own cultures rather than deconstructing Native viewpoints and arguing for their European underpinnings or even concentrating on white atrocities and Indian victims. When cultural contact between Native Americans and Europeans has occurred throughout history, I am assuming that it is just as likely that things European are Indianized rather than the anthropological assumption that things Indian are always swallowed up by European culture. I reject, in other words, the supremacist notion that assimilation can only go in one direction, that white culture always overpowers Indian culture, that white is inherently more powerful than red, that Indian resistance has never occurred in such a fashion that things European have been radically subverted by Indians.

In terms of Native literature, I relate this to a more radical "Red Stick" approach — the assumption that Indian viewpoints cohere, that Indian resistance can be successful, that Native critical centers are possible, that working from within the nation, rather than looking toward the outside, is a legitimate way of examining literature, that subverting the literary status quo rather than being subverted *by* it constitutes a meaningful alternative.

I am not claiming that such a task is a particularly easy one, especially given that we have had five hundred years of being whipped into believing we have no intellectual history of our own making that might provide such frameworks for analysis, and we have critics who would still have us believe this to be the case — that the ones we do have are not "pure enough" to be taken seriously as Indian, that Europe is as much the center of these writings as Native cultures.

If we take the Spanish book burnings of the Mayan codices in the 1540s as an example, we might describe this act of cultural genocide as one culture finding itself threatened by the profundity of the Other's literacy. These were illiteracy campaigns, sponsored by the group claiming to be the most literate. Symbolically, and literally, this campaign still continues; how many Native writers have commented on their long struggle simply to believe in the legitimacy of tribal voices in racist America, where they have been taught that such voices are not possible? In dominant culture, the term "Indian intellectual" is an oxymoron. Yet we have produced written intellectual texts for centuries, not to mention indigenous-based intellectual knowledge so much a part of the oral tradition.

And in contemporary literary criticism, it is still a struggle simply to legitimate Native approaches to Native texts, to say that it is OK for Indians to do it their own way. Indian critics, like any others, should be subject to critique, but sometimes the critique has approached the absurd when they have been accused of being atheoretical for wanting to examine their own cultures or for using their own authors as sources for building literary ideas, or when their ideas about looking at Native intellectual history have been characterized as a belief in the pristine quality of all things Indian. Rather than taking more time to present counterarguments against the ridiculous, I hope this study provides a positive example of why looking toward primary Native cultures, authors, and histories can enrich Native literature. If we Native critics share the fault of being "theoryless," my contention would be that this comes from not looking *enough* at our home cultures, not from looking *too much* at them. Naturally, this process does not call for abandoning literary theory, and if one examines the work of most Native critics, one will find that few of us have anyway.

Even postcolonial approaches, with so much emphasis on how the settler culture views the other, largely miss an incredibly important point: how do Indians view Indians? Literature departments have done little to answer this question, and this area of history we must dig up ourselves. Let me give a concrete example of Indian literary history not being uncovered by postcolonial or other approaches. In its thirty-year history, the Institute of American Indian Arts (IAIA) at Santa Fe, New Mexico, has turned out a tremendous number of Native artists, more than three hundred. The way art was taught at IAIA, especially from the mid-1960s to the early 1970s, and the movements that have come out of this school (such as Native abstractionism) have had a tremendous influence on Native poetry and, to a lesser extent, Native fiction. Yet none of this literary history has been uncovered by those practicing conventional Native literary criticism. This is a missed opportunity, and our understanding of contemporary Native literature suffers as a result.

Native literature, and Native literary criticism, written by Native authors, is part of sovereignty: Indian people exercising the right to present images of themselves and to discuss those images. Tribes recognizing their own extant literatures, writing new ones, and asserting the right to explicate them constitute a move toward nationhood. While this literary aspect of sovereignty is not the same thing as the political status of Native nations, the two are, nonetheless, interdependent. A key component of nationhood is a people's idea of themselves, their imaginings of who they are. The ongoing expression of a tribal voice, through imagination, language, and literature, contributes to keeping sovereignty alive in the citizens of a nation and gives sovereignty a meaning that is defined within the tribe rather than by external sources.

The point that Elizabeth Cook-Lynn makes so well is that there *already* exists a Native literary critical school:

> The second worry for the nativist is the question of whether or not opening up the American literary canon to include native literary traditions and contemporary works will have much relevance, given its own set of unique aims — the interest in establishing the myths and metaphors of sovereign nationalism; the places, the mythological beings, the genre structures and plots of the oral traditions; the wars and war leaders, the treaties and accords with other nations as the so-called gold standard against which everything can be judged. These are the elements of nationalism which have always fueled the literary canon of tribal peoples and their literary lives. In my own tribal literary traditions, there is a fairly long list of Dakota/Lakota writers and storytellers as well as a huge body of ritual and ceremony against which everything may be compared. Reference to the body of nationalistic myths, legends, metaphors, symbols, historical persons and events, writers and their writings must form the basis of the critical discourse that functions in the name of the people; the presence of the Indian nation as cultural force a matter of principle.[9]

Tribal authors have the right, as well as the responsibility, to explore these national literary tendencies in order to pass on the traditions of their respective tribal nations to the next generation. If Indian writers write only about tribes other than their own, and if critics fail to look at Native philosophies and philosophers in developing their criticism, what happens to the next generation in their own communities back home? What have we left for them? Perhaps it is time to really dig in, to entrench ourselves with what we have inherited from our home cultures.

Standing Rock Lakota scholar Kelly Morgan makes an impassioned plea for national literatures. She argues that imaginative literature — fiction and poetry — is a more accurate gauge of cultural realities than the ethnographic, anthropological, and historical record; that in fact, given the absence of Lakota women at all in non-Indian accounts (except for women as docile drudges), the imaginative writings of Lakota women are vital. Literature, Morgan posits, contributes to Lakota cultural survival because it extends knowledge of cultural practices to future generations. In comparison to rigid non-Indian "scientific" depictions, literature is unfixed, ever growing and evolving, and influenced by "the diversity of Lakota people themselves."[10] As an example, Morgan states that traditional Lakota oral stories, even in their written forms, can teach Lakotas valuable kinship roles that have been a part of Lakota worldviews for centuries. She goes on to say that these texts have the potential to aid in the cultural survival of the people, especially for young people who have suffered a loss of self-esteem from racism and stereotypical dominant culture depictions of Indians. One way this loss of identity occurs is when Native children have replaced what they have learned at home with external definitions of Indianness from fixed anthropological, ethnographic, and historical texts, or portrayals from popular culture. Morgan believes that the primary audience for Lakota texts are Lakota people themselves, and she sees the written word as a vehicle for carrying forward oral stories. This kind of nation building, I believe, is vital to the authorship and critical response of the future.

To legitimize a space for national critical studies and native intellectual history, scholars of Native literature need to break down the oppositional thinking that separates orality and literacy wherein the oral constitutes authentic culture and the written contaminated culture. The aforementioned Mayan codices, written in Mayan pictoglyphic symbols before contact, and in Mayan in the Latin alphabet afterward, are a fascinating study in these regards because recent scholarship has shown that these books were used as a *complement* of oral tradition rather than a *replacement*.[11] The books were recited and even read in precontact schools to educate the young in the oral tradition.

The idea, then, of books as a valid means of passing on vital cultural information is an ancient one, consistent with the oral tradition itself in the case of the Mayans. This example opens up a space for Native intellectual discussion, in the form of textual production, in contact, not competition, with the oral tradition. Surely, in today's literate society, this represents one hope for Native people in terms of passing on culture. In these regards, the Mayan codices are also interesting in terms of their national literary character; the texts taught Mayans what it meant to be Mayan — their history, their cosmogony, the evolution of their political system, and so on.

Another aspect of Native literatures that needs to be discussed in terms of their national character is their mimetic function, the link between literature and social realities that is a natural part of the oral tradition. Many authors have discussed the pragmatic nature of literatures in oral traditions where a song, poem, or chant is used toward utilitarian ends such as fostering successful hunting relationships, warding off evil, germinating crops, curing illnesses, going through the day with respectful thoughts and actions, and so on. In a classroom essay, Kirk Zebolksky, one of my Native literature students at the University of Nebraska at Omaha, made an interesting comment on the way Native literatures continue to link themselves with Native politics, a contemporary form of this unique mimesis:

> Implicit in this description of the U.S. as "stolen" is the presumption that parts or all of it should be returned. Thus Louis and other Native authors have an important role in dialogue about Native land rights. Perhaps they have the most important role in terms of getting across the point that indigenous land rights have been grossly violated. American Indian writers are asssuming a unique role — being the primary and most articulate voices in calling for major political changes and property transfers in the country which is the world's only superpower and the most militarily powerful nation in history.[12]

Native artistry is not pure aesthetics, or art for art's sake: as often as not Indian writers are trying to *invoke* as much as *evoke*. The idea behind ceremonial chant is that language, spoken in the appropriate ritual contexts, will actually cause a change in the physical universe. This element exists in contemporary Native writing and must be continuously explored in building up a national body of literature and criticism — language as invocation that will upset the balance of power, even to the point, as Zebolsky argues, where stories will be preeminent factors in land redress.

The early part of this book assumes that the political history of the Creek Nation, the ceremonies that form the ritual knowledge of the tribe, and the oral tradition, are central to an understanding of Creek literature. Chapter 1, "The Creek Nation," historicizes Creek government, beginning with the origin story, and describes the most important event of the Muskogean religious calendar, the Green Corn ceremony. Although individual Creeks, like members of other tribes, vary in terms of their degree of acculturation, I do not know of any Creek writers who have never witnessed the night dances between the arbors, and I argue that the sound of shells shaking and the responsorial rhythms of Creek singing show up in Creek literature.

Chapter 2, "Reading the Oral Tradition for Nationalist Themes: Beyond Ethnography," seeks to politicize the oral tradition and argue for a deeper investigation of narratives that goes beyond the simple structual categories of creation, hero, journey, monster slayer, and so on, in which the stories most frequently get cast. The chapter seeks to point out that nationhood and sovereignty are not European constructs but that Creeks had their version of such notions in terms of actual political practice as well as embodied in their literature. This is where the structural categories become problematic — they separate the stories from their political contexts. To demonstrate this interdependency of politics and literature, I use as an example Creek elder Phillip Deere's contemporary telling of the Muskogean origin story, and the political gloss he includes throughout his telling. The last part of the chapter deals with the ramifications of opening up the oral tradition to political readings.

Chapter 3, "In the Storyway," features Creek elder Linda Alexander's telling of the story of how turtle got his shell busted. Alexander is an extraordinarily talented word weaver, as well as a great shell shaker at the grounds, and an elder respected for her knowledge and many abilities. The turtle story is referenced throughout this book, and I have heard Linda tell it many times. I feel as if her turtle story is one of the factors that keeps this book from busting up, that has sung the words back together and, at times, has sung my own life into place. I include Linda's version in both Creek and English, as well as her comments and interpretation of the story. I attempt an analysis of the story myself, especially as part of a national body of literature.

Next I discuss a Creek writer who marks an important, if thorny, beginning point, in chapter 4, titled "Alice Callahan's *Wynema:* A Fledgling Attempt." Alice Callahan is the first Native woman to write a novel, a work, as it happens, quite problematic in its depiction of Creeks. Callahan's novel, nonetheless, causes us to ask important questions: What should a Creek novel do? What are some reasonable demands on Creek writers and their writings?

In chapter 5, I take up a discussion of a writer who may be one of the most effective Native literary artists in terms of using writing to address national concerns given the immediacy of the dangers his nation faced and his degree of involvement in response to perhaps the greatest threat to Creek nationhood in Creek history — the dissolution of tribal government under the Dawes Act. In "Fus Fixico: A Literary Voice against the Extinction of Tribal Government," I argue that the primary purpose of the Fus Fixico letters was not satire, caricature, or dialect writing but the thwarting of the Oklahoma statehood interests. Further, Posey is used as an example of the complexity of the Creek world, one that, like any other nation, contains a diverse population. Posey's life demonstrates that reductive categories like "assimilationist" or "traditionalist" are often more complicated than they seem.

In chapter 6, entitled "Louis Oliver: Searching for a Creek Intellectual Center," I argue that a central feature of Oliver's creative work is an intense journey toward understanding what it means to be a Creek intellectual. Similar to Phillip Deere, the Creek elder discussed in chapter 2, who glosses his creation account with political commentary, Oliver glosses his stories as well, but with philosophical reflection. Oliver's singular contribution to Creek intellectualism is that he places this pursuit of knowledge in the context of ethical questions involving the responsibilities of writers to their cultures and to the community of Native writers, past and present.

One of the obvious areas of inquiry in Native studies in the future will have to be the effect of pan-tribalism on Native cultures, from boarding schools to the urban demography of Native populations, to the powwow circuit, to beginning global alliances and awareness among indigenous populations worldwide, to name a few examples (not that these few phenomena mark the beginning and ending of pan-tribalism, but they seem like cogent ones). How does a study such as this, with its intense concentration on tribal specificity, deal with pan-tribalism? To answer this question, I look at a Muskogee poet whose work is solidly rooted in both Oklahoma Creek Indian realities and national, and international, indigenous perspectives. "Joy Harjo: Creek Writer from the End of the Twentieth Century" explains how Harjo's Creek nationalism strengthens, rather than weakens, her ability to take on pan-tribal concerns.

The final chapter may seem like a strange departure in that, in a study devoted to Creeks, I shift to a Cherokee writer, yet I feel the inclusion of Lynn Rollie Riggs an important one because of the way in which Riggs formulated actual written theories about Oklahoma. Further, inquiry into Riggs's life and writings opens up Native studies to the subject of sexual orientation, a topic long overdue in our field given the tremendous contributions of Native gays and lesbians to Native cultures and Native literatures. The chapter also attempts to set a record for the longest and most obnoxious title in the book: "Lynn Riggs as Code Talker: Toward a Queer Oklahomo Theory and the Radicalization of Native American Studies." I do a reading of Riggs's play *The Cherokee Night* that some may feel approaches the bizarre, but nonetheless, I hope to point out that the troubling phenomena of many writers earlier this century, endorsing vanishing viewpoints and tragic portrayals of Indians, is wrapped up in a complicated set of historical and personal factors. For Riggs, this had to do with the incredibly oppressive larger social milieu an Indian gay guy faced in the thirties, and I hope to show that Riggs's portrayal of doomed and tragic Cherokees has everything to do with his closeted condition. As a Native gay guy who, like Riggs, has walked the halls of the English Department of the University of Oklahoma, taught freshman composition classes there, demonstrated the same old mixed-blood proclivity for picking up a guitar and warbling out cowboy songs, and felt both the beauty and terror of life in Oklahoma, sometimes having to flee from home to survive, I must say that reading Riggs's biography was a spiritual unfolding for me. Riggs too is an ancestral voice, his an emergence story that needs to be brought out into the light so that the people can "come out" into the larger landscape, provided with an example through imagining and historicizing

Riggs's struggle. Or instead of the white gay notion of "coming out," we might coin Beth Brant's phrasing in her beautiful book *Writing as Witness* and say that such stories might teach us how to "present ourselves" to our communities as whole persons.[13]

If anything, I hope this study encourages young Creek writers to keep writing; to trust their own voices; to tell the stories of family, home, and nation; and to know the history of those who told such stories before us.

What identifies a Creek work, in my mind, in addition to its authorship by a Creek person, is the depiction of geographically specific Creek landscape and the language and stories that are born out of that landscape. The character Hotgun steps out of Creek literary history — that is, out of the letters of Alexander Posey published in the *Eufaula Indian Journal* just before Oklahoma statehood and into the letters written by Jim Chibbo to his buddy Hotgun in the pages of this book, *Red on Red*. Jim Chibbo says he done this because he wants to convey to his readers what it feels like in his little part of the world that is his home, his nation. In his past experience, he has found that reading literary criticism has done little, if anything, to spark that feeling. He's not satisfied with explicating Creek texts if he has never tried his hand at creating anything Creek himself. He wants you to drive around McIntosh County and take a look-see for yourself, maybe get out, walk a spell, and watch a couple turtles slip off their sunny spots on half-submerged logs in the Canadian River and plop down into the brown swirling water; or you might even consider stopping inside Keck's grocery store in Weleetka and see if they tell you the story of that awful murder that occurred there when my dad was a boy.

Pardon me if I jump out of the end row into a new furrow, but I gone on to explain to Hotgun and Jim that the university is about the meanest business any fool could ever find himself in. After I laid it all out, and they kind of studied it for a spell, Hotgun told me that he'd been through most everything, but that if he were ever to become a university professor, he wanted me to beat him over the head with a hickory ballstick and put him out of his misery. To avoid the nastiness of a profession that is just pitiful mean, Jim tries to tell a few funny stories here and again to consider the most serious critical issues in the book without becoming mean hisself. Him and Hotgun found that they could get to the heart of matters quicker by funning each other than by writing literary criticism, and they could use jokes instead of taking up the hickory stick themselves as a bloody cudgel on everybody who disagrees with them. Hotgun said they might reconsider, though, in the case of one or two individuals who been asking for a whupping, but that they was very special exceptions.

What's more, they suspicioned that what happened was that Creek writers read other Creek writers, and anyhows, if they don't, they ought to, and that Creek written tradition is passed on as well as oral tradition. They come up with the notion that the best way of going about all this was to get Stijaati Thlaako, Big Man, and Rabbit together to talk to some of these Creek authors and trace the history of how one influences the other, and Jim and him would write back and report on what their friends had to say about all this. They felt that as Creek critics, or just Creeks who talk a lot, if they abandoned their role as storytellers, something very significant would be missing from their criticism. They didn't want merely to write a book *about* Creek literature; they wanted to write a Creek book.

Hotgun and Jim was had remind me on the same occasion of the special symbolism of the Fus Fixico letters — they represent Indians addressing other Indians because they were published inside Indian Territory, inside the Creek Nation, and in the *Eufaula Indian Journal*, which was an Indian newspaper at the time. If we take a look at the nineteenth century, we might note two facts: lots of whites spoke on behalf of Indians, and when Indians did author their own books, they had to address a white audience, since they were writing in English, and their people, for the most part, couldn't read them. Those days are over. Educating white folks about Indians can only be taken so far. Hotgun claims it's like teaching hogs to sing: it wastes your time and only frustrates the hog. Now it's time to direct our literary efforts toward our own folks, and personal letters symbolize insider efforts, speaking a special language recognized by a particular community. Posey himself resisted having his letters published outside of Indian Territory because he was trying to get things stirred up *within* the territory, among the tribes, as will be discussed further in chapter 5.

Finally, Jim and Hotgun just clean didn't cotton to reading another dang work on *House Made of Dawn, Love Medicine, Ceremony, Winter in the Blood,* and *Darkness in Saint Louis Bearheart,* even though they're great admirers of all those novels. Most of all they didn't care a lick to hear critics talk about how these authors and their characters were a bunch of mongrelized mixed-bloods who weren't sure if they were Indians as they muddled about in some kind of hybridized culture, serving as the footpath between whites and Indians.

I tell you what's the truth: by and large, they just wanted to write something that was *different* and something that was fun. They tried their best to do it right, but if they done it wrong, then they hope you'll write your book too and improve on the overall situation.

Mado,
Craig

Dear Hotgun:

While Stijaati Thlaako drag ass like squared-up mule on last furrow and Big Man bawl loud as a weaned calf from his recliner OU football game and Rabbit pretend like he cain't find no clean shirt and mebeso they wives hollering them out to they Indian cars to get going to the gospel singing at Indian Methodist Church just south of Sapulpa where Rabbit's cousin Yahola Choffee is master of ceremonies for the evening, Chebon all out of breath from writing down his long-winded literary introduction take more time than getting them guys loaded up for singing hymns. They was to go a whole lot easier if it was catfish fry with white filet, beans, and coleslaw like last week, and Chebon's work go a whole lot easier if he didn't have to write the whole book before he was to understand what it was about so he could go back to make up the introduction.

Hymn singing went on forty pages too long, like most chapters in Chebon's book, and Rabbit poke his paw a little bit over the edge of the pew, turn it over palm up, and let his Zippo flash at Stijaati in row behind him. This Indian sign language for time to slip out and smoke during the next letup when old ladies start rustling pages to find next song. Big Man done sitting in back to make his way out first chance he get.

They slip behind one of the camping-in houses and light up, breathing deep and sighing along with the cicadas singing in the trees who sound purtier to them than the second verse of "Cesus Momis Apeyakathles." And that's purty.

Or mebeso it'd be more like what with the woods surrounding them, and the cicadas stuttering in the wet air, it sounded out kindy like twin fiddles on "Maiden's prayer" kin to what Stijaati was heard play in Johnny Lee Will's music shop in Tulsa.

Meanwhile, out back of the church house, Rabbit was had exhale smoke and say, "The Surgeon General has determined that hymn singing causes lung cancer in Indian men."

Stijaati was ask, "Isn't that Jimmy Johnny's Zippo?" He suspicioned Rabbit might was got holt of Jimmy's lighter, and he notice the small circle of *red earth* Rabbit is standing in. "That thing sure gets around."

Stijaati holds up his red-and-white package of Marlboros and was say, "How's this pack of cigarettes like Chebon's book?"

Big Man wonder, "Is this a quiz?"

Rabbit was say, "It turns your fingers yellow?"

Stijaati actually asking oratorical question, wants to lecture. "It ain't," he answers hisself, "Chebon's book about the Red, not the white."

Rabbit was exclaim, "I love trick questions!"

Big Man was say, "Ain't that a little naive? A Red book?"

Rabbit was answer, "Only if you believe white always swallows up Red. I think Red stays Red, most ever time, even throwed in with white. Especially around white. It stands out more."

Stijaati ignores interruptions and shakes out his tail feathers and swells up, ready now for sure. "They's a literary critic who was quote he got into Native literature on account of bring it up to a higher level, from its 'virtually pre-technological level of sophistication,' he says."

Rabbit was got a wild onion showing on his front tooth when he talk and say, "I believe Chebon is in it to bring Native literature down to a lower level."

Stijaati snubs out his cigarette. "Nothing wrong with the Lower World," he mumbles, as he takes his cowboy hat back off and wanders slowly toward the church house, listening to the hymns make their way toward the woods.

Sincerely,
Jim Chibbo

CHAPTER ONE

The Creek Nation

Contrary to *The Road to Disappearance,* the title of one of the most comprehensive books about Creek history, the Creeks have anything but disappeared. As of 1994, members of the Oklahoma Creek Nation numbered 36,695, and they make up a sovereign country existing within the borders of the United States and covering ten counties in East Central Oklahoma. Their Alabama kinfolk aound Poarch, Alabama, also a federally recognized nation, descendants of Creeks who escaped removal from their homelands in the 1830s, number 2,106. In addition, there are a number of state-recognized bands of Creeks in Alabama and Florida.[1] Taking into account the first census after Indian Removal in 1859, which enumerated Oklahoma Creeks at 13,537,[2] a decrease of as much as half the population of the nation due to the forced removal, today's numbers are amazing. The size of the nation has tripled compared to its population shortly after removal and is even double the number it was before Creeks were forced from Alabama. Oklahoma Creeks, owing to their larger numbers, have perhaps remained more traditional than their Alabama relatives, still maintaining around eighteen of their ceremonial grounds, where they continue to practice the stomp dance religion and retain the Creek language that many adults still speak. In recent years, however, there has been much contact between Oklahoma and Alabama Creeks, Oklahomans making trips to Alabama to teach their relatives stories, language, stickball, and stomp dancing.

Because I believe that one approach to Native literatures should be a study of the primary culture that produces them (for instance, learning something about Anishinabes to understand *Love Medicine*,[3] or about Jemez and Navajos and Kiowas to understand *House Made of Dawn*,[4] or about Lagunas to understand *Ceremony*, or about Creeks to understand the poetry of Joy Harjo), I wish to begin with a brief discussion of Creek history and culture.

According to traditional Creek storytelling, the nation was born when the earth opened up in the West near the Continental Divide and spit the people up from below its surface out into the broader landscape. The people journeyed eastward on a quest to discover the origin of the sun until they reached the Atlantic and could travel no more. Turning back, they decided to settle in the area of the Chattahoochee River in Alabama. One of the most evocative tellings of this powerful story is a contemporary one that Creek elder Louis Oliver includes in his book *Chasers of the Sun: Creek Indian Thoughts*. Mr. Oliver, in naturally poetic language and with a good measure of what can only be called Indian humor, recounts the ancient journey as if he were on it himself, employing the first-person plural "we" throughout: "We came pouring out of the backbone of this continent like ants."[5] This "we" point of view is something akin to Momaday's oft misunderstood notion called "racial memory," which some critics have seemingly mistaken for racist memory. The idea, however, has to do with the way narrative shapes communal consciousness: through imagination and storytelling, people in oral cultures reexperience history. This concept of ancestral memory relates to nationalism in that sovereignty is an intersection of the political, imaginary, and literary. To exist as a nation, the community needs a perception of nationhood, that is, stories (like the migration account) that help them imagine who they are as a people, how they came to be, and what cultural values they wish to preserve. According to Momaday, in *The Way to Rainy Mountain*, Momaday himself took part in the migration of the Kiowas from the headwaters of the Yellowstone out onto the great plains, a setting forth that occurred in the 1700s, as did the old woman Ko-sahn whom he writes about.[6] Within the telling, the event is reexperienced so that the people are reconstituted as a nation as they hear about their origins in ancient stories of creations and journeyings. The oral tradition has always had, and continues to have, a nationalist perspective. This notion will be explored more fully in the next chapter.

Recalling the story through living memory as a result of his upbringing in the oral tradition, Mr. Oliver tells of Creek experience as they head off toward the dawn: they follow an arrow for direction, and they encounter prophets who come down from the sun and instruct the people in their most important rituals. These include the maintenance of the ceremonial grounds, culminating in the annual Green Corn ceremony that takes place in late July or early August, the layout of the arbors and the proper seating of the clans, the correct use of medicines during the ceremonies, and instruction for the stickball game at which Creeks excel.

It is important to note, as does Mr. Oliver, that this knowledge and the practice of it at the ceremonial grounds is ongoing and relevant, not the remnants of a vanishing culture. This is key — the fact that the culture survives — because it is the basis for a recognition of a national literature, since living cultures produce ongoing literatures rather than merely preserve the ethnographic past. Stomp dancing, one of the religious rituals learned during the ancient migration, is still very popular among Creeks today, and Mr. Oliver describes it beautifully:

> They have been doing this for many hundreds of years and not one iota of the songs have been changed.
>
> So, in this instance, a leader is found and the dance starts. He walks slowly around the fire counter-clockwise, four times. The women with turtle shells strapped around their legs fall in line behind the leaders. There is a man carrying a stickball racket and acting like a deacon of a church, urging others to join in.
>
> After his fourth round the leader sounds out a long drawn out "yodel" so to speak, and those who have joined him, answer with a sharp "hoop." As the leader continues the man with the ball club shouts out: "Locha! Locha! Locha!" urging the shellshakers to join in. As the whole begins to "warm-up" so to speak, he again pleads "Tokas Che! hayomofa! hayomofa! Emvmiycvlke! emamiycvlke!" (Now-Attention, attention, helpers, helpers, come on!)
>
> To describe the action and the sound is very difficult as it involves entering into the sphere of the supernatural. Gradually the leader invokes, by stronger verses, the spirits of the other world and as the dance progresses they are all lifted up seemingly in a cloud. Many other leaders will come forward to continue the euphoria until daybreak.[7]

In Mr. Oliver's story there are many compelling elements that make a vast difference in its meaning compared to non-Native accounts of Creek origins. There is discussion of the supernatural aspect of the dancing, the belief in the spiritual powers it calls forth. There is the participatory level of the narrative, as well as the employment of Creek language to describe the event. As the passage demonstrates, because of Mr. Oliver's use of the present tense, the cultural life of the nation continues in a vital way into the present day. The overwhelming majority of books written about Creeks are written by non-Native authors who write in the past tense and assume that the people whom they are writing about no longer exist. Somehow, though it is not explained in these books quite how this occurred, the Creeks supposedly disappeared from the face of the earth the very year Oklahoma became a state (the terrible title of Angie Debo's book is a case in point). A good deal of this pessimism has to do with the dissolution of tribal governments under the Dawes Act of the late nineteenth century. In this chapter, however, I will discuss ways in which Creek government continued even after it was no longer recognized by the United States. Most of these historical texts, quite literally, end in 1907, the year of statehood. Some, but not many, have a very few pages about Creek life in the first part of the twentieth century. These texts still contain a good deal of value in terms of historical information; however, readers need to think about the ways in which the "vanishing American" mentality shapes the narratives these historians write, and how a reading of the books is modified by the fact that tribal governments were restored in 1934 under the Indian Reorganization Act and by 1936 in Oklahoma. In the following decades, tribal governments continued to evolve.

In terms of going beyond the facts and dates of history, Mr. Oliver's story reveals key aspects of Creek national experience and character — it foreshadows future migrations that culminated in Indian Removal in the 1830s when the Creeks were forcibly removed from their homelands in Alabama and Georgia; it shows the importance of earth relationship, since Creeks emerged from below the landscape; it explains the most important Creek religious symbols such as fire and the sun; it accounts for the beginnings of Creek ceremonialism. I will take up Oliver's work more fully in chapter 6.

David H. Corkran, author of *The Creek Frontier: 1540–1783*, a study of Creek history during the colonial period, discusses the word "Creek," which the eighteenth-century writer and trader James Adair claimed derived from the many streams and rivers in Creek country. Corkran gives the dominant-culture anthropological classification of Creeks:

> From their name, "Muskhoge," anthropologists have classified as
> Muskogeans a large group of Indian tribes who speak related languages.

Lately it has been suggested that the Muskogeans are related to the northern Algonkians.

Creek legends state that the tribe came to the Southeast by way of the Red River. When they came is obscure, but it is possible that they were part of the great intrusion of northern Indians which entered the southwest by way of the eastern Rockies in the period A.D. 800–1000. Archaeologists classify prehistoric Creek culture late Mississippian, or late temple mound, as distinguished from the early Mississippian or early temple mound which characterizes the builders of the great mound near Macon, Georgia. The early mound builders belong to the period A.D. 800–1200. Whether they were destroyed, dispersed, or incorporated by the invading Creeks is not known. . . . Though of disparate tribes, the Creeks considered themselves a nation distinct from the Cherokees in the mountains to the north, the coastal tribes to the east, the Timucas [*sic*] and Mobiles to the south, and Choctaws and Chickasaws to the west.[8]

For many Creeks, their own narratives about Creek origins are more important for explaining Creek beginnings than the anthropological and historical mythologies. This is a right that belongs to Creeks and other Native people. When Creek people assume they have the inherent right to interpret their own literature and history, even when their interpretations differ from those of dominant culture, they are setting themselves apart as a nation of people with distinct worldviews that deserve to be taken seriously. This is an important exercise of sovereignty.

The most comprehensive non-Native study of Creek history is Angie Debo's *The Road to Disappearance.* In spite of the book's unfortunate title and some of Debo's patronizing attitudes — she does not seem to transcend the typical attitude of her time, common among scholars, which tended not to take Indian people very seriously in terms of their own narratives — the book is nonetheless a powerful indictment of white land theft that deserves credit for its accurate naming and detailing of some of the ugliest aspects of American history, a stand that cost Debo dearly in terms of her career and her relationship to the state of Oklahoma and its institutions. Debo gives the geographic boundaries of Creek country before their land base began to be diminished as the English, and later the Americans, stole it from them: "Their domain comprised a large portion of the present states of Alabama and Georgia; it was bounded on the north by the lands of the Cherokees, on the west by the Choctaw and Chickasaw nations, on the east by the English settlements, and on the south by the Spanish and French outposts and the broken tribes of the Florida peninsula."⁹ She also points out an important characteristic of the Creek Nation — its tendency to "swallow up" smaller groups that moved into Creek country (these groups would often become assimilated Creeks, most eventually adopting the Creek language). This vast diversity accounts for much of the dialectical differences that exist even today from town to town, the individual township usually originating from one of these splinter groups. Debo goes on to say:

It soon became the habit of the Creeks to annex the tribes they conquered in war; and when the white men began to drive out the Indians in the neighborhood of the settlements, these refugees also were incorporated into the Confederacy. In this way they received the Alabamas, the Koasatas, the Hitchitees, and the Tuskegees very early in their history. These tribes were not Muskogees, but they all belonged to the Muskhogean stock. A still more distinctive tribe was the Natchez, a distantly related Muskhogean people with an elaborate system of sun worship, a hereditary nobility, and a royal family of divine attributes and prerogatives. They were almost exterminated in warfare with the French in Louisiana, but a few survivors fled to the Creek country, formed a town on the Coosa, and became incorporated eventually with the Arbekas. The Euchees, an alien people who had formerly been hostile to the Creeks, were crowded by the English, and they too joined the Confederacy, forming a strong settlement on the Chattahoochee [More recently, according to Charles Hudson in *The Southeastern Indians,* the Euchees have been determined to be a Siouan offshoot]. They spoke a distinct language unrelated, so far as is known, to that of any other Indian tribe, and they showed a marked clannishness in their social relations, but they followed the Confederacy in peace and war. A considerable number of Shawnees also lived in the Creek country, detached bands from their tribe which by this time was living on the Ohio. Although they were an Algonquin people, they were bound to the Tuckabatchees by strong ties of traditional friendship. They formed temporary towns in various places, but they showed a tendency to settle among the Euchees, so that traders often made the mistake of classing them as a kindred tribe. The Creeks also received individual accessions from the Catawbas, a Siouan people of the Carolina region, who had been almost exterminated in wars with other Indians, and the Biloxis, another Siouan tribe from southern Mississippi. Detached bands of Chickasaws also settled temporarily in the Creek country, attracted apparently by a legendary friendship for the Cussetas.¹⁰

This "swallowing-up" effect is important because it demonstrates that Creeks were able to view nationalism as a dynamic, rather than a static, process. Creeks, in constant contact with other peoples, especially as tribes fled toward the interior from the onslaught of the English, Spanish, and French, were always experiencing cultural change. Very early on, Creeks learned how to adopt not only new people but new ways of being as well. Yet Native cultures are most often analyzed as if change is something they faced only after European contact, and as if, in every instance, contact with other cultures threatens "cultural purity." Creeks, however, who experienced exposure to new cultures for hundreds of years, still managed to maintain their language, worldview, and government, even in a system of constant flux. Indian cultures are the only cultures where it is assumed that if they change they are no longer a culture. In most other cultures, change is viewed as a sign that the culture is vibrant and alive, capable of surviving. Creeks provide an interesting historical example in terms of the way an indigenous culture might actually flourish in the face of change.

Muskogean local and national government, a powerful legal system that featured autonomous local towns that met annually in national councils, frequently in regional councils, and almost daily on the town level, predates European contact by centuries, dating back at least to A.D. 800 to 1000.[11] The *talwa* (town) was the basic unit òf Muskogean governing structure and consisted of a group of people "united in having a single square ground and a single sacred fire kept in the center of the square."[12] These tribal towns, it is important to note, still exist and function in Oklahoma. Before contact, after which centralization became increasingly important in order for the Creek Nation to join in a united front against land theft, towns enjoyed a great deal of autonomy, really possessing local sovereignty as part of a confederacy. Towns, for example, could "go to war or refuse to go to war, unilaterally, and there was no higher coercive power" (Lankford, 57).

Within the town councils there was a dualistic division of red and white functions. The red group comprised young men competing in a military ranking system for specific titles such as *tasikayalgi* (young warriors), *imathlas* (those who had achieved valorous war deeds), and *tastanagalgi* (distinguished warriors who led the less-accomplished ones and spoke in council about matters of war). They also had a war chief, an assistant war chief, and a war speaker, "a major orator who articulated the views of the war chief in council deliberations" (Lankford, 57).

The white side, the peace division, was made up of older men, already accomplished in war, who had the role of primary leadership in council—the white peace division had precedence over the red. The white group included the head chief of the town, called the *micco*; his assistant, the *henneha*, who was part of a group of second-level leaders called the *hennehalgi*; a *yatika*, who was an orator who expressed the views of the *micco* before the council; and the *isti atcacagi*, who were elders no longer physically able to go to war (Lankford, 58). Lankford points out that the red and white divisions are consistent with Muskogean cosmological distinctions between the Lower World, This World, and the Upper World, in which the white chiefs would be more closely aligned with the stability of the Upper World (the periodicity and stability of sun, moon, and planets) and the red warriors with the violence and chaos of the Lower World (the realm of caves, rivers, water) (77).

The next higher level of the red and white duality was the way it affected the division of the towns on a national level, that is, the relationship of towns to other towns. Even though the town was balanced internally by red and white functions, externally towns as an entity were designated either red or white. This affected criminal law and social functions such as ball games. During Green Corn certain criminals could flee to white peace towns for sanctuary. Ball games were played with towns of the opposite color. Ball games were more than just athletic events—they were/are tied to important religious notions and served as a substitute for war, as well as a symbolic embodiment of the delicate balance between the need for war and the need for peace and stable governing. The red and white division was made up of a complicated array of symbols that affected Creek life in many ways, and the red and white designation of towns allowed for a structure in which the towns could come together on a national level as part of the confederacy and work with each other, rather than one particular town becoming too independent or powerful (Lankford, 67).

This points out a seeming contradiction, but one that makes a good deal of sense in terms of Muskogean worldviews—a person functioning on a red level, as a warrior in his town, might have to function on a white level as a national representative of a peace town. Yet as Lankford points out:

> If one really believes that balance is the desired outcome, and that the entire dualistic system is larger than the self, then one's personal

viewpoint is relatively unimportant in the larger structure. Like lawyers, the representatives of the red and white must espouse their sworn positions, knowing that they contribute to the larger solution by fitting harmoniously into the dualistic confrontation. The point is not to be red *or* white, but red *and* white. (78)

The first contact of Creeks with Europeans occurred in March 1540. Corkran says that "when Hernando De Soto's six hundred gold-seeking European adventurers marched out of the pines and ponds of northwest Florida into southwest Georgia, the Lower Creeks were well east of the Chattahoochee River, occupying an area on the Ocmulgee and Flint rivers south and west of present-day Macon."[13] In the later quarter of the seventeenth century, the Creeks evolved from a loosely held confederacy to one of the most formidable groups of warriors in the Southeast. After the Yamasee War from 1716 to 1733, the Creeks tried to maintain a policy of neutrality in struggles between the French, Spanish, and English. The policy did not always hold, however, and the Creeks ended up involved in the Spanish Border War of 1739 to 1748, French-English hostilities from 1745 to 1748, war with the Cherokees from 1750 to 1752, and many other skirmishes, including involvement in the American Revolution, which split the Creek Nation into opposing parties.

After the American colonial period, Muskogean government is marked by flexibility and survival in the face of extreme adversity as the result of a U.S. government constantly engaged in illegal maneuverings, in defiance of its own laws, in order to steal land—a challenge that far exceeded prior dealings with the French and English. The late 1700s saw a strengthening of Muskogean government on a national level, a response to the ever-increasing pressures of colonial settlement, which the Muskogees had to present a united front against:

> For the next several years [after the 1790 treaty with the United States recognizing Muskogean land holdings] the Muskogees continued to strengthen and centralize their national council. Each town sent five or six delegates to the council, which, in turn, appointed the principal chief and passed laws of national concern. Towns were grouped into districts, and each district was governed by one man responsible for enforcing the nation's laws. By 1818 these laws had been codified into a written document.[14]

The most far-reaching changes for the Creeks occurred when during the Jackson administration, they were illegally removed from their homelands in Alabama and western Georgia in a forced removal to Indian Territory in the 1830s that resulted in the death of as many as half the nation, including the many people who died the first year of arrival in what is now Oklahoma. Before removal, the Creeks had

> repeatedly refused to negotiate land cessions and even passed a law, in 1818 or 1819, declaring that no tribal lands could be sold without approval of the national council, under penalty of death. Federal negotiators, however, ignored the nation's refusal to negotiate and concluded a series of illegal treaties. In 1825 federal officials bribed William McIntosh, Speaker of the Lower Towns, and a handful of his followers into signing the Treaty of Indian Springs, which ceded all Muscogee lands in Georgia and two-thirds of their Alabama lands in return for new land in what is now Oklahoma. (O'Brien, 122)

McIntosh suffered dearly for treason — he was executed — but despite President John Adams's recognition of the illegality of the treaty, removal continued irrevocably forward. This was not the first, nor the last, of many serious divisions between the Lower Creek towns, where McIntosh resided, and the Upper Creek towns; the former generally being more favorably disposed to white culture and cooperation, the latter more closely allied with staunch traditionalism and resistance. This split has played an important role throughout Creek postcontact history, up to the present day.

Historian Grant Foreman records the results of the genocidal policies of Andrew Jackson, one of the most maniacal dictators in world history, in his book *Indian Removal: The Emigration of the Five Civilized Tribes:*

> A population of 21,792 Creeks was enrolled under the Treaty of 1832, which with the McIntosh emigrants brought the number accounted for by name and town well above twenty-three thousand. No subsequent enumeration was made until 1859 when the Indians had partially recovered from the terrible losses of the journey; but a careful census taken that year showed a population of 13,537. Obviously not more than half the Creeks who were uprooted from the loved soil of Alabama ever lived to thrive again in the rude land into which they were transplanted.[15]

The next crisis for the Creeks was the American Civil War. Because the lower towns had sided with the Confederacy, the Creek Nation was forced to make a disastrous land cession in 1866, as a punishment imposed by the victorious Union. The Creeks ceded almost half their lands, in spite of the fact that the Upper Creeks had vehemently opposed the Confederacy and fought in the Union's armies to protect the United States. Nonetheless, Creek constitutional life rebounded. In October 1867 a new constitution and code of laws was adopted, and Okmulgee was chosen as the nation's capital.

Although many historians point out that the constitutional government was patterned after the U.S. system of executive, legislative, and judicial branches, I would argue that the government remained distinctly Creek because it retained the most important feature of traditional Muskogean political organization — representation on the basis of *talwa*, or town, a form of governing old as dirt in Creek country.

> The new government was patterned after the U.S. system. The legislative branch, or national council, was made up of a House of Kings (like the Senate) and a House of Warriors (like the House of Representatives). Each of the forty-eight towns (forty-five Indian towns, three freedmen towns) elected one representative to the House of Kings, and at least one representative, plus an additional delegate for every two hundered people, to the house of Warriors. (O'Brien, 126)

Given our discussion of the red and white divisions, might we argue that the House of Kings was somewhat, at the very least symbolically, like the white peace town division of the national council, and the House of Warriors like the red division? At any rate, at the very heart of the matter is the fact that Muskogees chose representation on the basis of the *talwa*, a system quite *unlike* U.S. government. And when one considers the traditional reality that town membership was/is determined by matrilineal descent, a factor built in to the total political system, surely this creates a government of difference, quite distinct from the U.S. system, much more of an accomplishment than simply borrowing European parlimentary forms.

There were executive and judicial branches of the government, and, to be sure, there were significant changes, such as the shifting of clan responsibility for policing members to the role of district courts; yet again, very Muskogean ideas permeated even these systems. One famous example is the Creek propensity to show up faithfully for their own hangings. After receiving the death penalty, the person convicted was given several months of freedom to go home and take care of his affairs, and then he would show up of his own free will for his execution, which was often performed, according to Creek custom, by his best friend. This is consistent with one's role within a clan. If an offender does not allow the proper punishment to be meted out to him, another clan relative will have to take the punishment in his place, so it is important to subsume one's individual will to the good of the larger clan. The political system retained important traditional Creek features, and additionally, inside Muskogean towns, the clans remained strong.

The most serious change of the 1867 constitution was the adoption of the secret ballot. O'Brien says, "Under the traditional system nominations had been made from the floor at council meetings. Nominees then stood in different areas of the council grounds, surrounded by their supporters" (128). In other words, people would stand around the nominee they wanted to vote for, and there was an important notion of taking responsibility for language, uniting word and deed, making physically evident what one stood for. The new method of voting caused a revolt by Creek traditionals in 1871 known as the Sands Rebellion.

After the Civil War, the Creeks faced an even greater crisis in terms of national government. Beginning in the 1890s, the United States government illegally forced the Creeks and other Indian nations to accept individual land allotments, dissolve their nations, and become citizens of Oklahoma. This left millions of acres open for theft by the "sooners," settlers trying to get into Oklahoma, a criminal act that the state continues to flagrantly and proudly celebrate today. As Angie Debo in *And Still the Waters Run*[16] and many other historians have documented, almost every member of the Dawes Commission, the congressional commission responsible for dissolving the tribes, was involved in land scandals.

Creek history is a history of resistance, and Creeks fought vigorously against these efforts of legislative genocide. As early as 1870, the Creeks had hosted the Okmulgee Council, an intertribal gathering of the general council of Indian Territory, and had adopted the Okmulgee constitution, which proposed an Indian state in which the tribes would retain their autonomy. The hope was that by banding together, the tribes could thwart the Oklahoma statehood interests. During the full-blood Isparhecher's administration in the early 1890s, the Muskogee National Council "passed memorials requesting that Congress respect the treaties" (O'Brien, 129). After the Dawes workers began enrolling people, "an intertribal council of the Five Civilized Tribes again petitioned Congress to allow them to retain their lands" (129). Congress ignored the will of the tribes, the treaty of 1832, and their legal right to exist as a nation on their lands, and passed the Curtis Act, an illegal piece of legislation that forced tribes to accept allotment "by force if necessary, dissolving tribal courts, putting tribal funds under the control of the Secretary of the Interior, and requiring presidential approval of all tribal laws. The Muscogee National Council appropriated twenty thousand dollars for lawyers' fees to test the act's legality. President William McKinley nullified the Creek nation's attempt to protect itself by vetoing the tribal law appropriating the lawyers' fees" (130).

Yet Muskogee resistance continued, along with joint efforts that combined the will of the so-called Five Civilized Tribes. A full-blood faction among Creeks that became known as the Snakes, so called because of one of the leaders of the movement, Chitto Harjo, whose first name means "snake" in Creek, began meeting at Hickory Grounds in 1901. They simply decided to continue Creek national government whether or not it was recognized by the United States. They elected a full government — executive, legislative, and judicial branches, including a Lighthorse brigade (the Creek police force) — and Harjo became a powerful and bothersome presence in Washington, showing up in senators' and congressmen's offices and spreading the treaty of 1832 out on their desks, demanding they explain why it was no longer valid. The Snakes' efforts were a tremendous act of faith, testament to the fact that Creeks have *never* been mere victims or pawns. They continued meeting at Hickory Grounds long after Harjo's death until the early 1930s, sending representatives to Washington to argue for the recognition of tribal government. Other tribes had similar full-blood factions resisting statehood — the Cherokee Nighthawks and Keetoowahs, and the Choctaw Ishki Oshta clan, for example. In addition to these traditionalist societies were nationalist parties within tribal government.

An important pan-tribal effort to continue tribal government was the Sequoyah Convention of 1904, a united front of the five tribes, which drafted a 35,000-word constitution and proposed separate statehood for Indian Territory as planned earlier at the Okmulgee Council. In Daniel Littlefield's editorial comments in *The Fus Fixico Letters,* he says that the Creek constitution contained "among other provisions — a bill of rights with thirty-one articles, the prohibition of child labor and farming out of convicts for labor, and a provision for a vote on woman's suffrage."[17] Congress simply ignored the request for a separate Indian state because of the tremendous pressure of the railroads, who would get clear title to right-of-way through the areas crossed by their lines as soon as Indian title was extinguished; and additionally, these railroads wanted to engage in broader land speculation. There were also pressures from whites who had managed in various ways to get into Indian Territory, since their land title was not really legally secure unless Oklahoma became a state, and then there were those in surrounding states clamoring to get in as well. These pressures forced Oklahoma statehood on the tribes—a state without clear title to the land, in reality an occupied territory.

And statehood, by anyone's account, was disastrous for the tribes. Before statehood, Creeks and Cherokees were more educated than their white neighbors, had their own school systems, and maintained facilities and funds for orphans as well as other social programs. After statehood, within a few short years, they were dispossessed of virtually all of their allotments through fraud by whites and found themselves living in poverty, in a nation that, in the late nineteenth century, was an exporter of corn to foreign countries such as Ireland. This was a complete failure, of course, of the claims of assimilation ideology, which promised that individual land ownership and U.S. citizenship would make Creeks successful farmers with access to white culture and material success.

In a WPA interview, a Choctaw elder, one of the few who still owned an allotment in the 1930s, described the actual effect of the allotment process thus:

> Despite all the wealth which had been placed in the laps of the Choctaws through the inheritance of the Choctaw Nation with its wealth of natural resources, this poor old full-blood Choctaw woman finds herself in her advanced age with nothing but one hundred and sixty acres of land, which she can neither sell nor eat, nor can she find a properly equipped farmer to whom she can rent it with the view of making it productive of a living for her. She is highly intelligent and wonders if, after all, it would not have been better had the Nationals had their way.[18]

Another Choctaw says:

> Then after allotment was over the Indians held a vote on whether we should have statehood or not, but I, for one, saw that our election meant little. Statehood had been inevitable ever since the discovery of coal in the Choctaw Nation.

And I just want to say this before I am through: I felt safer against robbery and violence when I was under the Choctaw law than I do now. A man never had to worry about thieves because an Indian wouldn't steal. There are more killings in one year now than there were during all the years of the Choctaw rule.[19]

Or as Creek writer and national politician G. W. Grayson says of statehood in the stinging indictment that closes his autobiography:

Here was a proposal which paralyzed the Indians for a time with its bold effrontery. Here we, a people who had been a self-governing people for hundreds and possibly a thousand years, who had a government and administered its affairs ages before such an entity as the United States was ever dreamed of, are asked and admonished that we must give up all idea of local government, change our system of land holding to that which we confidently believed has pauperized thousands of white people — all for why; not because we had violated any treaties with the United States which guaranteed in solemn terms our undisturbed possession of these; not because of any respectable number of intelligent Indians were clamoring for a change of conditions; not because any non-enforcement of law prevailed to a greater extent in the Indian territory than elsewhere; but simply because regardless of the plain dictates of justice and a Christian conscience, the ruthless restless white man demanded it. Demanded it because in the general upheaval that would follow the change he, the white man, hoped and expected to obtain for a song, lands from ignorant Indians as others had done in other older states.[20]

Creek resistance, as Grayson hints when he says the proposal paralyzed Indians "for a time," nonetheless continued throughout this catastrophic period. Although the U.S. government had declared that Creek government no longer existed, the United States still appointed a chief handpicked by the Bureau of Indian Affairs (BIA). Tribal elections were not allowed, a real irony for a nation whose role always seems to be protecting democracy and free elections for the entire planet. The Muskogees, however, "refused to concede the end of their tribal government. In 1909 the towns elected delegates and convened the Creek Convention. Although unrecognized by the federal government, which continued to deal only with its illegally appointed chief, the convention held regular meetings to discuss and decide tribal issues" (O'Brien, 132).

These efforts eventually culminated in the restoration of tribal governments with the passage of the Oklahoma Indian Welfare Act on June 26, 1936. Although the successful passage of this act has been associated with the deplorable conditions in Indian country made public through the Merriam Report, the Indian reforms of John Collier, and the Indian Reorganization Act, it should also be noted that Creeks, and other tribes as well, never completely capitulated, and the resistance leaders, who refused to acknowledge defeat and never gave up their governments, had something to do with this restoration. Although the Indian Reorganization Act, and its Oklahoma version, are highly contested even today because of their limited sovereignty and the continuing paternalism of the federal government, Chitto Harjo and other traditional leaders of his ilk are real heroes, much neglected in the study of Indian history in terms of what role they play as the predecessors to modern tribal sovereignty.

Since the thirties, Muskogean national government has had ups and downs: for example, from the mid-fifties, when the United States was aggressively forcing termination policy on tribes, to 1970, when the Creek Nation was again forced to accept BIA-appointed chiefs. In 1970, however, "Congress passed a law allowing the Five Civilized Tribes to select their own principal officers" (O'Brien, 132), and the last two decades have shown Creeks, and other tribes, practicing increasingly powerful forms of sovereignty.

The structure of modern Creek national government shares some powerful continuities with the 1867 Creek constitutional government. In 1979 the Creek Nation adopted a new constitution as a successor to the 1867 constitution. The complexities of modern life have created a wider array of programs and services; nonetheless, many basic areas, such as Creek health and education, are age-old concerns, and before the destruction wrought by statehood Creeks had an exemplary school system and social legislation that provided funds for handicapped and elderly citizens. These concerns continue today.

One difference in modern Creek government from the 1867 constitution is representation based on districts rather than tribal towns, but on the other hand, the tribe maintains relations with twenty-seven Creek communities, a growing number of which have their own tribal charters to determine their own affairs (O'Brien, 137). Creek government, then, might be characterized as "ever changing, ever remaining the same." At the core of modern Creek national life is a continuation of adapted forms of Muskogean traditionalism.

Today's government is composed of three separate branches — executive, legislative, and judicial. Principal chief and second chief, the executive branch, are voted on by enrolled tribal members over eighteen years of age, and the chiefs serve four-year terms. "The principal chief, with council approval, also appoints a five-member election board, a five-member citizenship board, and six Supreme Court judges," says O'Brien (133). The election board oversees tribal elections; the citizenship board oversees the nation's rolls of tribal members; and the court judges, appointed for six-year terms, rule "on tribal ordinances and traditional law and [interpret] the Muskogee constitution" (134). Under the executive branch, tribal programs are administered, funded by revenue from tribal businesses such as agribusiness and gambling operations, as well as federal monies. This is a very basic overview of a complex governing body, and those further interested should read the nation's newspaper, the *Muskogee Nation News*, to see the ins and outs of Creek government and services within Creek country. Hopefully, what has been demonstrated is the amazing successes of Creek cultural and national survival.

Before embarking on an explanation of Creek traditionalism — along with government, a second factor that constitutes national identity — I should note again that Creek traditions, customs, and beliefs are still viable in the Creek Nation. The existence of a number of strong traditionalists is indisputable; however, on an individual basis there is a good deal of variation among Creeks. Not every Creek is a traditionalist; nor is every Creek assimilated, embracing white cultural values. Neither are all traditionalists old people; the ceremonials are quite well attended by Creek youth. Creeks exhibit a wide range of knowledge about their culture. Some barely know that they are Creek and, for all practical purposes, are culturally white. In Oklahoma, however, simply being visibly identifiable as an Indian person sometimes subjects a person to racism and social stigmata, no matter how assimilated he or she might be. In contrast to assimilated Creeks, others view their identity in terms of the Creek Nation and are strongly connected to Creek language, ceremonies, and social events. In addition, there is a wide range of variability in between. Relative to other tribal groups in the so-called Five Civilized Tribes — specifically Oklahoma Choctaws and Chickasaws — the Creeks, Seminoles, and some Cherokees have retained more elements of traditional culture, especially language.

To avoid creating the problematic impression that precontact lifeways have disappeared, this study will employ the term "traditional Creek life" rather than precontact and postcontact culture. I acknowledge that the very term "traditionalism" is problematic, especially in the way it is sometimes perceived as dealing only with the past. I wish to posit an alternative definition of traditionalism as anything that is useful to Indian people in retaining their values and worldviews, no matter how much it deviates from what people did one or two hundred years ago. The nostalgic anthropological view, by contrast, creates a self-fulfilling prophecy. Only cultures that are able to adapt to change remain living cultures; otherwise they become no longer relevant and are abandoned. Yet anthropology often prioritizes the "pristine." Anthrospeak claims that things must be recorded because they are soon to die out, yet the anthropological definition of culture denies cultures the very thing that will allow them to survive: the possibility of changing and evolving with the times. Literature, as will be argued in the rest of the book, allows for this kind of creative change.

Traditionally Creeks are a matrilineal culture. Clan identity is passed down from one's mother. Clans, on a pragmatic level, provide a means of keeping track of relations and avoiding intermarriage. No one can marry within the clan from a traditional perspective. On a social and spiritual level, clans provide instruction and identification with a totemic element of nature. To name a few examples, there is the Raccoon Clan, the Bird Clan, the Wind Clan, the Sweet Potato Clan, the Alligator Clan. Today some leeway is given in determining clan identity. If a person's mother is not Creek, or a member of another tribe, the person might take the clan name of her father or be assigned to a clan. What is fascinating about the fluidity at the stomp grounds is the way in which clan identity retains its own flexibility while still maintaining the community's criteria for membership.

Traditionally, a person's clan uncle — her mother's oldest brother — would be her most important relative. More than any other relative, the clan uncle is responsible for teaching the young person Creek culture. Today, in most families, one learns traditionalism from whoever is willing and available to teach it, yet a special attachment to clan uncles is still often evident.

A Creek not only views himself as a Creek and a member of a particular clan but, traditionally, is also a tribal town member. A town, or *talwa,* as discussed earlier, consists of a body of people who have their own square ground, a *cokofa.* The square ground is an arrangement of arbors with specific seating arrangements based on clan membership around a circle where ceremonial dancing and medicine taking occurs. Outside of the arbors, around their perimeter, people camp during ceremonies. One belongs to his or her mother's town. Today people still commonly affiliate with a particular town; they will say, "I belong to Greenleaf Grounds," for instance.

Traditionally, as touched on earlier, the towns are divided into two classifications — red and white, or war and peace towns. In earlier times, the red towns took the initiative in deciding whether or not to go to war, and the war councils were held there; councils were held at the white towns "for the conclusion of peace, the adoption of conquered tribes, and to a certain extent the enactment of laws and the regulation of internal affairs."[21] Charles Hudson, who gives a more accurate and detailed account of red and white town relations than Debo, notes that redness and whiteness could easily change. A red town, for instance, could overnight become a white town; in other words, redness and whiteness were not constants.[22] In terms of national representation of the autonomous towns, councils were held at the leading war or peace town of the time, usually a town that had abundant food and adequate facilities for encampments.

Towns of the same color are said to be of the same fire, and towns of different fires are rivals, displaying, for instance, a keen sense of competition (to put it mildly) during stickball games. Games between rival towns were known to erupt into violence. When a town plays its own members at its home ground, which is often the case in recent times, the games are friendly, and the leader lines the opposing sides up in a pregame ritual and admonishes them in Creek to display goodwill and to put aside negative feelings.

In terms of religious life, the highlight of the Creek year is the Green Corn ceremony, which takes place in July or early August and must be observed before the new corn crop can be eaten. Green Corn is a time of renewal, the beginning of a new year, when individuals and communities are ritualistically purified and focused on living in right relationship with earth and kin.

A skillful description of the Green Corn ceremony is contained in Willie Lena's book *Oklahoma Seminoles: Medicine, Magic, and Religion*.[23] Unfortunately, the book's jacket lists the author as the white anthropologist James H. Howard "in collaboration with Willie Lena," but I feel that Willie Lena is, at the very least, the coauthor of the book, and not a collaborator. The information was dictated to James Howard by Willie Lena, and Howard organized, edited, and commented on what Mr. Lena told him.

Mr. Lena is *micco* of Tallahassee Grounds. Oklahoma Creeks and Seminoles are closely related. First, the Seminoles were part of the Creek Confederacy until they split off and moved to Florida in the late 1700s. Second, during Indian Removal in the 1830s, most of the Seminoles were removed to Oklahoma and resettled adjacent to Creek lands. The U.S. government even planned to remerge the Seminoles with the Creek Nation, but this did not happen. Thus, in Oklahoma, there is much interaction between Creeks and Seminoles. In fact, the distinction between elements within the two groups is somewhat blurred, though they are officially recognized as separate nations. Oklahoma Creeks and Seminoles speak the same language, whereas their relatives in Florida speak a dialect of Muskogee that is a little different but nonetheless mutually intelligible.[24]

Lena and Howard give a detailed, step-by-step description of the activities at the grounds during Green Corn. The description that follows is a summary of their work.

> The Green Corn Ceremony (*vcf-opvnka*, "corn dance"; *posketv*, "fasting") of the Oklahoma Seminoles has several purposes: first, to renew and purify the sacred fire, and hence insure the continued health and prosperity of the members of the square ground and their families; second, to provide the purification required before the men can eat the now-ripening green corn (hence the English name for the ceremony), although women may eat the new corn at any time; third, to bestow Indian names upon and assign clan seats to young men not previously initiated, likewise men being adopted into the town; and fourth, to recognize the tutelary spirits of certain animal species, such as birds, snakes, and bison, and hence maintain their continued good will. (Lena and Howard, 123)

Lena and Howard begin by describing the first day, which begins on Thursday. Since many Creeks or Seminoles arrive from out of town or even out of state, the first day involves setting up family camps, though some local people camp in all week and are already at the grounds getting things ready. Grounds members participate in cleaning up the grounds and getting them ready for dancing. As evening falls, starting around 7:00 but varying from dance to dance and depending on "Indian time," the *henneha*, the speaker, will make rounds every half hour, calling out to the people to prepare for an evening of dancing. Some time after the last call, the women begin to strap on turtle shells attached to leggings that the women fasten around their legs. The women sit just outside of the square, and the men and boy participants sit inside the arbors. The stomp dancing begins but lasts only until around midnight rather than continuing on until dawn as on other days of the dance. Anyone who has seen these women dancing counterclockwise around the fire in the middle of the arbors and under the stars, creating their compelling beat with a skillful toe-heel action that shakes the shells and sounds like a continuous *shúguta shúguta shúguta* while the male leader sings and the men behind him echo their responses, will not soon forget this event. The dancing ends early, around midnight, with the *henneha's* admonition that the following day will begin bright and early.

Around 5:30 A.M. the men and boys, working in a counterclockwise direction beginning with the *micco's* arbor, start work on the arbors, cleaning them and making necessary repairs, replacing rotten timbers and covering the tops with willow boughs as need be. In addition to cleanup, an important ceremony on this day is "killing the green wood" to protect the worshipers "from any potential harm which might have entered the ground with the repair materials" (Lena and Howard, 126). This is a very Creek notion of protection from harmful influences whose intentions are directed toward ill will.

A highlight of the second day is the women's Ribbon Dance. Although Creeks and Seminoles do not dance wearing fancy powwow regalia like beads and bustles, it is during the Ribbon Dance that they are decked out to their fullest.

> Some are dressed in a style approximating the traditional dress of Florida Seminole women and known to the Oklahoma Seminoles and Creeks as "Florida style." This outfit has a long, full skirt with rows of Seminole patchwork, a tight-fitting bodice on the upper body, and over it a long, wide, cape-like garment of gauzy material. Other Seminole women and girls wear the same general costume worn by the neighboring Creeks. This consists of a wide, single-color skirt with two or three rows of ribbon trim near the hem, over it a long apron, generally white or of a pastel color much lighter than the skirt, a yarn sash with large tassels at the waist, and a loose, sleeveless blouse. With either costume a large silver or German silver comb is worn in the hair at the back of the head, and from it varicolored ribbons are suspended

to hang nearly to the ground. Sometimes additional ribbons are attached to the shoulders of the upper garment in front and in back. It is from these supernumerary ribbons that the women's dance derives its most common English name. Many bead necklaces are worn, also earrings, and some women carry wild turkey-tail-fans. Every woman and girl, if she owns a pair, wears either terrapin-shell or condensed-milk-can leg rattles tied around her calves. The long skirts must be cut wide enough to allow space for these leg rattles. Some women paint a single red dot on either cheek....

Although this is not their day, nor their dance, and they will be spectators for the most part, the men and boys also dress in their best for the Ribbon Dance. For most Oklahoma Seminole men and boys today, the ceremonial costume consists of a pair of fancy cowboy boots, a pair of dark trousers, a homemade "Indian" shirt, and around the waist a yarn sash with yarn tassels that fall to the wearer's knees when the sash is in place. Over the shirt, trousers, and sash some men wear a red "hunting coat" with fancy rick-rack or braid trim, or a vest decorated with Seminole patchwork. A few wear "Florida style" patchwork jackets with blousy sleeves. At the neck, some men may wear a bright silk scarf with a sachet of *kaptucka* (*Teucreium canadense L.*) perfume tied in it at the back of the neck. One or two older men may wear a crescent-shaped silver gorget, a family heirloom. On the head is a western-style hat, either felt or straw, with a beaded hatband, and at the right side, near the front, a white crane feather with the vane shaved so that it trembles or vibrates in the slightest breeze. Some of the men wear a white horsehair roach with a single eagle or hawk tail-feather in its center, fastened to the back of the hat so that the center feather droops elegantly down in back. Others wear an upright feather fixed in a spring tube so that it constantly sways back and forth. Thus attired, the men and boys assume their clan seats in the various arbors. (Lena and Howard, 127–29)

There is a stickball game in the afternoon, and, in the evening, a session of stomp dancing that lasts from about 9:00 P.M. until about midnight.

On the third day of Green Corn, the sacred fire is carefully and ritualistically prepared. The fire and the sun are closely related in Creek story and ritual. According to the precise directions of the *hilis heyya*, the medicine person, the ashes of the old fire are removed, a new mound is built in the center of the square, four logs are placed in the sacred directions, four ears of corn are prayed over by the medicine person, and the four ears are sacrificed and consumed in the new fire. The fire is kept burning until the end of the ceremony, and four young men take coals from the new fire throughout the camp to start up the cooking fires that have been extinguished. This act, perhaps, is reminiscent of the Creek story of how Rabbit steals fire and spreads it all around, making it available for human use, a connection of the oral tradition to traditional ceremony in contemporary Creek society.

It is also on the third day that the medicines are prepared. Two plants are involved in medicine taking at the grounds—*pasa* (button snakeroot) and *hoyanica* (small pussy willow). Two young men are sent into the woods to procure these roots, and then the *hilis heyya* blows through a bubbling tube into a tub of water containing the medicine and prays over it.

The women and children are the first to take the medicine and to be scratched, if they so choose. Scratching is done with an ordinary steel needle and induces endurance during the ceremonies, which require staying up long hours, as well as good health: "Four scratches are made on each upper arm, four on each lower arm, and four on the back of each calf," say Lena and Howard (137).

Whereas the women take the willow root medicine, the men, who take medicine next, take the button snakeroot and then walk to the eastern limits of the ground and vomit. As Lena and Howard state, "The *pasa* is administered only to initiated men, and to them only during the first episode of medicine-taking, not during the last three, when only *hoyvnijv* is employed" (137). The scratching for the men takes place next. There is a second session of medicine taking, followed by names being given to new members of the grounds who may be sons of women who belong to that particular ground or adult males being taken into that ground if their mother, for instance, is not Creek.

After the naming ceremony, the Feather Dance, led by members of the Bird Clan, is performed. The dancers carry feathered wands made of native river cane containing alternating white and blue crane feathers. Lena and Howard describe the dance:

> The dance begins with each of the dancers taking a wand from the bunch at the front of the chief's arbor and moving to form a cluster around the three musicians, who face toward the east. They wear no special costume except for the shaved crane feather stuck in the hat or cap mentioned earlier in connection with the Ribbon Dance. Most of the men, in fact, are probably wearing second-best clothing, since they are in the midst of taking medicine, which involves kneeling in the mud

before the tub of *hoyvnijv* and pouring some of the medicine over their heads, and also vomiting up the medicine they have imbibed.

In the dance they hold the lower end of the feathered wand at waist level and dance in place, patting the left foot on the ground before them, drawing it back, and then patting the right foot and drawing it back, and so on. As they execute this step they also manipulate the wand, moving it back and forth at the top. The dancers sing in unison with the musicians. The head singer calls out the words "*apiu, apiu,*" and all the dancers whoop. He then begins to sing. Once he has sung the key phrase and the song is recognized, all who know it join in. In spite of the shabby dress of the dancers, the Feather Dance is strangely compelling and beautiful. The swaying of the feathered wands in time with the music creates the odd illusion of a flock of small birds hovering just above the dancers' heads. The songs are quite melodic and attractive as well. Each episode has four parts, and each part employs only one song, which is sung and danced to at four stations. The first station is in front of the west arbor, the second in front of the south arbor, the third in front of the east arbor, the fourth in front of the north arbor. These locations vary from one ground to another, however, and at some grounds there is a station at the *tajo*, or mound. At some grounds the dancers and singers march slowly from one station to another, intoning the cry "Hi-i-i" as long as they can hold their breath, then ending with a whoop. At others the dancers run pell mell from one station to the next. During the fourth episode the dancers do not stop at the last three stations but merely march slowly around the ground, dancing and singing. (Lena and Howard, 140–41)

Following the Ribbon Dance, there is more medicine taking and the "going to the water," an act of ritual bathing. A great feast ensues in the late afternoon for the ravenous dancers, who have been fasting since the previous evening. Creek dishes include *sofki*,[25] blue dumplings, sour corn bread, wild onions, salt meat, boiled beef, chicken, and rice, accompanied by familiar American foods.

In the early evening, the Buffalo Dance takes place, for which the dancers dress in their best. The men carry a single ballstick or a buffalo cane on which they lean during the dance, imitating the movement of bison. Lena and Howard state that "the Creek-Seminole Buffalo Dance is . . . one of the most colorful and exciting American Indian music and dance events in North America. The insistent duple beat of the shell shakers punctuated by the 'bellowing' of the 'buffalo bulls' and the juggernaut-like progression of the dancers, raising great clouds of dust, is incomparable" (Lena and Howard, 146).

Following the Buffalo Dance, there is more eating, and then the last night of stomp dancing begins, which will continue until after sunup. The men take medicine a final time and go to water, after which the *micco* gives a final talk.[26]

The two major foci of this chapter—Muskogean government and the Muskogean ceremonial complex—form the backdrop for the rest of the book, which will take up an application of Creek nationalism and Creek politics to Creek literature and, further, explore some of the ways Creek literature is deeply affected by Creek worldviews, which are embodied in Creek ceremony. Basic institutions of any nation include government and tradition, as well as a body of literature that defines a people's national character.

Sitting under the stars, finding a place on the plank under the willow boughs, or outside the square on a lawn chair when visiting, looking toward the sacred fire, waiting for the leaders to call for the next dance.

Loca. Turtles. Women shaking shells. Night dances under the arbors. Fireflies flitting around the willow boughs that roof them. Fire embers slithering up the night sky. *Shúguta shúguta shúguta,* women stepping toe to heel, the sound of shells shaking, the turtle voices.

CHAPTER TWO
Reading the Oral Tradition for Nationalist Themes: Beyond Ethnography

Tribal sovereignty was not invented by Chief Justice John Marshall nor extended throughout Indian country via federal Indian law, though these political definitions affect tribes in very important ways. Sovereignty is inherent as an intellectual idea in Native cultures, a political practice, and a theme of oral traditions; and the concept, as well as the practice, predates European contact. Creeks, for example, had local representation in autonomous towns, which met in regional and national assemblies, as early as A.D. 800.[1] Further, contact narratives tell us that Creek oral tradition articulated concepts of nationhood and politics:

> Bossu, who visited the Creeks in 1759, stated of the annual assembly: "They have an annual general assembly in the principal village of the nation. They build a large cabin for the occasion and each one takes his place according to rank. Each one speaks in turn, depending upon his age, his ability, his wisdom, and the services he has rendered the nation. The great chief of the tribe opens the meeting with a speech on the history and traditions of their land. He tells of the military exploits of his ancestors who distinguished themselves defending the nation, and urges his subjects to imitate the virtues of these men by bearing hardships and misery without muttering against the great spirit, who is the master of all living beings. He advises them to face adversity courageously and to sacrifice everything for the love of nation and of liberty."[2]

The idea that the oral tradition has always been a deeply politicized forum for nationalistic literary expression is developed well by Joel Martin in his analysis of the Red Stick War of 1813 to 1814 when Muskogees revolted against European infiltrators and their tribal collaborators. Upper-town Muskogees were involved in assassinations of Creeks who had assassinated other Creeks who in turn had assassinated whites as well as those who were friendly with the Indian agent Benjamin Hawkins, who had been making demands for Muskogee lands[3] (thus the name Red Sticks, for their war clubs painted symbolically red). It was a war against both internal traitors and outside oppression.

Martin discusses earthquakes that preceded the war, and how that Muskogee geography, the very land itself, was transformed into a deeply politicized oral tradition that took up national concerns. The land was speaking through these earthquakes, issuing political and cosmological warnings that were interpreted through prophets by means of oral tradition. Muskogees had been influenced by the anticolonial message of the Shawnee resistance leader Tecumseh, and the Creeks had a "vibrant oral tradition that delineated precisely which lands had been lost."[4] At this time there was a rise in prominence of medicine people who could interpret these rumblings from the Lower World and place them in their colonialistic framework through means of the oral traditon:

> Between 1812 and 1814, the Maker of Breath inspired the critical shamans and disclosed to them the great revelation that the time was ripe for anticolonial revolt. Speaking prophetically, these shamans declared to the people that the cosmos itself opposed the colonial invasion and despiritualization of Muskogee. If the earth shook, it was because the Maker of Breath could no longer stand the evils that Anglo-Americans forced on creation and on the people of the land. The Maker of Breath, the land, the cosmos, and the ancestors demanded that the Muskogee people repel the invaders — and their native collaborators as well. Thus, it was the spirit of order, not the spirit of chaos, that motivated the prophetic shamans to lead a political rebellion. Invoking the power of order and balance, the shamans gained great political authority and led the Muskogees in revolt, a revolt to restore proper balance to a terribly imbalanced reality.[5]

Martin goes on to note the deep interaction between political, spiritual, and oral stories: "The actions of these shamans reflected deep involvement with and acute awareness of spiritual powers. Just as they interpreted earthly events through the symbolic template of sacred stories about the Maker of Breath, so they now acted politically in a way directly patterned after their most sacred rituals."[6]

The Red Sticks help to answer an important dilemma: Given the sacred religious nature of many stories, is it appropriate to look for political meaning when dealing with the sacred? This is a question of considerable complexity, since traditional stories teach the origins not only of the material culture but of the worldview, values, and religious beliefs of the nation. I believe, however, as best as I can understand it, that there is always an interrelationship between the political and spiritual. The Red Stick traditionalists sought a spiritual response to a political problem. The Red Sticks' politics were deeply rooted in a Creek religious revival. The original layout of the Creek Square Ground itself served both spiritual and political ends, a place for busk and Creek assembly. As Corkran says, "The meeting places of the Creek governing councils were the square and the town house, the former for the daily public meeting in clement weather, the latter for ceremonial and winter meetings and also for meetings of a less public character."[7]

Is spirituality diminished when influenced by the political? I suppose it depends, perhaps, on matters of balance. Politics without spirituality is not only out of balance but potentially oppressive. Traditional spirituality, without a commitment to intellectual growth, can result in a state of affairs little better than the worst of tribal politics. We need to lift ourselves up spiritually *and* intellectually. And spirituality without politics appropriates belief systems without taking responsibility for human liberation. This, I believe, is the case with the New Age movement. Part of the problem with the New Agers, among many others, is the desire to appropriate Indian spirituality without any of the commensurate political responsibility that goes with it. The New Agers will talk all day about medicine wheels and sweats, but who has ever heard them talk about Indian land claims? They have managed a perverse separation of the spiritual and political that leans toward the grotesque and is more influenced by traditional Western Christianity's spirit/flesh bifurcation than they realize.

More generally, to return to things Creek, in addition to their religious value, literary acts, particularly metaphor, were/are an important part of Creek political society. One example is the dual organization of Creek national life through the red and white divisions — that is, the war and peace towns, and the associated symbols of these institutions, which constitute a rich set of myriad meanings that affect delicate social balances in the tribe such as the young men's needs to go to war and achieve rank (a red activity) and the old men's needs to govern the town and work toward stability and peace (a white endeavor). George Lankford, drawing on conversations with Choctaw writer Scott Morrison, reports on this political symbology, which is so pervasive it affects not only social political ranking but daily personal emotions:

> From these two realms of male identity and adult self-awareness stem a lifelong personal use of the red/white metaphor. Not only is one's long-term identity as a male in society either red or white, one is also red or white at any given moment. If one is experiencing anger or other hostile feelings, one is in the red mode, but if one is calm, reasoning, dispassionate, one is white. The spectrum of feelings and mental states thus tend to become dichotomized — one is either red or white most of the time. From this use of the metaphor to assess one's current state comes a logical extension — personal relationships. When one finds that a hostile relationship exists with another person — either or both wish the other harm, expect harm from the other, and live in a state of readiness for hostile acts — then one is on the "red path" or "red road" in relation to the other person.[8]

Some of the very building blocks of Creek society are literary — that is, metaphorical — and are invested with deep political, as well as personal, meaning.

Evidence for the interrelationship between Creek storytelling and Creek politics can be seen in the way people continue to tell stories in Creek country. Phillip Deere, a full-blood traditionalist from Nuyaka Grounds, gives a version of the Creek origin story which combines emergence with Creek national concerns. Deere begins his account by expressing that one should understand the meaning of the square grounds if one participates. He tells his story in order that Creeks might understand the evolution of their ceremonialism and its significance, the religious meanings of the grounds so that they understand when they participate there. The transcribed version of Deere's story is in David Michael Lambeth's collection of elders telling stories entitled *The World and Way of the Creek People.*[9]

> It's needed, the study of the Creek culture and what the significance of the tribal grounds or what is sacred to them and to the creation and where did the ceremonial grounds begin and how important it was to our ancestors should be brought out. But, since it hasn't been brought out a lot of the traditions have died down and much of it has been put

down and was never held as anything sacred anymore. It is more like just a recreation area to a lot of our Indian people and the non-Indian, of course, are a long ways from understanding what it's all about.

There was no ceremonial ground in the beginning and the history tells us that the beginning of the Muscogee people, or the Creek tribe, which are both the same, began as two sets of people made up the tribe.[10]

Next follows Deere's version of the origin story and his commentary on its meaning. I will not repeat Deere's telling here, since another version of the story is discussed in the chapter on Louis Oliver and the entire telling is very long; however, I do want to focus on how Deere provides a political gloss to the story of Creek migration. Deere's narration style is informed by Creek nationalism—he says that stories should be told in order that Creek people can be good Creeks, knowledgeable of the meaning of their traditions. Like Oliver, Deere explains the migration beginning with a search for the sun—the beginning, perhaps, of Creek reverence for sun and fire—and the people journeying toward the east because "they thought the sun was the purest thing of anything that eyes could see."[11] After dealing with the migration story and then discussing Creek prophecy regarding language and ceremonial loss, the storyteller begins actively "unfixing" his narrative—glossing his own story, politicizing it, and relating it to contemporary political events in Indian country. Rather than ethnographic artifact, for Deere, Creek narratives serve as warnings for Creeks if they want to continue as a recognizable nation of people:

I think a lot about these things. Sometimes it makes me wonder how many of our people will be destroyed? How many of them will be lost forever? I keep looking around. I keep a thinking and I hope that I'm not the only Indian left because of knowing this. We may look like Indians, we have the color of an Indian, but what are we thinking? What are we doing to our own children who are losing their language, their own ways.

I sometimes think that even within the government, there's an all-out effort to lose Mr. Indian. Even Reagan, his new Federalism or whatever it is, it means cutting off all the funding from the Indian people. There's two new bills in there right now that's going to do that, unless something is done about it. All these programs that are being cut off, it may not affect me that much, but it's going to hurt a lot of my people. But on the other hand, what's our people acting like? What are they doing? Are they still trying to be Indians or are they just benefit Indians, a three-day Indian, a clinic Indian, or BIA-school Indian, what kind of Indians are we?

It makes me think about that and sometimes I think that one of these days we are going to find in our mail box, an application to fill out to be an Indian. Are you an Indian? Yes. How do you know? I've got a roll number. Do you speak your language? Probably be a lot of them that will be "No." Did you go to ceremonies? "No." Can you sing? "No." What makes you an Indian?

I wouldn't be a bit surprised if something similar to that happens, that we will have to answer those questions, each and every one of us someday. Because I feel like the precedent was set in Boston not too long ago when the Matchbe Indians went to court over the land claim in Maine and around that New England states. These Indians were claiming half of Maine and when they went to court, just like I've been saying for five or six years, these things came out. But when this case came up, the judge directed his questions to the leader of the Matchbe Indians and asked him if they have their language. Matchbe Indians don't have their language. They say they don't, just a few words. Do you have Pow-wows? Yes, we have Pow-wows. Do you go, he said directing his question at the leader of the Matchbe? Yes, I go. What do you do? I go and watch them have Pow-wow; everytime they go, I'm there. Everything was turned over to the jury. After that, the question comes out do white people go there? Yes, they go. What do they do? They observe. Turned over to the jury and the jury rules they (Matchbes) are not American Indians. They have been trying to appeal that case all this time, but I don't know if they're going to gain anything or not. But that's the very thing I've been talking about. It's going to take more than a number to be an Indian. And those were the questions that came out of this court.

I think that from here on in, we as Muscogee people maybe facing the same thing in the future years. So, it is important that we preserve our language, try to know more and more about our culture. If that man would have said, "I beat on a drum," or "I put on my costume," or "I get out there and I sing with them," the jury would have something to think about. But they compared him to the whites and they were not any different so that's how come they were losing.[12]

Deere goes on to warn about the link between loss of culture and loss of sovereignty, astutely observing that being recognized as a nation requires an ongoing living culture. He follows through with advice for Indian college students, encouraging them both in applying themselves to their studies and in continuing cultural relations with their tribe. Is this a freak occurrence, the heavy investment of the political within the same telling as the Creek creation account? Did this begin with Phillip Deere? Has the tradition lost its authenticity because it now speaks of political matters rather than stories about talking animals and tricksters?

I would argue that oral tradition has always contained within it this level of political critique — responses to the overriding concerns of nationhood — and what we have represented in Swanton's and Tuggle's and many other ethnographic collections and anthologies of oral traditions has been divested of political commentary because of a perception that such matters were outside the purview of oral tradition and ethnography. (W. O. Tuggle was an ethnographer who collected stories in 1881 while he was Creek agent in Indian Territory. John Swanton collected stories in the Creek Nation between 1908 and 1914 and later published them as *Myths and Tales of the Southeastern Indians.* A little more than half of Swanton's collection is a reworking of the stories previously collected by Tuggle.) Throughout Deere's story is an interweaving of traditional narratives, such as the beginning of the Muskogee's cooperative relationship with plants and the origins of the red and white divisions in the tribe, with commentary on the tribe's current political, cultural, religious, and social state. This makes his storytelling quite distinct from Swanton's and Tuggle's representations, which are stripped of political commentary.

Do ethnographers ever depoliticize the narratives they record? Consider Theda Perdue's introduction to her recent work entitled *Nations Remembered: An Oral History of the Cherokees, Chickasaws, Choctaws, Creeks, and Seminoles in Oklahoma, 1865–1907,* published in 1980 and reprinted in 1993. Perdue's collection is from the massive oral histories work done as part of the WPA projects of the 1930s. Perdue says, "Generally omitted from this particular work are mere chronicles of political events and controversies. Adequate factual accounts of treaty negotiations, elections, and tribal legislation can be found elsewhere, as the reader will see in the notes following relevant chapters. Furthermore, the presentation of a comprehensive history of the southeastern Indian nations is not the intent of this book."[13] Obviously, from Perdue's comments here, she encountered a number of politicized narratives in the stories that Indians were telling during the thirties. Although one respects her choice not to make that the focus of her book, I might nonetheless suggest that just such a work is needed: a collection of oral political narratives that could provide Native perspectives on tribal politics.

Not only is there the problematic separation between oral tradition and the "factual" in Perdue's statement, as if treaties, elections, and tribal legislation constitute a social reality constructed only through written discourse and somehow separated from oral stories and community. There is the further problem that stories that show the way Indians viewed and negotiated treaties, conducted their governments, and passed laws are vital to Native cultural survival, both historically and contemporarily. This is as important as collections of "folklore," "mythology," or "cultural practices." During any time period — but especially the years Perdue's book covers, from the Civil War to Oklahoma statehood, when the tribes faced the biggest disaster of their history, the forced extermination of their governments — how could oral stories possibly be separated from their political content? Fortunately, the stories of Perdue's collection contradict this — in the narratives she records, political matters such as Oklahoma statehood are hot topics on everyone's mind, and the interviews are deeply politicized in spite of Perdue's claims to the contrary. Perhaps the thorny sentence simply fails to describe the book well rather than constituting a statement of the author's philosophy. Indian people were certainly talking politics when they told stories, then as now. If one considers Alexander Posey's Fus Fixico letters, it is apparent that at the turn of the century people throughout Creek country, and the rest of Oklahoma, were discussing statehood, political factions, legislation, resistance movements — from the stomp grounds to porch stoops to mercantiles to church meetings. There is a huge body of discourse that backs this up — letters, newspapers, books (one interesting example is the scholarship of the Kilpatricks, both native Cherokee speakers, who have collected scores of Cherokee social and ceremonial documents).[14] Politics, land, and story are deeply intertwined entities. The Dawes Act was planned legislative genocide, intended to shift communal land sharing to individual ownership. Not only land base was being stolen. Creek land and its communal ownership are at the heart of Creek culture; matrilineal systems of town membership are tied to Creek land, and communal maintenance operates on the basis of shared resources in these autonomous towns. As the Red Stick discussion indicated, this was not the first time that land and politics were the subject of Creek storytelling.

There are many ramifications to looking at the oral tradition as a politicized, rather than merely ethnographic, body of narratives. We might, for example, begin to see forums, such as the aforementioned political journalism of Alexander Posey, contextualized in a new way, as a variant of a pretty traditional Creek national activity. Given their deep engagement in Creek politics, Posey's letters, it might be argued, are just as authentic a representation of Creek communal storytelling as the Swanton and Tuggle collections. This will be covered in greater depth in the chapter on Posey.

This inclusion of political journalism as an example of Creek culture challenges, to some degree, the anthropological sense of what constitutes Creek traditionalism, though I believe a more fluid definition is consistent with Creek history. Looking at the stories collected in *The World and Way of the Creek People,* it is interesting to note that the Creek elders telling stories are a widely diverse group — from medicine people to church people to educators — and I would argue that traditionalism has always been a complicated matrix of social, religious, political, and cultural aspects. Susanna Factor, a Creek involved in bilingual education, comments on the possibility of more than one fixed definition of traditionalism.

Factor has an interesting discussion of how clan values can be passed on today, and she observes that while language preservation continues to be a critical issue for the tribe, many Creeks are still culturally intact in other ways, active either at the Creek Baptist and Methodist churches or at the grounds. Factor classifies church people as traditionals because "within the church group there are those who want to continue to use the language and continue their hymns and their traditions and carry on in this matter. I still classify them as a traditional Indian."[15] Factor, then, opens up traditionalism to more than one possibility. She implies that Creek identity has several components, but two of the important ones are language and culture. Some people, as her example illustrates, may be low on the language scale but high on cultural connections.

In addition to expanding the notion of traditionalism, studying the oral tradition as political discourse might contribute to a discussion of tribal sovereignty. Sovereignty, it seems to me, like the oral tradition, is an ongoing, dynamic process, rather than a fixed creed, and evolves according to the changing needs of the nation. This "unfixing" of the idea of nationhood is needed to avoid some of the problems that Edward Said and other postcolonial writers discuss regarding the problem of the emergent nation simply becoming a "colored" version of the old oppression — to borrow Gerald Vizenor's phrase, a "terminal creed." Creek oral tradition, then, with its many layers of meaning, contains great possibilities for teaching us about nationalism, since it lends itself well to this flexibility.

The concept of nationhood itself is an intermingling of politics, imagination, and spirituality. Nationhood encompasses ongoing treaty relationships with the U.S. government. Nationhood has to do with federal Indian law, and tribes' testing of the sovereignty waters through new economic developments and other practices. Nationhood is affected by imagination in the way that the citizens of tribal nations perceive their cultural and political identity. Nationhood recognizes spiritual practices, since culture is part of what gives people an understanding of their uniqueness, their difference, from other nations of people. Literature plays a vital role in all of this, since it is part of what constitutes the idea of nationhood; people formulate a notion of themselves as an imagined community through stories.

Further, literary origins of sovereignty in the oral tradition, which predate European treaty relationships with Native nations, are much more radical in conception than "domestic dependent nations"; that is to say, outright nationhood is assumed, without the qualification of being subsumed by another government. Although these days the government of the occupiers is widely accepted, and though this government controls most of the power, it is not a fact that colonial governments and their constitutions are inherently superior to indigenous ones. Native sovereignty is recognized in the U.S. Constitution, but it also precedes the Constitution. Some might even argue that it supersedes it, and that limitations of tribal sovereignty are an encroachment, to use Howard Adams's phrase, a form of "constitutional colonialism"[16] favoring one constitution over another.

Extending the discussion of sovereignty beyond the legal realm to include the literary realm opens up the oral tradition to be read contemporarily by tribal nations so that definitions of sovereignty, which come from the oral tradition, might be used as a model for building nations in a way that revises, modifies, or rejects, rather than accepts as a model, the European and American nation. Oral tradition then becomes a useful tool rather than an ethnographic artifact.

This is not to deny the very real legal limitations that tribes have to work with in colonialistic America, like the plenary powers of Congress, for instance. Yet tribes also have the right, in their own critical discourse, rhetoric, storytelling, and literary discussions, to advocate something quite different, to discuss other possibilities, and to consider activism that might bring to reality ever-increasingly powerful forms of sovereignty—perhaps advocating for reopening discussions of full national status rather than working within the current limiting legal definitions as if they are set in stone.

If one accepts the deep politicization of traditional stories, then another issue that arises is whether we have been interpreting the narratives to their fullest potential. Might the symbolism of oral tradition, like Creek symbolism more generally, as with our discussion of the red and white dualism in the tribe, be deeply political? For example, when we consider the story of Turtle's broken shell and his concomitant recovery through singing a medicine song (the subject of the next chapter), might this story illustrate not only the power of chant but a critique of colonialism and a comment on Native resurgence and recovery? If so, this opens up a new/old way to teach the stories to Creeks, as a body of symbols that deal with Indian pride, Indian activism, Indian resistance. This makes the stories much more subversive than the anthropological discussion in which they are usually cast. Little wonder Swanton and Tuggle would avoid discussing these political contexts. When one considers the vast body of motifs dealing with tricks—encounters with opponents, disguises, transformations; little guys facing off with more powerful enemies and winning through ingenuity; rapacious tricksters and their victims; stories of flight and dispossession—how can we overlook the fact that these stories may also function as postcolonial critique, in addition to explanations of the spiritual and material origins of the culture?

Howard Adams says: "Of course, having Métis and Indians explore their identity and culture is not necessarily dangerous nor negative, providing self-awareness includes a political consciousness. Cultural imperialism does not. It is a false form of nationalism stressing legends and myths the state uses to direct Natives' attention away from revolutionary nationalism."[17] I would argue that oral traditions—legends and myths, if you will—performed in their cultural contexts have always been nationalistic and are told for the purpose of cultivating a political consciousness. If one considers the comments of the elders telling stories in *The World and Way of the Creek People*, virtually all of them indicate the purpose of the stories is to inculcate a sense of Creekness in Creek listeners—what it means to be from a clan, a town, a nation; their storytelling constitutes an act of Creek survival. Creek nationalism is created through Creek narrative; the two form an interdependency, not an oppositional discourse. Although Adams is surely justified in critiquing the way "legends and myths" are often used as a diversion from political discussion, this is not an inherent characteristic of the discourse itself. "Legends and myths" might provide strategies for nationalism instead of functioning as a distraction, and this may be more closely linked to their original purpose.

But no wonder Adams reacts this way, given the pablum out there in terms of coffee table books of myths and legends and complicated narratives turned into kiddie stories. "Indian stories" are popular stuff, as long as the creation, hero, trickster, and coyote stories fail to explicate the tribally specific cultural meanings, especially the political ones. I've had New York City editors call me wanting to take on these projects for big bucks, and the minute I started talking about the complications of the stories, the translation issues, the political ramifications, they say, "Oh, but we don't want anything that academic." My own biased view makes me strongly suspicious that what they do want are children's stories, nice stuff that presents white people with images of themselves, all mixed together in a highly palatable pan-tribal stew. In contemporary times, stories from the oral tradition that teach, for instance, earth connection, are charged with additional meaning when the earth is overrun by foreign invaders, and the colonized are engaged in struggles for the return of the land and recognition of their very status as a people, as a nation, within that landscape.

My concern has to do with the way we play into colonial discourse with these stories, the way we depoliticize our own literatures in an oral tradition genre that was once strongly nationalistic, and the way significant tribal differences are blurred and a sense of specific sovereignty is diminished. I am concerned about what happens to the political intent of the stories when they are separated from their tribal contexts, removed from a total existential situation. For example, in the case of Creek stories, a pan-tribal context—simply throwing a story about Rabbit, for example, into a chapter on tricksters in a cross-tribal offering—might cause a divorce from a sense of "Creekness." The collection might obscure knowledge of what it means to be from a clan, a town, a nation where these narratives are contextualized with other stories, songs, and ceremonies from within the Creek Nation rather than performed as iso-lated fragments alongside a confusing array of tellings from other tribal traditions. Would these stories better serve our own folks in the context of the passed-on tribally specific traditions, histories, religious prac-tices, and political thought that create their meanings? In that way, lit-erature is moved closer to activism and politics rather than farther away. This is not an attempt at anthology bashing per se—there are some wonderful collections out there that preserve in one place stories, es-says, fictions, and poems central to Native literature. Some of the most powerful and underappreciated work, however, has come from mem-bers of tribal nations authoring or editing books that contain the liter-atures of their particular tribe. For example, Percy Bullchild's book of Blackfoot traditional narratives entitled *The Sun Came Down*[18] deals with an entire corpus of Blackfoot stories and seeks Blackfoot contexts; other books that come to mind are the many works of Basil Johnston on Ojibway narrative,[19] and the previously mentioned Kilpatrick books.[20] The strength of these works is that they deal with the narratives of a specific tribal nation rather than lumping together stories from many different tribes in the usual structural categories such as creation, hero, trickster, and monster slayer tales, and so on.

The scholarly focus on oral traditions among Native literary special-ists has largely concerned itself with translation and performance, with much attention given to the way in which Dennis Tedlock, Dell Hymes, and Jerome Rothenberg have dealt with these issues. As important as the scholarship of the last two decades on these issues has been, my pur-pose in this chapter is to look at oral tradition in a new way, to expand the parameters of what we normally consider as the tradition itself, to argue not only that the literal versus literary translation problem is a dilemma, or the performative aspects that are lost in writing, but that often some of the best stories are not even considered as possibilities for translation because we have too narrow a view concerning what con-stitutes traditional "material." In cultures that operate under the cir-cumstances Walter Ong calls "primary orality," all information is passed on by word of mouth. Everything is narrativized, including political in-formation. What we often see in collections of oral traditions is only a small part of the tradition with a focus on the stories most popular with ethnographers, the ones that usually get cast in the aforementioned struc-tural categories. Hopefully, what has been demonstrated is that the tradition is a politicized one and that treating it as such may enhance its cultural integrity rather than diminish it.

When talking to both Native and non-Native students, I find that there is a huge dark cloud that surrounds the issue of translation of Native languages. While we assume that every other body of literature in the world is translatable, we seem to hold out a different set of expectations for indigenous literatures. The very reason we read García Márquez, for example, is that we assume that in the English translation something of the integrity of the original will be retained. When reading translations of Native literatures in English, however, the assumption seems to work in the opposite direction — that is, readers always tend to note what is lost. In regards to translated Latin American literature, one often hears of the superlative job of a particular translator, but how frequently do we hear of Native literatures that are examples of exemplary translations?

I would like to argue that Native literatures, like the literatures of many other nations, have sufficient literary excellence that they often retain something of their power in translation. I would like to argue, further, that Native literature is of equal merit to other literatures, so much so that it can, in fact, be translated, just like other literatures of excellence. What happens when Native literatures are rendered to the realm of problem (like the Indian problem, we have the translation problem) is that Native cultural production is then examined as ethnography rather than tribal national literatures. Rather than assuming that outside approaches have been the problem, we assume that the literature itself is the problem, and it is placed in this special ethnographic category that has a unique set of rules that apply to static cultures located in the past rather than viable nations facing contemporary political realities.

This is not to diminish the very real fact, one quite well established in the ethnography discussions, that translations vary in quality, and there are very real differences between a reader's experience of a written text and the oral perfomance of that text in a Native community. Many of the ramifications of this, in terms of both performative and cultural contexts, have been discussed endlessly. What I wish to emphasize here is the assumptions that may exist behind the Native translation skepticism. The diminishment argument seems to liken storytelling to copying a videotape — each telling is a poorer copy of the original. Like assimilation doctrine, this seems to me to assume that sameness is always good and difference is always something to be avoided. Assimilation, the so-called Indian problem, assumes that Indians are, in fact, problematic, that they ought to act like white folks; and the translation problem assumes that Native stories are problematic, that they should always remain the same, to deviate as little as possible from their correct original version. Stories have a correct cultural context and meaning, and translation always messes that up. The irony here is that stories supposedly retain their integrity by remaining authentically Indian, whereas in assimilation, the point is to erase Indianness. However, narratives are allowed to remain Indian, while Indians are not, because the narratives are relegated to quaint objects of the past, as will be discussed shortly.

I realize that opening up the idea of translation can be taken to a dangerous extreme, that it could be used to validate the very loose transliterations (Jerome Rothenberg's work comes to mind, loose literary translations of previously translated materials, many generations removed from original languages and contexts). This is not my intention, however. Instead, I want to point out some new ways to think about Native studies. The problem with the "translation problem," with its skepticism and emphasis on literary diminishment, is that it places us within a "pure versus tainted" framework that so much of Native studies gets cast in:

Pure	Tainted
oral tradition	writing
performance	print
original language	translation
precontact	postcontact
Indian religion	Indian Christians
Indian culture	Indian politics

We could go on and on with our short list here, but the problem is pretty obvious — this locks Native studies into a system that does not allow the discipline to evolve; it is the way in which we have inherited the vanishing mentality. I might argue that the translation controversy has as much to do with the vanishing notion as with linguistic realities. In other words, I think there are ways to talk about very real critical differences in the quality of translations of Native narratives without succumbing to this "the Indian world is falling apart" trap, where nothing is as good as it used to be, which is implied by the pure versus tainted framework. This is to say that by redirecting our language we can use our energies to concentrate on cultural survival rather than cultural disintegration.

What I have noticed in discussions with Native students regarding their own skepticism about translation of Native languages is that this dark view is wrapped up in very sensitive and important issues of literary self-determination. Their skepticism seems to originate from the fact that in their home communities, translation has almost always involved work done by outsiders — whites telling Indians the true meaning of their stories and the right way to speak their languages. What I hear in my students' skepticism seems to have relatively more to do with white people taking over the discourse than an endorsement of the vanishing mentality or strong belief that Native literature is untranslatable; though, to be sure, these anthropological assumptions can creep into Native communities, as well as Native studies departments.

The point I wish to make is that this very system just described is part of what has caused the depoliticization of the oral tradition in the first place — operating under the assumption that the oral tradition is a static body of narratives located inside areas of translation problems, performance problems, and textual representation problems, among other "Indian problems," scholars have glossed over their political meanings. This is not to say that all translation problems have been resolved already, but in the future, this kind of work will be done increasingly by Indian people who speak the languages of their tribe and are interested in recovering their literatures rather than by Native lit critics simply rehashing the discussion that surrounds the scholarship of Tedlock, Hymes, and Rothenberg.

The oral tradition is a living literary tradition, the standard by which Creek stories, oral and written, are judged. Like any other literary tradition, it consists of a complex body of genres, characters, settings, plots, images, symbolic systems, structuring devices, as well as a relationship to larger Creek ceremony, society, politics, and government, that need to be explored in terms of formulating and analyzing approaches to Creek literary texts. These two aspects of the tradition have been most often overlooked — its central place in establishing contemporary literary criteria and its political meanings. Critics create literary theory in relation to literature, and one would expect nothing less from national literatures — that the oral tradition would generate vital approaches for examining Native literatures. Oral tradition, then, becomes central to Native political analysis and the development of Native literary theory rather than fodder for backing up critics' pet theses on performance and translation, a discussion that has become largely redundant.

Dear Hotgun:

Well, so here it's come wintertime and all the leaves has dropped off the trees. The birds perched on bare branches just sitting there biding time like they blood's too froze to take off. Overcast days and rain, a little sleet.

So it was while the coonhound's water bowl start to freeze of a morning and longhandle underwears pulled out of the bottom of chest of drawers and days getting dark before supper that Stijaati Thlaako was had taking advantage of the cold weather by organizing deer hunt with Big Man. A sudden cold snap good sign for deer chances, and the last day of season you can shoot a doe; Stijaati think his probabilities of deer steaks in the freezer and jerky in the cabinet might be about as good as they gonna get. Both of them been cleaning out the cobwebs from they old muskets and talking about where to go on closing day. As usual neither one done a lick of homework scoping out hotspots for deer stand and the like. Big Man got a twelve gauge he gonna try to shoot slugs out of since he don't got no deer rifle and Stijaati has infantry days gun to sling over his shoulder. Rabbit don't take part in no hunt mebeso get shot at too often.

They pert near kicked up a dust cloud arguing so much hot air where to go while spit-shining they firearms. They was finally to agree on a spot down by the Oktahutche, the Canadian River, just the other side of a cow pasture where they'd seen deer grazing amongst the cattle toward dusk. Seen 'em from they cars that is. They parked Stijaati's truck on a field road that goes to a sorghum patch next to the cattle. Then they was cross over the bob wire, and walked to the edge of the field while the cows watch them on the other side. They gotta cross the wire again to get to the woods that leads downhill to the river then pick a tree that ain't so far back in that they cain't see out into where the cows is grazing.

Then Stijaati he say, "Be careful you don't shoot one of them Herefords," while Big Man use a fallen log to lean against a tree and shimmy up to the first branch. Stijaati can see this gonna take awhile maybe half the day but he has to stay put in order to hand the gun up. Big Man don't make no more than the second branch nohows when he huffs out. Stijaati knows they ain't got no time to lose beings how it's the last day of season and he decides to go for the long shot of kicking a deer up while he's walking around. Truth is he don't had no patience for sitting still in deer stand in the cold. They agree to meet up back at the truck come dark.

Stijaati decided to walk as close to the river as he could to keep his bearings. And Stijaati he go on and says to himself, "I'll just keep to the top of the bank," but he found that too close to the river's edge he had to fight brush and bramble and fallen scrub trees and the more he veered a little away from the Oktahutche, the easier going it was. He was only give a big grunt and say, "I'll just stick to these bluffs and keep the river within sight on my right." In order to stay on the hilltops he couldn't walk a perfect straight line, naturally, and pretty soon he'd lost sight of the river but he still knowed where it was. "I'll just walk a little ways until I can see the river again," he got to thinking and headed back toward the Canadian. He suspicioned that in no more than a couple hunerd yards the sandbars would come back into view. About a half mile later he hadn't seen the river and a light snow commenced to falling. He didn't know which direction to turn. "They's only four choices," he thought hopefully, "and I done eliminated one of them." Getting colder and the snow falling in big flakes now. What's more starting to get dark out there in the trees. He was dressed for cold but not for snow. Just then a big doe come bounding along out in front of him and he had a clear shot in easy range. A gift before Christmas.

So it was Stijaati sighted in just behind her shoulder for a heart shot and thinks good kill for bleeding and the doe making her way through the oak trees easy as a dogtrot around third base after knocking the ball clean outta the park and she hadn't even smelled him there upwind from her or heard him quiet as he'd been where he stopped to puzzle out where he was.

He lifted up his gun and sighted along the bead . . . "But what if I don't miss?" he was think. "How am I gonna pack this doe out in the snow and the dark when I ain't sure exactly which direction to walk, not that I'm lost, of course. But it might be just as easy to tell Big Man I didn't kick up nothing. My nephew is liable to bring over a few deer steaks nohows like he does every year." By this time too late to shoot and he was had go on and think "gol-dang, if she waddn't just too fast barely got sight of her before she go on."

This situation of being lost in Oklahoma is one you gotta work special hard at on account a country road was come out of purty nearly every woods. You cain't see the back of a tree stand for the road on the other side of it, so if you was to just keep walking in a straight line, you'll run into a dirt road, and then if you was to walk another section or two down that road, you'll come to a house. It ain't like being lost in the Rocky Mountains. That's what Stijaati done. He reached the dirt driveway of a little gray clapboard shack with a tool shed behind it fixing to cave in on itself. He was see a rusty yellow '78 Toyota pickup with country mud caked on the runners and underside parked in front, so most likely somebody's home. Stijaati stood on the porch and knocked on the door. A black kid answered, high-school age. Stijaati just stood there blinking with his antique rifle slung over his shoulder. See, he'd expected someone he knew to come to the door, and then maybe he'd know where he was as soon as he saw a familiar face. Before that he'd even hoped to seen a mailbox with a name and a rural route number, and then he wouldn't have had to even knock in the first place, just figured it out and walked back to the truck. But this young black kid wasn't a black Creek kid who he surely would have known him or his family. He didn't see no way out of admitting he was clean lost.

Stijaati he was say, "Um, are your parents here?" Mebeso feel like a little kid who didn't know his way home from school.

The young man says, "No, they went to town." He looked at Stijaati's rifle. "But they'll be back soon," he added quickly.

So it was at least he didn't have to admit he was lost to the kid's folks. "Could you mebeso give me a ride over to the paved road that goes to Four Corners? I'm meeting my hunting buddy over thataways." Maybe he could get out of admitting he was lost after all.

The kid looked at Stijaati's gun again and didn't say anything. Just stood there inside the house. Pert near a hunerd percent he waddn't gonna give Stijaati a ride. Who could blame him? Smart kid. That waddn't Stijaati's only problem. Big Man probably give up his tree stand a long time ago but Stijaati had the truck keys meaning Big Man standing out in the snow. He'd locked his truck on account of it sitting there bigger than Dallas on a well-traveled country road full of tools and a little money hidden in a Folger's coffee can behind the front seat.

Stijaati was ask, "How do you get back up to the oil road?"

The young man was say, "Up here half a mile is a road that runs north to the pavement."

Stijaati he go on and say, "Thank you," and started his long walk in the dark. Now that he knew where he was he was think to hisself, "I shoulda killed that doe." They was no moon out, and it gets pitch dark out here in the country what with no streetlights or lit-up porches, but you already know that, I reckon. Stijaati only stayed in the middle of the road by keeping the gravel under his boots and the dark shape of trees on both sides of the ditches. He might as well work on his story, and it had better be a damned good one too since Big Man must be sitting in the back of the pickup hunkered down against the cab teeth knocking together and cussing him in between chattering spells. Let's see. He had heard a "Rifle Shots," he recollected, the story coming to him as he walked in the dark, the crack of a 30–06 booming through the trees. He was make up now how he walked toward the hill where the sound come from. Might as well check it out on account of not having any luck hisself nohows was what he gonna tell. A big doe come crashing in front of him, her left leg was swinging wild as she bound off on her three good ones. He was almost start to see her more he took to lining out his story. Stijaati could see her white tail disappearing into a clump of trees. He knew she was going down soon, and mebeso he decided to follow her in case she'd run far and the hunter had lost track of her. The guy might need some help packing her out, who knows? She reappeared coming down the side of a hill just ahead, then she disappeared again in a heavily wooded bottom. Stijaati run over to the trees and begin following the blood trail until he found her in a clearing. Her eyes was already glazed over. Stijaati fired a shot in the air and hollered "Over here!" and five minutes later a young teenager run into the clearing. The kid was excited and out of breath. Who should he call this guy? How about Nathan, a black kid? It was the young man's first kill and Stijaati helped him string the doe up and clean her and they both took turns carrying her to the kid's pickup — he better not say to his house because Big Man or Rabbit liable not to know of any black kid named Nathan out thisaways.

Stijaati finished his story making reached the road that ran north and he could barely make it out as a dark tunnel through the trees. He hurried along the last mile and breathed out a sigh of relief when he found the crossroads and felt asphalt under his boots. The kid knew his stuff, sure enough. He could see his truck up ahead, and Big Man must be laying down in back by now, most likely covered up with the old tarp laying in the bed. Stijaati pitched a stone at the tailgate and hollered, "Yo, Big!"

No sound other than the rock pinging off the tailgate. He walked up and looked in back.

Not a sign of Big Man. Shit! Maybe he got stuck in the fork of the Blackjack he'd shimmied. Now he'd have to go back to the tree stand and pry him out. God a-mighty. At least he had a flashlight in the cab. He got a tire iron too in case he had to dislodge Big Man's big Indian ass from a tree jam. He made his way over to the sorghum field. He ripped the nylon liner of his jacket ducking under the first wire so at the next fence he stood on the bottom strand near a post and climbed over and ripped out the crotch of his pants on that one. The cows watched him, and he seen in their dumb brown eyes, "Back *again*?" He hollered, "BOO!" at them, and waved his hands in the air. He thought of a joke an Indian buddy had told him in the army: "What's the difference between white ghost and Indian ghost?"

The white ghost says, "BOO!"

Indian ghost says, "BOO! aieeeeeee..."

He shined the light on the trees, looking for Big Man's stand, and he seen something white blowing in the breeze against the trunk of the one he was looking for. What the hell? It was a note tacked to the tree. He shined the light up into the branches like a hunter searching for a treed coon to shake out, while mebeso coon dogs jumping against the tree baying. He walked over and pulled the note off the nail.

Dear Stijaati:
Hi!

    I was had. wait at the truck for a spell then caught a ride when Walter driven by.

Why didn't Big Man leave the note on the truck where they were supposed to meet? Stijaati wondered. Under the wiper blade or something. Only one answer. Big Man must have forgotten they was to meet back at the pickup and thought Stijaati was s'posed to walk back to the stand where he started out. "Or was I the one forget the right meeting place what with getting lost and making up the story about Nathan?" Maybe they *was* supposed to meet right here at the tree stand after all. But then how did Walter see Big Man and offer him a ride? From the road he couldn't have spotted him sitting in the tree and even if he did he wouldn't park his car and come strolling up to a man's deer stand for a little friendly conversation. Only one thing possible. Big Man must had petered out deer hunting most likely twenty minutes into the damned thing all stove up sitting in tree fork and throwed his gun down to the ground and jumped out and wandered back to the truck gonna pretend like he been scouting deer from the tree all day long whenever Stijaati got back except Walter come along first.

This ain't the story that Big Man tells about suffering cold and worried past dark in a tree stand waiting for Stijaati who he never seen again until two days later when he saw him talking to the Creek Lighthorse officer outside of Keck's Grocery in Weleetka. This ain't the story Stijaati tells of hunting until just before dark then going to his truck as they'd agreed and waiting around for Big Man until he finally went back to the tree stand and walked the river both ways for an hour looking for him. This is my own speculations, based on what I know about them two. This is what we call Indian oral tradition, the real stuff, not tales and legends.

They didn't talk to each other for as long as three days, but then since deer hunt didn't pan fry, they decided to try their luck at Karaokeing instead. Except they drove up to Tahlequah to do their crooning so they was had call it Chereeokieing mebeso. By the end of the evening, after getting wiser from Bud, they stopped arguing about who left who and where during deer hunt. Stijaati sung, "I'm Proud to Be a *Muskogee* from Muskogee," and Big Man sung an old Bob Wills classic, "Roly Poly," and Rabbit sung "Mamas Don't Let Your Babies Grow Up to Kill Cowboys" while Stijaati and Big Man two-stepped to it around the hardwood dance floor which was when some rednecks in straw Resistol hats chased them out of the bar and they was had to get the hell out of Tahlequah and clean out of the Cherokee Nation altogether I mean just a-hooking it toward Highway 69, which put a quick end to an evening of Chereeokieing.

Sincerely,
Jim Chibbo

CHAPTER THREE

In the Storyway

The chapter that follows represents a real struggle for me. When I first began my doctoral dissertation at the University of Oklahoma, I had grandiose plans to do a good deal of translation from Creek to English, collecting stories that Creek people are still telling in the Muskogee language and contrasting them with the versions that are represented in John Swanton's well-known collection. Two things happened that made my plan difficult: (1) I got a job away from home in Nebraska, which cut off regular contact with Creek language that I had been trying to relearn (relearn it in the sense that relatives knew it but not me), and (2) I had a crisis of faith regarding ethnographic work. I had begun to wonder if ethnography could be accomplished under any circumstances without objectifying people—that is, turning them into objects of study instead of representing the depth of their humanity.

While experiencing these doubts, I nonetheless felt—and continue to feel—the need for tribal people to build up their own national body of discourse for the sake of educating themselves about their cultures, and I believe that at least for their own purposes, Native people should be the ones doing this rather than outsiders (although certainly Native scholars engaged in these efforts need to know about works written about their tribes by non-Indians and be actively engaged in analyzing those books).

In regards to teaching and writing about Native literature, I believe we have too easily accepted an inheritance handed down to us largely by English departments experienced in dealing with American and British canons (but not necessarily the Native one) when we have our own canon, a large body of written and oral work authored and spoken by Indian people, both primary literatures and commentaries on those literatures in written and oral forms, which have existed for centuries and must surely provide models for interpretation and principles of literary aesthetics. I have felt that literature rises out of land and language and stories, and given that tribal nations have different landscapes, different languages, and different stories from the United States and England (and, importantly, tribal members and their nations are defined, legally, differently from the rest of the American citizenry, including America's minorities), those differences must suggest rejection of the approach to teaching Native literature as simply some kind of "minority extension" of the American canon.

Looking at language and oral tradition and land, the places of origin for Native literature, makes a lot of sense. We scholars haven't yet done enough to articulate how the oral tradition provides the principles for interpreting our national literatures — the genres; the unique approaches to character development, plot, theme, setting, and so on; the effect on the structuring of stories; the philosophies that come out of this tradition; the contexts it provides for understanding politics, religion, and society. Many works of anthropology have been written in these regards, but few take up the obvious question: since the oral tradition is a body of narratives — that is, of literature — what does it teach us about interpreting literary texts written by tribal people influenced by this very tradition? It is toward this end that I present "In the Storyway," as an example that certain key stories need to be examined really thoroughly; and when we have looked at enough of these stories, we need to ask ourselves what we have learned from them that might help us formulate interpretive strategies.

I examine only one story here, so I am hoping others will take up the call, especially those more proficient in Creek language than I, and begin to explicate others. If nothing else, I hope to use one story as an example of how profound the literary nuances of Creek traditional narratives can be so that the next phase of work might become obvious to others: the need to examine them for the interpretive principles they provide. The weakness of this chapter is that I have not yet attempted to articulate these literary "rules"; I've merely tried to demonstrate the potential for that through one particularly rich narrative and to encourage others, and myself, to examine enough of them that we can construct just such a criticism. I have suggested one conclusion about Creek national narratives: the technique of persona writing is deeply Creek, and the fact that so many Creek writers employ this form is no accident — its very roots may be seen in Creek oral tradition.

Further, as Hotgun and Jim Chibbo said in the introduction, they didn't merely want to explicate Creek texts; they wanted to write a Creek book. I don't know what could make this book feel any more Creek than this powerful story about *Loca,* given the centrality of turtle in Creek ceremonial life through women's shell shaking. Symbolically, Turtle traverses earth and water, This World and the Lower World. He is a primordial reptile, a link to looking back at an ancestral past, more specifically at women's ancestral ceremonial roles.

The story that follows is Creek elder Linda Alexander's version of how turtle got his broken shell. Linda is a much-respected Creek traditionalist and member of Greenleaf Grounds. I heard this version of the story at Linda's house in Norman, Oklahoma, where she told the story to me, her daughter Bertha Alexander, and the anthropologist and Southeastern Indian specialist Pam Innes. What follows is the transcript from that evening, including:

1. The conversation that leads up to the Turtle story (see the subheading "Conversations").
2. The version told in Creek by Linda ("Creek Language Version"). There is an interlinear translation in English attempted by Pam Innes and me. It should be noted that because neither of us is a fluent Creek speaker (though Pam is certainly much more advanced in the language than I am), the translation must be taken as a very crude attempt and not as an authoritative or expert rendering. Consequently, the interpretations offered on the basis of the translation are speculative, although they are undertaken with larger Creek cultural contexts in mind and Linda's own translation of the story into English as a counterbalance. Perhaps a Creek scholar fluent in the language, at some future date, will find the story valuable and provide a better translation. (I mentioned my frustrations at the beginning of the chapter, and this is a further one: the presentation in print of this speculative interlinear English translation given my

inadequacies in the Creek language. In fact, I was simply unable to translate the last line of the story, and I must admit that this is not an ideal scholarly situation. I feel nonetheless that the story is important enough that discussing it as Creek literature supersedes these inadequacies and that publishing it is clearly preferable to leaving the story out of the book. My hope would be that the story provides a reference for Creek scholars in the future, and that someone will improve on my feeble beginning.)

3. Linda's translation of the story in English and our post-storytelling discussion ("English Version"). I have deviated from the usual ethnographic approach in that I asked Linda Alexander to translate her own story; in other words, she told the story once in Creek and then in English. This to me only makes sense, to ask the storyteller's opinion on the story translation, especially given my own limitations in Creek.

4. The ethnographer John Swanton's two English versions of the story from his collection *Myths and Tales of the Southeastern Indians* ("Swanton's Version"). It should be noted that in the case of these two stories, Swanton rewrote versions that were in the earlier Tuggle collection.

5. My interpretive efforts at analyzing the story ("Analysis").

Conversations

CRAIG WOMACK: Where did you hear the Turtle story?

LINDA ALEXANDER: My daddy. See, my dad, uh, told us all these stories and stuff that I guess he'd heard it from his brothers and uncles. They used to — old people used to gather around on Saturday nights and smoke tobacco, chew tobacco, and just tell stories one at a time, and I guess that's where he got them. Cause he used to tell stories, tell us stories whenever he got through working in the field. He used to work the field, and on Saturday night, well, he'd gather up some potatoes, sweet potatoes, and he'd bake them for us to eat, and then he'd sit around and tell us those stories. Course, I didn't know the meaning of anything, but I'd just laugh because the boys laughed [she laughs now]. I had two brothers. Then, later on, after I was to remember those stories, I'd say, "God, Dad" [laughs]. But he said, though, whenever he was telling us these stories, he said that "this is the way the old folks used to tell their young people to behave and not do these things." In the olden days he said that the old folks didn't wanna come right out and tell their children. They were kind of ashamed to talk about things like that, he said. But, in the story way, after they'd get through, he said, "you mustn't do that because it'll get you in trouble," he used to say.

BERTHA ALEXANDER: Would you like some coffee or tea before we get started?

CW: Sure.

PAM INNES: Sure.

CW: Coffee will do me.

PI: Coffee would be great.

CW: Did he [Linda's father] say anything about the Turtle story?

LA: Well, uhm, he told it in two different ways, and two different stories. And so I usually leave that — you know where they got the pubic hair and put it around that turtle's neck — and this old turtle just kind of pranced out of there and said, "Oh, those women gave me a silk scarf, and here I am just — I'm gonna parade around among my turtles and show off," he says.

CW: When he told the one with the silk scarf, did he only tell that around certain people?

LA: My daddy?

CW: Yeah. Why did he tell one sometimes, and the other one other times?

LA: Oh, I guess he just — sometimes he just felt like telling — like sometimes you feel like telling the whole thing; sometimes you feel like leaving some out. I guess that's the way he felt. That's the way I gathered, you know.

BA: Some people might get offended. Any cream or sugar?

PI: Not for me.

CW: No thanks.

[Long silence. We drink our coffee for a spell.]

CW: Is the thing that's kind of funny about this whole deal the fact that he [Turtle] was prancing around showing off that scarf to his turtle friends?

LA: Uh, hum. Yeah, but these other turtles didn't pay no attention to him cause that's what Daddy showed that — in his story that these other turtles weren't interested in it cause they had never seen anything like that [laughs a lot]. If they'd known where it was from and all they'd say [uses voice to indicate prurient interest], "Where'd you get it?" you know [we laugh; the indication seems to be that the turtles would be aroused and want a "silk scarf" of their own]. I guess those women were crazy, too, I guess. I don't know what they aim was in that story. I just never could, you know, make out what—I guess being to show off. That would be the only thing I could think of, the turtle to show off. [Silence ensues.]

PI: Well, we can leave it up to Craig to come up with something.

LA: Something, OK [laughs].

CW: For me to come up with something? What?

PI: About the meaning of the story.

CW: Oh, yeah. That's my job [we laugh].

LA: Whenever y'all are ready, I'm ready.

PI: We're rolling.

LA: I'm gonna tell it in Indian, and then I'll tell it in English after that.

Creek Language Version

1 hofónof hoktaki hokolin wiilakatiis coko
   long time ago women two around were house

2 itskalkiit apokiitontowin
   they lived there

3 caakitatitvn
   the two lived there

4 aaciihocvks keykin hocin wilaa acii hocasaa wiilakin
   ground corn they were pounding, grinding corn they were there

5 Loca roratiis, Loca roraan
   Turtle wandering around a long time ago, Turtle wandering

6 maan moyii iilawitaaron kicapit
   he then hungry wandered around the pestle

7 kico ocat anahan aharsiiton
   the mortar somebody had by him was near

8 aariin arton, hiinscey? iheyn
   he went around and said, "Hello," uh . . .

9 ikoman atticiisatonsis keysaktatin
   he wanted to get in there and look up their dresses

10 maan Loca iilaawiitaankin manahtahaarin
    he Turtle was hungry and was fixing to be sick from hunger

11 hankitaweyk taweykin oweys ahnahin
    one of the women tossed the turtle away

12 anahtahin pomaboheycikitotaaton kiicabicoheys keycofan Loca
    man iilawitonka raatit
    *tossed him away, "Listen to us! Go away!" he heard them say as they
    were around the pestle, they said while Turtle, still hungry, came
    around*

13 keycotinbinahan rimankin
    next to the one with the mortar, again he came around

14 hankito
    that one

15 naakstowiisahaanahin ayiibitii
    near them he went where those two were

16 iiston iheyn
    he snapped up some corn uh . . .

17 ciinlanisins liimat iinokwaan siiwaneyitsofa keycit
    pubic hair she plucked around his neck she tied it on

18 mowin, iinhey insitowin leykit
    and . . . uh, there he sat with it

19 mahaleykit ciskeycin leykitihin ranis liwinmitcit Loca
    inokosonwaneyyinont owatin ahaarimankin okit
    *"Stay there! Do that!" they said, "Stay!" but Turtle because of
    hunger sickness he wanted to go around them again*

20 eyyitscikey tokis cey?
    "Didn't you go away?"

21 heyohatahin nakhinrocis ciwanaatowiis
    around here something good he wanted

22 eyyas keycaktowin Loca iikoteyyin oweysan
    *"Go!" they said. Turtle was still poking around looking up (their
    dresses)*

23   kiicabii nisit matas nafkas tocit toheyn spaansitmicit iheyn
     citakatiis ma loca ciitaktot haamoná
     pestle with it hit had uhm . . . she swept him out with uhm . . .
     busted up that turtle mashed, they say

24   iinocaata iimankiin monkton
     his blood he was losing badly

25   aaaa . . . iiteheyn iiton
     he got up next to the woods

26   stowitáaa . . . yis iitiileykeyteyatiis
     there he was, he lay next to it, stayed right there

27   toríiii . . . n ceyaamahkaktos makatis
     there, next to the log, he was, he didn't make a noise, they say

28   iinmitat aakireycaat
     What to do? he thought

29   toriin ceyaamakata tahoskon
     there, next to the log, he made a noise, all by himself

30   áaaa . . . iiteheyn
     next to the log

31   iitowaakiton raleykit
     next to the log, stayed behind it

32   tofmaan awaalapkiik oteyyaton taleykit
     that log he could not cross it and go on, so there he lay

33   léeee . . . kton stoyin itileykita iiteleykeyt eyyes sowatii
     he lay . . . ed there, he lay there and stayed, stayed right there for a
     long time

34   kontakiireysa akireystaa iinhinskaat
     he couldn't cross it, he knew it, and it was good

35   yaheykeyn owatiin acaatileyka
     he started singing, he sang it a long time ago

36   kowaa atiireyheyt
     as he lay there

caato sokoso
rock rough, rough

cato leyh leyh
rock is, is

cato sokoso
rock rough, rough

cato leyh leyh
rock is, is

37   maakit ostin mahkatin
said it four times, he said it

38   áaaa . . . yin sitiileykin aatiin aatin abiswa citakatito
he went while he was sitting there, he went, he went, the meat that was torn apart started to come together

39   ofa hahkit Loca onapowatii tikabakosii hakaa iiheyn   tikiileykin mamowaan baakin
inside Turtle made a noise, up above him his shell was still separate, still he lay there, and his shell began to resume his shape

40   mamowaano baakin iiheyn okit
he resumed his shape uhm . . . after a while

41   man heyvnka eyyit heyn loca abalwafolat iiheyn ririimakakey taakoskits
that here went that turtle, the rest of him came back together, his shell melded

42   irseyyokit seyyokit
he carried his shell, carried himself

43   seyyinuhin Loca tatii aatiilokti hicakton
carrying it Turtle uhm . . . his insides realigned, he was remade, he thought

44   hoktakeyhin notska . . . notska hiirin aacohey . . . acaacon . . . acaakon . . . acahoneyyiiceycaktownin okhon ohhonoceyyiit aktoweys keyciitii
The women's scarf was pretty, he thought, he woke up and started telling [the other turtles] what happened

45   stameyman keycaktat iimoneykikotatiis
     where? they said, he wouldn't say

46   iimoneykikoteyyat áaaa . . . yit iiheyn
     he wouldn't tell where he went

47   iiman simiisomakiit aastowaatiss iiheyn
     gift they were envious that he got over there

48   wii . . . nak . . . iraneyseysiisii . . . nokosiiwaaneyyowasti isteyca
     [we couldn't figure out this line]

English Version

LA: One time there was a couple women that lived in this house with their parents, and their parents always give them things to do, detailed them to do, whatever they needed to do that day. So she told them to pound corn cause we gotta have some food, so those women were out there pounding corn, and, uh, while they were pounding corn this turtle was under their feet; he had come up, they didn't notice anything around there, and they were just talking to each other back and forth and that turtle kinda touched one of the women's feet. And she looked down, and she said, "Get away from here."

"What's a-matter?" [the other woman said].

"Turtle's down there."

Said, uh, "Tell him to get away from here." She kicked him away, then, and he fell. And then, finally, Turtle has a hard time kinda getting hisself over. So he finally got over and come back again around the mug there where they were pounding the corn, and the other one says, in a laughing way—they were young women—so she says, "Why don't you pull your pubic hair and put it around his neck. Maybe he'll choke on that."

So they went around and she said, "OK." So she went and pulled her pubic hair, and tied it around that turtle's neck, and while she was doing that she kinda threw him to the side there. "Go on!" But he never did go, he just came back again, just kept bothering them, and around that mug he was hungry.

He's slow, and coming around there and that mug there and those girls were talking and laughing and pretty soon the other one says, "That old turtle just won't go away, so I'm gonna just pound the heck out of him," just pound him; they didn't say heck. Said pound him. So she took that *kicapii* and pounded him; she pounded him real good, and so he finally...

"How am I gonna get away from here?" Said, "I'm really beat up," he said to himself. And finally he just drug himself slowly until he come to a log, and he knew he couldn't climb that log, so he sat against that and he said, "Well, what shall I do?" he thought to himself. And, finally, something just came to him and said, "Why don't you sing this song and get yourself back together?" So he sang this song, saying,

> caato sokoso
> caato leyh leyh
>
> caato sokoso
> caato leyh leyh

He sung that four times, and he began to get his shell back together, but it had little creases in his shell, and he says, "Well, that's better than nothing," so he started out, and out in the forest area he went on around the tree, log rather, and he told these other turtles if he met any; he said, "Look what the women gave me! This silk scarf, and you can see it." And boy he was strutting around and all, and so those turtles didn't pay no attention to him cause they didn't know what that silk scarf was, so there he goes, just out in the forest, thinking he's the only one that has the silk scarf, and he didn't know what that scarf was [we all laugh].

And then that "caato sokoso, caato leyh leyh"; in English it means that the rock can kinda be rubbed together and get me together, and that's what he said. Rub that rock together and get me together. And just kept on saying that four times, and he got himself back hard shell, and that's the reason the turtle's back is that way.

There's Turtle down there, shells, where you can tell it.

CW: Where?

LA: Right there by the end of the ...

BA: Got it covered up [uncovers the turtle shells].

CW: So we can check out and see if the story's true.

LA: Yeah [shells rattle as Bertha hands them to me]. See those little creases?

CW: Yeah.

LA: That's where he put himself back together.

CW: [examining shells] Uh hum.

BA: I'll have to put these turtles back together! [Shells are loose from the leggings. We laugh.]

PI: You've got some work cut out for you.

BA: Yeah.

LA: Is that the only story you wanted?

CW: That's the main one I had in mind, yeah.

BA: The main one? [making fun of how much I like to listen to stories].

LA: I think that's kind of, you know, interesting to know that wooded area animals like that can sing and get himself together, but it's an old Indians used to say that something from the good Lord sends those words to you, so I imagine they send the words to the turtle to sing that. That's what my dad said, so I kinda think that, too, you know. After he told us that — that things come to you as you're sitting there if you're injured or whatever.

CW: So if you get hurt like that, sometimes, a medicine song will come to you, a song like that?

LA: Yeah, back in the olden days. It don't come to me, though [laughs].

PI: You been waiting and waiting, huh?

LA: Yeah, I'll probably just have to wait — forever [laughs].

CW: That's why they got Indian Health Service for us.

LA: Yeah, really [we all laugh].

BA: If you wanna die.

PI: For waiting forever and ever.

LA: Yeah, really.

Swanton's Version

35. *How the Terrapin's Back Came to Be in Checks (Tuggle Collection)*

A woman was beating sofki in a mortar out in her yard when she heard someone calling to her and making fun of her. She stopped and looked around, but saw no one. She began beating the corn again, and again heard the voice ridiculing her. She stopped and searched but in vain. Again she heard the voice, which seemed to come from under the wooden mortar, so she lifted the mortar and there found a Terrapin. As he was the guilty one, she took the pestle and beat him on the back until she broke his shell into little pieces and left him as dead. After she left, the Terrapin began to sing in a faint voice:

Char-tee-lee-lee (tcatilili)	*I come together.*
Char-tee-lee-lee	*I come together.*
Char-tee-lee-lee	*I come together.*
Char-tee-lee-lee	*I come together.*

The pieces came together as he sang, but his back always looked scarred, and terrapins have ever since then had checkered backs.

36. *How the Terrapin's Back Came to Be in Checks (Second version, Tuggle Collection)*

A Terrapin went hunting and met a woman. She accused him of having slandered her. He denied it, but when they passed a hollow tree into which he thought he could crawl, he said: "Yes, I did it; I am the man."

He tried to crawl into the tree but his shot bag got caught and he stuck fast. The woman caught him and beat his back to pieces.

By and by the ants came and he said:

I will give you my blood,
I will give you my fat,
If you will help me mend my back.

They consented and brought him some tar with which he mended his shell, but it was always in checks, and he never afterwards had any fat, nor any blood.

Analysis

The Turtle story is a potent healing narrative that contains a medicine song that Turtle voices to sing himself back together after two women violently smash him to the point of near death. Like much of Indian chant, from an Indian worldview, the song contains the medicine that sets the cure into motion as the language of the chant unleashes physical forces in the universe, Turtle's shell beginning to mend as he sings. Linda has told me the story many times. I like to believe that this is because she knows I need to hear it; at least that is the way I imagine my response to it as a listener. The story is very much a story of Creek nationalism, helping listeners to understand Creek culture and the ancient practice, still very much alive, of Creeks returning to the stomp grounds, four times a year, where they go out into the woods and sing themselves back together. Many non-Native Oklahomans assume that Indians have all been assimilated, not realizing that these ancient ceremonies continue right under their noses, just outside the small rural eastern Oklahoma towns they live in. The Turtle story, in terms of its intrinsic relationship to the ceremonial grounds, is part of an ongoing, vibrant nationalism that remains central to many Creeks' understanding of what it means to be part of the nation.

Linda begins the Creek version of the tale with a conventional Creek storytelling mannerism, "hofonof," meaning a long time ago. The Creek language has many more forms of past tenses than does English, and "hofonof," the way I understand it from talking to Linda, means back in mythical times when many unusual things happened that still affect our world today. The storyteller presents us with an opening image of two women pounding corn, and they are making *sofki,* a fact the Creek listener understands without explanation by the description of the *kico* and the *kicapii,* the mortar and pestle used in the preparation of this favorite drink made from corn. In the old days, a jar of *sofki* was kept next to the door in case of visitors; these days one gets to eat *sofki* at Creek ceremonial or social gatherings like out at the stomp grounds or camping in at Indian Baptist Church meetings.

In lines 2 to 5, one notices a classic oral storytelling technique — the repetition of words and phrases that create a heightened rhythmic language whose cadences are unlike those of ordinary conversational speech. In Creek, this heightened language has its most extreme form in Creek oratory — speeches before ball games or the calling of the *henneha,* the chief's speaker, before the dancing begins at the stomp grounds, for instance. Even those who do not speak or understand Creek can easily hear the sung quality of the lines in this type of oratory, the consistent meter, and the end rhymes. Here, in the storytelling voice Linda uses to convey the Turtle story, these formalisms are much less pronounced than in Creek oratory, the repetition being the main rhetorical device: "they lived there," "the two lived there," "ground corn they were pounding," "grinding corn they were there," "Turtle wandering around long time ago," "Turtle wandering."

Turtle addresses the women, as is appropriate when approaching strangers, but in an aside, Linda reveals to us in lines 9 and 10 that Turtle has ulterior motives. He is hungry to the point of sickness, and he is "horny." He wants to look up the women's dresses. Although Rabbit, rather than Turtle, is the central trickster in Creek literature, Turtle occasionally functions as trickster as well, and this is amply demonstrated in Creek literature. A Creek classic in this regard is the time Turtle rigs a race against Deer in which Turtle arranges for fresh replacements to step in for him at the top of each hill, unbeknownst to his competitor. In Linda's Turtle story, the narrative begins to follow the trickster pattern because Turtle has ulterior motives; he begins to plan a way to meet immediate physical needs, his behavior involves a comic sexual element, and the trick backfires on him at the end. Although it encompasses another discussion, suffice it to say that it is interesting to note that this particular story, as do countless other trickster narratives, contradicts Paul Radin's Jungian analysis in his book *The Trickster,*[1] which claims that the trickster acts on primordial instinct without volition or premeditation, the trickster thus representing humanity's undeveloped psyche before "civilization." Turtle clearly knows what he is about here and plans his actions out beforehand.

With the hunger elements, the storyteller introduces tension, heightening the listener's interest, causing her to wonder how Turtle will satiate his needs. Linda mentions, in a skillfully understated aside in line 7, that there is a mortar nearby. The listener in an oral tradition already knows the outcome of the story because she has heard it many times. *How* the story is told, then, and especially the performance of it, becomes almost as important as what is told. Linda Alexander emphasizes repeatedly the fact of Turtle going around and around the pestle with the mortar nearby in the first sixteen lines of the story. The repetition is a performative ploy, like a jazz player riffing on the same note for a sustained period of time, the technique increasing tension even though the listener knows what note the sustained pitch will resolve into. The listener can feel the women getting madder and madder with the sustained emphasis of Turtle going around and around up under their feet, ignoring their warnings.

In line 17, Linda introduces a theme completely missing from both of John Swanton's versions of the story. The women pluck pubic hair from their crotches and tie it around Turtle's neck. To a Western audience, this action seems inexplicable, yet it is not unusual in light of Indian humor in the oral tradition, which often contains sexual elements, as with this particular image of Turtle and his extraordinary neck piece. The women continue to warn Turtle to stay away; he continues to ignore them and persistently plods around the pestle.

The story mixes humor and poignancy, the serious elements weaving in and out of comic treatments. In oral tradition stories, humor is less of a distinct genre than in Euramerican literature, the comic often being an element of creation stories, religious stories, migration stories, hero stories, and many other kinds of narrative. The inclusion of comic elements is not the same as tragicomedy in that it flows in and out of many kinds of narratives more fluidly; the term "tragicomedy" itself indicates that these two genres are generally seen as oppositions and their merger as something unique. As the Turtle story unfolds, the serious element reveals Turtle's suffering, beginning with the fact that Turtle is not only hungry but sick from hunger (lines 10 and 19) and culminating with the turtle bashing.

A transition occurs in line 23 with the introduction of the communal point of view, "they busted up that turtle, they say." The teller reminds us that she is not the author of the story but the vehicle of a tradition. The individual artistic ego is subsumed by the will of the community. The communal point of view introduced in the "they say" transition marks a turning point in the story. After this culmination of violence when the frustrated women pound Turtle nearly to death, the story goes from ordinary events into the sphere of the supernatural. In a traditional worldview, the natural and supernatural are two sides of the same coin, so the story does not really change in direction but rather, one might say, becomes supercharged. Beginning in line 25 and continuing through line 28, the storyteller uses stretched-out syllables in the ritualistic pattern of four to emphasize how serious matters are and that the medicine, the main focus of the story, is coming into play. One is reminded here of the language features of Southeastern tribal incantations wherein images are repeated in a cumulative fashion until a kind of literary crescendo occurs by which the words being spoken no longer serve a mere linguistic function but actually unleash supernatural forces. This is a critical moment in the narrative in which Turtle must conserve his physical and spiritual strength to get through the rest of the story. The stretched-out syllables, the more formal oratory, underscore the climax of Turtle's predicament and his need for medicine. He is hurt, he is suffering, he is mashed nearly to pieces, and he has reached a log he cannot cross over, so severely is he wounded. Turtle's stasis is mentioned repetitively in nine lines that precede the moment when he begins to sing his medicine song.

Line 35 contains another transition that refers back to the beginning of the story. Just as line 23 marked the communal point of view leading to the climax of Turtle's suffering, so line 35 marks the time frame: "he sang it a long time ago." The listener is reminded again, as with the storytelling mannerism in the opening line, that the storyteller is taking us back to mythical beginnings. I wish to emphasize here that I use the word "mythical" as a descriptive term for stories that deal with supernatural realities, and I realize the problematic connotations of the phrase in popular culture that associates "myth" with fantasy, falsity, or metaphoric rather than literal treatments. The emphasis on "long time ago," from a traditional perspective, does not mean the medicine is outdated and no longer functional in contemporary society. "Long time ago" increases rather than diminishes the validity of the story because of the reverence for the past and the extraordinary happenings of myth. It does not serve the same function as "once upon a time." "Long time ago" reminds the audience that the story's origins date back to that time when the culture's most important developments took place.

Turtle, realizing his need for help, goes beyond his own natural abilities, starts to sing. Linda comments that the way her dad explained the medicine song was that whenever a person is beside himself and in a fix, he may be given a medicine song in this emergency ("English Version"). Turtle's song acknowledges roughness and imperfection, a gradual and progressive cure: "rough rock, that's what I'm becoming." But as Linda has also said about Turtle's mending, "that's better than nothing" ("English Version"). The song and the story's denouement seem to emphasize that healing is an ongoing process. Something is set in motion the moment Turtle starts to sing, but the working out of it takes time.

He sings the medicine song in the appropriate ritualistic pattern of four, and his busted-up self starts pulling back together. In addition to the physical mending, there is a movement in the story in which Turtle progresses from an inarticulate state to an articulate one. Until the medicine song, Turtle hasn't uttered a word other than greeting the women in line 8 and wondering what to do about his injured condition in the internal monologue in line 28. Until the medicine song, he is manipulated by the language of others, silenced, and at the mercy of the women's speech. Perhaps if he'd had a voice, he could have talked himself out of a beating; we don't know. Because he is unable to speak, he suffers. Here we find a thematic element common to Indian stories old and new. Compare, for instance, the following passage about Abel, the protagonist of

N. Scott Momaday's 1968 Pulitzer Prize–winning novel *House Made of Dawn:*

> Had he been able to say it, anything of his own language — even the
> commonplace formula of greeting "Where are you going" — which had
> no being beyond sound, no visible substance, would once again have
> shown him whole to himself; but he was dumb. Not dumb — silence was
> the older and better part of custom still — but inarticulate...
>   He was alone, and he wanted to make a song out of the colored
> canyon, the way the women of Torréon made songs upon their looms
> out of colored yarn, but he had not got the right words together. It
> would have been a creation song; he would have sung lowly of the first
> world, of fire and flood, and of the emergence of dawn from the hills.[2]

Turtle's healing begins when he speaks. Speech, in traditional thought, has great potential for both healing and destruction. Speech can be medicine or witchery. The women's talk leads to a violent beating; Turtle's song leads to things being set right.

After the demonstration of the polarities of speech, the story leads to a mediating ground of language: words that cause laughter. This is not to suggest that the story becomes less serious. The word "baakin" in line 39 conveys the sense of leavened bread rising, and Turtle is still in the process of recovering his former state, even as he makes something of a fool of himself.

Realigned and remade, he gets to thinking about how pretty the women's scarf is he is wearing about his neck. Turtle, in his tricksterish naïveté, does not fully realize the humor of sporting a scarf that originated from somebody's crotch. The humor lies in the irony of Turtle's lack of understanding of how highly unusual is his neck piece.

Turtle is vague and mysterious about how he acquired the scarf when he tells the other animals in the woods of his new acquisition, yet they show little interest. The irony is doubled because Turtle's friends also lack knowledge concerning the gift's origin; thus it does not seem interesting enough to arouse their curiosity, a point Linda brings out in the section "Conversations." Had they known of the scarf's sexual origin, it might have had a prurient appeal. The storyteller's audience, however, has a fuller understanding than Turtle and his admirers. In the section "English Version," Linda says that Turtle thinks he is the only one who has such a scarf (not recognizing it as universal physiological "apparel" among humans), and the other turtles don't pay any attention because they have no context for Turtle's adornment—they don't know what it is.

The humorous ending is not gratuitous. It is a strong indicator that the cure has "taken" as the medicine moves from Turtle out to the storyteller's audience, who can, because of their distance, see things that Turtle and his friends cannot and laugh. Irony and distance, getting outside oneself enough to see things in a new light, are essential to psychic health, making humor, which relies heavily on these two elements, part of the healing process.

Before comparing Linda's versions of the Turtle story with the ones John Swanton borrowed from Tuggle's collection, let me first say something about this prolific ethnographer. Altogether Swanton wrote twenty monographs, whereas most of his contemporaries at the Bureau of American Ethnology produced only one. For example, his monumental work on the Creeks, the *Forty-Second Annual Report,* is a huge, encyclopedic work that records everything from linguistic details regarding the Creek language to the layout of the Creek square grounds. Though Swanton's knowledge was comprehensive, his biases shaped much of what he heard, a subject worthy of its own book in terms of the racist statements in Swanton's ethnography.[3] Swanton's work is a major source for all the books written about Creeks, many of which are shaped—some subtly, some more overtly—by his attitudes.

Swanton presents two versions of the Turtle story[4] as represented here under the subheading "Swanton's Version." In number 35, which Swanton titles "How the Terrapin's Back Came to Be in Checks," Turtle angers a woman pounding corn, leading to his beating. In this version, Turtle makes the woman angry by ridiculing her, though we are not told what he says. When she locates Turtle under the mortar, she "took the pestle and beat him on the back until she broke his shell into little pieces and left him as dead."[5] Swanton mentions that Turtle "began to sing in a faint voice," an element that Linda's story does not include, but one that nonetheless seems authentic in light of the story's movement toward progressive healing in all versions. The medicine song that Turtle sings in the Swanton version is a variant of the one he sings in Linda's version. It is, in fact, one half of the same song. Swanton actually gives the song in Creek, something he almost never does in his renderings, spelling it "Char-tee-lee-lee," that is, "caato leyh leyh," in Linda's version. Swanton translates the song roughly the same as well, rendering it as "I come together," a very similar phrasing to Linda's explanation of the meaning of the Creek. The Swanton story, unlike Linda's, makes the healing immediate rather than a longer process, yet it does suggest a similar notion of accepting imperfection: "The pieces came together as he sang, but his back always looked scarred, and terrapins have ever since then had checkered backs."[6] Unlike Linda's story, Swanton's ends with the explanatory moral, whereas Linda's version lapses somewhat into mystery — Turtle being evasive about where he got his scarf and leaving the other animals puzzled.

In Swanton's story 36 (he numbers the narratives consecutively), as in story 35, any allusion to Turtle's "silk" scarf is completely missing. Both stories are borrowed from the Tuggle collection, a body of stories Swanton revised considerably.[7] Given the time they were writing in, either Swanton or Tuggle before him would most likely have edited out the sexual material; or the storyteller could have edited it out herself, knowing she or he was talking to a non-Indian with a different understanding of the place of sexuality in narrative.

Linda herself does this. I have seen her, for instance, when there are certain people around, such as a Creek Baptist preacher or other Indian Baptist Church folk, leave out what that particular audience would consider offensive. I am speculating that this self-censoring is more of a contemporary phenomenon than an older, traditional one, and that this editing nowadays results from a contemporary teller's awareness that dominant culture expects certain behavior in public settings. This may be demonstrated by the fact that Bertha, Linda's daughter, from a younger generation, explains that certain people may get offended, whereas Linda, of the older generation, simply attributes the omission of the silk scarf to length — she says sometimes her dad didn't feel like telling the longer version.

In Swanton's story 36, Turtle goes hunting and meets a woman. As in the previous story, Turtle says something to ridicule the woman, but we are not told what he says. Turtle's shot bag gets caught as he is trying to crawl into a tree. The woman comes along and beats his back to pieces. When the ants come by, Turtle sings a song that Swanton renders only in English. Curiously, the song has only three lines instead of the ritualistic pattern of four, but this could be due to the English translation, Swanton not thinking the repetition of a line necessary. The translation is arranged into a rhyming pattern, and one wonders if Swanton, or Tuggle, sacrificed a line to make the rhyme:

> I will give you my blood,
> I will give you my fat,
> If you will help me mend my back.[8]

Turtle agrees to a reciprocal arrangement, and the ants bring him some tar. Swanton also ends story 36 with the explanatory moral: "They consented and brought him some tar with which he mended his shell, but it was always in checks, and he never afterwards had any fat, nor any blood."[9]

Swanton does not provide the cultural context for the story. For the Creek listener, this story will have a lyrical and haunting effect because of the larger context that shapes it. Creek women place turtle shells on top of red ants' hills, where the feeding activity of the ants cleans the shells; that is, the ants clean out the blood and fat. Then women attach the shells to the leggings that they wear during stomp dancing, creating a unique rhythm with a skillful heel-toe action (the shells have pebbles in them that rattle). The story explains the origins of shell cleaning, an activity related to the most important of Creek social and religious institutions, stomp dancing, and traces the origins of the shell cleaning to the reciprocal relationship between turtles and ants. There is something beautiful about the possibility that a religion could be partially dependent on the smallest of living things and the most minute relationships, a fragile balance.

The story is metonymic. Because the Creek listener knows so much already from her ceremonial and cultural experience, she makes dynamic connections across her culture that deepen her understanding of Creek earth relationship and religion. The story can be minimalistic in style because so much of its meaning resides in Creek experience already understood by the community. The natural world and the ceremonial world provide tangible evidence that backs up the story — turtles everywhere in eastern Oklahoma, women cleaning shells on anthills, shell shaking at the night dances. Thus, in an oral culture, the narratives are not viewed as "mythical" in the sense that contemporary culture understands that word in association with metaphorical, make-believe, or imaginary; indeed, the stories can be verified with physical evidence in the natural world.

In terms of style, as in all of Swanton's narratives, both versions of the Turtle story sound as if they have been written by the same person rather than told by different storytellers. Swanton's literary style is easily verified. Looking at Linda's English version for an immediate contrast, one notices a complete lack of parataxis in Swanton's stories. Linda links sentences and phrases together with "and" or "so"; Swanton uses complex sentences with dependent clauses rather than stringing together thoughts with conjunctions. The former technique, the use of subordination, is a written form; the latter, a cumulative and additive style, is the way of organizing information in cultures highly influenced by orality. The aggregative style of oral storytelling has been much discussed by Milman Parry and Albert Lord, Walter Ong, Eric Havelock, and all those writing about oral formulaic theory.

The diction in the Swanton versions is far removed from the Indian English of eastern Oklahoma. Swanton's stories abound with phrases common to writing, but not oral speech: "but in vain," "and there found a terrapin," "as he was the guilty one," "and left him as dead," "terrapins have ever since then had checkered backs," "brought him some tar with which he mended his shell," "and he never afterwards had any fat." In short, this is not the way storytellers talk; this is the way writers write (at least writers of Swanton's time, who were still influenced by Victorian prose). Even educated people, to whom Swanton and Tuggle may have talked, do not speak this way; they write this way.

When compared to Linda's story version, Swanton's narratives seem encapsulated, paraphrased in the extreme. Even in the main body of the story, not including the conversations that frame it, Linda's English version contains 552 words. Swanton's story 35 contains 152 words, and story 36 contains 126 words. Even if one does not include the silk scarf motif present in Linda's story and missing in Swanton's, Linda's story is much longer. Tuggle and Swanton, working before the advent of tape recorders, probably had little choice but to take notes, then rewrite the stories based on sketchy outlines of the main plot details.

Another reason for the shorter length of the Swanton versions is possibly his leaving out some other sexual elements of the stories in addition to the scarf (though this would be a much smaller source of word depletion than the paraphrasing and summarizing). In story 35 we are told that Turtle was "making fun of her," and that the woman "heard the voice ridiculing her." In story 36 the woman "accused him of having slandered her."[10] The conflict is highlighted a little more strongly in story 36 with the accusation of slander. Turtle denies the charge and leaves and passes a hollow tree rather than Linda's log; unlike Linda's version, he has not been beaten up yet. Right before attempting to crawl into the tree, for some reason, Turtle admits his guilt, saying, "Yes; I did it; I am the man."[11] What he is guilty of is left unstated.

Because we have Linda's story for a comparison, we might speculate that the reason Swanton omits this conversation and summarizes it, rather than giving the actual dialogue, is because Turtle's comments to the women may be sexual in nature. The way Linda tells it, Turtle's hunger is both physical and sexual—he wants to get under the women's feet in case they drop some food, *and* he wants to look up their dresses. Swanton's choice of the word "slander," at any rate, is interesting. It is a strong word that makes us wonder, as readers, what Turtle has said that is so inappropriate.

One question concerning Linda's story that needs further investigation has to do with the reason Turtle is looking up the women's dresses in the first place, other than the most obvious reason, which is his horniness. In other Creek stories (for instance, the story explaining how Turtle got red eyes), Turtle likes blood and bloody meat. Evidently this is the case literally as well; Linda told me that turtles like raw meat. Were these women menstruating, and if so, does this come to play in the Swanton stories? This is an interesting possibility, since it merges the sexual motif of the story with the hunger motif. In a traditional Indian worldview, menstruating women are extraordinarily powerful. In traditional Creek culture, there are certain ritualistic separations that women go through during menstruation. They don't cook, and they don't dance, at the time they are menstruating. They are at the peak of their power at this time and are a competing source with the community's medicine, or common power. This may explain the women's violent reaction—could Turtle be making fun of their sexuality, making light of sacred matters? Perhaps, even, the silk scarf could function as a kind of dunce cap, a literal reminder that Turtle does not understand women's sexuality and how to respond appropriately to it. The mixture of sacred and profane elements—Turtle's slander and Turtle's healing—would not be unusual if the story contains trickster elements. Admittedly, these are speculative possibilities—I'm guessing here—but ones undertaken with a consideration of the larger cultural contexts in which the stories occur.

One of these larger cultural issues is particularly important in story 36. Linda's story, unlike Swanton's, is contextualized by a conversation that occurs both before and after the main story. After the telling, Linda handed me some women's shells so that I could verify the veracity of the story by looking at their checkered pattern. Swanton's stories never contain any of the narrator's commentary, another omission that accounts for their brevity and indicates extensive reworking. Linda's meta-narrative and "visual aids" provide vital cultural information — there is a relationship between Turtle's story and Creek religion. At first, I experimented with representing Linda's storytelling in regular prose lines, but end punctuation seemed completely artificial when listening to the tape. The Creek version had more pronounced pauses that indicated line breaks, and I believe this is because in Creek, Linda uses a more heightened and formal style than in English. I based line breaks on the pauses in the Creek version, which seemed marked, regularly occurring, and at consistent intervals. If nothing else, the arrangement according to pauses gives a feeling of the continuous quality of the narrative, which is not the same as the pause after end punctuation.

Unlike Linda with her extranarrative comments before, after, and within the story, Swanton's narrators are completely erased, leaving no tracks within their tellings. The effect of the erased narrator is a fragmenting one — the stories do not connect to a living human community. The tellings occur in a vacuum. They are artifacts; they have no bearing on contemporary concerns. They are self-fulfilling evidence amassed by the BAE to prove the popular "vanishing American" theory so widespread during Swanton's time.

In the way Linda tells the story, the performance becomes instructive concerning the act of storytelling itself rather than mere plot details as in Swanton: "First Turtle . . . next Turtle . . . then Turtle . . . ." For instance, in one of Linda's asides, she shows that in an oral tradition exemplification is just as important as abstraction: "In the olden days he said that the old folks didn't wanna come right out and tell their children. They were kind of ashamed to talk about things like that, he said. But, in the story way, after they'd get through he said, 'you mustn't do that because it'll get you in trouble,' he used to say."

Point of view is much more complex in Linda's story than in Swanton's. She continually shifts from Turtle's and the women's viewpoints to her father's viewpoint (as in "Daddy useta say...") to the community's passed-on tradition ("the women busted up that turtle, they say").

Tense shifts are more complex as well. Linda will shift into present tense, connecting the turtle of the past to the turtle of the present: "He's slow," she says, speaking of Turtle's persistence in plodding around the pestle. It is a little arbitrary to say just where the story leaves off and the commentary begins. After telling about Turtle showing off in the woods, near the "end" of the story, Linda begins translating and explicating the Creek medicine song. Then, in a powerful contemporary manifestation of the story, she hands me the shells, and the turtle voices rattle as she places them in my hands. There is a lot of medicine here, and as she reaches across the table, handing the shells to me, might not this be part of the story also? Maybe it is this moment that *is* the main narrative, at least in terms of my experience of it. At this point, "real life" and "story" merge into a single identity. This synthesis marks the oral tradition: songs, chants, poems, and stories — that is to say, literature — are acted out in ritual, ceremony, and verified by a tangible presence in the physical world.

We felt the reality of the story that evening, its rootedness in "real-life" experience, because we started acting out its movement toward comedy ourselves. The end of our conversation consists of jokes about the inefficacy of Indian Health Service. And this, I would suggest, is also part of the Turtle story — its context that particular evening and relationship to the contemporary life of the people.

When comparing Linda's Creek and English versions, it is difficult to give an exact word count for the original Creek because of variability in trying to determine what constitutes a Creek word (someone with more skill in the language might do this more easily than I). Yet it is obvious that the English is more detailed than the Creek. In the way I have printed out the stories, Linda's English version contains 552 words compared to 203 words in the Creek version.

There are two possibilities here. The most certain is that Creek (especially because of the complexity of its verbs, which can express many nuances of tense, and even locations where actions take place, not available in English) takes fewer words in the original to express the same story in English. In other words, one Creek verb might take many English words to render its meaning, and like many oral stories dense with narrative action, this story is verb intense. Second, as has been previously stated, oral stories tend to be metonymic because the audience already knows so much context that need not be repeated. Thus, in the Creek version, Linda probably followed the traditional minimalistic presentation; in English, she may have followed the dominant culture's paradigm of fuller explanations.

Turtle sings himself back together, and his discovery of the power of language empowers him to play the fool, to cast himself as a clown inside his own fiction, in which he creates a story about his wonderful luck being presented with the fabulous gift of a silk scarf—I can almost see it trailing wildly behind him as he parades through the post oaks toward his audience. The fool has moved from being the inarticulate victim who gets the tar knocked out of him with a big *sofki* paddle to the narrator who rescues his reputation with a story. In the chapters to come, we shall see other Creek authors pulling such tricks out of their hats as well.

In terms of rescuing oneself through a story, we may be reminded here of a quintessentially Creek literary form, that of persona writing, an author pretending to be someone else. In lines 44 to 48, in the section "Creek Language Version," the interlinear translation reads:

44   The women's scarf was pretty, he thought, he woke up and started telling [the other turtles] what happened

45   where? they said, he wouldn't say

46   he wouldn't tell where he went

47   gift they were envious that he got over there

In Linda's version in English, she says:

> So he started out, and out in the forest area he went on around the tree, log rather, and he told these other turtles if he met any; he said, "Look what the women gave me! This silk scarf, and you can see it." And boy he was strutting around and all, and so those turtles didn't pay no attention to him cause they didn't know what that silk scarf was, so there he goes, just out in the forest, thinking he's the only one that has the silk scarf, and he didn't know what that scarf was [we all laugh].

The Creek version emphasizes Turtle's secrecy and even seems to imply that he comes up with an alternative story about where he went. The English conveys a sense of naïveté on the part of both Turtle and his

friends. If we combine the two elements together, we may have the beginnings of a central Creek writing feature, that of the persona in which
the author's true identity is obscured, secrecy is donned through a literary disguise, and the writer takes on the role of a naive innocent, telling
stories about what has happened to him, reporting on what he has seen
and heard.

This technique, in which later authors will employ the vernacular of
the person they are imitating, will be taken up not only by Alexander
Posey but by other Creek writers such as Louis Littlecoon Oliver, who
is also discussed in this book, as well as authors such as Charles Gibson
and Thomas Moore (writing as William Harjo). Beginning with the persona's roots in the oral tradition, and definitely further establishing its
"Creekness" through the successive use of the form by many Creek writers, we have a literary technique that is identifiably Creek and passed
on by both oral and literate generations. Other ways a persona, that of
Alexander Posey's character Fus Fixico, is rooted in Creek oral tradition will be discussed in a later chapter.

The question of the so-called purity of the form that some literary critics might bring up — this is to say, they might argue that Europeans and,
especially, American humorists have used the persona before Creeks —
is immaterial. It is a literary technique Creeks have found useful for presenting Creek voices, maintaining Creek viewpoints, continuing Creek
oral tradition, and speaking to a Creek audience. It is a Creek form that
is identifiably Southeastern Indian in its contents and structure, as well
as the forums where it has been presented (most often inside tribal nations in Indian Territory newspapers; or, in the case of Thomas Moore
in more recent times, in the Tulsa newspaper, also within modern Creek
jurisdiction). The uniqueness of the Creek persona, in terms of content, audience, and place of publication, at the very least, creates a significant difference from the way European or American humorists may
have employed personae, a difference that suggests an analysis of such
forms through the study of tribal oral and written literary production.
This may suggest that other national literatures have unique forms of
tribal literary expression best identified by searching out the tribe's oral
and written literary history, and that these primary sources have been
underexplored because of the way in which these literatures have mostly
been analyzed under the practices of the American literary canon.

Dear Hotgun:

I was hear Stijaati Thlaako tell the time when he was to visit the high school in Weleetka to talk about old-timey Creek culture to the kids so they wouldn't forget their ways. Chebon's dad was borned in Weleetka, you know. Stijaati was had give a lecture on long time ago arrow shoot where fifty or sixty guys and gals would meet up at a church or school or field at someone's house, park they wagons, or horse or cars on the edge of the field. Anyplace they could set up bales of hay and hang cardboard targets was where they was to have it. The shooters would ante-up they money — Lord, I couldn't believe it when I was a kid — seeing them grown-ups lay down anywhere as much as three or four cents a round. Then they was a sight to see when they'd let fly with their arrows, from their homemade bows, busting that cardboard up, I mean just a-gettin-it. Whoever hosted the doin's provided prizes, and lots of other folks would pitch in something too. The highest scorer each round got hisself a little ole can of coffee or maybe a jar of peanut butter or a bag of sugar or a little syrup or grease or cookies or some other traditional Creek food. The shooters would commence to accumulating their winnings and setting them there in front of they little old shooting stand where ever body could see how good they was a-doing.

Stijaati clean in the middle of old days talk when he notice his students not too inersted anymore, kindy like the teacher who turns around from the blackboard too quick. Stijaati stopped for a minute to garner his bearings and got so innersted himself in the silence he forgot his own lecture. He hunted what his students was a-tracking and followed their line of gaze to the classroom floor in front of their desks. Mrs. Pringle, the old lady high school teacher pry been there since Chebon's granddaddy graduated from first grade to cotton chopping, let her horn-rims fall off her nose to the end of the string of pearls they was a-hung on. She got all anxious and nervous and started tapping the toe of her high-heel shoe on the floor waiting for Stijaati to take up where he left off. Probably an Indian thing.

Stijaati was had seen what the kids seen — the biggest cockroach he'd ever laid aholt of within eyeshot, we're talking a huge BIA HUD HOUSE SIZE cockroach, maybe one that with a few more meals could eat McIntosh County.

Stijaati knowed no teacher even him could compete with a giant cockroach making its way out the door to escape class. Dang if he wasn't just about to the part about the time he won the arrow shoot too before he had to stop. Stijaati just walked over to that cockroach and unceremonially ground the giant bug into the floor except he didn't take into account the thing, as large as it *was,* would make such a big mess, so he headed out toward the bathroom to get some tissue paper to lay the bug to rest in the trash can and clean up the tops of his new Justin Ropers whose red calfskin didn't match roach innards particular well. He was coming down the hallway with a good-sized wad in his hand, when he heard all kind of ruckus and commotion and carrying on and voices coming out of that classroom he just left. He thought to hisself, "What in the *world?*"

He didn't know that giant cockroach had revived itself while he was gone away kinda miraculous-like. The roach was dragging its poor crippled maimed-up self toward the door of the classroom fixing to light out toward its favorite crack, as best it could.

When Stijaati walked back in, all the Indian kids was cheering that cockroach on!

Mrs. Pringle told Stijaati just go on home, class dismissed early. Pert near ever one of them kids told Stijaati how much they liked his lecture and when was he coming back?

Stijaati was had go home. Big Man and Rabbit already sitting in the shade of the catalpa tree when Stijaati was had pull up same place where Chebon's grandpa used to shoot squirrels out of hims branches long time before Stijaati's brick HUD house sat in the midst of the little oak grove there. They was waiting for him come home and shovel out his experience as Creek lecturer in public school system competing with cockroaches. Stijaati made Big Man get out of his favorite garage sale yard chair. Big Man always hard on chairs him all busted down mebeso no count with only a few threads keep Stijaati's butt from falling down between aluminum frame. Big Man set down arms resting on wooden picnic table top painted red. Best part got a pitcher of ice tea and the top covered with saran wrap so the bugs don't drop down into it. Stijaati finish his story and get up and pour hisself another glass. Sucks on a lemon and makes a sour face, then spits out seed.

Big Man he was say, "These young folks have forgotten everything. They more innersted in cockroaches than the Creek Nation."

Stijaati was shook his head and say, "Mebeso they mapping out their own nation." Then Stijaati was had stretch his legs out in front of him and lay his head back ag'in' the tree, recovered now from teaching experience since he told about it.

Big Man look kindy puzzled but don't move much on account of the heat. "You mean they planning on running as future National Council members from Okfuskee District?"

Stijaati he was go on and say, "That's part of it. That's a tough enough job what with all the meetings and paperwork and stuff you gotta read up on. I mean more along the lines of the notion that the Creek government stretches out long time before U.S. ever borned. In that amount of time Creek government has changed her ways all the time but still stayed Creek. She started out with most of the power in the towns whose alliances was with other towns of the same fire. Then she had to put on a more united national front to deal with the Spaniards and the British and the Americans wanting to steal land everywhere in Muskogee country. Then she got her own constitution. Then she got removed to Oklahoma. Then she went from lining up behind people you wanted to vote for to casting a ballot. Next thing was representation based on districts rather than towns. The government keeps changing, always has, before whites ever come here, and kept changing afterwards too. I wonder what the next changes will be? What will be the Creek government of the twenty-first century? What do these kids imagine as *their* Creek Nation? Maybe we ought to ask them since whatever they dream themselves to be is what Creek culture gonna be in the future. All the Indian experts was write books about Creek history, Creek stories, Creek language, Creek dances, Creek medicine, Creek customs, but not about Creek politics and Creek government. *But it's all part of the same ole sofki pot!* You can't understand Creek storytelling or Creek language or Creek customs without knowing something about Creek government, and these kids are gonna be the ones making up the new stories and running the next government."

Big Man was hold a sweating glass of ice tea up against his forehead and say, "I'll be. Mebeso cockroach stories is gol-durned important!"

Stijaati was settle down into his chair to take a snooze in the afternoon heat and shut his eyes and say, "I think that cockroach might had been singing himself back together."

Big Man he was say, "I think maybe them kids was."

Sincerely,
Jim Chibbo

CHAPTER FOUR

Alice Callahan's *Wynema:* A Fledgling Attempt

In LaVonne Ruoff's useful introduction to Alice Callahan's novel *Wynema: A Child of the Forest*,[1] Ruoff points out that this work has the distinction of being the first novel authored by a Native woman. Although this is an achievement of note, to be sure, I feel that the novel needs to be problematized because of its failure to engage Creek culture, history, and politics. I make this claim based on the novel's erasure of Creek voices, the characters' rejection of Creek culture, the many instances of cultural misrepresentation throughout, the lack of any depictions of the nuances of Creek life, the protagonist's repudiation of Muskogean matrilinearity, and the author's choice of a non-Creek and non-Indian viewpoint.

Despite the novel's failings as a Creek novel and its literary weaknesses, it is nonetheless an interesting work, especially as a document of Christian supremacism and assimilation. Two aspects of the novel make it worth reading. The characters have a debate concerning allotment under the Dawes Act, so as readers we get an early-1890s perspective of that major assault against tribal governments. Further, the assimilationist dogma in the book unintentionally subverts itself, constantly calling into question its own theology through the very symbols chosen to represent it. These aspects of the book, I believe, are where the most potent critical discussions may lie in terms of future scholarship that surrounds *Wynema*. For my purposes here, however, I want to use the novel as an example of some of the problems and pitfalls involved in writing a Creek novel.

In terms of erasure, one might note that few Creek voices exist in the novel. The protagonist, Wynema, a young girl living somewhere in Creek country (exactly where we are never told), is the wunderkind of Methodist missionary and teacher Genevieve Weir—her star pupil with straight As in whiteness, miraculously transformed under Genevieve's tutelage from inarticulate full-blood to Victorian lady. Wynema, virtually the only Creek character who ever gets to speak in the novel at all, suffers a complete erasure of her thoughts and opinions, which are subsumed by the white characters who speak on her behalf, and this is presented as normative.

There are some rare exceptions to the *complete* silencing of Creeks in the novel—Wynema's father speaks five short sentences on pages 3 and 4 of the novel and a short paragraph on both pages 30 and 31; Wynema's mother is given two very short sentences on page 12; and someone whom the Methodist preacher and teacher Gerald Keithly calls "ole Masse Hadjo" writes an editorial to an unnamed paper (though even this is read aloud by Gerald, not by a Creek person, and constitutes one long paragraph (Callahan, 73–74). Creek voices, to say the very least, are shockingly missing. When political topics like allotment are discussed, the utter lack of any Creek opinions renders invisible the tremendous acts of resistance against Oklahoma statehood that were going on both within the Creek Nation and in alliance with other tribes in Indian Territory. The thoughts, comments, and dialogue of Genevieve Weir and Gerald Keithly, the two Methodist missionaries come to Indian Territory to save Indians, predominate the book.

In Wynema's case, seldom has a protagonist's viewpoint been so thoroughly filtered through others outside herself. If this is a novel about strong, independent women expressing political viewpoints, it works only for the white women characters. In terms of the Native protagonist, we see a complete colonization of her thoughts and speech. For example, during an important discussion on the allotment issue, which I shall return to more fully later, Wynema takes the assimilationist position and argues the standard party line—lazy Indians will be turned toward industriousness through the magic of land ownership (50–51). Genevieve articulates the counterargument: Indians are not sophisticated enough to be U.S. citizens and will be duped out of their land because of their simplicity (52). As soon as Genevieve makes her case for the Indian-as-simpleton, ending with a question about the lack of civilization among the western tribes, without follow-up discussion, without further question, without time to think or consider matters further, without a pause of even a few seconds, Wynema completely defers to Genevieve's opinions, saying, "Oh, no indeed! Far from it! What a superficial thinker I am not to have understood this!" (52).

Genevieve continues by discussing inevitable land theft, which, sadly, ended up being the case after Oklahoma statehood, with a rapid loss of allotted land from Indian control to white control, though this had to do with illegal activities of whites who had power, not with stupid Indians. At any rate, after this discussion, again without a pause, Wynema says, " 'Oh, I am so sorry, dear Mihia [teacher]—so sorry I was so foolish! Pray, forgive me! It is always the way with me, and I dare say I should be one of the first to sell myself out of house and home,' and the girl hung her head, looking the picture of humiliation" (53).

Although I am glad to see Wynema won over to the anti-allotment position, one assumes she could have reached this decision by virtue of some reasoning process of her own (and for much better reasons, perhaps, such as the continuance of Creeks as a nation of people), and the scene is indicative of a general pattern in the novel where Creek opinions are taken hostage by Gerald and Genevieve. Further, Wynema, as a character, is simply painted over white, created in Genevieve's (possibly Callahan's as well?) own image as a Victorian lady. She does not come through as a Creek character. With no transitions, no character development, and few explanations except that under Genevieve's influence she takes a shine to reading Dickens, Scott, and Shakespeare, Wynema magically transforms from a young girl speaking some kind of gobbledygook baby talk that is supposed to represent Creek English dialect ("Oh, Mihia! It is Blue Dumpling. I luf it. Do you love it?") (10) to Victorian speech that never sounds like spoken dialogue:

> "Are you sick, Monsieur Gerald, that you are so pale and quiet? You have not asked me a question when you generally ask me so many," teased Wynema. The years had turned the tables and made her the tease. "Did you know that Miss Genevieve and I are going back to her home on a visit, in a few weeks? Yes? Who told you? We can never surprise you, for I believe you keep a particular courier running back and forth all the time to keep you informed concerning our doings and misdoings." (37)

The silencing of Wynema is seen further in her marriage to Genevieve's brother, Robin. Given the novel's primary function as an assimilationist and Christian supremacist tract, it is no surprise that Wynema ends up marrying a non-Indian. Total whitewashing seems to be the book's highest aim (Wynema's daughter is even blond, though the narrator does make the concession that she has brown eyes). Wynema's loss of self and culture is so complete by this point that when her white husband wants to name their child after her, Wynema herself objects: "Wynema would not have it so. 'Call it Genevieve for the dearest friend I ever had'; and so she was named" (76). Throughout the book, Wynema never has a single moment of doubt, irony, or resistance to Genevieve's "saintliness," nor do any Creek people ever question a single action or intention of Genevieve or her sidekick, Gerald, the founder of the mission among the Creeks. The same is to be said about the assimilation dogma of the novel. Not one Creek voice is raised in protest. In fact, the narrator comments, "Railroads and telegraphs were also welcomed, as the Indians are always pleased with progress in the right direction" (103). The advent of the railroads in the 1880s, however, contrary to the narrator's claims, marked the beginning of whites pouring into Indian Territory in large numbers, and the railroads were hotly contested by the tribes. And to bring matters a little closer to the theme of the novel, Creeks, to this day, are divided on the issue of the light of the gospel, divisions between stomp dance folks and Christian folks being profound (though this may be changing somewhat in recent years, and there have always been those individuals who have somehow managed to be faithful to both). Church people used to have a "backsliders' row" where Creek traditionalists were made to sit if they visited the church, and the stomp grounds were associated with the old life of carnality that was to be mortified after salvation.

Let me return to Wynema and her family. Regarding Wynema's daughter's nicknames, the narrator makes the following comment: "But various were this little lady's sobriquets. She was 'Angel,' 'Pet,' 'Love,' and 'Darling,' to mamma, and 'Dada,' 'Sweetheart' and 'Duchess,' to auntie and uncle; 'Bebee,' to Gerlie, and all the pet names in the Indian vocabulary, to 'Damma' and 'Dampa'" (77). It is interesting to note that although the nicknames in English are actually mentioned, the nicknames in Creek are completely totalized and erased. This is indicative of a larger problem in the book—there is no Creek language in the text. One wonders if the saccharine "Damma" and "Dampa," given in reference to the little girl's Creek full-blood grandparents, are either a conscious or unconscious play on "damn ma" and "damn pa," a repudiation of the Indian side of the little girl's family.

What further sets *Wynema* apart as a decidedly "un-Creek" novel, in addition to its erasure of Creek voices, is the rejection of Creek culture by both white and Indian characters, as well as the narrator. The narrator tells us that Genevieve, while tasting blue dumplings, a Creek dish made from corn and beans, "was not prepossessed with its looks, and ate it with difficulty for it was rough and tasteless" (10). The narrator goes on to say, regarding *sofki*, a drink made out of hominy, that

> the Indians, as a general thing, prefer it after it has soured and smells more like a swill-barrel than anything else. Besides the sofke, were soaked corn bread, which is both sour and heavy; dried venison; a soup with an unspellable name [!] made of corn and dried beef, which is really the most palatable of all the Indian dishes; and opuske, a drink composed of meal made from green corn roasted until perfectly dry and brown, and beaten in a stone mortar until quite fine; mixed with water. (11)

The appraisal of the dinner is a metaphor for the attitude expressed in the novel as a whole: Creek culture is rough and tasteless, perhaps not even worth sampling, since the author for the most part acts like no such culture exists, given that she renders it invisible on the pages of her novel. Following the narrator's general trashing of Creek cooking, there is a follow-up apology that points out the general health of the Indians, but as Ruoff points out in her introduction, when Creek culture is defended by the narrator or Gerald Keithly, the apology just barely exceeds the revulsion. Further, Creek people never get a chance to speak on behalf of their culture, only the narrator and the two missionaries.

The narrator's seeming defense of Creek cooking is undercut when Genevieve becomes quite ill in the very next passage. We do not know how long this occurs after the Creek feast, but because of the scene's placement, we cannot help but associate Genevieve's sickness with what she seems to have just eaten. It is also interesting to note that these comments of revulsion come from the narrator, not from a character, in which case one might argue that the statements reflect the biases of a particular person depicted in the novel, not the book as a whole. The narrator seems to depict the Creeks as grotesques, and this mentality is omnipresent throughout the novel. Even if Genevieve or Gerald had spoken these words in dialogue, however, neither character is ever presented ironically. Both are the incarnation, civilization made flesh. When Genevieve heeds the call in "the great Methodist assembly" to go teach in Indian Territory, the narrator comments, "Thus came civilization among the Teepee Indians" (5).

What is more disturbing about the food passage is Genevieve's blatant dishonesty when she intentionally deceives the *hilis heyya*, the medi-cine maker, and how that repudiation of Creek culture is celebrated throughout the novel. When Genevieve reports her illness, Wynema's full-blood mother, in hackneyed broken English (this is the only page where she speaks), says, "Seek [sick?!] ... What eat?" (12). Genevieve replies, " 'Yes; I do not care for anything to eat'... thinking, 'Oh, I shall starve to death here if I am sick long!' " (12). Wynema's mother calls for the medicine person to come:

> After the blowing had been going on for some time and the incan-tation repeated and re-repeated the medicine was offered to the patient, who made a pretense of taking it.
> "Tell him I am better now, Wynema, and he may go," she said to the child who was taking the performance in.
> After that dignitary, the "medicine man," had retired, Genevieve used the few simple remedies at hand, known to herself, and to her joy and surprise, was able to resume her school duties on the following day.
> The "medicine man" was never called in to wait upon Miss Weir again. (13)

Genevieve's pretense of taking Indian medicine, belief in the superiority of European cures, and intentional dishonesty mark the passage; these traits, seemingly, are Methodist virtues.

In the few instances Creek culture is described, one is reminded of early contact narratives that describe the languages of Native people as guttural and ugly sounding, and their music as the most unpleasant of sounds; hissing, wailing, and so on. For instance, here is how the stomp dance is described:

> In the middle of the plain sat the medicine man, who seemed to be master of ceremonies, and all around him, in single file, danced first the men then the women. Danced? Well, not as you understand the word, my reader, but in a kind of a hop, up and down — a motion not in the least graceful or rhythmic, but it was in accordance with the music. The medicine man directed all the motions and figures by the tune he sang. He droned one tune and the company started; another and they stopped. And what music, or rather queer noises this savage musician

made! No Chinese love-song could have compared with it. His voice was accompanied by the jingling and clanking of shot and shells, bound on the ankles of the dancers. What a strange, weird scene it all was for this girl [Genevieve] unaccustomed to such sights! She looked at it with amaze; the plain, with its semi-circle border of tents; the gaudily and fantastically dressed dancers; the medicine man with his strange ceremonies; and above and beyond all, the clanking of the shells and shot, mixed with the groaning and grunting of the musicians tended more to strike with terror than admiration. Gerald Keithly laughed at his companion's look of consternation. (20–21)

Sophisticated antiphonal music, with a complex narrative, religious, and ceremonial context that provides its meaning, is reduced to "a kind of hop…not in the least graceful or rhythmic," "a drone," "queer noises," "a strange weird scene," "gaudily and fantastically dressed dancers," "strange ceremonies," and "groaning and grunting." Later we will see how strikingly different this is from contemporary Creek writer Louis Oliver's description of the stomp dance. Even conceding that Callahan wrote during a very different historical period than Oliver, compared to other Creek writers close to her own era (such as Alex Posey and Charles Gibson), Callahan's description of Creeks and their culture is bizarre. Although Posey and Gibson poke fun at Creek traditionalists through comic caricatures, there is also a great deal of admiration — rather than revulsion and a sense of total "Otherness" — in their relationship to those characters.

As mentioned earlier, when Genevieve reacts this way with her trenchant monoculturism, she has the saintly Methodist preacher Gerald Keithly to challenge her (when I say "saintly," this is in keeping with the formulaic language of the novel used to describe the characters — upon their first meeting, Gerald is described as the "long-expected Mr. Keithly," and Genevieve as the "well-beloved Miss Weir" (15). They are often introduced with these classical name tags, similar to epic conventions such as "the wing-heeled Achilles." Keithly's modus operandi for getting Genevieve to examine her biases is to provide her with Eurocentric comparative examples that demonstrate that Creek life is not to be despised any more than the worst tendencies in white people. Creek traditionalists who stomp dance, for instance, are not any worse than floozies in low-cut dresses at white "galas":

"Do you think, Miss Weir, that if our Indian brother yonder, now full of the enjoyment of the hour, could step into a ball-room, say in Mobile, with its lights and flowers, its gaudily, and if you will allow it, indecently dressed dancers—do you think he would consider us more civilized than he? Of course that is because he is an uncouth savage," with a slight tinge of irony. "Now, I am going to be ignorant and uncouth enough to agree with him in some things. In the first place, he is more sensible in the *place* he chooses. The Indians select an open space, in the fresh, pure air, in preference to a high, heated room—an evidence of their savagery. In the second place, the squaws always buy enough cloth to make a full dress, even if it be red calico. You may go among them so long and often as you choose, and you will never find a low-necked, short-sleeved dress—which is another evidence of their ignorance. In the third place, they are more moderate in their dancing. A few nights during the year are sufficient for the untaught savage to indulge in the 'light fantastic,' whereas, every night in the week, during 'the season,' hardly suffices for the Caucasian." (21–22)

Keithly's instruction of Weir maintains white society safely at the center as the barometer of all things right and wrong, and Creek culture on the margins. Further, Keithly is only saintly from a non-Indian perspective. In one passage, which has all kinds of strange implications from a more modern psychosexual viewpoint, Keithly teases the young girl Wynema with a piece of candy to get her to say she loves him. Wynema, clearly uncomfortable, avoids Keithly's demands, finally relenting by saying that she "likes" him but "loves" Genevieve. Keithly, not getting the desired response, withholds the candy from the little girl: " 'I don't think I can give this to you, now, since you care so little for me,' and he held up the sack tantalizingly; Wynema turned away proudly disappointed, but deigned not to reply" (20). Keithly is a real prick in this scene, pun intended.

The novel is rigidly formulaic in technique, and following Genevieve's and Gerald's observation of the stomp dance, they see another—to use the words of the novel—"strange ceremony." What they actually witness are some Creeks going to water, a prayer ritual performed next to running water at dawn. This scene is presented to the reader in the same fashion as all the other major scenes in the novel. There are always two voices, a "for" voice and an "against" voice, and the first one makes his or her case, followed by the second one's rebuttal. So as in the stomp dance scene, Genevieve protests, and Gerald defends. Genevieve objects to Gerald's participation in the going-to-water ritual and shows deep consternation that his behavior validates the reality of the ritual. Gerald, in his "defense" of Creek culture, totally negates the religious meaning of what he has just seen. He explains that he does not believe in the ritual either, but the ceremony corroborates a good sense of Methodist hygiene:

> "Surely, Miss Genevieve," he replied, "when I am in Rome I strive to do as Rome does when the doing so does not harm me nor any one else. The Indians believe that the water will keep off the disease, and they have an inkling of the truth. I don't mean to say that I believe the sprinkling of water, as I did just now, will have any effect, either good or bad, on the human system; but it is declared in Holy Writ that 'Cleanliness is next to godliness,' and truly a clean body is almost proof against disease." (27–28)

Probably, Gerald needs to study his "Holy Writ" a little more closely, since the "cleanliness" aphorism is a popular maxim, not a scriptural verse; but more importantly, there is a deep level of duplicity surrounding much of these missionaries' behavior, since they pretend to go along with Indian medicine knowing that they do not believe, as in the earlier scene when the medicine man is called in. These behaviors and discussions are presented not with irony but as moral and spiritual centers from which to judge the cultures being represented in the book.

In addition to the rejection of Creek culture, there is misrepresentation of culture, but misrepresentation of a particularly interesting ilk. In the novel's opening scene, in fact in the first sentence, in a scene striking for both its pastoral romanticism and its simultaneous use of words such as "buck" and "savage," Callahan reports of Creek life in "teepees." What interests me here is not merely that Callahan's depiction is grossly inaccurate, not that she gets it wrong. I am struck by *how* wrong she gets it, and by the fact that she has to be purposefully, not accidentally, misrepresenting culture. As Ruoff points out, Callahan spent a very limited time actually living in Creek country. She grew up in Sulphur, Texas, and spent some time teaching Creek youth at Okmulgee in 1886; attended the Wesleyan Female Institute in Staunton, Virginia, for ten months in 1887 to 1888; taught Creek and white kids at Muskogee's private Methodist high school, the Harrell International Institute, in 1891; and taught Creeks at the Creek boarding school, Wealaka, in 1892 to 1893.[2] Yet even *one month* in Creek country, much less several months teaching Creek children and dealing with Creek families, would be enough to reveal that Creeks do not live in teepees. This has to be intentional misrepresentation. What do we make of this author, then, who is purposefully writing to satisfy white stereotypes? Creek writers, like authors from any other nation, are capable of writing lousy books.

The point I wish to make here is that Callahan's novel is more interesting as an assimilationist and Christian supremacist tract than it is as a Creek novel; these subjects could provide a full study, though that is not my purpose here, since I am trying to examine the book's Creek integrity. As propaganda, Indians in teepees probably need converting a good deal more than those living in log cabins, farming, and attending Methodist and Baptist Creek churches (this is meant to make a point, not to dismiss the equally strong traditionalist faction that maintained its religious life at the square grounds in Callahan's time and does so today).

What strikes me further about the novel's lack of a Creek sensibility is simply the way in which few, if any, nuances of Creek life — political, social, religious, historical — seem to be depicted. It is difficult to prove a negative, but where does the reader of *Wynema* gain any insights into elements of Creek society such as Creek Baptist and Methodist churches and the monthly times of camping in at the church grounds; the age-old division between lower towns and upper towns; the white and red, or so-called peace and war, divisions of the tribe; the political bicameral structure of the House of Kings and House of Warriors that affected the offices Callahan's own father held; Creek clans, which are the vital matrilineal aspect of Creek life; Creek autonomous towns, another strong form of matrilinearity; stickball games; or even any sense of the natural landscape of Creek country?

Ruoff values the suffragette themes mentioned in the book, and the strong women characters who are allowed to address important political issues of their day. Wynema is such a character, though when *she* expresses such an opinion, as demonstrated earlier, her thoughts and words are subsumed by Gerald and Genevieve. Whether this represents some kind of gain for her as a woman seems doubtful to me. Further, to gain the right to speak, she pays a price the other non-Indian women do not — complete cultural loss. It is interesting to note that her character development does not even allow for a period of time when she has difficulties making the transition from savagery to civilization. Like Christ, who sneaks off from his parents to hear the rabbis teach in the temple, Wynema is found by her parents at the feet of Gerald Keithly, captivated by his teaching (3). She is a prodigy, "smarter" than the rest of her uncivilized classmates, and she soaks up Methodist indoctrination and the classics of Western literature like a sponge (23). The novel assumes that Wynema's advanced learning has to do with the fact that she is smart and her other classmates "simple," not that Indian children are being subjected to a racist Christian schooling system that crushes any signs of their intelligence. She is Keithly and Weir's greatest success story, the one they literally write home about, but the exchange is somewhat Faustian considering what little is left of Wynema as a Creek woman.

This is demonstrated by her views on the role of women in her own tribe. Robin, Genevieve's brother, the white man Wynema eventually ends up marrying, says:

> "I am afraid you are a regular suffragist! . . .
> "Hear! Hear! How much the 'cause' loses by not having you to publicly advocate it! Say, didn't sister teach you all this along with the rest? I think you must have imbibed those strong suffrage principles and ideas from her," said Robin teasingly.
> She went on earnestly, ignoring his jesting manner: "Your sister and I hold many opinions in common, and doubtless, I have imbibed some of hers, as I have the greatest respect for her opinions; but the idea of freedom and liberty was born in me. It is true the women of my country have no voice in the councils; we do not speak in any public gathering, not even in our churches; but we are waiting for our more civilized white sisters to gain their liberty, and thus set us an example which we shall not be slow to follow." (45).

Generally, Wynema is correct in asserting that historically women did not speak in the councils (though this is not always the case, and throughout history there have been *emarthlas,* "beloved women," who were quite strong in council among the men). Women are also asked to pray and lead songs in Creek churches, I believe (I have to admit that my experience at Creek Baptist and Methodist church meetings is limited), though men hold the offices. What is more important here is that Wynema has been so thoroughly brainwashed that she fails to see she has erased at least half the culture. Creek traditional culture involves a delicate balance of women and men wherein clan is based on matrilineal descent and town membership of one's mother's town. These two institutions are two of the strongest in Creek society, in which exists a unique sovereignty of autonomous towns that are part of a larger confederation. The councils would literally not be able to exist without women's clans and women's towns. It seems to me that any suffragist viewpoint that

Wynema might express has been stripped of any real power, since she is simply reliant on white women to formulate her consciousness, and she cannot see the power of Creek women that already surrounds her and surpasses the rights of the white women in the Methodist circles in which she worships.

Although Callahan was biologically Creek, the extent to which she was culturally Creek is harder to ascertain. Her biography, what little we know of it, most closely resembles the white southern genteel background of her character Genevieve Weir, the school marm who rejects Creek culture at every turn. The issue of insider/outsider status is seldom a simple one, as recent literary theory often points out, but the balance of evidence seems to indicate that Callahan wrote more from a non-Creek perspective than from a Creek one. In this regard, I acknowledge that defining just what a "Creek perspective" is remains problematic, since there are many Creeks with many different perspectives. But as an act of nation building, it seems to me that Callahan's novel fails dismally.

The novel *does* express sympathy for Creek people, and those of other tribes, as victims of the white man's avarice. The problem with this reasoning, as with many other depictions of Native Americans that place Indian people in tragic frameworks, is that it completely ignores the active and successful resistance of Creek traditionalist groups such as the so-called Snakes who refused to acknowledge the dissolution of tribal government and the illegal state of Oklahoma and, further, carried out their defiance by continuing Creek tribal government at Hickory Grounds into the 1930s. Further, the novel's sympathy for Indian victimization fits into its assimilationist doctrine quite well, since the abuse of Native people is argued as unjust but nonetheless inevitable under the unrelenting advance of progress.

There were factions in Creek country, however, such as the Snakes, who had a different argument — not only was land rip-off unjust, it was not fated. They recognized the continued validity of the treaty of 1832, which promised them their land in Indian Territory into perpetuity. They continued Creek government even after it was declared nonexistent and fought the good fight, sending delegates to Washington until, in fact, tribal governments were restored in the 1930s. Part of their power was their refusal to accept the ideology of victimization, opting instead for continuation.

Callahan, it seems to me, is a Creek writer who rejects many Creek points of view, even a Creek Christian one, which would have to acknowledge the existence of Creek pastors and congregations preaching in Creek and reading Creek Bibles and singing out of Creek hymnals for decades before the saintly Keithly and Weir (presented in the novel as the first missionaries in Indian Territory) heed the call to save Indians. In fact, there was a body of Creeks who migrated to Oklahoma voluntarily with William McIntosh after the ratification of the Treaty of Washington in 1826. They preceded the rest of the nation by ten years before the forced removal of 1836 to 1837, and these Creeks established Methodist, Baptist, and Presbyterian congregations in the Arkansas Valley by the time the main body arrived.[3]

Creek Christianity, then, precedes Gerald Keithly's putative pioneer missionary efforts by at least sixty years (we know Callahan's novel takes place in the early 1890s because of the allotment references and the discussion of Wounded Knee in the latter part of the book). In the early years after removal, between 1836 and 1841, no white missionaries were allowed inside the Creek Nation because Opothle Yohola had opposed white Christianity.[4] Churches were run exclusively by Creek pastors. The novel completely erases the work of Creek preachers and their congregations; one can only guess that the gospel always begins with white folks. By 1840 Creeks had an orthography, a hymnal, portions of the Bible, and several readers. By 1848 white Methodists had established the Asbury School at North Fork Town,[5] so Callahan does not even get her own Methodist history right when she places Methodism's origins in Oklahoma in the 1890s.

Samuel Checote was the first principal chief elected after the Civil War in 1867. He is a man Callahan's father *had* to have known about, since Samuel Callahan was a captain in the Confederate Creek regiment as well as a member of the Confederate Congress, and Checote was in the Confederate Creek regiment as well. More importantly, Samuel Callahan served as a clerk in the Muskogee House of Kings from 1868 to 1872,[6] under the Checote administration. Checote was a Methodist minister himself. Surely Alice Callahan knew about the history of Creek Methodism, at least that it did not begin in 1890! Yet she chooses to erase Creek contributions to Methodism totally. For a full-length (and much more informed) study of the history of Methodism among Creeks, and other

Southeastern tribes, both before and after removal, readers would be better served perusing Choctaw Methodist pastor and writer Homer Noley's *First White Frost: Native Americans and United Methodism.*[7]

Even Callahan's own experience as part of the mixed-blood "progressive" Creek element, certainly an important faction in the tribe, especially in terms of its political leadership, is missing from the novel. Her own father held various offices, including clerk in the House of Kings, after the Civil War, and he was justice in the Muskogee Supreme Court in 1901, superintendent of Wealaka Boarding School from 1892 to 1894, and often a tribal delegate to negotiations in Washington D.C.[8] Yet this mixed-blood, so-called "progressive" element of the tribe is completely missing from Callahan's work. Perhaps, given that many were Creek Christians who had been born and raised in the faith and whose families did not need saving, they did not very well fit Callahan's propagandistic aims to satisfy a white audience hungry for heathens. Obviously the novel is not written for Creeks, another factor that sets it apart from Posey's and Gibson's work, which was read by a local Indian audience. Callahan's novel is a remarkably "un-Creek" work, which is not the same thing as saying that she is not a Creek writer. She is a bad Creek writer who has written a marginally Creek novel, at least from one Creek reader's perspective, and I would say that her novel squelches any Creek voices, or any other Native perspectives.

Inherent in this kind of analysis is an argument that Native American novels should have some kind of integrity in terms of their representation of the nations they purport to be written about. Whereas different novels will vary in terms of their emphasis on history, culture, politics, and land, these nonetheless seem to me important aesthetic considerations. No matter how we look at *Wynema*, even if we place it within the context of the sentimental fiction of its time, it is bad writing. We might point to its failure on technical grounds (even its 1891 publisher apologizes in the preface for the book's crudeness and incompleteness), noting the lack of character development, the unconvincing dialogue that sounds more like written than oral speech, the awkward self-referentiality when the narrator refers to other passages in the book, the abandonment of any attention to sense of place, and the unbelievability of many of its events. Under literary analysis that pays attention to nationalism, however, there are also the considerations mentioned earlier. In what ways does the novel record Creek history, create a sense of place on Creek land, advance Creek culture, or strengthen Creek autonomy? How deeply is it engaged in things Creek? And this is not even to mention the god-awful depictions of Sioux people in the book's artificially tacked-on ending, but I will leave that to Lakota scholars.

To be sure, Callahan had virtually no models on which to base an attempt at writing a Creek novel or even an Indian novel. There were, however, widespread opportunities in Indian Territory to read literary representations of Southeastern Indian voices. As Dan Littlefield has pointed out, the tradition of dialect writing, often in the form of comic portrayals of full-bloods who were more comfortable in their nation's language than English, was going strong in the 1880s, and these columns appeared in papers throughout Indian Territory.[9] Although many of these writers rendered somewhat hackneyed depictions of Indian life, they had one thing in common — they represented Indian voices in their work; in fact, that was the most salient characteristic of the genre. So although we have to give Callahan credit for writing in a kind of vacuum in terms of novelistic production, and perhaps we can attribute some of her aesthetic failings to this, it seems to me we can critique the lack of Creek voices in Callahan's writing, given the rich tradition of Indian written speech represented in the literature of her surroundings.

Her position as a complete accommodationist is harder to justify. If we look at other Native women writers of Callahan's time (for example, Paiute author Sarah Winnemucca, who wrote before Callahan in the late 1880s, and Sioux author Gertrude Bonnin, who wrote a little after Callahan, around the turn of the century), the differences are glaring. Winnemucca and Bonnin are themselves the products of a Christian education, but both present stinging indictments of Christian schooling and practice, sometimes overtly criticizing the relationship between church and land theft and cultural loss, other times employing strong irony in their Christian depictions. It is not difficult to imagine that Callahan could have written a very different novel had she chosen to do so.

Callahan is a Creek writer who has written a novel; but is it a *Creek* novel, and further, is it an accomplished Creek novel? What her writing does for me, as a Creek reader, is to confront me with a challenging question: What are the minimal requirements for a tribally specific work? Perhaps Creek readers will answer this question differently, but Callahan's failures might suggest that a sense of Creek land, Creek character, Creek speech and Creek speakers, Creek language, Creek oral and written literature, Creek history, Creek politics, and Creek government might be potential considerations in our growing understanding of what constitutes an exemplary work in a national tribal literature.

Oh, and did I forget to say? It also has to tell a good story.

Dear Hotgun:

Well, here it come the middle of August and the tomatoes are turning red so fast you can hardly catch them before they fall off the vines and it's too hot to go fishing though Stijaati Thlaako tells it that late in the evening when it cools off they was had hitting on top water lures and I put up the last jar of snap green peas with new potatoes and just a little bit of bacon rind (I can just about taste them now with those sliced fresh tomatoes making little red rivers into the beans) and we was had our only tornado siren this year which brung in a big blow and much hailstones and black clouds and wind which reminds me of the time Lucille come in plumb frazzled from picking cotton all day and throwed herself down on the bed too give out to move and here come a big storm and her husband cain't rouse her for nothing so he gotta gather up the kids hisself and finally he tells her, "You can lay there on ye goddammed ass and git blowed away, but I'm taking my kids to the cellar!"

Good thing for him too Stijaati made it in before the big storm but bad luck on the way back from lake Eufaula driving past Raiford on number nine highway was where he got pulled over by trooper. Stijaati sitting there waiting not knowing what him done wrong. At least didn't had no beer cans in the car, thank goodness, drank him all up between casting spinners in bass holes. Had an ice chest on the back seat but nothing more than two smallmouths inside, mebeso pound and a half, couple pounds apiece, not so bad, and oh so good fried up with a little cornmeal and some salad and them Texas cantayloupes he bought in Eufaula the kind you can smell they sweetness before you even pick them up and mebeso piece of chocolate cake afterwards if he spark his wife just right but here come that trooper nohows make him straighten up in his seat and practice his "Yes, officer."

Whenever Stijaati got stopped by polices he always made note of they badge. "Gerald Keithly," this one said. Officer Keithly was had wearing a little gold cross on a chain that stood out against his white tee shirt. He took off his sunglasses and put 'em in his pocket slow like a TV cop. Stijaati look up and couldn't believe he was looking into two of the bluest eyes he'd ever seen, pert near white clouds floating in them.

Officer Keithly was frown and ask, "Are those tribal plates?"

Stijaati he was answer proud, "Yes, sir. Creek Nation."

Keithly was had want to know, "Where's your Oklahoma plates?"

Stijaati didn't know what to tell the man, so he repeated, "I don't have Oklahoma plates. I have Creek Nation plates," and Stijaati reached toward his glove box, but Officer Keithly move so fast that before Stijaati was to pop the box open, Keithly was had drew a small green Gideon's New Testament out of his holster and pointed it at Stijaati's head.

Stijaati was stuck his hands in the air and holler, "DON'T SHOOT!" He got his arms put up far as he could except he had to stop when he reached the roof so he place his hands palm-up on the car top like holding her from caving in.

Officer Keithly snarled, "That last Indian I gave three wishes, but your luck is up!"

Stijaati confused good now. "I was just reaching for some papers, sir. I was gonna show you a letter from the state department of public safety that was issued to everyone with a tribal tag. It explains that Senate Bill 586, which don't allow Oklahoma residents to purchase motor vehicle tags issued by another state, don't apply to Indian governments issuing tags."

Officer Keithly waddn't listening. He pointed his ticket pad slow and mechanical. "Step back to the patrol car," he told Stijaati. Stijaati got out and did as told him. He say he could heared voices in the back of the cruiser, arguing. He opened up the door and was climbed in, surprised him pretty good to see three women already crowded on the seat. "This is Wynema, Alice, and Genevieve," Keithly said, pry amused at Stijaati crammed in elbow to elbow with a bunch of womenfolks. They had fell quiet when Stijaati opened the door. They stared at him for a spell, then didn't hardly miss a beat and went back to fussing. Wynema seemed like the youngest of the bunch, and she just clean busted loose: "What do *you* know, Alice? You weren't in Indian Territory long enough to know a Creek from a Comanche."

"Why you ungrateful..."

"*Indian*," Wynema replied quickly.

"No, I was thinking 'character,' " said Alice.

Then the girl turned to Genevieve: "And you and that preacher never gave anyone else half a chance to say anything! You stole nearly every line in the book!"

Keithly looked up from writing out the ticket, but he didn't say anything.

Stijaati try to referee and was say, "Ladies, ladies!" Mebeso afraid they might come to blows and him locked up in the back seat between them.

Officer Keithly was mutter from the front seat, "God, what a mess." Stijaati was begun to think that instead of going to jail, for what reason he can't recollect, his punishment was to sit here and listen.

"You know it wasn't easy writing in 1890," Alice said, defending herself, "being the first Indian woman to write a novel."

"You mean the *worst* novel written by an Indian woman," Wynema was fire back, "not the *first*."

"Some of the depictions of Creek life are inaccurate, to be sure," said Alice, "but look at other books during the time. Do you think the public would have read anything other than Creeks in teepees, ripe for salvation and the glories of progress? Maybe we can recognize the novel for what it *does* rather than what it doesn't. Doesn't the book allow women to express intelligent opinions?"

"White women, maybe," Wynema said, her eyes flashing. She'd been waiting a long time to speak, a hunerd and six years. "When did I ever get to express my opinion in that damn book?"

"My, you've changed from the little girl who used to call me 'teacher,'" said Genevieve, sadly.

Stijaati started to pick up interest in the argument. He remembered something, started to place the name. Callahans—wasn't they mixedbloods from around Muskogee? And an author by that name too, read a book of hers. Stijaati one of them Indians read everything on his tribe he can lay aholt of and besides that knows family histories all over Creek country.

Stijaati he was had say, "Hey, I read that book over at the Oklahoma Historical Society, how bout it? I reckon I gotta throw in with Wynema. I remember when I was reading thinking something ain't right here; they's a white man in the sofky pot. Let me expoundulate on my methodism: I found ever single little place in the book where an Indian got to say anything and counted their words. We talk, they listen on pages 3, 4, 10, 12, 14, 19, 20, 24, 27, 30, 31, 35, 37, 38, 43, 44, 45, 46, 50, 51, 52, 53, 61, 62, 63, 64, 67, 68, 69, 77, 78, 80, 81, 82, 83, 84, 85, 86, 87, 88, 89, 90, 91, 92, 94, 95, 96, 97, 98, 99, 100, 103, and 104. I made a running count for each page of how many words the Indian on that page spoke, then I used the calculator function under the Apple icon on my laptop to add up the total. There are 5,528 words spoken by Indians in *Wynema: Child of the Forest*. Next, I counted the number of words on a purty fair to middling average-looking page, page 39. They's 335 words on page 39 but I ain't saying I might not have missed one or added an extry, but let's say 335. Then I gone home because they wouldn't let me brung in a cup of coffee I bought over in the cafeteria at the capitol building across the street during study break. I gone home and multiplied 335 average words per page by the 104 pages that make up the novel not counting LaVonne's introduction (I hope she don't get mad at me neither for bringing all this up because not too long ago she bought me breakfast at Columbia, Missouri). My calculator was say they are 34,840 words in the novel. Of those 34,840 words, as we have established already, 5,528 belong to Indians. They's a lot of dialogue in the book, at least a third, maybe a half of the novel. No matter how you figger it, there's more white Methodist talk than Indian talk or Creek talk. What happened to a Creek viewpoint?"

"Until Officer Keithly put us in the back of this cruiser and I met Wynema," Alice said, clearing her throat, "I had never *heard* of such a thing as a Creek viewpoint. Maybe you have to realize I was just thinking of telling a story, not building up the Creek nation through writing. Nobody during my day ever heard of a thing called a Creek novel or an Indian novel. Part of my public appeal was the exotic notion of an Indian even writing. And surely I allowed you to speak a good many times," Alice continued, turning toward Wynema. "Stijaati counted a rather full page, thus overcounting the total words in the novel given the chapter beginnings with not nearly as much print on those pages. Indians *almost* got to speak as often as whites in my book if you take into account the lower total word count."

Wynema was just shook her head. "A further issue is the *quality* of that speech. What good is my dialogue if you simply created me in your own Methodist image? If the book is about women expressing opinions, it is also about a white woman completely overrunning an Indian woman's thoughts and the way the Indian woman is brainwashed into believing this is normal, submitting all her opinions to her white mentor, Genevieve, for approval. You speak of women's rights but ignore your, and Genevieve's, roles in suppressing Indian women's rights."

"But do you really think the book is of no value whatsoever as a Creek work?" Alice asked, now sniffling.

Stijaati was answer, "No, lady. I read it and I'm Creek. I think you contributed something. The book mebeso make us look at Creek writing as a historical specter with you being one point on that time line and today's writers carrying that forward. By studying what all you went through writing a Creek novel — even if you never knowed it was a Creek novel — we can understand lot better how far Creek writer was had come, what she can do today, and how he was to got there. You didn't write a great Creek book, mebeso not even a good Creek book, but your failure hep us ask questions. How do Creeks like Indian professor kind talking about books nowadays get feedback from Creek people themselves about what they read and what they expect from Creek writers or other Indian writers? So that we don't has similar problem as *Wynema* with no Creek voices. How can these here what you call literary criticizers, mebeso Native Lit Critters, include that feedback in their discussions of Creek literature? How can Native Lit Critters carry on a discussion of Creek culture as a conversation *with* Creek people rather than speaking *for* Creek people? How can white Lit Critters become helpers, rather than Indian experts? How can they promote the work of Native people over their own, and still was keep up their own good efforts at contributing to Native literary development? How can Indian Lit Critters do the same thing — encourage the budding talent in their own tribes, the young ones who have new things to say, the kids singing themselves back together?"

"Just wait a minute," Wynema says. "Here we go again. A man who wants to do all the talking. I still have some things to say. Whether or not Alice ever *heard* of a Creek viewpoint does not change the fact that one existed, and where it existed was among *us*. To only talk about her 'constraints' as a novelist begs the question. There is another half of the equation we are ignoring — in what ways were Creek people during her time expressing their views, amongst themselves and to the larger public? Why couldn't she express those opinions in her book? Especially given her father's prominent political history in the tribe, she must have heard stories about happenings and opinions among Creeks. What was stopping her from writing about them? Why, like several Creeks actively writing just after her — Alex Posey, G. W. Grayson, Charles Gibson — could she not at least take Creek characters, Creek speech, Creek ideas seriously? Posey and Gibson seemed to be fond of their characters; Grayson was a defender of Creek national life in his writings. Alice seems to be making fun of the Creeks in her book. Even before Creek writers like

Posey, Grayson, and Gibson, were the Indian dialect writers beginning to use Indian speech in the 1880s as a common forum in territory newspapers, readily available examples of Indian people speaking in fictional formats. Given its paucity of Indian voices, what is the novel *Wynema* really about? Is it about Indian people, or do they exist as props to give the missionaries something to talk about? What makes an Indian novel Indian? Is *Wynema* Indian enough to be an Indian novel? Did Callahan even *like* Creek people, given the revulsion expressed throughout the book at all things Creek? I know I don't sound like my character in *Wynema*, but I've got monologues of my own making, and I never was the 'little maid,' the book says I was on page 19. And one last thing," Wynema added, glaring at Alice, "Why did you force me to marry that white geek named Robin? Only you would think of a husband for me who later would be Tonto to Batman."

Stijaati getting hot in the back of the car. He wipes his forehead with bandanna in back pocket. In the front seat Officer Keithly is chewing the end of his pencil, short pause after writing long time. Stijaati expecting a paragraph, at least, describing his violations, maybe a page. I can just see him now when Keithly tore it off and handed it to him, the only thing it said was OPERATING WITHOUT A LICENSE TO CRITICIZE A NOVEL. The fine on the back said

$40 if you're only A.B.D.
$60 for only a master's degree
$80 if no more than a B.A.
$100 for nothing but a certificate from a vo-tech school
Indian: long-term financing available

Stijaati was asked, "Can I go now?" Plumb staggered by the possibility of the fee for a full-blood who'd dropped out of Bacone his second semester on a baseball scholarship, him. He'd better leave before Officer Keithly asked to see his diploma. Stijaati stepped out of the car. Officer Keithly started up the ignition.

"What about us?" asked Wynema.

"I'm taking you in," answered Keithly, dropping the transmission into drive.

"Where too?" Wynema insisted.

"Dwight Presbyterian Mission at Sallisaw. You'll be in the custody of James and Lucinda Sessions."

"But we're Methodists!" protested Alice and Genevieve together.

"OK, then," said Officer Keithly, slamming the car in reverse and stomping on the gas pedal.

The way Stijaati tells it last he seen was police car hooking it backwards down the shoulder of Highway 9 gravel flying ever whichaways and a young Indian woman leaning out the window black hair blowing all around her face and hollering at the top of her lungs into the wind.

Sincerely,
Jim Chibbo

CHAPTER FIVE

Fus Fixico: A Literary Voice against the Extinction of Tribal Government

A discussion of Creek writing would not be complete without including a forerunner who affected not only the Creek Nation but events in
Indian country at large, Alexander Posey. Posey's wide-ranging career,
which ended abruptly just after Oklahoma statehood when he drowned
in 1908, did not merely encompass writing; it also included many offices in Creek national politics, administration in Creek schools, stints
at journalism as owner of the *Eufaula Indian Journal,* periods spent la-
boring as a field-worker for the Dawes Commission, and involvement
in real estate dealings. Posey, a difficult figure to define, endorsed the
idea of progress and criticized traditionalists as "pull-back" Indians who
were doomed to be left behind by modern life. Yet he remains hard to
categorize as "progressivist"; such terms break down when applied to
Posey. He admired many of the full-bloods he caricatured because of
their knowledge of a past that he idealized and believed had passed
away. Further, in the Fus Fixico letters, the idea of progress is parodied
so frequently that getting a reading on Posey's relationship to assimilationist ideology is no simple matter.

In the letters, for example, his criticism of the Dawes Commission is
perhaps one of the strongest critiques of that political body to date, and
history has proven him right, since almost every single one of the commission's members was involved in swindling land from Indians or was
in collusion with the railroads and large real estate companies operating
illegally in Indian Territory. Yet after statehood, Posey became involved

in real estate himself, working with land companies to divest Indians of their allotments. Some Creek traditionalists believe that because of these unsavory activities, Posey died an early death, drowning in the very river, the Oktahutche, or the Canadian, that he so dearly loved.

Perhaps one of the strongest expressions of Native literary nationalism, however, comes to us via Posey in the form of the Fus Fixico letters. This may come as a surprise to some, since critics have presented Posey as a progressive who endorsed allotment and the inevitable role of "progress." Critics have often analyzed the bicultural elements of his writing as well, its European influences, and Posey himself as a writer torn between two cultures. In this chapter, I would like to present what I hope is a more Muskogee-centric portrait of Posey, arguing for his immersion in Creek nationalism, history, politics, and culture. Further, rather than analyzing the letters as humorous commentary *about* Oklahoma politics, I would like to emphasize the mimetic function of the letters — Posey's use of this literary format to actually thwart the Oklahoma statehood process and the dissolution of tribal government. Finally, in the last part of the chapter, I will discuss the style and structure of the letters.

Thanks to Daniel F. Littlefield Jr., professor of English at the University of Arkansas at Little Rock, a scholar with an impressive body of work on Southeastern Indians and Creeks in particular, we have two groundbreaking works on Posey's life: the biography *Alex Posey: Creek Poet, Journalist, and Humorist* and a collection of Posey's persona writings, *The Fus Fixico Letters*, the latter work begun by Carol Hunter and finished by Littlefield after Hunter's death.[1] Both books are excellent, and *The Fus Fixico Letters* is timely because there are so few substantive works on Indian humor. The scholarship that exists tends to emphasize Euro-American criticism over explicating oral traditions and the primary cultures that create Native literature. Littlefield's book provides the raw data that make possible such an analysis in the future. Although Littlefield's editing provides more of a historical context than an analysis of the humor in the letters, he does include a very good introduction that touches on Indian humor. The historical work is impeccable. The footnotes, so thorough as to almost constitute a book unto themselves, are an impressive chronicling of the events that led up to Oklahoma statehood. Littlefield does a beautiful job of contextualizing the letters, delving deeply into old census records, letters, territorial newspapers, and many other obscure sources. There are many recurring names, especially of Oklahoma politicians and Dawes Commission members, and Littlefield manages to say something different about these repetitions each time they occur in the letters, explaining the names in relation to their changing contexts.

Littlefield's book, as good as it is, could benefit by paying a little closer attention to traditional elements of Creek culture; for instance, the belief of some Creeks that Posey's compelling poem about drowning prefigures his death. Some Creek traditionalists believe that Posey's death came about as the result of his real estate dealings after Oklahoma statehood when Posey was beginning to become involved in the sale of Indian allotments. For these reasons, some say, Posey was drowned by Tie-Snake, swallowed up by the very river he loved, the Oktahutche. The book would be better served if these oral and communal viewpoints were, at the very least, acknowledged or, better yet, included to balance out the extensive reliance on written sources. In Hunter's preface, she acknowledges that she talked to Creek people, in the area Posey lived, about him (Posey, xiv). These responses from the community would have been valuable had they been made part of the discussion, especially given the tendency of critics to reduce Posey's life to reductive generalizations such as calling him a Creek "progressivist," a term that may not necessarily resonate among Creeks as an accurate description of Posey. Perhaps inclusion of the interview materials was difficult because of Hunter's untimely death. I have talked to some Creeks who were related to Posey, and I do not recall them describing him as a "progressivist," and I think this matter needs further clarification from oral history sources — those related to Posey and other Creeks who knew of him. One cannot help but wonder to what degree terms such as "progressivist" actually resonate with meaning among Creeks. Perhaps they would judge Posey by different criteria than the either-or categories of "traditionalist" or "progressivist."

Posey was born "on August 3, 1873, in a remote section of the Creek Nation known as the Tulladega Hills, about fifteen miles northwest of Eufaula" (Posey, 6). His mother was from Tuskeegee, and thus Posey was born as a member of that particular tribal town. As contemporary Creek writer Louis Oliver recalls in his poem "Alexander Posey":

His mother was the daughter of
  Pohos Harjo,
and a member of the Wind Clan
  of the town of Taskegee
  it is said.[2]

This makes Posey a Wind Clan member like his mother. Posey's father
claimed to be Creek, yet there is some doubt whether he actually had
Creek blood. There is little doubt, however, that his father was culturally Creek; Posey's father was raised in the Creek Nation from orphan-
hood, a member of Broken Arrow tribal town and a fluent Creek speaker.
An early, telling event in Posey's life was "when the younger Posey reached
age fourteen, his father insisted that he speak English" (Posey, 6–7). Given
that his father, Hence Posey, would punish his son for speaking Creek,
it is not surprising that Posey would display ambivalent feelings about
Creek traditionalism throughout his lifetime. As Oliver says in the aforementioned poem:

It is said he was not a fullblood Indian
  and estranged from his people
  by the Whiteman's ways.[3]

Yet in Oliver's work, which will be discussed in the next chapter, the
commentary concerning Posey is placed in shifting contexts. In many
ways, Oliver holds Posey up as the quintessential Creek writer.

Posey began writing while he was a student at Bacone (Posey, 7). Some
of his early work includes retellings of Creek traditional stories that, as
Littlefield says, are hackneyed attempts to turn Creek myths into Euro-
American fables that satirize human foibles. Posey's main early interest
was poetry. Although he had some arresting images in his poems, his
skill was not as a poet, and whether he would have overcome his limitations in the writing of poetry will never be known because of his
early death. The poems, imitative and overly influenced by the romantics and popular sentimental poets of the era, depict a generic landscape based on romantic pastorals rather than a concrete naming of the
natural world around the Eufaula area that Posey knew so intimately.
As Alexia Kosmider points out in her dissertation and upcoming University of Idaho book publication entitled "Tricky Tribal Discourse," it
is whenever Posey links his work most closely to Creek oral tradition
that he is most effective, whether in the poems, his stories, or the letters.[4]

Embodied in the language, in the Creek English that his full-bloods speak, comes a worldview and a sense of place missing in the poems' "elevated" diction. The dialect of the Fus Fixico letters, in contrast to the poems, is striking in terms of its originality. This makes the letters considerably more powerful than much of the poetry, since the letters are representations of oral Creek voices in dialogue.

Further, the switch from poetry to dialect writing underscores a major political turning point for Posey. The dialect, unlike the poetry, by presenting Indian language, even if Indian English language, is anti-assimilationist in the sense that it represents a refusal to become something else—that is, proper English or English more accessible to white readers (Posey also includes here and there untranslated Creek words and sentences). The switch in languages, I believe, is one of the factors that enables Posey to move from the largely apolitical poems to the letters completely immersed in Creek, Territorial, and Oklahoma politics. This radical transformation from poet to letter writer also impacts our assessment of Posey's life. How can we easily describe him as a progressivist when he immersed himself in such a uniquely Creek literary form, one that we might describe as a refusal to write in English (standard English, that is) and a privileging of the language of full-blood Creeks?

Posey hit his stride, then, in a big way, with the appearance of the first Fus Fixico letter on October 14, 1902, in the *Indian Journal*, the Eufaula weekly paper. Fus Fixico is the persona Posey assumed, pretending to be a Creek full-blood writing letters to the editor of the Eufaula paper. Fus Fixico would report overheard conversations between a group of Creek men who were his friends. Fus Fixico is, as Littlefield has pointed out, the detached listener, the outsider who reports events with humor. Students of African American literature might be reminded of Langston Hughes's Jesse B. Semple letters, which portrayed Mr. Semple as a wise fool commenting in black dialect on politics and conditions for African Americans in the 1940s, using comedy as a technique for underscoring serious issues. Similarly, Posey uses Fus Fixico and friends, initially, to comment on local events around Eufaula, often reporting meetings, socials, and gossip in a mock-epic style, blowing up little events in an exaggerated manner. As the letters evolved, Posey's subject changed to more serious matters concerning the theft of Indian Territory from the Indian nations, who were under extreme pressure to give up their lands, and reporting on the corruption of federal officials who were members of the Dawes Commission. Like Hughes, Posey uses dialect, what Posey characterized as *este charte* (more likely to be pronounced *stijaati* in Creek country, literally, red person, i.e., Indian) English.

In all the ways that Posey's poetry fails, his letters succeed. They create an extremely strong sense of place, evoking a feeling for the countryside around Eufaula: the town's streets and buildings, the speech of its citizens, natural details in the surrounding woods, the stomp grounds outside of town, Creek farming patches and Indian houses, a whole world, what the American realist William Faulkner, referring to his own fiction, called "his own little postage stamp of native soil." Altogether, Posey published seventy-three letters, a sizable body of dialect literature.

Non-Natives are often unable to connect comedy with Indian people because of the American guilt complex over Indians and the oft-embraced tragic view of the vanishing American. The Fus Fixico letters, however, as is the case with much tribal literature, contain strong elements of humor. The humor in Posey's letters often derives from the perspective of the characters as full-bloods bumping up against a changing world. At other times, the humor involves the ways in which some Indian people themselves are complicitous in scandals that threaten the well-being of the Creek Nation. Naming plays a big part in the humor, and the names of characters are little caricatures of their personalities. Slang, unusual expressions, reworked clichés, botched English, and understatement are used as comic devices as well. As Littlefield sums it up, "In short, in Fus Fixico's and his friends' efforts to assess matters in a foreign language, their assessment becomes a tour de force of humorous effects" (Posey, 39). It is important to note, however, that the characters are not being made fun of by the author as "dummies"; they are, rather, intelligent people making astute comments about important events in Indian Territory. The characters, people of detached critical intelligence, maintain their dignity while exposing political corruption. To summarize, Posey is fond of Fus and his friends.

Alexia Kosmider's "Tricky Tribal Discourse" is a useful work in terms of its engaging voice and original research on Posey. Especially important is her attention to Posey's poetry, which had not come under critical analsyis before her manuscript. At the time of this writing, I was only able to look at the dissertation rather than the completed book for this promising work, which was still unavailable from the University of

Idaho Press. I wish to point out, however, some of the ways I feel her work is influenced by the popular "bicultural" and "mediative" theories that have dominated Native literary analysis, and I will argue that such theories sometimes fail to incorporate tribal realities. Biculturalism looks at Native literature as a hybrid discourse, influenced by European literary forms. Native artists, according to this view, are "adaptors" and "adopters" rather than originators, incorporating tribal worldviews into extant forms such as the novel, the short story, and the poem, the argument being that such expression is not indigenous to tribal cultures. The works themselves, according to the theorists, have a "mediating" function between white and Indian worlds, and in terms of the authors, their mixed-bloodedness is emphasized, as well as their positionality between cultures. Marginality becomes a huge concern. In examining Kosmider's discussion of Posey, I wish to point out that the history of Native authors needs to be examined more fully before simply assigning them to these "torn between two worlds" approaches.

Kosmider's introduction begins with a personal anecdote regarding a well-known photograph of Posey in a tweed jacket and derby, looking very much the romantic, and a rather handsome one at that. Kosmider finds herself sometimes "glancing over at this picture, puzzled at its meaning" (1). The meaning may be as much a reflection of Kosmider, however, as it is of Posey, since she comes to the conclusion that

> we may speculate that Posey, a Creek Indian writer and poet, living in Indian Territory at the turn-of-the-century, may have been trying to emulate one of his favorite poets in this photograph. Like Burns, Posey is situated between two worlds, Euroamerican and Indian. In this photograph, we may ask, does Posey want to erase his culture-boundedness, creating a new representation of self? But at the same time, he seems to create a vision that speaks of cultural conflict. (1–2)

Wow! All of that on account of poor Alex just getting cleaned up and getting his picture took! Just what, I would like to ask, is an Indian in a tweed coat and a derby hat trying to erase? Many Creek people, just about all of them that I have ever seen from photos taken during this time period, got dressed up to go to town and get photographed. What might Posey have worn that would have been more appropriate? He wasn't at the stomp grounds, mind you, he was at the photo studio.

Of course, at stake here are larger issues than Posey's attire. Rather than historicizing Posey's Creek world, Kosmider uses as her paradigm the popular literary assumptions about biculturalism and otherness. This juxtaposes current sensibilities against turn-of-the-century Creekness, a strategy that does not work all that well, here and elsewhere in her analysis. Kosmider goes on to say that "Alex Posey at times emulates dominant cultures' beliefs — at other times, he celebrates and tries to dispel negative Indian stereotypes. His vacillation is the act of an individual who has difficulty understanding who he is — and perhaps accepting his Indian identity" (20). Where does this statement come from? There isn't a lick of evidence anywhere that would indicate Posey did not know whether he was a Creek guy and an Indian. Throughout his lifetime, Posey spoke, wrote, and thought of himself as a Creek, an Indian, and a Creek Indian writer. Equally as important, Creeks, then and now, think of him as a Creek, as a Creek writer, and a Creek politician. Posey grew up speaking Creek, not English, until he was fourteen. His mother immersed him in Creek oral tradition. He held political offices in Creek national government all his adult life. If Posey wasn't Creek, then who is?

In talking to Creek people, in Creek country, about Posey, some of whom were kin to him, I can never recall anyone saying that Posey did not know whether he was Creek and Indian. I have to wonder, then, to what degree all this erasure business has anything to do with Posey. This does not mean that we have to romanticize everything that Posey did, turn him into a "Super-Creek," a staunch traditionalist, or overlook the history of his more unsavory activities such as working for the Dawes Commission or his later real estate dealings. What this does call for, perhaps, is historicizing Posey according to the realities of Creek national life during Posey's time.

Many Creek families, though operating businesses, running large cattle ranches, attending Indian Baptist and Methodist churches, and so on, were still totally immersed in the political, social, economic, and cultural life of the nation — a nation, like any other, with a diverse population. We can say that these families, who were often from the Creek lower towns and had a very long history of difference from the largely full-blood traditionalists of the Creek upper towns, were *different* Creeks, to be sure, than the full-blood faction; but does this necessarily make them torn between two cultures, given that Creek reality had included contact with other cultures — white, black, and Indian — for hundreds of years? It is difficult to imagine how anyone could be rooted any more solidly in "Creekness" than Alex Posey, given his total immersion in Creek language, Creek oral tradition, Creek social life, and Creek politics. Kosmider's analysis depends on static assumptions that the"real" Indian world is a pristine one rather than a complex, dynamic state of evolving nationhood.

For example, in analyzing the putative Europeanization of Creek education and government, Kosmider says, "Thus the five southeastern nations' pursuit of education links them more closely with Euroamericans, setting them apart from 'other' Indian tribes.... Along with educational interests, their governing systems, although differing from one another, resemble Euroamerican models" (11). Why Euro-American models? The last I heard, the U.S. Congress did not have a House of Kings and a House of Warriors at that time, nor representation based on matriarchally inherited autonomous tribal towns. True, the Creeks had a constitution, framed in 1867 after semirecovery from the Civil War, which established a court sytem and electoral districts. Yet the newly emergent United States did not become Iroquoian when it borrowed its most important political document from the Indians. What is the point of these bicultural, mediative arguments? That any cultural contact whatsoever diminishes personal or national identity? That "pure" Indianness is no longer possible? So what — has pure anything ever existed?

Kosmider goes on to say that Posey, like Burns, wanted acceptance from mainstream society: "It is probable that Posey, who admired Burns's poetry, identified unconsciously with the 'Ayrshire Plowman.' Like Burns, Posey sought to be accepted in a world that tried to deny him a literary voice. Both Posey and his hero, Burns, understood their positions between two worlds" (88–89). Yet Posey's life and literary production seem to contradict this. He resisted, not accommodated, literary acceptance outside of tribal culture. Littlefield says:

> With such literary achievement, why did Posey not gain greater recognition as a humorist? Some blame rests with Posey himself. Twice in his life he had opportunities to reach a wider audience with his writings, and twice he refused. In 1900, at the height of his reputation as a poet, he was urged to submit his poems to eastern publications, but he refused, arguing that he wrote for a local audience and that eastern audiences would not appreciate his local references. In like fashion, in the summer of 1903 at the height of his popularity with Fus Fixico, he

was asked to seek a wider readership for the letters by expanding their scope to take in the American national scene. Again he refused, citing his concern for territorial issues and characters and his belief that eastern readers would probably not understand him. (Posey, 40)

Rather than saying the "blame" lies with Posey for this local audience and attributing Posey's reluctance for a larger following to a translation problem wherein easterners might not understand his writing, might we praise him and surmise that the reason for this choice had to do with seeking a Creek audience, alerting that audience to the disaster of statehood in hopes that the population of the nation might be roused and dissolution of tribal government might be thwarted? That is to say, Posey was engaged in the concerns of Creeks and Indian Territory, not the American mainstream. This, to me, does not sound like seeking "accept[ance] in a world that tried to deny him a literary voice," as Kosmider seems to assert (88).

Kosmider even applies the "torn between two worlds" argument to the characters Hotgun and Tookpafka Micco, two full-blood traditionalists allied with the most rabidly anti-assimilationist faction in the nation, the Snakes: "Hotgun and Tookpafka Micco use down-home sayings, but their words mediate between two worlds, Indian and white" (125). Yet it seems to me problematic to say that these characters, who sometimes comment on white society, are "mediat[ing] between two worlds, Indian and white," especially given that their commentary about whites functions as such a strong, resistant critique to the white forces threatening the Creek nation at that time. Saying anything about white people, including criticizing them, somehow, is an act of mediation? Here and elsewhere Kosmider would be better served by examining Creek political, social, and religious history rather than awkwardly juxtaposing bicultural and mediation theory.

When examining the bigger picture of contemporary Native literary criticism, one could discuss the lesser problems with this type of analysis — its old-school roots in the tragic Indian notions of the early part of this century, the half-breed torn between cultures, and all of the either/or assumptions that go along with this type of thinking. One could also point to the anthropological underpinnings that suggest that Indians, because they have survived into the twentieth century, are now somehow tainted, contaminated; nothing they do is as good as it was during their heyday, when men were men and buffaloes were scared.

Someone even more cynical might try to point out that the bicultural arguments work out nicely for white critics who, by deconstructing insider/outsider status, can carve out a huge place for themselves in Native literary studies, since we really need a heaping helping of non-Indian critical theory to understand the stuff, given its European underpinnings; and they aren't really outsiders to the literature, since their cultures helped to produce it anyway!

These possible fallacies are important, but a primary aspect that is often overlooked has to do with very basic sovereignty issues. If another nation, let's just say Mexico, for example, makes steps toward modernization, nobody says, "Oh, they're no longer Mexicans"; we just say, "Oh, they've got computers," or "They improved their public transportation system," and so forth. If one of the changes is reading new books or learning about other cultures, we do not assume that this somehow means they are no longer Mexicans. Kosmider's second chapter, " 'Hedged In, Shut Up, and Hidden from the World,' " attempts to trace Posey's Thoreauvian influences. There is nothing wrong with saying that Posey was influenced by Thoreau. My concern is the possible implications of that kind of study, given the bicultural framework in which it occurs. I would simply point out that reading Thoreau does not — any more than an American's reading Shakespeare — constitute a loss of identity. This is an argument that is only applied to Indians who, once they defy the stereotypes prevalent in popular imaginings, become suddenly less Indian.

The tendency to put Native people in this reductive tainted/untainted framework occurs, at least partially, because Indians are thought of not in terms of their true legal status, which is as members of nations, but as cultural artifacts. Native people are seldom regarded in terms of the political and legal ramifications of tribal nationalism. Alexander Posey, no matter how much Burns he read, was a member of the Creek Nation — a real, viable, ongoing political entity, recognized historically in terms of treaties with European nations, its sovereignty and that of other tribal nations recognized by the U.S. Constitution, and, most importantly, recognized by Creeks for centuries through a complex system of local and national representation. The Creek Nation during Posey's time had a full range of social, political, and religious practices, making Posey not at all torn between two cultures — he was very solidly in the midst of Creek culture in all its complexity.

The character of this national culture at the turn of the century varied from Creek full-bloods taking medicine at the stomp grounds to Creek Baptist and Methodist preachers explicating the gospel in Creek, reading out of Creek Bibles and singing out of Creek hymnals; from merchants and cattle ranchers to subsistence farmers practicing Creek agriculture; from those who didn't speak English (a large portion of the tribe during Posey's time) to those, like Posey himself, who had gone to Bacone and studied classical literature; from medicine men (*hilis heyya*) and town chiefs (*miccos*) to tribal judges who worked for the nation; and a whole slew of other nuances of Creek life too numerous to mention here. Rather than arguing for Posey's biculturalism, I would argue that he was thoroughly immersed in a Creek world, and that Creek world, *like other nations,* was a complex one that cannot be simply analyzed inversely to its relationship to the pristine; that is to say, its cultural power does not diminish to the degree it evolves.

It seems to me this applies to the bicultural theorists more generally—they lack sovereignty contexts that could lift their analyses out of dependence on intellectual and cultural purity where they must argue that tribal authors are influenced by Europe; therefore, an Indian viewpoint is impossible. Contrary to this argument, tribal viewpoints continue because they originate from living nations that are recognized both legally and imaginatively. Further, does the idea of hybridization (which I suppose is useful to those searching for new varieties of seed corn) necessarily say much about the historical and contemporary challenges of Native authors?

Perhaps what we can say about Posey is that given a range of practices and beliefs within the Creek nation during his time, Posey was relatively closer to an assimilationist position than a traditionalist one, both factions fitting easily within Creek national life of that time period. He would probably be less traditional in outlook than the contemporary Creek writer Louis Oliver, for example, or, in terms of Posey's characters, Hotgun and friends, who contemplate emigrating to Mexico with the Snakes to carry on unabated Creek government and tradition. It is interesting to note that Oliver himself seems to see Posey as an artistic and intellectual role model rather than simply as a sellout. The categorization of Posey as a progressivist is far too simplistic—at almost every juncture in the Fus Fixico letters, Posey is parodying progress, manifest destiny, Oklahoma and national politics, federal Indian policy, statehood, education, and so on. Here is just one passage taken from hundreds of possibilities throughout the letters. Hotgun, one of the full-blood characters, reports on the opening prayer for the convention on Oklahoma statehood:

> He say, "This was a grand and glorious country. It was the land a the brave and the home a the brave. Everybody was created free and equal— subject to later developments. Greece and Rome was the greatest countries of olden times, but the United States was the grandest domain the moon or sun ever shone upon. From the dashing waves a the Atlantic to the rolling billows a the Pacific—from the icy mountains a the North Pole to the everglades a Florida the Stars and Stripes was the emblem a liberty. I was glad to stand before you today in the short-grass country. Injin Territory was clasp hands with Oklahoma. We was the cream a civilization—if you don't mind the whey. But we was not in the Union, so we better butt in." (Posey, 209)

You don't exactly have to be a literary critic to detect irony here. Or how can we ignore this sly subversion of General Sheridan's infamous genocidal statement: "Well, so I was tell you bad news about my old friend Choela. He was gone to be good Injin, like whiteman say when Injin die" (Posey, 76). In another letter, Hotgun says, "The Injin is civilized and aint extinct no more than a rabbit. He's just beginning to feel his breakfast food" (217). At the very least, there is a strong subversive element in these statements rather than outright faith in white progress. Posey's supposed endorsement of progress may have been a simple recognition that Native people could and would move into the future, that is, a rejection of the vanishing notion. These kind of passages do not stand alone—literally, there are scores of like statements, making any surefire conclusions that Posey was a progressivist pretty tenuous.

Why is it always assumed, furthermore, that Native is assimilated by white, not the other way around? For studies of Native cultures, this assumption has broad implications that contradict anthropology. Given, especially, the history of Oklahoma, how many white bloodlines have been subsumed by marriage into tribes where the mixed-blood descendants become culturally Indian, speaking Native languages, acquiring communal worldviews, and becoming active in the social, political, and religious life of the tribe? How do we know that whatever "whiteness" existed in Posey's background was not swallowed up by Creek culture rather than vice versa? In what ways were Posey's ideas regarding progress modified, revised, and subverted by a traditional Creek upbringing and lifelong residence in the Creek Nation and active involvement in Creek politics? Contemporary Mohawk lesbian writer Beth Brant says:

> When a non-Native becomes part of a Native household or family group, whether through marriage or companionship, the Native family takes over. This is assimilation of a kind that is never discussed or written about. The non-Native often has to put up small battles to hang on to a separate personality rather than the personality of the Native group.
>
> I have seen this happen in my own family with my non-Native uncles, mother and my lover. Soon they are talking like Natives, joking like Natives; the prevailing Native culture and worldview is assimilated by the non-Native. I suspect this process is not discussed because the dominant culture does not want to admit that another way of *seeing* may be a more integrated way of being in the world, as opposed to Manifest Destiny. Again, this process of assimilation is *not* becoming Indigenous. It is a recognition that every part of what constitutes life, *makes* life.[5]

These comments become especially cogent in light of Creek history, given that in the eighteenth century, Scotch-Irish traders married Creek women, whose culture is a matrilineal one. It was in these traders' best interest to locate in the woman's *talwa,* her maternally inherited tribal town, and set up trade there, given the spouse's matrilineal clan and town connections. Simply put, it was good business for the trader, who would have lots of relatives to sell his goods to. The mixed-blood children's clan connections would remain intact, since they come down through the mother's line, and tradition dictated that a Creek's most important mentor would be the clan uncle, the mother's oldest brother. In other words, for children who had a Creek mother and a white father, the connection to Creek life could remain entirely unbroken. The Indian side of the family, in terms of its relationship to Creek traditional life, could thrive in spite of mixed marriage. This, of course, is not the situation with all tribes, but marrying whites and maintaining clan relationships with the new Indian relatives was typical of Creek postcontact life. Whiteness was often subsumed, or at the very least modified, by Creekness.

Further, before assigning Posey too easily to the progressives' camp, it is interesting to note the separatist leanings his life and literature took. Both Posey and his Creek friend Charles Gibson, who wrote a column called "Rifle Shots" in Territory newspapers, were quite critical of whites writing *stijaati* English. Posey and Gibson believed that *stijaati* could not be produced by outsiders. In 1908 Gibson complained about hackneyed attempts at dialect writing appearing in the Checotah newspaper, a town near Eufaula: "It's the poorest dialect stuff that was ever forced upon the reading public. Don't dodge behind 'Este Charte,' white man, but get up your rot in straight English, if you can write it.... Get from behind 'Este Charte' and wash the paint off your pale face. Take off the turkey feathers. They don't become you" (17). Posey echoed Gibson's stinging critique: "Those cigar store Indian dialect stories being published in the Checotah papers and the Hoffman Herald Auxiliary will fool no one who has lived 'six months in the precinct.' Like the wooden aborigine, they are the product of a white man's factory, and bear no resemblance to the real article" (17). It is interesting to note Posey's literary separatism here and the corroboration between Posey's political and literary efforts: just as he is claiming Indian Territory for Indians, so he is staking out intellectual territory, claiming Creek literature for Creeks. Note that Posey's very life stood for Indian separatism through his efforts to get Indian Territory admitted as a separate state, controlled by the tribes, rather than annexed to Oklahoma. In the letters, Hotgun links separate statehood with maintaining tribal autonomy:

> And Hotgun he go on and say: "Well, so somebody was had to take the lead for separate statehood, and the Injin say 'might as well be me.' So he report for duty first and was immortalized himself. He wait purt near a hundred years and Opportunity didn't find him asleep in the wigwam. He was watch faithful at his post and make good when the time came. You could call the movement for separate statehood bosh, or fiasco, or sentiment, and names like that if you want to, but I was call it a declaration a independence that was had its foundation on every hearthstone in Injin Territory." (218)

The readings of Posey as a progressive are reductionist; he was a complicated man. While endorsing many notions of "progress," he also worked on behalf of preserving the autonomy of Oklahoma tribal nations. And autonomy was a central issue because history has proven that once Oklahoma became a state, Native participation was no longer welcome; politics became the white man's business, and tribes were left completely without representation. The almost complete absence of Indians in the Oklahoma legislature, then and now, in a territory that was once completely controlled by tribal nations, is indicative of the disaster of Oklahoma statehood for the tribes. Posey's vision was a far-reaching one.

In fact, the very reason Posey gives such authority to full-blood conservative voices may relate to the complexity of the issues and his own uncertainty as to the best path for national survival. Posey's support for allotment in the Fus Fixico letters comes after the Curtis Act, when the legislative arm of the U.S. government, though illegally and without agreement of the tribes, had made allotment inevitable. One full-blood traditionalist faction, the Snakes (so called after their leader Chitto Harjo, whose first name means "snake" in Creek), simply refused to recognize the allotments or to sign up for them. The Snakes sent out their Lighthorsemen to inflict corporal punishment—whippings—on those who accepted allotment deeds. In terms of the future, if the Snakes could have gotten the Creek national government to follow their policies of noncompliance, Creek national government and land title would have remained clear at least in the sense that the Creek Nation would never have signed anything that accepted the allotment of tribal land and the dissolution of tribal government (both would have occurred anyway through the illegalities of the U.S. government, but they would not be recognized by Creeks). This would have been a powerful act of resistance. This would bank everything on the future when, perhaps, the illegal occupation could be remedied through legal, or other, means. The difficult question that Posey and others faced was what would Creeks do in the mean time? Where would Creeks live? They would be completely dispossessed of land until whenever it could be won back; perhaps, like the Métis of Canada, Creeks would end up squatters in roadside ditches. Accepting allotment and U.S. citizenship at least meant gaining a few rights in the here and now. The Snakes' position was a superior, albeit extremely difficult, one that might exact a heavy toll. As it was, the Snakes, as a faction, were able to resist effectively even though the Creek government gave in, and the Snakes continued to hold their own Creek government at Hickory Grounds and send delegations to Washington to argue the validity of the treaty of 1832, even though the United States did not recognize their government. The Snakes continued this resistance until the 1930s, when the United States again recognized Creek government.

Regarding the Snakes, Littlefield says:

> The advent of a new year, 1904, was an opportunity for Hotgun and his friends to assess the condition of the conservative Creeks in the face of social and economic change in Indian Territory. Like Posey, they nostalgically looked back to the Creek Nation of twenty-five years earlier; present-day realities indicated that economic well-being depended on the removal of restrictions from the sale of allotments and that the efforts of Snakes like Chitto Harjo to have the old treaties reaffirmed and old lifeways maintained were detriments to progress. (Posey, 152)

Yet the Snakes, it seems to me, were doing exactly the opposite. Rather than backward-looking romantics, more than any other element of the tribe, they were looking toward the *future,* though, to be sure, their position was an extremely difficult (others might even argue impossible) one. By insisting on the validity of the treaty of 1832, the Snakes were banking on the future, instituting a holdout policy until Creek tribal government and Creek land tenure could be restored. In the meantime, they elected their own tribal government, sort of saying the hell with whether anyone recognized it — *we* recognize it, they seemed to be saying — and they refused to accept the illegal activities of the United States.

Posey's letters, with their privileging of full-blood voices, reflect this overwhelming complexity the nation faced. Rather than simply presenting the progressivist argument for disbanding the tribe and turning everyone into white farmers, ranchers, and businesspeople — a position the critics say he endorsed — Posey presents something much more complicated. If anything, traditionalist full-blood opinions get more attention in the letters than any others. Fus, the narrator, is a full-blood moderate who is pro-allotment, but his friends he reports on, the subject of his letters, are conservative Snakes.

The second aspect of the letters, which I believe warrants further critical examination, is the way they function beyond mere political commentary (which is important in its own right) and seek further actually to influence events during Indian Territory's most critical time, when entire nations of people faced extermination by U.S. legislative fiat. The letters, as political discourse, need to be examined in light of a whole body of resistance movements going on in Oklahoma during this same period — the Creek Snakes, the Cherokee Nighthawks and Keetoowahs, the so-called Cherokee outlaws, some of whom Robert Conley has analyzed as Cherokee nationalists fighting for the continuance of Cherokee

government, to name just a few groups actively fighting against statehood. It is interesting to note that Posey knew Chitto Harjo and interviewed him.[6]

Although critics may speak of marginalization, biculturalism, and mediation between cultures, I believe that another factor limiting the usefulness of these approaches has to do with the mimetic function of the
letters. Posey had a much more important set of concerns than his personal marginalization and angst over identity—he and his people faced
the imminent dissolution of tribal government under the very real threat
of Oklahoma statehood. Posey's writing was empowered by the immediacy of this threat his nation was facing. His voice, as an Indian journalist and well-known Creek active in national politics, in concert with
the aforementioned radical traditionalist movements and the more cen-
trist attempts to achieve separate statehood for Indian Territory rather
than simply annexing it to Oklahoma, had the potential actually to
sway events in the Territory. I believe that Posey was trying to strike a
death blow to the crooks from Washington trying to take over his nation, or to quote Tookpafka Micco, "Well, maybe so if we could had
that investigation and put Dam Big Pie and Jay Gouge Right and Break
in Rich and Plenty So Far and Tom Needs It and grafters like that out a
business" (Posey, 132–33). The way Posey uses the letters to influence political outcomes tends to get downplayed.

Kosmider says:

> What makes this humor so powerful is it's like a slice of real life. It is a
> way of expressing frustrations and hostilities. As Paula Gunn Allen's
> comment suggests, Hotgun and Tookpafka Micco laugh to survive; they
> make jokes to renew themselves and others; their comic vision is to
> overcome erasure, denial, invisibility, and annihilation. They create
> humor to encircle and to contain the humiliation and the bitterness that
> being an Indian encompasses. Humor, as Lincoln suggests, "refuses to
> give in to the pain; it administers an aesthetic to make pain the very
> subject of its pleasure." (126)

Littlefield echoes this sentiment in a somewhat similar fashion:

> Though Posey believed that allotment of lands and statehood were
> inevitable, he was not blind to their impact on the Indian peoples of
> Indian Territory. Perhaps his letters made the process "more palatable"
> to many in the Indian nations. For others, perhaps the letters offered a
> diversion from the realities of greed, deception, fraud, political

arrogance, illegalities, and political chicanery, realities that Angie Debo has described in her study of the allotment period and the making of Oklahoma. Though some of the contexts for Posey's humor have been lost, readers today, with a little editorial help, can find most of the letters not only readable but downright funny. That is the primary reason they should be read. (Posey, 48)

Both these quotes tend to underrate the mimetic function of the letters. I do not believe that the primary purpose of Posey's humor was expressing frustrations and hostilities. I do not believe he was merely laughing to survive. I especially do not believe that he or his characters needed to overcome identity problems or issues of marginality, or to contain the humiliation and bitterness about being an Indian (what does *that* mean, anyway?). Nor do I believe that Posey was administering an anesthetic, making the criminality of land theft more palatable, or offering a diversion. I believe Posey was trying to get Indian Territory admitted as a separate state and retain tribal autonomy. A bigger issue was at stake than relieving personal pain — the survival of the Creek Nation. I believe that Posey was trying to overturn the very events causing all of this pain, especially through his efforts to achieve separate statehood for Indian Territory.

This is a key issue of importance to Native literature more generally, maybe the most important issue that faces Native literary studies. Are tribal literatures merely a salve, or should they engage in active critical political commentary? Should they concern themselves with tribal history and politics? Should they be a means of exploring more radical approaches to sovereignty? Should they seek the return of tribal lands? This book argues that the answer to such questions is a resounding "yes."

In comparing Posey to contemporary Native fiction writers, one observation that might explain Posey's immersion in local politics and today's writers aversion to them is the very different backgrounds that constitute the forming of the Native writer in the two different time periods. Today's writer is trained in the academy or in creative writing schools, whereas Posey's training, besides his short stint at Bacone, which would be something like the equivalent of high school college prep, was in Creek national government, where he was elected to the House of Warriors, served as superintendent of the Creek Orphan Asylum at Okmulgee, superintendent of Public Instruction for the Creek Nation, and superintendent of the Creek boarding schools at Eufaula and Wetumka.

This is a different experience from that of today's writers and poets who are trained in Iowa City at the famous writers workshop. This is an exaggerated statement, but one intended to make a point. He already had a literary bent from his earliest days at Bacone, and his life in Creek national service groomed him to merge politics and literature, enabling him to create a body of creative work thoroughly immersed in the tribal politics of his nation. Posey was so politically engaged, in fact, that his literary efforts covered "Creek national affairs: activities of the Creek delegation in Washington, potential candidates for the Creek principal chief to be elected in the summer of 1903, allotment policies, and efforts to achieve statehood" (Posey, 16). Today's writers are more likely to undergo training away from home and end up having to teach far from their original tribal community, making such immersion more difficult for all of us.

Another important factor for modern writers is the very real pressures from agents and publishers that steer writers away from engaging in political discourse — the taboos that immediately assign the political to the didactic and anti-aesthetic. These mindless formulations need to be challenged, and means of creative literary politics explored. Posey's letters enjoyed wide popularity, so the public, at least during his time, was interested in political and literary syntheses. We are seeing some encouraging beginnings with writers such as Ray Young Bear and his semifictional explorations of Mesquakie life, culture, politics, and religion written from where Young Bear resides on the Mesquakie Settlement. Hopefully the efforts of Young Bear and others will inspire more of this tribally specific writing, closely connected to original languages and landscapes and immersed in the political life of tribal nations, emerging in the future. Although there are many possibilities for what constitutes a Native text, certainly the ones that maintain a national sensibility and a sense of intact culture are as important as the works about marginalization and identity struggles.

The content of the Fus Fixico letters, because of their discussion of factual events in a fictional format, demonstrates Posey's attempts to affect the outcome of Oklahoma politics, not simply to make his readers feel better. The subject matter covers issues Posey was personally working for or against in Creek government and as a member of Territorial committees. For example, the very names of the characters are people alive in the Creek Nation at the time of the letters, and Posey even speculates about their reactions to being cast inside his fictions (33–34). Fus takes up the "real-life" topic of Pleasant Porter's bid for reelection to national office, (begrudgingly) endorsing Porter's campaign, believing Porter to be the only viable candidate, given his opponents. Fus uses the names of other living Creeks holding offices in the House of Kings and Warriors. In the letters, Fus discusses and supports the Sequoyah Convention, of which Posey was secretary, whose aim was to achieve separate statehood apart from Oklahoma wherein the new state, Sequoyah, would remain under the control of the tribes. Fus even refers to Creek writer Charles Gibson's popular column "Rifle Shots"; Gibson was a friend of Posey's and another commenter on Territorial politics.

Fus's political commentary regarding statehood waxes and wanes depending on the degree of intensity regarding the issue in Congress, which shows the concern Posey had for dealing with real events as they became important. Fus takes up specific treaty issues, including the Loyal Creek Treaty, which had guaranteed a settlement for losses incurred by Creeks loyal to the Union during the Civil War; Fus strongly critiques the fact that nearly forty years later, the United States had not settled the matter. Once Posey got on the separate-statehood bandwagon, after initially resisting it for a short time because he believed it did not have solid political underpinnings, he used the letters to argue for the benefits of Indian Territory remaining under the control of the tribes rather than being annexed to Oklahoma. These are just a very few examples; in short, the evidence is overwhelming that the letters are an attempt to influence Oklahoma politics; in fact, they are only marginally fictional. All of this goes beyond some kind of early postmodern intertextuality; Posey is using his editorial voice to sway events and his column as the format.

Further, if one looks at the elaborate nature of the trickster disguise that Posey dons, certainly there are political ramifications. Posey, a very literate Creek, is writing in the voice of a full-blood who has difficulty speaking English. Another level of the joke is that because Posey was actually editor of the *Eufaula Indian Journal,* a paper that is still published in my grandmother's hometown (though no longer as an Indian newspaper), Posey was actually writing to himself while disguising his letters under the name Fus Fixico.

Given the political nature of the letters, a political reading of trickster might be called for. In Creek tradition, trickster is often a little guy using his wit to overcome a larger, predominant force; thus there is Rabbit tricking Wolf, Turtle outrunning Deer, and so on. Sometimes things backfire when the little guy gets beat up by the larger, quicker, or more powerful adversary as in Linda Alexander's story of Turtle getting bashed by the women with the *sofki* pestle recorded in chapter 3 of this book. Disguises are necessary against an enemy with more power—one cannot win by means of brawn, so more subversive methods are employed. Societal norms are both reified (when trickster serves as a negative example by getting in trouble when he transgresses social boundaries) and challenged (when he pulls off a transgressive act successfully). Trickster stories are one means of testing the waters, seeing what communal limits are, how far one can go, where the boundaries really lie.

What does this mean politically? Posey's world is complicated because the transgressive act, in white culture, is Indians who are a "roadblock" to opening up Indian Territory; however, within Creek country, this resistance means cultural and political survival. If Fus Fixico is "fearless or heartless bird," as his name translates in English, he may be going where no other dares to go. This is the power of transgression, entering waters others are afraid of, and Fus shows such ability by diving headfirst into Creek and Territorial politics. Further, Posey takes the stereotypes surrounding full-blood Indians—laziness, illiteracy, simplicity, and so on—and inverts them for his own purposes. This is a subversive move in and of itself, a tribal member appropriating language commonly used against the tribe.

The trickster disguise, then, provides Posey with the means to engage in guerrilla warfare, camouflage, and sneak attacks, the battle strategies of disadvantaged opponents facing more powerful adversaries; that is, the Creek Nation against the U.S. government. Posey's overt operations were through his separate statehood activism, including his participation on Territorial committees. His covert operation was the Fus Fixico letters, which provided an important form of literary resistance to the master narrative of the U.S. Congress and the Dawes Commission, which called for the political extermination of Indians through the termination of their nations. Fus and friends are able to enter the troubled waters of Territorial politics, take a stand on vital issues, and make fellow citizens aware of the dangers through an elaborate system of code understood by Creek residents of Indian Territory and inscrutable to outsiders, the many political wranglers trying to wrest Creek resources, primarily land, from Creek citizens. This code talk, a means of communicating in order to avoid detection by the enemy, is evident, for example, in the way Posey develops a unique system of political metaphors throughout the letters. Littlefield says:

> Fus Fixico and his friends also have a propensity for metaphor: pie comes to represent graft; the sofky patch, or corn field, Creek allotments; the lightning-rod salesman, materialism; and Bud Weiser, legalized drink. Political maneuvering is described in terms of a poker game or a parody of the Twenty-third Psalm. Common expressions such as that connecting politics and strange bedfellows, are given new force: "maybe so politics was not make a stranger sleep with you." Colloquial expressions abound; people "light a shuck" for town, and a political campaign that gains momentum is "96 in the shade." (Posey, 39)

In addition to providing a forum for insiders to communicate safely, a significant political factor in trickster strategies—as Gerald Vizenor has pointed out so often—is introducing play. By this means, Posey can critique one system of oppression without simply advocating some authoritarian system of his own, and further, he is able to present a dialogue, a range of interpretations concerning what is going on in Indian Territory, rather than one monolithic narrative like the U.S. propaganda about the benefits of the dissolution of tribes and turning Native people into ordinary citizens. Through gossip, overheard conversations, and dialogue as the vehicle for transmission of political information, Posey is able to present a humanized politics.

Not only are Posey's letters a political tour de force, they are a stylistic achievement as well, demonstrating that politics and aesthetics are not mutually exclusive. Consider, for instance, the balanced statement, the parallelism, and the repetition in the following passage concerning assimilation:

> So he [white and Indian progressivists] was called you all together to hear his will. He want you to take his sofky patch and make a big farm out of it, and raise wheat and oats and prunes and things like that instead a flint corn and gourds. He want you to tear down his log hut and build a big white farm house with green window blinds. He want you to take his three-hundred pound filly with the pestle tail and raise Kentucky thoroughbreds. He wants you to round up his mass-fed razorback hogs and raise Berkshires and Poland Chinas. He want you to make bulldogs and lap poodles out a his sofky curs. He want you to had no understanding with Oklahoma. (Posey, 220)

This passage employs a highly oratorical style, closely related to speechifying, and is in fact a reference to a speech made by Chief Pleasant Porter at the convention for separate statehood.

Another example of stylistic accomplishment is the following long dependent clause joined together by a string of conjunctions. The sentence has a cumulative effect in that by the time the reader gets to the main body of the sentence, a beautiful little picture has been created that evokes a complete setting:

> Well, so while the ducks was scooping up the juice a the watermelon
> rinds and the old squirrel dog was stretched out dozing in the shade a
> the ash hopper and the locust singing lonesome in the blackjack grove,
> Hotgun he was get a good holt on the bottom round a his hickory chair
> with his heel and lean back again the catapa tree and ask Tookpafka
> Micco, "Well, so what was you thought about the future state, anyhow?"
> (222)

The sentence builds in momentum with each clause, and the style parallels the lazy summer feeling of Hotgun working up to getting around to asking Tookpafka Micco a political question. Style, here, reinforces content, and we see an author influenced by both oral forms and literary styles in his development of politicized fictions.

Posey's stylistic features have their strongest origin in the Creek oral tradition. Even though Posey drew widely from Western literature, and his work might somewhat resemble that of the American Southwestern humorists, each allusion is filtered so that it is rendered as a full-blood would think it and speak it and feel it. Whether full-bloods would know these allusions is beside the point. By the time Posey gets through with these quotes, they sound as if the full-bloods originated them rather than Shakespeare or Homer. Creek thought can encompass European literature and effectively Indianize it, another instance where literary style makes a political point.

For Posey's time, the very role of the Indian journalist, perhaps, required a trickster spirit. The idea of the Indian journalist, the Indian speaking for himself, was an oxymoron, and this novelty may have contributed to some of the interest in Posey's work. Many nineteenth-century works about Indians are collaborative autobiographies involving an Indian subject and a white recorder-editor, or biographies written by whites without any Indian involvement whatsoever (some important exceptions include Native-authored autobiographies by Sam Occom, William Apess, George Copway, Sarah Winnemucca, and others). In Posey, the public was exposed to the literate Indian who could quote a wide range of Western literature. The Indian with his own articulate voice — the Indian who can speak for himself without the mediation of the colonizer — is an oppressive culture's worst nightmare, and Posey, in fact, was a cog in the wheel of the Oklahoma statehood process.

Posey's trickster nature dated back to his earliest experiences. As a child, Posey played pranks on his father's renters, posed irreverently in family photos, and carried a comic sensibility into adulthood when he terrorized his employees at the Creek Orphan Asylum with many practical jokes (9–10). Posey heard traditional stories from his mother, so he must have learned about Choffee, one of the key players in Creek traditional storytelling. Reading Posey's life as a trickster narrative goes a long way in trying to make sense of his contradictory actions — I mean here his later real estate dealings and drowning shortly thereafter — since Rabbit seeks first and foremost to satiate his own needs, often falling victim to his own greediness but also sometimes bringing about cultural transformation in spite of his avarice and victimizations.

Posey's style in the Fus Fixico letters is marked by "coined words, slang, western expressions, Latin phrases, puns and other plays on words, literary allusions, and understatement in reporting not only insignificant events and odd occurrences but more ordinary local news as well" (10). Posey's letters were partially stylized and contained a good deal of stereotypical speech, what one might today call "Tonto talk." In contrast, however, to representations of Indians in print common to Posey's day, what Littlefield calls cigar store dialect, Posey's letters contain an impressive degree of realism. Other dialect writers preceded Posey in the Territory. One example is Unakah (probably a corruption of the Cherokee word for white man), who wrote letters to the *Cherokee Advocate* between 1878 and 1886 (11). The first authors to write in Red English were Choo-noo-lus-ky and Ah-sto-la-ta from 1890 to 1893, and the careers of several Indian Territory dialect writers followed (26–27). These letters, like Posey's, create a persona who observes a community of characters and concerns himself with changing affairs within his nation (28).

Posey's work, however, surpasses that of the local dialect writers in many ways. The cigar store dialect is characterized by dropped articles, elimination of "to be" verbs, no use of nominative personal pronouns as reflexives or possessives, and the use of "maybe so" to indicate a conditional action or possibility. Posey avoids the staccato effect of all the aforementioned techniques. The dialect writers were also more dependent on typographical tricks and misspellings (Posey, 26, 29). Unlike Posey's work, the dialect writing does not reflect a vast knowledge of Western literature and history (26); Posey created a real cultural synthesis. The presentation of the complicitous role some greedy landgrubbing Indians played in the allotment process also contributes to the complexity of the letters. Posey's Indians are humans rather than idealized noble savages.

The letters serve multiple roles as a forum for literary creativity as well as political statement, editorials, humor, and news. A key element of the letters is the reporter who is detached from events, the outsider who can report with humor and a sense of detachment, thus making Fus's role in recalling the overheard conversations of his friends imporant (Posey, 12). Yet Fus's "outsiderness," unlike some contemporary depictions of Native life, does not come from mixed-blood marginality. A mixedblood progressive — for instance, a Creek farmer, rancher, or business owner — would not have the same stance toward white progress in the form of land scandals perpetrated by the Dawes Commission as Fus's friends have. Fus's outsiderness is a result of his position as a storyteller, listening and reporting, not the result of cultural confusion.

The overheard conversation provides the narrative framework for the letters. Point of view affects humor, comedy often centering around two differing viewpoints that come into contact and clash, the outsider providing the most natural means of observing and reporting this collision (this often provides the framework for jokes; for instance: "Hey, there were these two guys...").

The humor in the letters often derives from the characters' difficulty in comprehending white progress, which often as not takes the form of graft and corruption. These Indians' worldview often causes them "misunderstandings," which take the form of mispronounced words and inverted phrases in English and an attempt to translate white dealings into a language they can understand. Their "misunderstandings," however, do not arise from Indian stupidity; the misunderstandings very frequently point to the failing of white progress itself, once more making Posey's simple assignment to the progressivist camp dubious. The misunderstanding is more on a linguistic level as the full-bloods try to express these thoughts in English rather than a lack of knowledge on the part of the characters about events. The reader of the letters is exposed to different ways of looking at the same event from varying reference points, the aforementioned comic collision. The translation of white ways into the semiotic system of the full-bloods often involves unusual metaphors and the subversion of popular clichés and hackneyed expressions. Metaphor works particularly well in the letters because of the way in which it links things that on the surface would not appear to have any overt connection; in other words, when dealing with cultural differences, metaphor is an effective device for revealing the chasms between varying cultural vantage points.

Naming also plays a big role in the humor. Traditionally, in many tribal cultures, naming, of course, is serious business, and a link exists between a name and a person's identity. This works on a comic level as well, and Indian people love nicknames, which often function as caricatures, metonymic devices in that behind the name is a story about the person. The name captures some fundamental part of this story and the named one's personality. In the Fus Fixico letters, "the names of the Dawes Commissioners, other petty Federal bureaucrats, and local politicians reflect the grasping, avaricious, greedy behavior in which these men were engaged: Tams Big Pie, C. R. Break In Rich, J. Gouge Right, J. Bear Sho 'amfat, Plenty So Far, Rob It L. Owing, Toms Needs It, Charlie Divide Some, and so [on]" (Posey, 38). These men's real names are Tams Bixby, C. R. Breckenridge, J. George Wright, J. Blair Shoenfelt, Pliny Leland Soper, Robert L. Owen, Thomas B. Needles, and Charles A. Davidson. Littlefield lists ninety-six such name caricatures in an appendix that names the persons' real identities (267). This is another strong body of evidence for the mimetic function of the letters and Posey's interest in affecting real events through his critique of living politicians whose name caricatures do not obscure their real identities but incorporate a stinging criticism into the new spelling of the name.

The roots of Posey's brand of humor can be located more in the Creek oral tradition than in a study of the American rural humorists and dialect writers. Punning, as the aforementioned names attest, is an important part of the letters, and examples abound in the oral tradition where the denouement of a story centers around a pun. In one such story told by Linda Alexander, the Creek elder and member of Greenleaf Grounds who tells the Turtle story in chapter 3, Rabbit visits a farmer who is busy mending fence. Rabbit wants to borrow a pair of pliers. He asks the Creek farmer, who tells him to go up to the house and get them. When Rabbit gets inside, he sees that the farmer has two beautiful daughters. He sees that the pliers are lying next to the post hole digger, so he hollers back at the farmer, "Can I have both of them?" But Rabbit is really looking at the daughters, and the farmer hollers back, "Yeah, take them both," Rabbit interpreting this as permission to have sex with both women. In Creek, the punning is much more intricate, but that is the gist of the story, and many stories exist that demonstrate a delight in this kind of wordplay; in fact, these stories culminate in the revelation of the pun.

There also exist a good number of uses of onomatopoeia. In one very sexual story, another one that I have heard Mrs. Alexander tell, the sound a dog makes licking sounds like the Creek word *slaks,* which means "Come back soon." This story is fairly graphic, so I won't go into detail here, but the Fus Fixico letters contain their share of this type of punning, though not on a sexual level because they were printed in turn-of-the-century newspapers. Consider the intricacy of the following pun in Posey's letters:

> "Well, reckon so," Tookpafka Micco he say, "everything be a whole lots different then. Maybe so when the big change was set in, in Nineteen Hundred and Six, it was continued till old Gabriel was blowed on his horn to call in the chasers after the bucks if they was not gone out a hearing." (222)

Littlefield explains in a footnote that "the Five Civilized Tribes were supposed to cease to exist on March 4, 1906. The pun in this passage is elaborate. 'Bucks' refers to both money and deer; the 'chasers' are grafters and dogs. Gabriel's horn on Judgment Day calls the grafters to account just as the hunter's horn calls the dogs in — if they are not too far gone" (Posey, 225). Again, we have an example of code talking, a critique of the grafters meant for a particular audience who could break the code, who were affected by these catastrophic events in the Territory.

The use of rampant understatement found in Posey's letters can also be traced back to the oral tradition. In another story I have heard from Linda Alexander, this one about adultery, a man and woman in the middle of consummating an affair notice the husband returning. The man climbs up into the rafters where the saddles and tack are hung while the woman lets the husband inside and acts like everything is normal. The husband and wife later go to bed and engage in sexual relations, arousing the prurient interest of the adulterer, who leans over the rafters and watches, but in the shifting about he loses his balance and falls to the floor with a saddle. He turns to the shocked husband and says, "I just thought I'd bring back that saddle I borrowed."

Posey also uses understatement, especially in quoted dialogue, similar to the last line of the aforementioned oral story. With this device, Posey critiques white politicians, their faults being so understated as to draw even more attention to their misdoings. For instance, behind this seemingly straightforward report of President Theodore Roosevelt's "hunting" in Oklahoma — straightforward in the sense that there is a kind of journalistic reporting of events with little commentary — is a critique of Roosevelt's disrespect for the natural world:

> Then Hotgun he go on and say, "Well, so the next stop the Great White Father make was out in Oklahoma in a big pasture, where they was lots of cayotes [sic]. He was got after one a horse-back and crowd it over the prairies till he was get good results and captured it alive. He was had lots of fun with it before he was run it down. The President was a great hunter and was kill big game well as a cayote or jackrabbit. So he was go on to the Rocky Mountains to beard the bear and lion in they den." (205)

The critique is all the more ironic for its minimalism. Roosevelt, during his politicking in the weeks that Fus is reporting on, left a wide swath of coyote and bear corpses — the president was often out gunning down wildlife while his aides conducted national business in the towns he was supposedly visiting (206–7).

Fus's friends take confusing political events and relate them to the natural world to understand the way politics spin out of control when white men are deciding Indians' destiny apart from their own consent. Though, as mentioned earlier, Posey plays on stereotypes, in this case the stereotype of the unsophisticated and innocent full-blood, Posey subverts the stereotype by moving his characters beyond their innocence through their efforts to understand their experiences through metaphor and imagination. Unlike the innocent, the joke really isn't on them; white oppression becomes the larger subject of the critique.

The Creek oral tradition is replete with depictions of characters who are a little outside of the norms of the community: orphans, the poor, those persons a little geeky or strange, and even nonhumans, small creatures that one might judge insignificant at first glance. By the end of the story, these characters do something powerful, perhaps even to transform the culture (see, for instance, in Swanton, "How Day and Night Were Divided," "The Orphan," "Thunder Helper," "The Orphan and the Origin of Corn," "The Only Son and Rabbit," "Man-Eater and the Little Girl," "The Water Panther," "Story of the Bat," "The Friendly Dogs," "The Hunter and His Dogs," "Rabbit Gets Man-Eater Over to the Other Side of the Ocean," "Raccoon Gets a Deer for Panther," "Terrapin Races," "How Rabbit Got the Widow's Daughter," "Rabbit Rides Wolf," "The Flight to the Tree," "The Boy and the Lion," and "The Creation of the Earth").[7] The stories seem to demonstrate that one should take care in prejudging someone before one knows the person's full spiritual potential.

In the Fus Fixico letters, the unfolding of the stories borrows from this traditional pattern in an interesting way. In the letters, one observes what literary theorists might call dissonant narration. This is to say that Fus Fixico, who functions much like an omniscient third-person narrator in his ability to report conversations and actions of multiple participants without being dramatized as a character himself, indirectly points out foibles and ironies in his characters' statements and behavior. Yet just as the reader gets the feeling that the narrator is making fun of the characters, it is revealed that their assessments are correct and insightful. What appears at first glance to be superstition, ignorance, laziness, and backwardness ends up providing a unique vantage point that reveals social ills, especially the criminality of the statehood process. These characters, akin to their likes in the oral tradition, are little guys with big ideas, cultural transformers with a lot of power and the ability to see the truth through all the sham in the Oklahoma political process.

Another element of the Creek oral tradition, this one an imagistic motif, is the image of bones picked clean, sitting on a table, which can be traced back to an old Creek story I have heard that involves Buzzard and Rabbit. Rabbit has a bellyache, and Buzzard volunteers to doctor him. Buzzard sends all the attendees out of the room and begins his "medicine." Every time Buzzard pecks at Rabbit, Rabbit cries out in pain, causing consternation among Rabbit's kinfolk listening outside the room. They keep inquiring, "Is everything going OK?" and Buzzard, gorging himself, replies that everything is going great. Finally Buzzard flies off, and Rabbit's kin find nothing but a pile of bones left. In the Fus Fixico letters, on a larger thematic level, over and over again, the reader is reminded how Indians are being stripped of everything they own, down to the bones, in the statehood process. The voracity of white hunger is alarming. More specifically, the image of bones stripped clean is a recurring one. Fus says, for instance, "Well, I like to know who we going to had for next chief.... Porter was not say nothing yet, but I think he was had his eye on it like buzzard on dead cow in winter time" (Posey, 70). Or, concerning another election, Legus Perryman's and G. W. Grayson's opposing campaigns for principal chief, Tookpafka Micco says, "Well, so they was had a big fight over the last bone" (110). One of the name caricatures even plays on this image. Charles J. Bonaparte, who conducted an "investigation" of the Dawes Commission scandals (his powers were actually limited by higher-ups who kept him from really investigating anything), is referred to as Bony Parts:

> Well, so Hotgun and Tookpafka Micco and Wolf Warrior and Kono Harjo was all happened to meet up together last Sunday at the Weogufky stomp ground and was weighed Bony Parts in the balance and found him whitewashing.
> "Well, so," Hotgun he say, "I think Bony Parts could made a good organizer a secret societies, 'cause it come natural for him to do that kind of business." (149)

In the Buzzard and Rabbit story from the oral tradition, the humor is rooted in the absurd. The idea of such a carnivorous and predatory bird doctoring Rabbit seems headed for disaster from the outset. Whites looking out for Indians' best interests — a major claim of the statehood argument — and "Bony Parts" conducting a fair investigation are equally absurd.

Rabbit is the one who usually plays tricks on others, then steps back and laughs; in the "Buzzard and Rabbit" inversion, he becomes the victim. "Buzzard and Rabbit," then, is a metanarrative about the tricking of trickster. Oftentimes in Creek oral tradition, there is not merely one central protagonist who gets duped as in "Buzzard and Rabbit." In fact, many stories center around multiple trickster encounters where the duped in one sequence becomes the one playing the trick in the next (see Swanton's "The Fawn, the Wolves, and the Terrapin," "Rabbit Tries a Game of Scratch with Wildcat," "Rabbit Gets a Turkey for Wildcat," and "Rabbit's Imposition is Detected"). Trickster is a composite force for both good and evil in one being, and in the Fus Fixico letters, many characters have a similar complexity, as do their counterparts in the oral tradition.

In fact, a big theme is the way in which Indians themselves are complicitous in the land grubbing, an extension of the victim-becoming-victim-
izer theme in traditional stories (a similar criticism is sometimes directed
against Posey himself, who, shortly before his premature death, worked
in real estate acquiring Indian land allotments). The following conversation in the letters, regarding a convention at Checotah called to demand the lifting of restrictions on the sale of Indian allotments, takes
place between Hotgun and Tookpafka Micco:

> Then Tookpafka Micco he say: "Well, maybe so they was nobody
> mixed up in it but white people, 'cause no good Injin was help do
> anything like that."
> And Hotgun he say, "Well, so that's where you ain't on to it, 'cause
> Henry Clay Fisher was made his mark to the call and was a delegate to it
> and couldn't hardly wait for his badge." (124)

Fisher was a prominent Creek who had held a number of offices in Creek
government, including membership in the House of Warriors, to
which he was elected in 1895, and here Hotgun critiques Fisher's support of the allotment process.

The amazing thing about trickster in Creek tradition, and many other
tribal traditions, is his irrepressibility. Rabbit, like Coyote in other Native traditions, is always on the rebound—run over by a truck in one
story only to resurrect himself in another to carry forward his comic
potential. The humor of trickster, the ultimate survivor, provides Indian people with road maps for survival in the face of oppression.

Posey's depiction of the laziness of full-bloods is partially a stereotypical portrayal, and Posey at times seems to see them as backward, or
"pull-back," Indians. But getting a constant "fix" on this author is difficult—the stereotype is constantly subverted, and the characters are
shown to have roots in the trickster tradition, especially in the way their
laziness, on closer examination, reveals a spirit of resistance to white
encroachment and progressivism. What whites and progressive Indians
interpreted as laziness in the full-bloods was not laziness at all; it was a
communal spirit whites did not comprehend. The full-bloods did not
farm the way the whites did; instead, they Indianized agriculture to make
it suitable in light of the communal values they upheld. These full-bloods
never assimilated as agriculturalists in the white way, but this had nothing to do with an aversion to work. They valued communal maintenance,
the entire community working the town plot, for instance, for the widows

and orphans, taking care of the ceremonial grounds, and allegiance to one's town and clan, over production agriculture that measured success in terms of bushels per acre. Take these passages where Fus reports on full-blood laziness:

> Well, it was just stay raining all the time looks like, and come put near wash all my cotton off in Shell creek. I don't care nohow if it did. It's get too cold to pick cotton in the winter like white folks and take bad cough and die. (58)

> Hotgun was play fiddle more than he was work in his blacksmith shop. I was take him my plow to fix but he was let it stay outside and rust. (68)

> Choela's old red rooster was freeze to death on his roost that night, and Choela was stay in bed all day and say it was not daylight yet maybe. (69–70)

And the following passage, which depicts Indians spending windfall profits from land sells, then leaving their purchases, for which they paid an exorbitant price to white merchants, out in the yard unused:

> Then the white man he tell the Injin, "Well so your wagon was out of date and you better buy you a fine buggy; or, maybe so, a fine surrey." The Injin he grunt and say, "Well, so let's see um." Then the white man he say, "Well, so I sell it cheap like steal it — sell it to Injun the fine buggy and harness and all for hundred and fifty dollars. That was cheap, 'cause Injun he was sell land and got it lots a money and was out of date riding on two horse wagon." Then the Injin he look at fine buggy a long time and make good judgement and buy um. His little pony mare team look mighty weak and wooly and got colt, but they was pulled the fine buggy home all right. Then when the Injin was got home he was put the fine buggy under a tree to look at like fine painting. (165–66)

The passage reveals that the Indians with new money are unaccustomed to materialism, but more importantly, their actions reveal that the land sales have gotten them nowhere, except to divest them of property. In this duping of the Indian there is a trickster lesson about the way greed works; the Indian is worse off than ever after embracing everything the whites tell him is good.

In regards to dividing Indian Territory into two states, one for white settlement and one for the tribes, Fus makes the following comment:

> Well, so Hotgun he say he was for double statehood, 'cause they was too much long-tailed cyclones out in Oklahoma and people was had to

live right close to a hole in the ground like prairie dogs to keep out a
they way. Hotgun he say he was not used to that kind a living and was
get too old to learn to act like a prairie dog. Then he say sometime the
people what had a hole in the ground was not out a danger, 'cause the
rivers out in Oklahoma had no banks to um and was spread out all over
the country when they get up, like maple syrup on a hot flapjack. He say
he was druther be where he was had a show for his life. (102–3)

In this instance, the laziness — not wanting to build a storm cellar —
is underscored with a central irony: the arbitrary nature of the land
settlements. Hotgun wants a border that will separate the Indian-con-
trolled territory from the state of Oklahoma, hoping that this border
will also wall out western Oklahoma weather, and — unstated, but suggested strongly — other adverse elements (the western part of the state
had already been opened to white settlement). Hotgun is resistant to
giving away any more ground than what the Creek Nation has already
lost, and his laziness is the laziness of trickster. What seems at first glance
to be self-serving involves powerful cultural protection for remaining
Creek land the tribe still holds.

The wonderful accomplishment of these letters is that Posey makes
his politics deeply Creek, especially through his reworking of Creek oral
tradition. Turtle is a cultural icon in Creek stories and Creek life. In Swanton's collection, eleven of the ninety-one Creek stories deal directly with
turtles, and this does not include minor references to them in other
stories. Linda Alexander's story about Turtle (see chapter 3) is a major
contribution toward understanding his role in Creek life. The Fus Fixico
letters also contain recurring references to turtles, some direct, some in-
direct. Posey, who had been urging Creek chief Pleasant Porter to hurry
up and release the land deeds, says through Fus, "So I was quit talk about
Creek deeds this times. Maybe so Porter was get mad and say he won't
issue deeds soon if I was not shut up tight like terrapins" (66). Among
traditional Creek women, turtle shells are dried, filled with pebbles, and
sewn onto leather leggings that women wear to make the rhythmic rat-
tling that accompanies the men's singing during a stomp dance. The story
discussed in chapter 3, which explains how Turtle got his checkered shell,
involves Turtle getting up under some women's feet who get frustrated
and pound him with the *sofki* pestle. In the Fus Fixico letters, Fus says:

> Well, maybe so Chief Make Certain [Choctaw chief Green McCurtain]
> was just made a flash in the dish pan about statehood and they was

nothing to it nowhow like railroad talk. Maybe so he was better sneak
'way off and lay down like a yaller dog that was get hit on the head with
sofky pestle when he was poke his nose in the crackling. (84)

Whether or not Posey makes these oral-tradition allusions consciously,
we do know that he heard traditional stories from his mother, Nancy,
and they were formative in his upbringing, as Littlefield documents in
his biography. Posey's first writings, at Bacone, as Littlefield points out,
were reworkings of traditional Creek stories, and it seems more than
accidental that these references occur in the letters. Surely Posey's storytelling, in terms of both style and content, was influenced by oral stories, even if only subconsciously. Too many parallels exist between Posey's
letters and the oral tradition to ignore this possibility. Just to name one
more example, the numerous references to races and pursuit, such as
hounds trailing wolves, and races between unequals where, surprisingly,
the slower participant wins, occur many times in the Fus Fixico letters.
In Creek stories, these iconographic narratives occur frequently, such
as when Wolf is pursuing Rabbit, for instance, and when Turtle wins
races against more fleet opponents, like Deer. Compare the following
passages in the Fus Fixico letters:

> So it's look like Chief Porter was lose ground bad like coyote when
> grey hounds was after him on the prairie. (85)

> And Tookpafka Micco he say, "Well, so it's looked like a race between
> a thoroughbred and two scrub ponies that aint bridle wised yet and a
> old breachy hoss mule that had to hump up before it could strike a trot."
> (132)

These connections to the oral tradition may seem tenuous when considered individually, but taken as a whole, they suggest that Posey's writing contains a lot of overlap with the oral stories he heard as a child
from his parents and continued to hear throughout his lifetime. A more
reasonable question might be why *wouldn't* Posey's writing contain these
oral influences? Given this probability, it seems to me that the Creek
oral tradition would provide the most natural framework for analyzing
Posey's letters. Some letters even contain direct retellings of traditional
stories, such as letter 65, in which Posey tells the story of the animals
choosing their foods, and particularly of Rabbit making the dumb choice
of sycamore balls and nearly starving to death. Placed in the context of
the Fus Fixico letters, this traditional story is truly haunting: Who is ac-

tually making the choices regarding the future of Indian Territory—Indians or whites? If the wrong choice is made, will Native inhabitants of Oklahoma be left, like Rabbit, without the resources for bare subsistence?

As the Fus Fixico letters evolved over time, their emphasis shifted from local events around Eufaula and concerns of the full-blood community to Creek national affairs, statehood, and land allotment (15). Accompanying this change in content was a concomitant change in the central characters. Littlefield says that "by the summer of 1903, Fus Fixico had become more or less the recorder of conversations between Hotgun and Tookpafka Micco (Letters 22 and following). They added to their circle Wolf Warrior and Kono Harjo, who did little more than listen, smoke, and, like Washington Irving's Nicholas Vedder, grunt their assent to, or displeasure at, their friends' statements" (16).

Wolf Warrior and Kono Harjo may seem like minor characters, but they serve an important role that goes far beyond grunting their assent. They serve to dramatize a listening audience. Unlike most written works, we actually see, through description and dialogue, those listening to the stories. Normally, in Western written narratives, the writer imagines an audience; in the Fus Fixico letters, the writer dramatizes his audience and presents them to his readers. This, it should be noted, is not the eighteenth-century "Dear Reader" approach, which is still a generic form of address to an imagined audience, even if the second-person "you" is employed. Rather, this audience is specified, named, seen, and heard from as individual listeners and commentators. I would argue that Posey writes this way because of his borderlands position between orality and literacy. Walter Ong, in a well-known article entitled "The Writer's Audience Is Always a Fiction," [8] argues that one of the differences between oral and literate cultures is that writers do not address an immediately present audience. An oral storyteller reacts directly to the boredom or enthusiasm of his audience; thus the same story might take ten minutes or an hour depending on its reception on the part of the listeners. The oral storyteller responds directly to the audience, and writing is not the same two-way street in the immediate sense that spoken stories are. Ong discusses not only the way that writers imagine who they might be "addressing" but the ways in which readers play the author's game and become the reader the author intends. Ong uses the example of Hemingway, for instance, who casts his readers as boon companions; thus he need not tell them all the details. This allows Hemingway to write in his oft-discussed minimalist style. Whereas audiences reading texts, following an author like Hemingway's cues to his readers, may go along with the narrator's cues and *pretend* to already know much, thus accepting the narrator's sparse details, an oral audience *actually does* already know many of the details of the telling because of shared communal knowledge.

Posey, a literate Creek writing at the turn of the century, is in between these two systems. He has experienced and practiced *both* oral storytelling with a physically present audience *and* the writing process where he must imagine his audience. He comes from a literate background, but many, perhaps most, of his countrymen and -women during this time operate mostly in an oral world. In the letters, he presents a unique point of view through his dramatized listeners that reflects the way in which he is writing on this frontier where orality meets literacy. One of the unique effects of the dramatized listeners is that the reader of the letters not only gets the content of the story but also gets to see something about the ways in which stories are created. Attention is momentarily diverted away from the story itself to the process of story-making.

Each comment, though succinct, provides an observation and reaction to the story like a minimalist Greek chorus (a Creek chorus!). Additionally, it gives a little word caricature, a mini-portrait of full-blood behavior. A few examples:

(Tookpafka Micco and Wolf Warrior and Kono Harjo, they was kind a hold the smoke in their mouth and pay close attention and grunt some time.) (161)

(Then Tookpafka Micco and Wolf Warrior and Kono Harjo they was grunt and spit in the ashes again and say, "Well, so we vote it straight.") (166)

(Tookpafka Micco and Wolf Warrior and Kono Harjo they was grunt and look way off towards the creek like they want to go fishing.) (169)

(Tookpafka Micco and Wolf Warrior and Kono Harjo they was look mighty sorry.) (170)

(Tookpafka Micco and Wolf Warrior and Kono Harjo they was grunt soft and study about it, while Hotgun was filled his pipe so he could warm up to the occasion.) (172)

(Tookpafka Micco and Wolf Warrior and Kono Harjo they was listen so close they pipes was go out and they didn't know it.) (173)

(Tookpafka Micco and Wolf Warrior and Kono Harjo they was looked kind a mystified, like Hotgun was getting too far 'way from the sofky pots and they didn't know what he was driving at. But they was smoked slow and watched the red ants and paid close attention and wait for chance to grunt.) (178)

(Tookpafka Micco and Wolf Warrior and Kono Harjo they was looked like they was more interested in the red ants.) (179)

(Wolf Warrior and Kono Harjo they was propped theyselves on they elbows and look on the ground and pay close attention.) (182)

Space does not allow me to give the context for each of these commentaries, but they provide a forum for the narrator, for Fus, to respond to the contents of the discussion and to subtly indicate his approval or disapproval, channeled through the positive or negative reaction of the full-blood listeners. They show that stories are shaped by complicated contexts, some of which are nonverbal. They are also some of the best dialogue tags in literature—rather than just saying "he said," the narrator uses the description to develop character and scene. Further, it might be noted that the "grunters" are exaggerated comic caricatures of Creek men, their taciturnity, their mannerisms, traits recognizable to those who have been around Creek guys.

That Posey is writing in the borderlands between orality and literacy is actually made the subject of some of the discussions in the letters, and this is especially seen in the humor that satirizes the way the full-bloods see the world. In the full-bloods' worldview, speech is action, and this is carried over to the way that they understand writing. For instance, in regards to the slow process of releasing the allotment deeds to their respective owners, Fus criticizes Chief Pleasant Porter's administration: "Well, one thing I like to know is if Porter was quit trying to issue them deeds. I guess maybe so he was had so many deed to sign up he was just give out of breath and quit" (56). In this case, the act of writing is associated with a physical expenditure of energy that requires breath, as speaking does. In the following passage, in which Hotgun critiques the way some traditional Creeks have assimilated (and does so with some very stereotypical and hackneyed language), names are seen as physical entities: "He [the assimilated Creek] wear a white shirt now and black clothes and shoes that was look like a ripe musk melon. Then he was buy bon bons for his papoose and drop-stitch stockings for his squaw and part his name in the middle, J. Little Bear" (165). Here a name has physical attributes: it can be parted like one's hair. Both passages show a worldview that, because of the way it is rooted in the old orality, carries over the physicality of speech into the world of writing.

Everything in the letters, even abstract ideas about land fraud, is placed in the context of a narrative, which is the way that oral cultures pass on information. In the following passage, Roosevelt's lack of attention to the scandal in Indian Territory is treated like the story of a treed coon:

> Then Hotgun he say, "Well, so it was like this way: President Rooster Feather was ordered Secretary It's Cocked to see what Brosius was had treed in Injin Territory, but It's Cocked was too busy in the office fixing up rules and sitting down on skin games to climb up in the tree and see what's up there. So he was go out and tried to find a honest man that could made a good investigation. But maybe so he was had bad luck same like Diogenes in olden times." (129)

In this borderlands position between speech and writing, the narrative is neither pure plot-driven story nor pure conceptual abtraction; it is in between. In terms of the politics of these oral features in Posey's written discourse (the dramatized audience members, the scenes of story making in progress in which the dialogue and actions of listeners are actually noted in the writing, and the interpretational clues are provided by the listening audience's reactions), these techniques create a represented scene not unlike a political forum with speakers, speeches, questions, and voiced dissent or approval. Posey uses the letters, essentially, to stage a political meeting and ingeniously adapts his literary style to accommodate community-based multivocal political discussion. Perhaps he felt this literary forum might be more effective than the actual meetings he was attending, and committees he was serving on, throughout the territory.

A final oral feature of the letters is earth related figurative language, the use of abundant local natural detail, which shows a close connection to the Creek oral tradition in its similar concern with the natural world. Virtually every simile in the Fus Fixico letters is a comparison to an element of nature: blackbirds, buzzards, turtles, cows and bulls, horses, jackrabbits, grub worms, mules, various dogs, coyotes, wolves, squirrels, different kinds of trees like elms, blackjacks, hickories, and many others, chinch bugs, hogs, snowstorms, cyclones, bedbugs, various features of landscapes, leaves, smoke, and river snags. In fact, there are few similes anywhere in the letters that do not name some element of nature. In addition to the figurative language, specific place-names of creeks, mountains, meadows, and other prominent features of landscape abound. This ties the letters closely to the oral world, where stories are most often earth related, and where oftentimes a place will have a story associated with it. In oral tribal cultures there is an equation between sacred place and sacred story. Stories differentiate points in the landscape and explain the community's relationship to such places. Often these places are the loci of supernatural events or the homes of supernaturals that are told about in stories (among Creeks, for instance, one could compare certain creeks and places along the Canadian River that are said to be the home of Tie-Snake, a supernatural who can pull one into the water).

Too late for inclusion in this book, unfortunately, I discovered Posey's nature journals in the Gilcrease Museum in Tulsa, Oklahoma. Posey's nature writings demonstrate his understanding that one aspect of tribal writing involves an intimate knowledge of a national homeland and the ability to capture its sense of place in terms of its natural details, and its spirit of place in terms of the meaning of the land. This subject will be the topic of an upcoming article in the *Wicazo Sa Review,* but suffice it to say for now that one of the greatest marks of the integrity of Posey as a tribal writer is his ability to write about the landscape of his upbringing.

Posey kept a journal of a June boating trip down the Canadian River in 1901. Posey intended the journal as notes, to be developed later into sketches of the outdoors. Given that Posey wrote about Creek landscape in many different forums — the river journal, his "Notes Afield," letters to friends, poetry, the Fux Fixico letters — it seems reasonable to speculate that Posey understood this notion that one of the distinctions of being an Indian writer is the ability to write about the land of one's own tribe.

The river journals and "Notes Afield" are sketches that he intended to develop more fully later. Had he lived long enough, it would have been interesting to see what became of Posey's nature writings, especially given that he was a better prose writer than a poet. Perhaps he would have come to a place of such retrospection that he could have, for instance, produced a work as accomplished as Osage writer John Joseph Matthews's *Talking to the Moon.* Matthews's masterpiece, a recollection of ten years living among the blackjack trees of Oklahoma Osage country during the years of the Great Depression, establishes something of a benchmark for tribal writers in terms of naming concrete details about their home landscape and exploring the significance of those details. Whether Posey could have written as artistically and evocatively as Matthews may be somewhat speculative, yet Posey certainly had as much lifelong experience in Creek country as Matthews had in Osage country. Posey's unusual — perhaps even cutting-edge — creativity, which he demonstrates in the Fus Fixico letters in his use of original narrative in a unique format full of arresting images and surprising phrasings, might indicate that he could have written a superlative work on the Creek natural world had he developed his nature journals.

The importance of this kind of place-specific writing, I believe, is, in fact, increasing over time, just as relevant to today's writers as to those of Posey's and Matthews's times, because the land provides a constant against cultural deterioration. No matter what happens with language and culture, the land remains if jurisdiction over it is protected, which means that tribes always have somewhere to return to as a people. Some element of culture will always continue if a relationship to the land is still possible. Native authors, through their writings, must create this sense of place and preserve and reinvent these relationships to tribally specific landscapes for the continuance of the tribes.

Posey's influence was far-reaching. Another Creek who followed his example was William Harjo, whose real name is Thomas E. Moore. Moore, also a mixed-blood and student at Bacone like Alexander Posey and Louis Oliver (though each was there at a different time), later got a law degree from the University of Oklahoma. He published his letters as the regular feature "Sour Sofkee" in Oklahoma City and Tulsa newspapers from late 1937 until early 1941. He wrote more than 150 letters under the persona of Chinubbie, borrowed from one of Posey's early characters.

In addition to these local influences, Posey's mixed-genre approach, with its inclusion of fictional characters and events blended with real people and happenings around Eufaula and Oklahoma, use of poetry in the letters, references to and retellings of traditional myths, and historical and political discussions, is a forerunner of contemporary Native American literature, which is often experimental from a Western literary perspective in the way that it blends genres. These experimental forms demonstrate that myth and history, the personal and political, public and private, fiction and nonfiction, poetry and prose are interconnected and cannot be compartmentalized as easily as is often assumed. What might be "experimental," however, in light of the Western canon, is a natural extension of the oral tradition where the lines between the arts are more fluid. In a traditional culture, a story may be acted out in ceremony where it is danced or painted or sung. Think about a Navajo sing, for instance, that incorporates art (sandpainting), music (sung chants), and narrative (stories of the Yei, Navajo supernaturals), all of these forms reinforcing one another for the sake of the health of the patient. Many contemporary Native works embody this viewpoint; one thinks of Leslie Marmon Silko's *Storyteller,* which contains photographs, poems, autobiographical selections, short stories, Laguna myths, historical references, and other art forms. We might think, then, of Posey's borrowings from the oral tradition as a forerunner of much of contemporary Native American literature. It might be noted in reference to the time period between Posey and these contemporary writers that Will Rogers, influenced by Creek and Cherokee newspapers, is the next link after Posey in developing a unique brand of Indian humor, and Rogers succeeded in bringing it into the American mainstream. Finally, Posey's potential influence on modern Native writers includes the possibility that Fus and friends might serve as a challenge to integrate politics and aesthetic excellence in contemporary Native writing in a manner much more effective than what has been written to date.

Dear Hotgun:

Well so it was Stijaati Thlaako go to bed early of a summer evening not long after supper dishes cleaned and put up and whippoorwill makes her first call from the woods. He keeps extry unusual hours on account of long before sunup he wake up and give his ole percolator a kick start and look way off out the front window where purty soon he sees Rabbit's headlights coming down the driveway and car stops and two doors open and shut and him and Big Man come on in and Stijaati says, "Lekibus," and they sit down and Rabbit puts the card deck on the oilcloth tabletop.

His friends was come over to play gin rummy at 3:30 in the morning, a regular habit of theirs. Rabbit was ask, "Do you have any *sofki?*" looking at Stijaati's cabinets suspicioning he was had secret stash on account of Rabbit knowed Stijaati's aunt give him a jar at the busk grounds. Stijaati had hid away the *sofki* for hisself, but he reached below the kitchen sink nohows and dug it out from under a pile of dishrags he'd covered her up with. Stijaati made mental note taking that Rabbit always asked for some *sofki* and never had none at Rabbit's own house. He had to be hospitable though, even to these two; for Stijaati so loved his *sofki* that he gave his only begrudged jar that whosoever come over to his house should not perish from hunger and throw an everlasting fit.

Rabbit spooned sugar into his bowl of sour *sofki* while Stijaati looked at him in disgust and Rabbit he was say, "They call them wolf hunters but they was only run coyotes."

Big Man he was say, "I seen the wolf hunters' trucks pulled off into Tommy Thompson's cow pasture. I reckon they was to have a big dog swap and wolf hunt. Did you know Tommy has one pig ear?"

Rabbit sensitive about the ear issue and he was go on and say, "Let's play cards," shuffling the deck between his front paws, but Big Man go on nohows.

"Tommy used to ride dirt bikes at meets in Arkansaw until his last race when his motor sickle throwed him over its handlebars and ground his nose down into razorback soil. His bike flipped up, back wheel over front, and twist around so that the tailpipe come down on Tommy's ear and was had burn it clean off. His wife run him over to Fayetteville where the surgeon sewed on latest medical technology replacement — ear transplant made out of hogskin. That's how Tommy got his pig ear."

Stijaati he was gather up his cards and drink *sofki* out of styrophone cup and say, "Did you know Chebon played a dance for the last wolf hunters' dog swap?" The wolf hunters first heard him play at a gig way over Perkins way except Chebon waddn't in the band. He'd been visiting kin who'd moved out thataways, and he was just trying to kill time of a Saturday night in the greater Perkins-Tryon area. The band's guitar player never showed up, and they was a-fixing to take down their sign:

ONE NIGHT ONLY

Indian Princesses's Castle

PLAYING HERE

Chebon's uncle told 'em, "My nephew can make a guitar hum like a strand of tight fence wire," and Chebon played the rest of the night on account of the real guitar player never made it in from the calaboose. Some of the wolf hunting bunch was there that evening, including Derek Stiff Rabbit.

So it was Big Man want to know if Derek any kin to Rabbit but Rabbit he say only shirt-tail.

Then Stijaati he was take up again where he done been and tell how the wolf hunters asked Chebon to play the next Saturday night after their dog run and swap meet and prize raffle and hunting supply auction, big event sure enough.

Stijaati he was go on and say, "Did you know that when the wolf hunters turn loose that pack of hounds, ever one of their blueticks, and treeing walkers, and black-and-tans and Louisiana Catahoula leopard dogs, that the coyotes around here run relays on them?"

Big Man and Rabbit they was paid close attention and put near let their spoons lay quiet in their *sofki* bowls.

Stijaati he was say, "Coyotes place themselves in strategic locations throughout McIntosh County the Saturday morning of a wolf hunt. The hounds, who ain't nearly as organized as coyotes, eventually stumble on a hot trail, and the whole bunch hits a note higher than Maria Callas and lights out across fields and under fences just wearing themselves out in earnest pursuit. But the coyote they're chasing will only run until he gets bored and loses inerest, mebeso then he'll pass by one of his buddies in a prearranged spot and tag his colleague and the new coyote will take over for him so that there's always a fresh coyote outrunning wore-out hounds.

"Chebon showed up to the wolf hunt at Tommy Thompson's around eight that night. Way he figured it the last of the dog swapping would be finishing and he could set up bandstand. The wolf hunters had even built him a plywood stage in back of Tommy's house. Chebon got out his guitar and sat down on top of his amplifier and started tuning up. He got up and turned on the floodlight the wolf hunters had rigged up on a wood pole to light up the dance area, and he reckoned that would signal them to finish they dog bidness and begin they drinking and dancing bidness. He hadn't seen none of their cars and thought they must had parked on the north side of the field next to the road. He went up to the clubhouse and all the lights was turned off, so he finally went and knocked on Tommy's door. He waited for a long time on Tommy's porch. Finally Tommy was had answer the door in his long-handled underwears and pulling the straps of his overhauls over his shoulders. Tommy said, 'Chebon, all the wolf hunters has gone on home and went to bed.'"

Rabbit he was check his wristwatch and say, "Mebeso they was had a gin rummy game in the morning."

Stijaati he go on and say, "No, they average about seventy years each, and they couldn't hunt wolves, trade dogs, and stay out late on the same night." Stijaati tell how Tommy Thompson is real honest for a white man and he was to pay Chebon anyway just for showing up.

Rabbit he was say, "You mean they paid Chebon not to sing?"

Stijaati was answered, "Yup, that was the first time Chebon got paid not to play."

Big Man was throw in with, "But maybe not the last."

Rabbit lean back in his chair all full of *sofki* and was say, "You know those coyote relay contests was remind me of the story of Turtle challenging Deer to a footrace and getting off to a slow crawl on account of you know how he is plodding along there and all but he had posted turtles out of sight who stepped in for him and took his place all along the race path most likely one turtle looks bout the same as another to Deer and at the end Deer come over the hill and seen the finish line but they was a turtle dragging hisself across it just before Deer could bound over. Maybe coyotes learned how to run dogs from listening to that story."

Stijaati picked up his cards and was say, "You know somebody who loved a good relay was Creek writer Alex Posey. He run tight race neck and neck Indian Territory ag'i'n Oklahoma statehood with the separate state of Sequoyah coming up in the backstretch. When Alex Posey wore out his words and letters and territory committee participation he passed the baton to Charlie Gibson who was had shot his rifle in Oklahoma newspapers and when Charlie's rifle run out of buckshot he hand off to G. W. Grayson who take the next leg of the race politicking in Creek Nation and he was had tag Alex again and they all was running their stories against the railroaders and the sooners and the boomers and the Dawes commisioners."

Big Man was wonder out loud, "What do you reckon Posey would say about his race against Oklahoma statehood if he was here?"

Rabbit was say, "You know Posey took a raft trip down the Canadian and wrote a nature journal about his trip? I was always wanted float-trip down the Canadian and lay back and finish my autobiography: *Tricking History: A Rabbit amongst Creeks.* I'd have liked to have taken that trip with Alex."

Stijaati Thlaako he was say, "If I was floating down the Oktahutche with Posey, I'd ask him what it means to be a Creek writer."

Big Man he was add, "I'd cast out my cane pole and try to catch a big ole channel cat, pry couldn't get a word in for you two anyways."

It is daylight, and the sun has come up on the Eastern Oklahoma horizon, a fiery globe resting on the low hills. Light has spread over Stijaati Thlaako's farmyard, bringing into view his black-shuttered brick house, the barnworkshed, the cow pasture, the gate, the water trough, the crossbred Angus and Hereford black baldies (white-faced black cattle) grazing behind the fence, and the oak trees at the edge of the field. Inside the barn, Rabbit is jumping up and down on a foot pump, and Big Man has a nozzle inserted inside the air hole of a two-man rubber raft. Stijaati has backed his pickup up to the barn and is tying down an aluminum boat in the back end. He instructs Rabbit and Big Man to wait until they get down to the river to blow up the raft.

They drive down to the Canadian and park by a two-lane bridge. They put the raft and all their gear into the boat, and half slide, half carry the boat down a steep embankment to the river, where they finish blowing up the raft and launch their craft in the reddish brown water. They tie off together, the boat to the raft, and throw over an anchor made out of a five-gallon bucket filled with concrete. Stijaati holds up three toothpicks in his hand, and each man draws.

STIJAATI: Short straw, Rabbit. You get to be Posey. Big Man, pull up the anchor.

They start drifting slowly down the river, and Big Man is in charge of pushing them off sandbars and shallow spots. He sits in the front of the aluminum boat, using the oar more as a pole than a paddle. Rabbit has the rubber raft all to himself, and he is being interviewed by Stijaati, who is sitting behind Big Man in the aluminum boat.

STIJAATI: Alex, did you think of yourself as a Creek writer?

RABBIT: What *else* would I think of myself as? The public thought of me as the Indian who could write, the reason Fus Fixico gained regional popularity. My Indianness overshadowed everything. The great bulk of my work was published in Indian Territory, much of it in the Creek Nation. In my own mind, I knew I was Creek, obviously, before I ever knew I was a writer. Growing up, I spoke Creek for many years before I even spoke English. My mother immersed me in the Creek oral tradition, as well as Creek Baptist tradition. I wasn't borned in the United States. I was borned in the Creek Nation in Indian Territory where I lived my entire life and held national political offices. These are the political facts of my upbringing and adult life until shortly before my death. There was no other way to imagine myself, even if I'd wanted to, and I didn't.

Rabbit looks down nervously at the red water eddying around the raft.

The most serious threat to that sense of being a Creek writer was the looming dissolution of Creek tribal government, the greatest national issue of my time, and I lived with that fear always present: What would become of my nation? All of this was going on at the same time I was learning to write and formulating ideas about writing. But that was an externally imposed threat; it didn't come from an identity crisis of my own or uncertainty that I was a Creek writer. That threat, in fact, created a kind of urgency around the issue of being a Creek writer; it intensified my sense of writing on behalf of the nation and the sense of using my writing as an extension of my political work in Creek national government.

Rabbit is sitting still as a statue, afraid of falling in the river if he upsets the raft. This makes the interview somewhat awkward, and he keeps insisting on anchoring up next to shore and being interviewed from the bank. Big Man simply ignores him and stays his course in the middle channel.

STIJAATI: When you was first begun writing at Bacone you was recreating Creek stories. Stories about Owl, Dog, Cricket, Possum, Skunk, and even "monkeys with their tails stamped off calling themselves people." It inerests me that *writing in the oral tradition* is the beginning point of your writing career that was come before your poetry or Fus Fixico. In what ways should a Creek writer pay attention to Creek language and stories, and in what ways did you pay attention to them?

RABBIT: That influence did not end at Bacone. As I continued as a Creek writer, I simply began developing Creek stories in new ways—both in terms of content and style. The early characters from Creek storytelling stayed with me until the end. In terms of subject, I wrote about Creek full-bloods and interesting prophets and medicine people in my poetry, and in the Fus Fixico letters I make allusions to Creek animals, as well, so I always worked with Creek traditional material.

(*huffily*) Including one rather unflattering reference to Rabbit's stupidity in choosing Sycamore balls as his meal of choice.

Rabbit's nose twitches wildly for a moment, then he regains his composure.

In the Fus Fixico letters the more overt references to Creek animals and Creek stories get transformed into Creekness, if you will, through the *way* those stories are told. The *manner* in which Fus tells about the doings and misdoings of his friends, even his approach to analyzing politics, makes these stories as deeply Creek, as rooted in Creek stories, as the earlier work that dealt more directly with references to Creek animals. Although I allude to Shakespeare and Burns and the Bible, and so forth, this is not what marks the stories. Many people during my time made allusions to great authors, but *nobody* so radically altered them the way I did by filtering the quotes through the voices of Indian characters whose borrowings from classical authors sound like *Talking Indian* when these guys get through with them. The point is that the literary allusion is Indianized, not that I was as much influenced by classical literature, or Thoreau, or anybody else, as Creek stories. You can never get away from the point of view of the stories — this is Shakespeare and Burns quoted by full-bloods, and they make these references according to their own unique Creek vision. This is reflected especially through the way they modify those allusions with Indian language — their Creek English, which carries a whole different viewpoint than the English of white people or the literate English of newspaper and periodical writing of my day. Further, listen to the political analysis in the letters. Many people in my day engaged in political commentary in newspapers. But this political commentary is different because Creek full-bloods are doing the commenting, and the way they see politics is completely different from the way American journalists were writing about politics. The Creekness of these characters is evident by the very words they use in describing the political situation around them, and the way they talk about politics through Creek ways of telling a story.

As far as my interest in all this classical literature, I was a young budding intellectual who wanted to know more about the world. I was not the first, nor the last, in the Creek Nation to have such a curiosity, and all cultures have individuals who hunger for knowledge about what goes on outside of their most immediate experience. This in no way indicated an uncertainty about my place inside the Muskogee Nation. If I had such doubts, I would have left and sought my fortune elsewhere, in the outside world. If anything, my work shows that Creeks exposed to Shakespeare, Creeks knowledgeable about U.S. national politics, still remain Creeks, and why wouldn't they?

STIJAATI: Yet you mebeso believed in a golden era, a Creek heyday, that was had passed away by your time.

RABBIT: But that conviction came as much from what the nation was facing when I was growing up as any steadfast belief that Creek life was not sustainable. When you are born into an age where one large country, the United States, is promising to wipe out a smaller country, the Creek Nation, by virtue of legislating them out of existence and breaking up their system of landholding that they had enjoyed for thousands of years prior to this time, this tends to darken your perceptions of the present, as well as the future, and make you look to the past for better times. And my "golden age" wasn't all romance. It reflected three decades of Creek life that had been better than others. After the disaster of Indian Removal in the 1830s, we had a brief period, two decades, of relative calm wherein we were left pretty much alone. During this time the ceremonial grounds and the town system were reestablished, two of the most important aspects of Creek life. In the 1860s, the nation was split apart again along the old lower and upper town divisions by the Civil War. This caused another major disruption, but afterward, things calmed down once more. This peace lasted until the decade of the 1880s with the coming of the railroads into Indian Territory, and whites pouring in, in such great numbers that they were soon to outnumber Indians.

Do you think such things don't affect one's literary sensibilities? The golden age that I depicted was a reflection of these two earlier historical periods of peace and prosperity. When, in my formative years, I saw the railroad towns springing up, white commerce, the outrage of the federal district court at Muskogee within the Creek Nation, and an increasingly hostile foreign government threatening to take over and declare our constitution, laws, courts, and branches of government null and void, I yearned for the days when things were more secure. I didn't have the luxury of a vantage point, like you all have, of seeing Creek culture, and Creek government, survive throughout this century. This is why in my writing the characters who come through with the most integrity are the full-blood traditionals — the medicine people, prophets, Chitto Harjo and the Snakes, Hotgun and friends. In my mind at that time, they were holdouts against impossible odds; tragic figures to be sure, but no less brave. My great mistake was my inability to imagine a Creek future for these men, a mistake most all the Indian writers of my time made. You can see this even in the group of writers just after me, the participants in the founding of the Society of American Indians, which came into existence in 1911, three years after my death. They presented only one alternative: assimilation into mainstream culture. But none of us believed that our way of life was inherently inferior; we simply saw overwhelming evidence that the cards were stacked against us. One of those involved with SAI, Charles Eastman, walked among the frozen corpses at Wounded Knee, treating the few survivors; and another, Carlos Montezuma, was kidnapped by Pimas at age five and sold to a white man for thirty dollars, separated from tribal life thereafter. Do you think these writers were likely to present a rosy prognosis for the future of things Indian?

Further, go back to my work and read it carefully. I surrounded my endorsement of progress with the strongest irony possible, with seething criticism of materialism, white politicians, Christianity, Indian reformers, and so on. Writers today, writing about the survival of Indian culture, need to know that there were those of us who came before them who prepared the way. Their writing comes out of a specific history, and it isn't merely the history of Indian-white relations, it's *a history of Indian writers.* In some ways we serve as negative examples, examples of what not to do, particularly in our endorsement of vanishing ideas and assimilation. Nonetheless, we do serve as examples. If nothing else, we provided narrative patterns and structures for stories to come later. Creation stories move from chaos to order, like the story of the Creek people lost in the fog, bumping into things and hurting themselves, then banding together until the fog lifts, when they take, for clan names, the name of the animal nearest to them. Indian writing has evolved from chaos to order as well, from uncertainty about an Indian future and the legitimacy of writing about tribal experience to today's possibilities of passing on tribal culture through books. That's a huge leap in a short amount of time — less than a century — and in my day, we hadn't even started to hop.

Big Man has run aground on a sandbar; tying the two craft together has made it harder to maneuver around low spots. The four men roll up their britches and wade a short distance over to the island. Rabbit has to be dragged out of the boat by Stijaati. As they approach, two turtles, sunning themselves on a log, slip into the water with a little plunk. The three friends find a fallen tree and sit down, wiggling their toes in the water, except for Rabbit, who cowers behind the log.

STIJAATI: How did your mom's Creek Baptist influence, and the Creek Baptist preachers who was in your family, affect you as a writer and as a Creek?

RABBIT: Lord, how could that bunch not influence me? Mom's dad was a founding member of Tuskeegee Indian Baptist Church and the pastor there. Her younger brother was a preacher, too, at Artussee Indian Church. Mom's uncles, Grandpa's brothers, were the first converts to Creek Christianity in the Tuskeegee area. This may sound surprising, since I endorsed agnosticism privately, but those were important influences on the way I saw Creek society and wrote about it. Creeks will understand this. As you know, especially during my time, there was a real rift between the church grounds and the stomp grounds. Church people did not go out to the stomp dances; that was part of the old life they were supposed to put away. Pauline doctrine of mortifying the flesh became associated with setting aside Creek ceremony when taking up the cross. I'm biased in these regards, but I always reckoned that church people were worse about it than stomp dance folks. I heard churchgoers criticizing the grounds and traditional people more often than I heard traditionalists putting down the church. As a result of my mother's Christian influence, we, like a lot of other Creeks, had a complicated relationship with the traditional life of our tribe. We spoke Creek, in most cases better than English, and in many cases our kin didn't speak English at all. We grew up hearing the stories central to Creek people's understanding of themselves as Muskokalkee. So we were both inside and outside of traditional life. We shared much in common with the traditionalists — language, stories, and Creek beliefs — but Creek Christians separated themselves from the very center of where those beliefs were practiced, the ceremonial grounds.

This is why the various full-blood personae I assumed in the poetry, and later in the Fus Fixico letters, became so very important to me personally. I guarded these letters jealousy, resisted having them read anywhere but within the Territory by a local audience. They were a way I could imaginatively bridge some of this distance. That is, by assuming the voice of a full-blood, in deep communion with other full-bloods, I found a way to bridge the chasm between myself and that traditional world, if only in my mind. I feel some sense of loss as a writer, and this too relates to my imaginings of a golden age for Creeks. It was part of a world I'd been separated from, even though it still existed all around me within the nation. I've always wondered what I would be like had I been raised squarely in that traditional world, as a regular participant in the ceremonial life of my mother's grounds, with all the responsibilities that go along with that in terms of the grounds' upkeep, maybe leading stomp dance songs, helping repair the arbors before Green Corn, and so on. What would I write like? Would I even feel the urge to write? The political need would still be just as urgent, the necessity of addressing the threats against the Creek Nation. But if I was living the life of a traditionalist, maybe I would not be a writer because rather than writing about it, I'd be living it, doing it instead of talking about it. Instead of writing newspaper columns, maybe I'd be meeting with Chitto out at Hickory Grounds and planning ways to fight Oklahoma statehood. This personal loss, this separation from Creek ceremony, I reckon, is somewhat behind what fuels my desire to take up the full-blood personae and imagine that world. Of course, like most Creeks, I've had some exposure to that world, been to the night dances, known medicine people, and so on. But this is different from being a regular participant at the grounds. The ironic detachment that comes through the comedy in the letters, and personae in the poems, is the residue of my life as an outsider, the tendency to see things with distance, and, at the same time, not being entirely outside due to commonalities of language, stories, and beliefs. Perhaps this is why in my letters, the depictions of traditionalists have the feeling of an author talking about "us" and, at the same time, "them." This irony, however, has nothing to do with being outside the Creek world; it is an irony that existed within the Creek Nation because there were, and always have been, many different kinds of Creeks.

In reference to my Christian influences, I'll let you in on a little secret. When an Indian converts to Christianity, not all of him gets converted, no matter how thorough his newfound convictions. I have sat and listened to my uncle, a Creek Baptist preacher, tell stories about *stikinis*, witches who could turn themselves into owls and "go about and do the devil's business." My uncle took these stories seriously and was frightened by their implications. Do you see my meaning here? This is evident in the church grounds as well, the many features borrowed from Creek ceremony, from the grounds, aspects of Creek Christian life that are quite unlike white Christianity.

We Creeks have to believe certain things; it's in our blood. There's a certain bridge by Bald Hill, a wooden one over a little stream that was forever washing out, and my dad had to fix the bridge constantly. Dad tells a story about walking over it when he was a kid and feeling like he was being followed, then hearing an owl hoot behind him. The owl kept flying from tree to tree, just behind Dad, as he walked down the road that night, until eventually he was running, as fast as his legs would carry him, toward home. No matter how much agnosticism I might profess, I can assure you that if I walk over that bridge after dark, my pace will quicken considerably.

Getting back to the Baptist preachers, I can sometimes hear their voices when I write. White readers might think this is where all my literary allusions come from, but this is not so; the literary allusions came from Eufaula Boarding School and Bacone. Back in those days, educating Indians meant a classical education, teaching Indian students the pinnacles of Western civilization. But Creek preaching, more than the inclusion of the literary allusions from Western culture, affects the language of the letters. Creek preachers are not like white preachers. I am thinking of a different quality of their preaching, a rhetorical earnestness so much a part of the Creek preachers trained on our own soil, the sound of their voice, their pleas, their silences as they let their words hang in the still hot air of a summer Sunday. I've seen these ministers off by themselves, though, when the seriousness slips away and a little playfulness creeps in; and even now I can see them sitting in the shade and talking to one another, looking down and smiling at what must have been a joke. When I imagine this, I can also hear the voices of Hotgun, Tookpafka Micco, Kono Harjo, and Wolf Warrior, and I feel the style of my writing is often influenced by the repetitious drive of preaching, and by the preacher's pauses when he stops and lets the cicadas take over the sermon for a spell, allowing his words to weigh on his listeners as the insect din from the woods chimes in and backs him up.

STIJAATI: One thing I was notice. Your writing looks easy but you can only realize the genius of it mebeso if you was to try your hand lifting up the pen yourself. I tried writing a Fus Fixico letter and was had mail him to my wife for a little joke like her old boyfriend Billy Harjo was trying to re-spark her. I never was learned easy, but my writing taught me something nohows about what you had accomplished in those letters. Making the letter sound like talk instead of writing. Throwing in little reminders that make us realize we been told something, not read something. Not slipping up and falling back into book language instead of conversations. Using literary techniques and still making it sound like Creek full-bloods. Capturing something Creek in a Shakespeare quote or a Bible verse. Turning common clichés into brand-new jokes or saying them some new way we never heard before.

But there's something more important I noticed and I think I can say this about Fus and his buddies. Ever once in a great while, a feller gets to go somewheres where they's all Indians listening to an Indian talking, whether that Indian is a poet reading her poems about Indian life, or a play put on by Indians, or just an ordinary speaker at a meeting. One thing about that audience — Indians is starved for images of Indians, most important, images that come from themselves, from their own people, instead of from outsiders. They is something that happens in such a setting that will just make you think it's put near supernatural. They's a level that everyone starts hearing all at onced, laughing at the same moment at some little ole Indian trait, or expression, or mannerism, or way of walking that ever body there recognizes. The recognition is borned out of shared experience that outsiders cain't know. I think that's what your writing presents, this recognition where Indian people experience the joy of seeing themselves. And even though we're being made fun of, we're being made fun of by one of our own who understands and who likes us. What I learned was getting that on a piece of paper is as much a feeling as a technique, a feeling that comes from deep immersion in Creek life, as well as powerful writing.

I wanna switch into high gear here. You was involved with the Dawes Commission as a field-worker. The Dawes Act, other than Indian Removal, mebeso was had the greatest disaster in Creek history. How can you justify that participation?

RABBIT: Did you ever read Mark Twain? Sitting here with our toes in the water reminds me of Huck and Jim sitting in the shallows of the river bottom, watching dawn come up over the Mississippi, except here we are and it's getting dusky from our long talk. Perhaps it's time to man our craft toward shore. I'd rather not be out on the water at night, even under a full moon. I haven't had good luck with boats.

Sun sets on the Canadian River as Rabbit pushes the stern of the boat while Stijaati and Big Man tug the bow up the steep embankment back toward the pickup.

And that was the end of Stijaati's, Big Man's, and Rabbit's playacting.

Sincerely,
Jim Chibbo

CHAPTER SIX

Louis Oliver: Searching for a Creek Intellectual Center

One of Louis Oliver's central concerns in his writing is the possibilities and difficulties of being a Creek intellectual. Some of the ways his poems and stories take up the intellectual theme directly include framing the Creek migration story as a national search for knowledge; linking the migration story to contemporary patterns in Creek life; placing Creek migration in a teleological context; making connections between Creek intellectualism and Creek geography; suggesting that intellectualism is a tribally specific activity in relation to a given nation of people; discussing what constitutes a Creek philosophy; searching for an integration of intellectual, moral, and spiritual concerns; taking up the cultural and social problems surrounding being a Creek intellectual; and, finally, analyzing Creek humor as part of Creek intellectualism.

A little background about Louis Oliver may help provide a backdrop for understanding his intellectual journey. Louis Oliver was born in 1904, three years before Oklahoma statehood. Traditional Creek life centers around autonomous towns, and one's tribal town is determined matriarchally, as is clan identity. Mr. Oliver is from Coweta town. He was orphaned as a child and raised by grandparents and aunts at Okfuskee, Creek Nation. His mother's clan identity, and thus his as well, is Raccoon (*wotkalgee* in Creek). Mr. Oliver graduated from high school at Bacone in 1926. He passed away in 1991, an inestimable loss to the Creek Nation.

Whenever anyone mentions Mr. Oliver's name among contemporary Indian writers, eyes begin to light up from their memories of his knowledge, wit, kindness, and comic trickster spirit. Unfortunately, Mr. Oliver only began writing later in life; consequently, we may never know his full potential. He was a remarkable man — he not only spoke Creek but also spoke several very old dialects of Southeastern tribal languages, such as Yuchi and Alabama, and also Cherokee, which he learned as a result of living in Tahlequah during the latter part of his life.

A story, perhaps, will serve best to try to convey something of Louis Oliver's personality and spirit. Joseph Bruchac, Abenaki author, publisher, and founder of the Greenfield Review Press, tells of his first meeting with Mr. Oliver at a writer's conference in Tahlequah where Mr. Oliver showed up with sheaves of his poetry and asked Bruchac to look it over. Mr. Oliver has written of his amazement at what he saw at the conference. He had not realized the abundance of writing by contemporary Native authors or the imaginative possibilities of recording one's history, both artistically and with an integrity true to tribal life. Bruchac took the poems back to his room and looked them over. The poetry, he quickly discerned, was highly redolent of nineteenth-century romanticism and popular sentimental poetry of that time. Unbeknownst to Bruchac, this was no accident, since Mr. Oliver was highly influenced by the work of Alexander Posey, who had been taken by the same group of poets. The next day, Bruchac did not quite know what to say to Mr. Oliver, for whom he had already begun to develop a good deal of affection, so he kind of stammered and hem-hawed around and finally told him, "Well, they scan real well." Finally, Bruchac managed to say to him that contemporary Native American poets were developing new forms and trying to express their works in ways that were consistent with tribal traditions. Mr. Oliver, not to be deterred, showed up the very next day with a whole new body of poetry, which he had written overnight, and reported to Bruchac that this new corpus was, as he put it, "written in the contemporary idiom."[1]

Such a statement underscores Mr. Oliver's playfulness with language: in his work, he will often use strings of abstract phrases and then mock his own pretentiousness with a follow-up phrase stated directly in concrete language that cuts to the heart of the matter. One Creek writer, Helen Chalakee Burgess, says this of his passing:

> Somehow, I couldn't connect Louis and a funeral home wake. The Louis
> I knew should be laid out, dressed to the Mvskoke max, under a full
> moon brush arbor with swirling swells of smoke spirits preparing the

way for his good journey. Those who stayed with him through the night would be comforted by the soft settling of the early morning dew — reassurance that all was well. . . .

The service started with hymns and a Creek preacher, who obviously had not known Louis, delivering a canned sermonette telling us about the path we must follow if we wanted forgiveness for our sins and everlasting life; then he commented that in a hundred years nobody would know who Brother Louis was — a dichotomy of confusion without explanation of either. Our people have been subjected to this retribution for over a century, some have accepted without question, some have questioned and some have, like Louis, steadfastly maintained as is accounted in his writings. . . .

Phasing in and out of the service, I kept hearing words like hereafter, saved, sin, etc. and more etc. I was also hearing another ceremony going on at the same time, familiar sounds, yet unfamiliar feelings. It was as if Louis was conducting his own wake somewhere else. Then Barney [Bush] went to the pulpit and began telling us about the Louis he knew and everything began to relax. We enjoyed hearing of his and Louis's encounters, especially on the literary trail throughout New England. Barney led us through a hilarious retrospect of our friend and he wistfully told us of Louis's more serious side. Barney brought Louis back to life in the hearts of those who knew and adored him and lent some excitement to those who didn't.[2]

Like much of what contemporary Native Americans are writing, as Helen Burgess's title suggests ("The Night Barney Bush Saved Louis Oliver"), the story of Mr. Oliver's funeral has to do with getting the words right, even "manipulating the enemy's language."[3] Fortunately, Barney Bush did just that and was able to offset the verbal violence of the Creek Baptist preacher and bring Mr. Oliver back to life through storytelling.

Now that I've told some stories *about* Mr. Oliver, I'd like to deal with some stories told *by* him. I'll begin at the beginning by turning to the Creek migration story — that is, to Mr. Oliver's singular treatment of it in his invaluable book *Chasers of the Sun: Creek Indian Thoughts*.[4] Mr. Oliver is a traditional full-blood writing in the language of a Creek person for whom English is a foreign language. In addition to writing in English, he wrote bilingual editions of his prose and poetry in *Estiyut Omayat*[5] and *The Horned Snake*.[6] Making a point about these bilingual books seems essential to me, since a Creek audience, to some degree, is being written to; and failure to recognize this causes uninformed responses to the work and debates about its "literariness," a literariness defined by Western standards rather than by Creek cultural integrity. This constitutes impossible criteria for works written in the Creek language, and even those written in English, whose purpose is to educate Creeks about their culture rather than white readers about Creeks.

What strikes me about Oliver's account of Creeks coming into the world is that he links their origins to a national search for knowledge. Creeks were looking for answers to a scientific inquiry (and from a Creek viewpoint, given the centrality of fire in ceremony, a religious one as well) in their search for the place where the sun originated. That intellectual questions were part of the national character, not a mere chance phenomenon, is made evident by the fact that the issue was deliberated in council: "We came pouring out of the backbone of this continent like ants. We saw for the first time a great ball of fire rising out of the earth in the east. We were astounded at the phenomena, but we had no fear of it. We held council and made a decision to go and find the place that it lived" (*Chasers*, 3).

Briefly stated, the migration story explains how the Creeks, after emerging from below the earth in the middle of the continent, followed the sun to the east coast. Discovering the origin of the sun and reaching the limits of their travels, they turned back and settled along the Okmulgee River in Alabama. Looking at Mr. Oliver's version of the migration story, one could say that a characteristic of Creek identity is moving, journeying, setting forth.

After migration, other types of journeys have characterized Creek life throughout Creek history. Forced removals have left the nation in flux; the first was the upheaval in Alabama during the 1830s when the Southeast was being emptied of Indians by Andrew Jackson's administration. There was only a brief reprieve of less than thirty years when full-blood traditionalist Creeks found themselves fleeing to Kansas during the Civil War to escape their own government, which had sided with the Confederacy. Another short thirty years later, the Civil War was followed by land theft under the Dawes Act, causing people to abandon communal sites and move to allotments at statehood. Within a few years after allotment, almost all of this land had been lost, owing in large part to white scheming to remove it from Indians, a fact well documented in Angie Debo's watershed work *And Still the Waters Run*.

Migration continues. My family members left Oklahoma again during the thirties and after World War II for economic reasons and went out to the San Joaquin valley to pick cotton and work in the oil fields. Other Creeks moved away from Oklahoma under federal relocation programs in the 1950s. This is a common experience for many Southeastern Indian people whose families have lived in transit back and forth along I-40 between California and Oklahoma. We are still living out the migration story, reaching the coast, turning back. The Creek migration story has served us well in explaining our history.

Contemporary Creek poet Joy Harjo feels the pull of Creek migration strongly in her poetry. She teaches in New Mexico, and when people ask her when she will return home to Oklahoma, she replies that she will go back whenever she has "enough money and the right words." The last part of the statement is fundamental, of course, because if she gets the words right, she *will* be home. Harjo, then, is creating contemporary migration stories of her own, a jazz improvisation off of the original (jazz is an important concept in her work, and she is an accomplished sax player), in an attempt to figure out what has happened to her people. Oklahoma, one of our many homes away from home, becomes a kind of metaphor, a place in our imaginations, as well as the place to which we return.

I grew up with grandparents who told stories about sharecropping for white people in eastern Oklahoma, and they created that landscape for me in my imagination, supplementing the tellings with physical journeys across I-40 and home to the "real" place, but the "real" locale was no more or no less "real" than their verbal creation of it.

That the concept of multiple homes is carried within Oklahoma Creek memory is evidenced by Mr. Oliver's geographic description of the Creeks' original home in Alabama as well as the setup of his tribal town, Coweta, as it existed 150 years earlier in Alabama before removal:

> The people in general knew only to obey and reasoned that the river Okmulgee did not produce enough water to care for the people, so willingly they marched westward to Chatahoche. Geographically in the southeast part of the United States there lay three rivers: Alabama, Chattahoche, and Talapoosa: the fork of the Chattahoche was the Flint river. On the Okmulgee river there existed only one Creek town by that name, but later disbanded.... The Cowetans found the old campground on the Chattahoche and went about the business of laying-out a much larger square and reseated the notables in this manner: In the west arbor, or bed which had two sections north and south were seated the Wind and Bird clan with the chief who was of the Bird clan. In the rear were

seated the Bear and Beaver. In the north bed were the Blues in this order: the greater Hemeha of the Bird clan, the Blue of the Fox clan and a Hemeha of the Beaver. Hemeha, as referred to, were called the Precious ones. In the east arbor were seated women and the children with the rest of the clans. (when there is no fast) In the south bed which is called the warrior's bed were seated the Panther and Potato (Kvtcha and Ahalaka) clan. The head warrior was of the Potato or Ahlakalke clan and the vice warrior chief (Meko apoktv) was of the Panther or Kvtcha clan. The two medicine pots were at the north end of the Chief's bed. The ball ground was at the northeast of the east arbor. (*Chasers*, 12)

Even the order of the ceremonial grounds is embedded in the migration story. In making migration central, Oliver's work demonstrates an important element in building new Native literary theories. Foremost is the importance of migration stories and the way these narratives move from chaos and pain at emergence toward settlement in a homeland. Oliver's work has everything to do with relationship to a specific landscape and a specific tribal culture. Perhaps the next phase of Native literature is destined to take up these migratory concerns. The most effective writers, I believe, will be those looking toward their tribe's culture to generate appropriate literary formats for their work. Oliver does this by encapsulating his poetry inside a philosophical reflection on Creek migration; the work that follows the migration essay continuously uses migration as its reference point.

Bigger migration questions, perhaps, lie ahead for the Native writer than what has been dealt with thus far in the evolution of Native writing. Can the reconnection of the tribal protagonist to home and tradition occur on a larger, communal level? How can Indian communities achieve the same level of health the literary protagonist achieves by the end of these novels, given the tremendous problems contemporary Indian people face in racist America and their own communities? Does the individual reconnection to tradition seen in the novels provide any survival strategies for broader communities? Can a community, rather than only a single individual, migrate home toward spiritual, cultural, and political wholeness, and can written literature help this process along?

Can Native literature, like the oral tradition where literatures such as chants, songs, poems, and stories are used to effect an outcome in the real world, achieve some similar form of mimesis where literature affects events in tribal society? Can written literature serve Indian people in discovering ways to protect sovereignty and maintain Native identities? These migratory questions all have to do with homecomings, and like the original migration story, modern Native life is complicated, involving much journeying forth as well as returning home.

The migration stories deal with larger issues than the struggle of a single protagonist; this is underscored by the choice of the "we" point of view for Oliver's narration. It is interesting to note that the "new wave" of works being written by Native authors seems to hearken back to this older pattern from the oral tradition. The "old wave," the homecoming novels of the 1920s and 1930s, followed by the major works of the "Native American Renaissance" of the 1970s and 1980s such as *Sundown* and *The Surrounded,* followed decades later by *House Made of Dawn, Ceremony,* and many others, featured single tribal protagonists attempting to reconnect with their cultures. More recent works, such as Leslie Silko's *Almanac of the Dead* or Ray Young Bear's *Black Eagle Child: The Facepaint Narratives,* have communal casts rather than focusing on a viewpoint character. These works are further marked by their rejection of literary conventions, notably the modernism that these earlier works embraced, and by their direct discussion of politics—in the case of *Black Eagle Child,* tribal politics, and in the case of *Almanac,* global indigenous issues.

Louis Oliver seems to see a connection between literature and the life of the people, possibilities for the former serving the latter. So close is the connection between narrative and life that Oliver emphasizes the teleological aspects of the migration story, the way the narrative supports an ordered world chosen for Creeks. In his bilingual book *Estiyut Omayat,* Oliver says that the Creek way of life is given to Creeks by the Maker of Breath because it is best suited for them. Creeks were placed in a particular landscape for a reason, not as a matter of chance: "The chief of the Tokepotchas once said, 'I was often told in my youth that there is a Hesaketamese, (giver of breath) who gave us our way of life which is best suited to us'" (6). Oliver quotes another Creek leader to establish a fundamental land/breath/blood equation: "Thus spoke Yahola Mekko of the Coweta town: 'Our land is the very life and breath of us, and if we part with it, we part with our blood'" (6).

Oliver's ideas concerning the relationship of land to writing apply to contemporay Indian literature: the Native writer who abandons a specific sense of landscape places himself in a schizophrenic state, cutting himself off from his own body, culture, and people. The preceding quotes appear in a passage entitled "Why I'm Writing This," and they follow a discussion of a trip to New York City to discuss Native writing with four other Indian writers, further linking the issue of tribal cultural specificity to contemporary Native writing.

So strong is this connection between specific tribal landscape and tribal writer that in Oliver's poetry he traces the way his particular Creek landscape affects his intellectual activities. One poem entitled "In Honor of Ya'ha" shows the way Oliver's clan animal affects his study, thinking, and reading patterns:

> True to my clan animal
> the Golden Raccoon
> I search the woods for wild grapes
> plump and sugary persimmons.
> True to that animal's instinct
> I leaf through anthologies
> and find my favorite fruits
> in lyrical prose and song
> by my kindred ones,
> I study the faces of those in print,
> but I love Ts'eekkaayah
> nectar and ambrosia
> of the author via the pen. (*Chasers*, 83)

Oliver, like Raccoon, is a scavenger — but for literary knowledge and insight. The natural world is not merely the subject of Oliver's work; it is the method of his work, so that geographic specificity affects both content and technique. One especially memorable poem in *Caught in a Willow Net*[7] is a beautiful evocation of the fish, insect, plant, and animal life of the Deep Fork of the Canadian River, the Oktahutche. This poem, entitled "Deep Fork" (*Willow Net*, 14), reminds one of the many parallels between Oliver and Posey, for Posey loved this same river and even produced a journal of his trip down the Canadian that records in great natural detail its life and landscape. In *Caught in a Willow Net*, Oliver says, "Much of my inspiration for writing poetry or prose comes from the surrounding area of the Deep Fork river and the community" (72). River and community, an important equation for this writer; place and people, an important equation for any writer.

Given Oliver's and Posey's examples, then, what do we make of recent trends in Native writing where the reader cannot even tell *where* the story takes place or *who* the story is about—that is to say, land and nation fall by the wayside? I am talking here about a generic impulse where tribe and place are erased. If not for the biographical blurb at the beginning or end of the story that names the author's tribal affiliation, it might be difficult for the reader to determine she is reading Native literature. Surely there is room for much diversity in Native writing, but can we afford to divorce our narratives from the landscapes that should give birth to them? Can a poem or story be "Indian" if it has lost all connection to land and a community of people? What about Oliver's quotation of Yahola Mekko, who links land with blood and breath?

This is not to dismiss urban writing, an important phenomenon given twentieth-century Native American demography and the federal programs that have relocated people in cities, but even a story in a city has to take place somewhere, has to occur in a landscape, an urban one. Some might argue that generic writing opens the literature up to a larger audience. Flannery O'Connor's comments are interesting in these regards. O'Connor pointed out an interesting paradox—the more a writer delves into her own home country, the more universal her writing becomes. Geographic and cultural specificity enriches narratives rather than limiting them. It is through the specific, through concrete details, that universal human truths are often revealed. In regards to broader accessibility for the non-Indian audience, non-Indian readers of Native literature do not simply need their own culture mirrored back at them; they also need to encounter cultures of difference.

This call for cultural specificity is not to advocate giving away tribal secrets. To the contrary, respecting the wishes of one's tribe in regards to what should be in print is a response to a particular community of people and a specific landscape.

Oliver's particular sense of Creek landscape often involves demonstrating the ways Oklahoma geography and Creek roots in the mother country in Alabama are interdependent, pointing out the renaming of Oklahoma towns and grounds after their Alabama precedents. Throughout his work can be seen lists of the original town names in Alabama. There is another important sense of Creek geography that affects Oliver's writing. In the migration story, Mr. Oliver's relationship to the story he narrates sets him fundamentally apart from ethnographers' and historians' accounts of Creek history because he is talking about his own landscape, the place of his youth and old age, his cultural center. Mr. Oliver, in recalling the origins of Creek people, uses first-person plural through-out: "*We* came pouring out of the backbone of this continent like ants" (*Chasers,* 3; italics mine).

This is of the utmost importance for two reasons. The first and most obvious is that Mr. Oliver is narrating his own history from an insider's viewpoint rather than as an outsider looking in at the culture. Second, as Mr. Oliver tells his story, *he* is emerging from below the earth out into the light of the broader landscape; *he* is on the migration trail with his people, searching for the origin of one of their most important symbols, the sun.[8] For him, history is his story, and the narrative comes to pass in the telling of it.

This is an important point because Mr. Oliver depicts intellectual activity as a relationship between an individual and a community of people; it is a "we" relationship. In fact, Oliver reports that the genesis of his own intellectual life resulted from both literal and spiritual contact with Creek and Indian writers and thinkers, and he traces that tradition from his own study of Alexander Posey's earlier work to the new ways he began to imagine himself as an Indian writer after talking to other Native writers in Tahlequah. So we see two strains of development in Oliver's intellectualism—contact with Creek writing and tradition and contact with other Indian writers. I would argue that the process analysis Oliver provides us of his journey as a Creek writer points to larger patterns in Native literature—the really vital discourse is coming about as the result of Indians talking to other Indians, in their own tribes, and with other Native people.

Mr. Oliver, in his telling of Creek history, often breaks off from his detailed description of the progress of the migration to discuss philosophical concerns rather than rendering an events-only account. More generally, Oliver's work often deals with trying to delineate a Creek philosophy, often by following concrete description with reflection. The book as a whole is a kind of cultural survey that attempts to mark some of the most important aspects of Creek national character, some of the cornerstones of the culture and analyses of their meanings. His series of numbered poems in *Caught in a Willow Net* entitled "Creek Indian Thoughts" (26–35) show that he is trying to write about philosophical concerns from a Creek perspective, and the concept of "thought" is a recurring one throughout all his work.

Chasers of the Sun is very much a philosophical meditation on the interrelationship between matter and spirit. Oliver's philosophical asides consciously center the migration story around the sacred fire and explicate the importance of Creek ceremonialism, an important theme throughout. No one who has been at a ceremonial ground and heard the women shaking shells and dancing counterclockwise around the fire, the steady *shúguta shúguta shúguta* of the turtle shells wafting through the arbors, can forget this sound. Mr. Oliver describes the stomp dance music with a philosophical reflection on its spiritual dimensions:

> To describe the action and the sound is very difficult as it involves
> entering into the sphere of the supernatural. Gradually the leader
> invokes, by stronger verses, the spirits of the other world and as the
> dance progresses they are all lifted up seemingly in a cloud. Many other
> leaders will come forward to continue the euphoria until daybreak.
> (*Chasers,* 9)

This description invokes the Indian idea of chant. As the words go forth, they cumulatively gather power until they begin to exert energy on the physical world, actually causing things to happen. As Leslie Silko says, in her well-known poem about the witches' storytelling contest, the words are set into motion.[9] Mr. Oliver's philosophical musing includes an explanation of the power of language and ways in which words are incarnated in ceremony.

Another example of a philosophical aside in Louis Oliver's version of the migration story is the following critique of contemporary society's ultrarationalism:

> I add here a note to further bolster our beliefs: Contemporary man
> although rejecting fantasy and myth, aspires to make it a reality. True for
> man to fly was a fantasy, but he does just that now, but only
> mechanically. What he cannot grasp is the irrelevance of Spirit to matter.
> Spirit, as the term is used, is in the sense of a broad generalization. The
> gods, and there are many gods, rule in this outer world, each delegated
> with a power peculiar to its governing law. This is one group of beings
> (spirits) as opposed to the theocratic governing body which is the
> fountain head of pristine laws. These spiritual entities are the true
> governors of mankind through the ages. (*Chasers,* 6–7)

Mr. Oliver's philosophizing involves a combination of facts, imagination, and spirituality, and he demonstrates a complex relationship to his materials, a relationship that necessitates his emotional involvement. The author draws on a remarkable variety of sources: Chikili's speech from the early eighteenth century, passed-down oral stories, personal meditation, and even quotations from religious texts like the Secret Doctrine as well as from various historians. The story breaks down discrete Western categories between fiction and nonfiction, history and myth, prose and poetry, philosophical abstraction and concrete details. Storytellers use whatever is at hand to make the story memorable rather than categorical.

In addition to drawing on a wide variety of sources to create narrative, one of the concerns of Oliver's philosophy is linking intellectualism with spiritual and moral concerns. In the essay entitled "Climbing the Mountain," Oliver discusses his own writing processes, but more importantly, he attempts to discuss moral and spiritual guidelines for tribal intellectual activities. He does not separate writing from contact with his tribe or with spiritual forces:

> I with only a very meagre education, no degrees, not much schooling, but spent years as a transient, then settled down and had an urge to write in my old age. My grandmother taught me songs to sing over roots and herbs made into a tea. She taught me how to pray or meditate in the Indian way on things I so desired. So I climbed a certain mountain here to rendezvous with the "Little people" or the ethereal spirits. (*Chasers*, 27)

After describing the details of his fast and isolation, he goes on to say:

> I prayed or concentrated on my wish and hope to be able to write, on these trips to the mountain top. It took me three trips before I could isolate all outside thoughts and saw only myself composing poetry and prose though they seemed nonsensical; varied subjects and objects were presented. Divine afflatus often occurs at this time. It seems the one theme that stood out in my mind went something like this: "I am earth in part — I belong to the earth. All of Creation is of the elements and shall return to it." (*Chasers*, 27)

The idea that keeps recurring is that Oliver's inspiration to write comes from cultural and spiritual grounding and contact with other Native writers and thinkers:

> So — to what avail, to what advantage has it been that I climbed that mountain and prayed in my Indian way, for expansion of my mind; to be able to recall past knowledge and experiences that are recorded in the files and indexes of my brain?

> I had never given a thought to the possibilities of my writing prose, poetry, the history of my people or of the Native American in general. Then I attended my first Conference of Native American writers. I felt very much out of place when I learned that those Indians of various tribes were professionals in the field of writing. . . . I was very much impressed by their urging that the Indian must write as a survival tactic. When they returned to their respective homes and businesses I received from them so much material and chapbooks by other writers, that I was overwhelmed and very much inspired to write. (*Chasers*, 28)

Not only does Oliver put writing in the category of spiritual quest, but he links his writing process to specific Creek spiritual entities. Native literary criticism, to my knowledge, has never taken up this important religious issue — the way that writing, for some tribal authors, is a result of visionary experience related to a tribally specific theology. The Little People (Stiloputchkogee) have already been mentioned. Oliver also links his writing process to Tie-Snake, the anomalous river dweller whose hypnotic pull can drown a victim but whose horns are valued for the most powerful of medicines (*Chasers*, 30). Oliver makes the link between writing and Tie-Snake by association rather than analytic comparison; he follows a statement about starting to write with his grandmother's instructions regarding Tie-Snake. After this story, he makes a direct connection, linking his grandmother's comments with his book in Creek and English: "This happened seventy years ago and in that lapse of time I learned more about it and wrote a bi-lingual book called *The Horned Snake*" (30).

Why Tie-Snake, and what does this have to do with writing? On the most obvious level, Oliver seems to say there is a pantheon of Creek spiritual entities, beings such as the Little People and Tie-Snake, and they deserve attention from a Creek writer, given their place in Creek cosmogony. On a less obvious level, it is interesting to note that not only were Creek writers Posey and Oliver linked in some way to Tie-Snake but that the same water creature surfaces in Joy Harjo's writing as well.

Harjo's encounter with Tie-Snake in "The Flood," one of the prose poems in *The Woman Who Fell from the Sky*,[10] unites tribal past and present, since the story moves back and forth between a contemporary sixteen year old who drowns while drinking and a Muskogean woman from the past for whom Tie-Snake's magnetic pull is a result of his appearing to her as the "most handsome man in the tribe" (Harjo, 14). The distinction between the woman from the past and the one of the present is blurred throughout the poem. For Harjo, Tie-Snake seems to represent the way we are part of larger ongoing, living mythical patterns that we often do not even realize: "Before I could deter the symbol we were in it" (14), and our blinding to such reality has to do with the way contemporary culture has provided us with a "proliferation of inventions that keep us from ourselves" (17), keep us from seeing the magic just barely below the surface.

Tie-Snake, who is part of the underworld realm in Creek cosmogony, is part of the balance of oppositions, that fragile tension wherein Upper World, Lower World, and This World cohere. Many Southeastern traditional narratives tell of the fight between an underworld snakelike creature and upper-world birdlike being, a battle that is a working out of this delicate balance. Or, as Harjo puts it much more beautifully, pointing out the symbolic Lower World water and Upper World sun connections: "Years later when she walked out of the lake and headed for town, no one recognized her, or themselves, in the drench of fire and rain" (16).

Surely Creek writing involves such a balance, cooling fever with water, bringing Upper and Lower Worlds back into balance, so that neither hot nor cold gets out of control and predominates, allowing for the inclusion of "queerness," anomalous animals like Tie-Snake who share in one body Lower World characteristics of snake/fish (water) and This World characteristics of deer (horns). Part of the answer to Tie-Snake's relationship to writing can be seen in Mr. Oliver's discussion of the social and cultural problems that surround the Creek writer, who must be more than amphibious, not unlike Tie-Snake, who is part land and part water. One reason that Oliver relates to Tie-Snake is because of the awkward state Oliver's education leaves him in as a Creek full-blood whose schooling sets him apart from the rest of the traditional community, the proverbial fish out of water.

The work of Creek writer Tsianina Lomawaima may provide us with some useful background before taking a look at what Oliver himself says about his experience of education. From *They Called It Prairie Light*,[11] Lomawaima's excellent book on the Chilocco boarding school attended by many Creeks and Cherokees, the reader can get an approximation of how some Creeks of Oliver's time may have viewed education and writing. Part of Lomawaima's argument is that historians writing about boarding schools have relied heavily on written sources and, at least partially, simply duplicated the federal record. Thus Lomawaima interviewed the students of Chilocco themselves and based her conclusions on their perceptions of life there.

As part of her findings, Lomawaima indicates that for those Indian parents who chose to send their children to Chilocco, such a choice was not necessarily out of a love for white education; other more practical reasons often took precedence. Some of the typical families sending children to Chilocco included large ones facing economic pressure during times of poverty like the Great Depression, single-parent homes struggling to make ends meet, guardian homes where families had taken in orphaned relatives, or cases of illness, invalidism, or unemployment of the parents (Lomawaima, 33–35).

Lomawaima also develops a direct link between federal Indian schools and divestiture of tribal lands through the allotment process, as well as part of a program to separate women from the culture of their mothers and grandmothers.

> Domesticity training for Indian women suited the goals of the federal government above and beyond training for subservience. It fit integrally into governmental plans for a fundamental alteration of Indian peoples' relationship to land. . . .
>
> Dispossession of communal tribal lands, coupled with the creation of small "Indian homesteads," supported the rationale of domestic education for Indian women.
>
> The struggle to reform and reshape the Indian home targeted the education of young women. They would serve as the matrons of allotment households, promoting a Christian, civilized lifestyle and supporting their husbands in the difficult transition from hunter, or pastoralist, to farmer. Women's capacity to bear this burden was taken for granted by the Victorian vision of Woman as Mother, influencing society and shaping the future through her nurture of her children (Richards 1900). An epigraph by Helen Hunt prefaced a description of "Home Economics Class Instruction" at Chilocco: "A woman who creates and sustains a home, and under whose hand children grow up to be strong and pure men and women, is a Creator, second only to God" (*Chilocco: School of Opportunity* 1938, 31). To create this Godly creature, Indian schools had to convince or force Indian girls to renounce the teaching of their own mothers and accept the dictates of the federal curriculum and the Allotment Act. Estelle Reel, superintendent of Indian Schools from 1898 to 1910, encouraged the matrons to assure Indian girls being trained in housekeeping that "because our grandmothers did things in a certain way is no reason why we should do the same." (Lomawaima, 86–87)

Especially informative is Lomawaima's analysis of domesticity training at Chilocco, which was directly linked to subservience. This type of education involved keeping the school itself running with its huge workload of cooking, cleaning, and sewing, rather than any kind of training for life outside Chilocco. The only future for Indian girls trained in such an educational system was as the next generation of matrons in boarding schools inculcating more of the same kind of "education" into their Indian wards, or as domestic help for white people. Another big aspect of Indian women's education was submission to federal authority (Lomawaima, 81–99).

It is a general perception that the "Five Civilized Tribes" have always valued education, and there is some truth to this; the Creek Nation itself, for example, ran its own schools inside the nation before statehood. Given, however, the U.S. federal agenda of boarding school education for the purpose of land divestiture, communal displacement, and the creation of a body of women servants, it would be surprising, indeed, if there were not some factions of ill will toward education in Creek communities, especially full-blood communities like the one Oliver came from. These full-blood communities were adamantly opposed to allotment, and Lomawaima makes the fascinating link between allotment policy and boarding school education. It is important to note that Lomawaima emphasizes the many creative ways Chilocco students resisted these external impositions of oppression and authority, yet it is also interesting to speculate what kind of feelings of ill will toward education may have been created back home in the students' communities by many generations of this type of treament (Chilocco operated from 1884 to 1980).

Further, in rural Oklahoma, those visibly identifiable as Indians were often simply not allowed by whites to attend public school, and some students' attendance at Chilocco was their first formal educational experience. Lomawaima says: "Many Indian children who attended Chilocco in the 1920s and 1930s came from isolated, rural communities where public schools were unavailable or unfriendly. Chilocco may have been the only option, especially for junior or senior high school" (32–33). Surely this kind of rampant racism in white Oklahoma communities could have contributed to bad feelings among Indians about education.

In his bilingual book *Estiyut Omayat,* Oliver himself says:

Many things they told me [his grandmother and Creek elders] which would have been of importance to me, I have forgotten. They and others stressed the need for an education and that I must try hard to learn.

By much coaxing and threats with a hickory whip, I did eventually attend school and graduated from high school. I thought that I had accomplished much and I expected praise and honor from my people, but that was not to be. I was accused of capitulating to the White Man's ways and because of my refinement in character, I was not looked upon as being a real Indian, so I caused much consternation.

As I think back to the days of my youth and under the circumstances we lived, we wanted for very little, being healthy and happy. Now, that my old ones have passed away, I have a deep felt sorrow for them. (4)

There are many complicated worlds that have to be negotiated here as a result of Oliver's burgeoning intellectualism — both value and disdain for education, a "healthy and happy" world at home and the school world that is unknown and unfamilar to him, praise and honor versus capitulation, real Indians versus those "refined in character," and on and on it goes. What budding intellectual could survive these circumstances other than someone who can move fluidly between land and water, between different worlds, a being not altogether unlike Tie-Snake?

This may explain, as well, the fluidity of Harjo's poetry, where distinctions between past and present, myth and history, natural and supernatural are blurred. First, the point seems to be that all these worlds continue to affect us, but second, the Creek writer simply faces a complicated existence that requires many powers of shape-shifting. There is power in this movement, being able to transcend boundaries and categories, but there is also much danger, the danger of losing one's geographic, cultural, and spiritual center as one crosses so many barriers. This complex relationship of both danger and power is demonstrated by the fact that Tie-Snake, though he may drown his victims, is also prized for the medicine from his horns.

Some Creeks say that the reason Tie-Snake pulled Posey under the waters of the Canadian, the very river that he loved and eulogized, was because of Posey's treacherous real estate dealings buying up Indian allotments. In other words, certain Creeks put Posey into a larger context than his writing alone by considering the life that surrounds that writing. Oliver himself, in *Estiyut Omayat*, says in the poem "Alexander Posey":

Had he not changed his name to
Chenube Harjo,
the river would not have taken him.
Many will believe my thought. (17)

"Chenube Harjo" was the writing persona Posey wrote under in his early
writings at Bacone. In the poem, Oliver talks about spiritual forces that
may have affected Posey's untimely death. He claims that "the Harjos
were strange and mystical people" (*Estiyut Omayat*, 17), and he names
a number of factions who may have had animosities against them. By
choosing the Harjo persona for his writing, Oliver suggests, Posey may
have brought on himself some of that ill will, even though the name
was a fictional one. Once again, as Oliver tells us throughout his work,
we are back to the notion of tribal writing as a moral and spiritual endeavor full of powerful potentialities as well as possibilities for abuse.
To put it succinctly, this is scary territory for all of us who write, and the
negotiations are complicated.

As has been mentioned, Mr. Oliver discusses the difficulty of being
judged an assimilationist by his own people simply for completing a
modest level of education, high school in his case. In Oliver's poem
"Powers to Be Had," he links the speaker's acculturation with a conscious choice to be a witch:

Acculturated, I speak English
so my people disown me.
I chose the power to be unseen
Hicka Seko it is called; (*Chasers*, 40)

There is often a glib association these days of shape-shifting with trickster's powers to transcend boundaries, but shape-shifting, the poem
makes clear, is not always a power for good. Often shape-shifting and
tricksters are used as tropes for the postmodern obsession to make everything amorphous, indefinable, and decentered. Some questions remain,
however, about these putative powers in relation to Native intellectualism.

To name one such question, is the language of postmodernism an effective means of analyzing tribal worldviews given postmodernism's
skepticism about language and literature and its tendency to place them
in the realm of nonrepresentation? In some ways, might these values be
antithetical to Native philosophies, as well as struggles for recognition
of national and intellectual sovereignty? What changes occur in "the

power of the word" concept when it is examined under a system that devalues any sense of word essence? What happens to spiritual possibilities? If we are going to liberate words from fixed meanings and celebrate their amorphous shape-shifting qualities, might we need to recognize not only that tricksters shape-shift but that witches shape-shift also, as Oliver would remind us? Is there a balance called for here, an acknowledgment that sometimes fixed meanings are necessary, other times free play, as well as an honest recognition that both can be abused? Are some creeds, especially ones that relate to tribal traditions and political strategies such as sovereignty, worth staking oneself down and defending? What happens to political struggles when a concept like identity is deconstructed?

It is interesting to note, in passing, a trend in a separate discipline that deals with a marginalized group, the hugely expanding field of queer theory. Many gay and lesbian theorists have by necessity had to come to the conclusion that certain essentialist strategies, especially in relation to identity, are necessary if theorists are to maintain any connection whatsoever to the real world. It is difficult to argue that a group faces oppression if you no longer believe the group exists because you have deconstructed its identity to death. This might serve as a potential warning for those of us trying to find critical centers consistent with our own cultures.

Further, when Native literature takes up the hypertheoretical jargon of postmodern theory, do the theorists, at times, limit their audience to a handful of academics, effectively cutting themselves off from Native people, except for those few who teach Native literature in English departments? Whereas some might argue that academics are being addressed on their own turf, with their own language, and Native Americanists are demonstrating that they can do theory as good as anyone else, I am waiting for the day when Native people will be addressed on *their* own terms.

Oliver reminds us that the positive powers of shape-shifting tell only half the story:

> voices, voices urging me
> to take the power of the elements
> that can open safes in banks
> with just a puff of my breath
> point my finger and a person dies.

Those were powers of the devil.
I had a choice and was urged
    to do good or evil.
I wrestled with the psychic forces
    ... drained myself and fell asleep. (*Chasers,* 40)

Perhaps the poem is a useful example for thinking about writing. The tribal writer goes through a process of spiritual warfare wherein the writer must decide the purpose of that writing because she or he is writing for the survival of a community of people. To ignore the place of writing for the health of the nation might place one in danger of witchery. This is a uniquely communal view of the writing process that rejects the Western view of writer as isolated and/or alienated artist. Knowledge for knowledge's sake is not necessarily an end; knowledge is valued in relation to the degree it makes a return to the tribe.

I feel the struggle acutely in my own writing as I try to write from some kind of Creek and Cherokee viewpoint. As a Native gay man, I want to include, rather than exclude, the concerns of Native gays and lesbians, including especially our struggles with the AIDS epidemic, which has hit our communities harder than any other minority group. To talk about this issue, in a very literal way, has everything to do with our survival as sovereign nations of people. Yet I have to find a language to speak about prevention, HIV, AIDS — as well as the health and spiritual strength of Native gays and lesbians — in a way that is culturally appropriate and consistent with the values of the Indian communities in which I operate. Finding such a balance is seldom easy, and for the writer who wants to be able to return home, the writer whose very identity is framed by a communal view of the world in relation to family and kin, the possiblity of rejection by one's own is terrifying. The alternative — hiding your story, and the stories of your brothers and sisters — is not any better than rejection. This creates a lot of fear — the fear of rejection, the fear of remaining silent. Creative strategies, new imaginings, brave thoughts, words, and deeds, powerful and inclusive forms of sovereignty, are called for.

Perhaps in these matters also we can look to the migration story, which, for Louis Oliver, is not a foregone myth but a road map for sensible ways to continue the journey in contemporary settings. In recalling the origin of clans, when people and animals were lost in the fog and formed bands based on the group they were with when the fog lifted, Mr. Oliver says, "In that obsidian darkness they wandered by feel and instinct" (*Chasers,* 5).

Another aspect of Oliver's attempt to define Creek intellectualism is by describing Creek humor. One of Mr. Oliver's poems in his book *Caught in a Willow Net* is a classic of Indian humor that parodies the speech of two Indian oil field workers, poking fun at their many prejudices:

Indian Macho

This black 'yeyhoo' said he's Seminole
I bragged of being Creek 'injun'
—tough guys, ya know—
tool dressers from the Seminole oil fields.
Pay-day and we hike for "Shanker" town—
There a makeshift bar—sawdust floor.
We don't know name brands of beer
We order two bottles of good ole "frogass"
Bartender say: "You mean, 'Progress,' don't cha?"
We take table where Indian girl sits
She pays no mind—munching salted peanuts.
'Yeyhoo' told me she is 'cherry-kee'
"I know," he said, "she come from 'tally-kaw'."
Table too high or chair too low for her
—So her 'boobs' were laying on the table
seeming to look right straight at us
reminding me of baldheaded beavers.
She listened to our 'bull' with her eyes.
After several rounds of 'speeded' beer
we began to 'show off' our manhood.
He took a bottle between his teeth—no hands
raised it straight up and emptied it.
We did an arm wrestle and he won.
I dropped a quarter for an excuse to
look around under the table and saw
She sat spraddle legged on her chair
I came up saying: "good god!"
She paid no mind—just munched her nuts.
He flaunted a five dollar bill in her face
—burned it up with a lighted match.
I wrote a check for ten thousand dollars
—tore it to bits and pitched it in the air.
She leaned over and whispered: "You go with me." (60)

The poem takes on issues of sexism and racism, parodying the absurdities of macho behavior. The poem is funny because of its use of puns, for instance, a carryover from Indian joking in original languages often involving much more complicated punning. The sound similarity of "frogass" and "progress" provides an irony in the poem, since the idea of progress has been used in so many ways to oppress Indian people, providing justification for various abuses.

The use of the term "black yeyhoo" reveals that Indian people are not without their own prejudices and also points to a source of controversy that goes back many years. Creeks and other members of the so-called Five Civilized Tribes owned slaves; usually these slave owners were the more wealthy and assimilated mixed-bloods. The slaves often became culturally Indian, and their offspring biologically Indian through intermarriage, many even speaking Native languages. After the Civil War, they were considered full members of the tribe with the same voting rights and privileges as other Indians. At statehood, freedmen received allotments as did other Creeks. Even today, there are many African Americans in eastern Oklahoma who are culturally Indian. Unfortunately, there is some ill feeling among some Creeks, and members of other Southeastern tribes, about whether their fellow tribal members who are black should receive the same privileges that they do. The poem reflects some of this old hostility.

The voice in the poem is redolent of one of Posey's personae with its use of localisms, terms common to a specific area, and its parody of the way people talk: "Shanker town," "frogass," "cherry-kee" for Cherokee, "tally-kaw" for Tahlequah. In other poems, Mr. Oliver will use long strings of malapropisms and then follow up with a short statement in simple language that cuts to the heart of the matter and makes fun of the speaker's use of pretentious speech. As in this example, many of the poems are self-deprecating. Many of the words in the poem have sexual double meanings because in Indian humor many aspects of sexuality are made fun of, and in a matrilineal culture such as that of the Creeks, male virility is open game for satiric treatment. In this regard, some of the images are comical, such as the comparison of breasts to "baldheaded beavers," an image no less funny for its absurdity — Indian humor often conveying a strong sense of the absurd. The poem ends with more male posturing, and the comic assertion that the men's machismo is not what matters in the end; it is really a matter of how much cash they are carrying, but even this is undercut by the tearing up of a check, which has no intrinsic value once it is destroyed. More important, there is a ground shift, a major inversion. The conclusion is decided by the woman; she calls the last shot, and no matter what the "machos" might think, she has had control of the situation all along.

Like the poem, Mr. Oliver's migration story also contains a good deal of tongue-in-cheek humor, an important factor in surviving migratory dislocations. For instance, he paints this Edenic picture:

> Now I must say here that the physical stature of the Creek Indians in those days, both men and women, was superb. No man was under six foot and no woman was "baggy" or paunchy. They were all the very picture of health as they bantered and fought for the ball, but all in good humour. (*Chasers*, 8)

In addition to the exaggerated physical description, any Creek knows that the ball is not always fought for in "good humor," one name for the stickball game being "Little War." Especially if rival towns are being played, towns of "different fires," the competition can be intense, to say the least. My aunt Barbara Coachman has told me about games she witnessed in her childhood that resulted in killings, injuries, wounded carried off to the hospital, and the spectators, including herself, running like hell, "just a-hooking it," as she likes to say, as the fight erupted. Today stickball is a kinder, gentler game, but even now the *micco* lines up the players before the game and gives a speech about goodwill and setting aside hostilities.

Louis adds a hyperbolic touch with the following statement: "At around noon or awhile afterwards, the men challenge the women to a stickball game. Usually the temperature was around 110, but they were urged to play hard until nearly sundown" (*Chasers*, 7). Mr. Oliver, in addition to these comic exaggerations, uses malapropisms consciously and slyly to work the humor of his stories, as in the following: "Much has been written about the religious beliefs and the medical practices of the Muskogee or Creek Indians by the Anglo-Americans, but nothing of its esoterics has been revealed by them. It would take a scholarly fullblood with a Ph.D. in *ethmology*, but there are none, and not likely to be any in the future" (13; my emphasis). Like much of Indian humor, the statement stings a little at the same time it makes us laugh. For those of us who are Native academics, there is a truth here that we immediately recognize: many scholars are more text oriented than personally knowledgeable of traditionalism, and the possibility of a traditional worldview being accepted in the academy is bleak indeed. That Mr. Oliver used malapropisms like "ethmology" consciously and for effect has been confirmed by many who knew him.

In Mr. Oliver's analysis of the workings of Creek humor, he points out that one of its characteristics is attention to the smallest of details — in fact, the microscopic focus may become the controlling idea of the joke. To make this point, he tells a story where the irony has to do with a single blade of grass — a wild onion blade, actually, which looks like a grass stem:

> How to put this into perspective I don't know, but it was spring and the wild onions were up big enough to gather Saturday and the Indians were in town to supply their cupboards. One Indian stood on the street corner just looking at the traffic and passers. He had eaten a good dish of wild onions at home. A friend came up to him and noticed a piece or a "blade" of onion on his teeth. Said the friend: "Are the onions up pretty good?" With a broad grin he simply answered: "I don't know." Was that the punch line? Where is the joke? Such as that the Creeks consider to be funny. They cannot discuss any serious matters without allowing humor to intervene. (*Chasers*, 54)

Often Creek jokes are marked by this lack of a punch line, since the humor occurs throughout the narrative through concentration on just such microsopic ironies as a single wild onion blade as well as the humor outside the story in aspects of the teller's performance such as mimicking of voices or caricatures of facial expressions or movements. In one of the stories that follows in Mr. Oliver's section on Indian humor, "An Indian Dog" (*Chasers*, 61), the story never does work its way to a comic revelation because the Creek dog is extraordinary from the very beginning of the story — funny in all his ways, since he knows that a squirrel gun means to head toward the post oaks, a shotgun means to head toward the cornfield to hunt quail, and a pole means to head toward the fishing hole. Because of his amazing intelligence, it is time to laugh at Che'coni the dog at the beginning of the story, and throughout the story's unfolding, not merely at the story's climax. I believe that Oliver's discussion and use of humor as part of his intellectual journey and understanding of Creek philosophy may indicate a potential direction for analyzing Native literature in a manner that Indian people can immediately recognize and relate to.

In her critical work, Elizabeth Cook-Lynn discusses what she identifies as a problem in Native literature when authors write from a mixed-blood perspective; her concern, as I understand it, is not degree of blood quantum but contemporary literary emphases that fail to incorporate tribal realities.[12] Cook-Lynn sees a trend where Native authors overly concern themselves with individual self-liberation rather than their place within the tribe; focus on first-person perspectives rather than the life of the people; discuss their own marginalization, which really becomes these authors' evaluations of their place in American culture rather than tribal culture; and depict cultural dysfunctionalism rather than healthy aspects of tribal life. I believe that authors such as Louis Oliver are the tonic for this kind of mixed-blood malaise, where blood and marginalization, rather than the ongoing life of the nation, become the overriding issue. In Oliver's work, we are always aware that we are reading about Creek life, the tradition of Creek intellectualism, the role of community and culture in forming Creek thinkers, and the ways in which such thought diverges from dominant culture.

Dear Hotgun:

Well, so Stijaati Thlaako been cleaning out his old car lot behind his house getting ready for the Thlaako family reunion. He done whittled the rust off the spark plug wires of his old Allis Chalmers tractor and pumped and primed and kicked and resuscitated that one sure enough until she cough out black smoke and sputter back alive. Then he hook on to his old junkers what he call "collector's items" and haul them out behind the post oaks to a little meadow where no one can see them until he got his backyard put near spit-shined for the kinfolks coming over.

Mebeso he have one last collector item to hide, a little old 1978 Honda Civic. This one run on her own, so Hondo don't have to arrange no date with Alice Chalmer to get a ride to the back forty. Stijaati just hop in her and drive lickety-split bouncing over cow field grinning and waving black cowboy hat out the winder and give big turkey gobble like leading stomp dance. Having fun, sho' good. He come up on his little one-acre museum where the junkers look like corpses, falling in on theyselves and axles resting right on the ground. Oughta build a little house over ever one of them, sure enough, but Stijaati tells his wife might need them for parts someday.

Stijaati seen a open spot next to a little ole Ford Fairlane, one of his prize possessions. He cain't see too good on account of the mushroom cloud surround Hondo when she slows down on final approach. He backs in next to the Ford Fairlane and waits for the smoke to clear before get out. He rolls down the window and smiles proud at the sagging vinyl roof of the Ford, a real classique. Stijaati hears a hiss, something like dropping a hot coal into a bucket of water. Sitting in the back seat of the Ford, torn headliner hanging all around its big red ugly head, is a turkey buzzard, blinking at Stijaati, like he's waiting for Stijaati to get in the front seat and chauffeur him to the next dead cow.

Stijaati let loose the most unmanly shriek you ever heard. Liked to scared the *sofki* out of him. All that hollering scare Buzzard pretty good too and he lowers his head and extends his wings as far as he can stretch in the Ford, giving an even louder hiss than before kin to Stijaati's wife snoring. Then Buzzard tries to get out the winder but cain't on account of flapping his wings too big. Like the old Indian said about the horse—rearin' to go but cain't go for rearin'. Finally squeezes out and falls to the ground with a plop, gathers hisself back up, and takes off uttering a low whine until plumb airborne and circling the car lot, rocking side to side in the blue sky while Stijaati hold his cowboy hat ag'in the sun and watch. Still ain't climbed out of Hondo clean in shock.

Kinfolks was start coming and parking all up and down the country road in front of Stijaati's house. Lucille was there, leaning on the porch rail and telling Chebon on the bottom step all bout how when she was a girl she useta smoke honeysuckle and grapevines for cigarettes. Lester Henneha was there, but hardly five minutes before he snuck out to his car to get away from his brother Ezequiel, who ever body called Zeke, and have a nip and already wishing he could go home. Jimmy Alexander was there, looking under the hood of Zeke's Toyota pickup on account of him had overheated on the way in from Newcastle. Jimmy had his shirt off and was standing back and unloosening the radiator cap with an old oil rag. Zeke hisself was there, sat down at the picnic table under the catalpa tree tuning up his old Epiphone six-string for a hymn sing. His twin daughters Docia Mae and Zadie Fay was there, and they was cutting up a cardboard box to make bases out in the cow pasture for their annual softball game. Big Man and Rabbit was there, but they hadn't showed up in time to hep Stijaati rearrange his car junkyard like they was promised but they did make it in before the big feed started.

While they was standing in line to eat, Stijaati told Rabbit about the buzzard in the backseat of his Ford and Rabbit told Stijaati how one time when he needed doctoring for the flu he went to Indian Health Service in Shawnee and sat and sat and waited and waited with a thermostat in his mouth and his tail hanging out the ass end of the skimpy white gown the nurse had hung over him until she finally come on back and took the thermostat out, and Rabbit tried to get her phone number, but she'd only let on that she lived in Oklahoma City and didn't say nomores than "Doctor will be in, in just a minute" nohows and "Lay down on that gurney." She was had shut the door and Rabbit could hear her out in the hallway arguing with the doctor. "You get his charts yourself, you old buzzard," she was had say and her voice disappear down the hallway. About an hour later the doctor come in, and he was a turkey buzzard with a stethoscope around his neck. Before Rabbit could recover his senses and jump up from the gurney, the doctor was slammed the door shut and jump on Rabbit and pecked out a large gouge of his hide. "Is everything alright in there?" the purty Indian nurse from Shawnee crooned out in the hallway, and the doctor answered back, "Just fine," but Rabbit slipped out of the doctor's claws and throwed open the door, like Lot don't even bother to look back at his salt-pillared wife or even gather up his overalls and Nike cross-trainers, running, I mean just a gittin' it, outta IHS with the back of his hospital gown flapping open in the breeze and head back to Weleetka faster than a jackrabbit don't even stop for Chinese food.

An Oldsmobile pulled up into Stijaati's driveway just about the time they was finished up buzzard talk. A young curly headed blonde woman stepped out, well dressed in a blue skirt and high heels. She was unloaded a wheelchair from the trunk of the car and unfolded it next to the passenger door. She opened the door and helped a right elderly man to his feet, then moved the chair underneath him. She wheeled him up to the end of the line, and Stijaati was said, "Well, hello, Seborn. And hello, Gracie. How's nursing school?" She was explained how she had finals but her great-uncle was want come and visit kinfolks so she'd picked him up at Creek Senior Citizens. None of his brothers and sister still alive to take him.

The old man was say, "Seborn Winfield Bigpond," like he forgot he was around kin and needed introduction.

Rabbit he was say, "Mr. Bigpond, I believe you went to Bacone with my dad, Opanka Choffee."

The old man was not say much just, "Don't recollect." Stijaati him a right good hand with recollections and old collections, and he got a whole stack of Bacone yearbooks amongst his treasures, one for ever year since the school begun in Indian Territory, and he picked these up at garage sales, kinfolks' attics, and thrift stores in Muskogee. Since he was graduated from there hisself—well, almost graduated, the way he tells it—he liked to keep up with Bacone alumni. Stijaati went into his house and come out with a box full of yearbooks. Stijaati pulled them outta the box until he was come to the year he wanted, and thumbed through to find a pitcher of Opanka Choffee. He handed the open yearbook to Seborn who set it on his lap and gently rested his hands on the pages. He studied the pitchers for a spell.

The old man light up and say, "Oh, yes. We was in Shakespeare Club together. We put on a production of *Troilus and Cressida*. We had a famous classmate, you know. Alex Posey, who later became the Creek writer. He played Troilus."

The old man was laugh and go on and say, "I'll tell you a funny story on Alex. This happened years after Bacone, the year Alex drowned. Well, let's see. Yes, I was gone over Eufaula way to visit Alex. You see, in the years after school, I'd become something of a local historian. Truth is I was the kind of fellow who people would run away from when they seen me coming on account of I was so full of facts and names and places and families I had to tell about. Out at the grounds they would tease me, cover their ears, call me history book. I was always pretty thick-skinned, though, and all that funning didn't hurt me none; fact is, it give me an idey. I had come upon the notion of putting together a book of my own, tell the history of what all I knew which seemed considerable. I waddn't shy neither. And maybe if I was to write it down, get it out of my system, I wouldn't have to burden friends and kin so much with all my knowledge. Naturally, I knew about Alex's writing for the school paper at Bacone, and everybody knowed he was a poet. I didn't have the least notion of how a feller might go about making stories into books, but I figured Alex must."

By now Stijaati was had remember his manners and go get food for Mr. Bigpond and set it down on the picnic table and hep him out of his chair and over to the table. Ernest put up his Epiphone into guitar case and waddles over to the line, man shall not live by hymn sing alone. Big Man and Rabbit show up I mean piled high with *sofki* and sour corn bread and grape dumplings and chicken and rice and salt pork and what all I mean sho, good. Wish I was there now. They set down. Stijaati go and get hisself a plate and come back, complaining that Rabbit took all the grape dumplings. That's one of my favorites too.

Stijaati he was go on and say, "So you was saying you knowed Alexander Posey, Mr. Bigpond?"

"That's right. Like I was telling I went over there and we sat on Alex's porch, and I commenced to pulling out old letters, newspaper clippings, family photographs, scraps of notes I'd written, and I explained the story of every one of them to Alex, down to the least scrap of paper writing. Alex was really quite busy them days, as editor of the Eufaula paper, and I think he could see that he might be sitting there with me recounting Eufaula history, and history of the old country in Alabama before that, for the next year or so. Alex was quite inersted in such things, but a person can only take so much before you start wearing him down, and I had the same effect on him as on most everybody—I just plumb overwhelmed him before I got all my stories laid out. So when Alex seen he had visitors, a wagon pulling into the farmyard, I think he was secretly happy.

"An old lady climbed down and straightened her dress and apron. Rough roads in them days, especially on a wagon. She held out her hands to a little toddler, nomores than four years old, who climbed down. He was barefooted and in overalls, nothing underneath them. The old lady was talking Indian to Alex, but Alex had never seen her before. She said, 'This is my grandson, Wotkoce Okisce, Little Coon. The Dawes Commission workers come through and called him Louis Oliver for their rolls. You worked for them, ain't it?'

" 'Yes, ma'am,' Alex offered.

" 'Well, this is my boy,' was what the old woman said. 'His mama and daddy's no longer living.'

"And that kid was a corker too. When she'd handed him down from the wagon, he'd hit the ground a-running, chasing hens under the porch and taking after the guinea fowl who was lighting off toward the woods, the whole farmyard in motion. The little boy just naturally appealed to Alex, all that orneriness was so much like hisself. He scooped him up in his arms when he went running by and walked him over to the fence-line where a pair of mules Alex's dad had give him was grazing quiet on the other side. Suddenly, it dawned on Alex. Most likely his dad was playing a prank on him, sending this strange old woman he never laid eyes on to come over and talk to him. That whole family was a mess. They went to so much trouble playing jokes on each other it would be like work to normal folks. Didn't even take a day off on Sundays. This woman was most likely someone his dad known from the Indian Baptist church Alex's mom went to. Alex decided to have a little fun hisself. They was a Creek preacher over to that church, Alex's granddaddy, and during ever sermon he preached, told the story of how be begun his ministry by practicing on mules. With the mules in the trace lines, while he was a-plowing, he'd preach to them. His congregation sometimes called him the mule preacher amongst each other when he waddn't around. 'That mule preacher, he preaches tough,' they'd say, then laugh. Alex hopped over the fence with the young'un in his arms, who was laughing and pulling the watch out of Alex's pocket. Alex went and stood behind a rusty old moldboard plow and started mimicking the preacher. The preacher had a certain way of screwing his face into a frown that

Alex knew how to exaggerate, and Alex give the mules a wicked look. Then Alex whistled, and the mules looked up, and Alex commenced to preaching to them. He preached a sermon on how Indians are better writers than white people and how Creeks are better writers than Indians. He ended his sermon by saying, 'Bonnie and Sally, this is Wotkoce Okisce, Little Coon, a beloved new Creek writer, of whom I'm right proud.'

"Alex give the little boy back to his grandmother who was grinning ear to ear. She smiled and thanked Alex, and just got back in the wagon with the boy and left. But here's the funny part of the story. Next time Alex seen his parents, he asked them, 'How's the mule preacher a-doing?' wanting to reap the benefits of his little joke. But they just stared at him like they didn't know what he was talking about. He told them about the old lady and the kid, and they let on like they didn't know a thing. Alex could never figure out if they was playing another trick on him or if they was telling the truth. Why had the old lady come all the way from Coweta to see Alex?

"The funny thing is, Alex died that year before he ever was to know that this young boy ended up going to Bacone, just like Alex did, and growing up to be a poet and writer, just like Alex had, and would even write, considerably, about Posey, including a poem written in Creek as a tribute to Alex in Littlecoon's bilingual book *Estiyut Omayat.*"

Rabbit was suck the juice off his paws and say, "Mebeso that's the rest of the story like Paul Harvey."

Mr. Bigpond seemed kindy wore out so Stijaati he was say, "Well, that boy was growed up to be a gol-durned sure enough Creek writer. In *Chasers of the Sun,* he wrote my favorite lines of poetry in the whole world." Stijaati he was stand up next to the picnic table in order to declaim:

> We gave turtles songs to sing
> > of the beginnings and the endings
> > of man.
> You tell them I said this,
> > without words,
> strapped to a woman's ankle.
> > You tell and don't forget.

The four Creeks mebeso look down and study red ants and hide tears in they eyes. Stijaati clear his throat and say, "You know I was read something about Littlecoon recently in that book I was buy at the gift shop at the Creek National Council House." Stijaati headed back to the house to rummage through his collections.

While Stijaati gone looking for his book, Rabbit was say, "One writer picked up the pen in his youth, the other in old age. Both of them's writing careers cut short. One writer wrote under the doom of statehood and end of tribal government, another under the rebirth of the Muskogee Nation, including its constitution, branches of government, tribal courts, representation by districts, Lighthorsemen, besides new social services that it never had before. One writer believed in a golden Creek past, the other wrote of his continued communion with Creek life. One writer looked admiringly and humorously at the life of traditionals, the other lived the life of a traditional with as much admiration and hilarity. One writer was educated in Territory schools in Western literary classics, the other writer received similar training but tried mostly to school hisself in Creek philosophy. One writer told Creek stories as if they were Greek myths, the other was able to tell the Creek migration story like he was there with the tribe when they was emerged from below the ground."

Stijaati come back from the house with just one book instead of big box like last time. On the cover it says, *Red on Red: Native American Literary Separatism*. Stijaati was say, "Here, page 219 and begins to read:

> The idea of the mixed-blood mediator, the Native writer who adopts European forms to record tribal stories, is especially irrelevant in Oliver's case. His understanding of the writing process is rooted in tribal vision, and, further, religious experience that is specifically Creek, including communion with the Stiloputchkogee, the Little People. In his book *Chasers of the Sun: Creek Indian Thoughts,* he says:
>
> > I with only a very meagre education, no degrees, not much schooling, but spent years as a transient, then settled down and had an urge to write in my old age. My grandmother taught me songs to sing over roots and herbs made into a tea. She taught me how to pray or meditate in the Indian way on things I so desired. So I climbed a certain mountain here to rendezvous with the "Little People" or the ethereal spirits. (*Chasers*, 27)
>
> The religious dimension of tribal writing, such a vital aspect of the artistry of more traditional writers in primary contact with their cultures, has not been recognized in recent literary analysis, perhaps because these Native authors do not easily fit into the mold of the

popular bicultural and mediation criticism. Mediation approaches emphasize the Indian writer as more of a revisionist than an artist, a borrower rather than an originator, schooled in forms known only to Native artists after contact with Europe. Oliver's example, however, shows that both the individuality of tribal vision, as in the individual seeker's quest, and the communal nature of that vision — that is, its roots in Creek ceremony — defy the notion of the simple adaptation of things European by the writer.

Oliver speaks of undergoing tribal vision as a part of his writing process that he must undertake before he can write with integrity as a tribal author. This is not to say, obviously, that Oliver was never influenced by literary forms outside of Creek culture, but so what if he was? Do we demand that any other world literature avoid contact with other cultures and then, if it fails to meet this unwieldy criteria, claim that the literature is not "pristine," no longer purely indigenous but some strange amalgamation, making analyses of the literature from indigenous perspectives impossible? Oliver's use of Western literary forms, to whatever degree he uses them, goes beyond transforming what is borrowed. Oliver *transforms himself* before he borrows them. He seeks communion with Creek spirits to learn how to write. The religious character of his writing, and that of other Native writers, cannot simply be ignored.

Further, might we be bold enough to speculate that since Indians have always had chants, songs, stories, poems, prayers, and many other types of literary and religious expression, that Oliver, and some other Native writers, might be borrowing from that tradition as much as from the novel, free-verse poem, or short story? In Oliver's writing, we see that he incorporates Creek deer songs, supernaturals from the Creek pantheon, characters out of Creek oral tradition, discussions of Creek humor, comic stories, various emphases on the relationship between narrative and Creek ceremony, and a host of other techniques that suggest this literature has its own set of rules, as unique as the literary techniques that one must study to achieve an understanding of European and American literatures.

Stijaati end his reading and close the book. Rabbit was had go to sleep under the catalpa tree, his eyes rolled back into his head and make a snore like the buzzard in Stijaati's Ford. His loud rip wakes hisself up. He begs, "Please, no more." Big Man had hepped Mr. Bigpond back into his chair, and the elder's head was had nodded over, and he is sleeping quietly in the shade of the catalpa. Big Man hisself has stretched out on the grass but can't sleep on account of a bee buzzing around his sody pop.

Big Man he was say, "Somebody must had made that guy mad sound like he got an ax to grind."

And that was as much about the Thlaako family reunion as I want to tell bout it before I get out of breath and my hand fall off.

Sincerely,
Jim Chibbo

CHAPTER SEVEN

Joy Harjo: Creek Writer from the End of the Twentieth Century

The Power of a Pan-Tribal Vision When the Writer Is Rooted in a Solid National Center

One of the strongest voices in contemporary poetry is Creek writer Joy Harjo. In the last twenty-five years, Native Americans have produced a tremendous body of first-rate poetry that often borrows from their own oral traditions of superlative song and chant and modifies the contemporary poetry scene through tribal vision. Harjo's 1989 book *Secrets from the Center of the World* and her 1990 book *In Mad Love and War* have received national critical attention and two prestigious awards, the William Carlos Williams Award and the Delmore Schwartz Memorial Poetry Prize. Harjo's themes often concern the Southwest, which has been her home for most of her adult life, but in every collection of her work there have also been poems that deal directly with Creek culture, and throughout the work a Creek sensibility pervades many of the poems. In interviews, Harjo has attributed her muse to an old Creek woman who speaks to her. In addition to writing poetry, Harjo is also a painter, filmmaker, and a musician.

Harjo's books to date include *The Last Song* (1975), *What Moon Drove Me to This?* (1980), *She Had Some Horses* (1983), *Secrets from the Center of the World* (1989), *In Mad Love and War* (1990), and *The Woman Who Fell from the Sky* (1995).[1] As John Scarry has pointed out in a useful essay on Harjo's work in the spring 1992 issue of *World Literature Today,* Harjo's poetry often contains overlapping images, perhaps influenced by her work as a painter, that move rapidly from one world to the next:

the world of dreams to the world of waking, subconsciousness to consciousness, myth to concrete experience, past to present, spiritual to physical.[2] In fact, the poetry demonstrates the ways physical and spiritual realities are constantly rubbing up against each other. As Scarry says, even though Harjo's poetry may sometimes occur in bleak landscapes filled with oppressed people, the poems show that "unity can be recovered . . . and a vision of Beauty can lead to a positive recapturing of something lost — and that all this can come to all of us at the most unlikely time and in the most unpromising place."[3]

Many critics have commented on the transformation of Harjo's poetry from the early books *The Last Song* and *What Moon Drove Me to This?* to *She Had Some Horses*, remarking that in the latter work, and the ones to follow, the poet's writing becomes more interiorized, riskier, complex, and fluid in breaking down boundaries between mythical and personal spaces. Cherokee/Quapaw critic Geary Hobson makes the observation that one of the earlier poems, "The Last Song," is a prediction that Harjo, who has spent much of her life outside of Oklahoma, will eventually return to writing about the Oklahoma landscape of her raising.[4] I wish to concur with Hobson's statement while pointing out that Harjo has never left Oklahoma as subject matter in her poetry. Hobson's prediction that the poems will, at some future date, deal more overtly with Oklahoma seems a logical one; because of the circular movement of Harjo's poetry, one would expect her to return to her last song, but the direction toward such an emphasis is already evident within her work. Harjo herself, when asked when she will physically return to Oklahoma, has said she will go back whenever she "has enough money and the right words."[5] It seems, then, that Harjo is already trying to get back to Oklahoma, and for her the journey will always be more than a physical return — the physical return, in fact, always being preceded by first trying the waters through language and imagination. If she can get the words right, she *will* be home, having incorporated Oklahoma into her sphere of experience.

Harjo's work demonstrates that connection to one's tribal nation vitalizes one's writing. For Harjo's artistry to be effective, Creekness is essential, even though this writer is pan-tribal in her concerns, lives away from Oklahoma, moves in many urban landscapes, and is influenced by feminism and other philosophies. In other words, contact with other cultures does not cancel out her Muskogean center. I would like to discuss ways in which Harjo's Creek grounding strengthens her pan-tribal vision. This brings us to an important issue. In a study such as this one, which advocates tribally specific literatures and critical approaches, how do we justify literary nationalism in relation to powerful pan-tribal movements? If we look at indigenous resistance worldwide, surely there is much to be learned from other movements, since Native peoples everywhere face some common issues, namely, the fact that the United States and other colonial powers make money by exploiting the resources of indigenous people in the Third World. That the United States enjoys the high standard of living it does has nothing to do with the myth that Americans are more hardworking than anyone else in the universe—it has to do with the fact that U.S. lifestyles are maintained by keeping the Third World in poverty and by the wealth built off the resources of Indian country, at home and abroad. Transnational corporations provide cheap consumer goods to the United States while making sure that Third World countries never develop their own resources. Howard Adams says:

> The world is awash in low-level wars today. There are almost 100 wars being fought around the globe that involve indigenous peoples, their nations and resources. Imperial nations, especially the USA, have crucial interests in every one of these conflicts. Inuit, Métis and Indian colonies have important similarities and relevance to these low-level conflicts because they contain vital rich resources, such as uranium, oil, gas, water, timber, etc. Despite the publicity of enormous aid to Third World countries, the First World (G7) takes from the Third World in raw materials twice the amount it sends in as aid. Furthermore, the debt and interest payments paid by Third World countries are three times more than all the aid they currently receive.[6]

Surely this stikes resonant historical chords with Indian country at home, where self-determination has remained an empty promise until land and resources are returned so that an economic base can be developed that will enable true self-determination. In other words, U.S. wealth is built on Native nations' poverty, specifically stolen land, water, and minerals. It is interesting to note that the Zapatista movement in Chiapas, Mexico, from its beginnings, has been anti-NAFTA, and their struggle has much to teach us about the connection between autonomy, cultural integrity, and economic issues such as taking back the land and controlling one's own resources.

Further, Leslie Silko's prophetic work *Almanac of the Dead*[7] predicts broad alliances between indigenous people, especially the tribal people of Latin America. The political reality is that U.S. Native numbers are around .5 percent of the total population, and though this is probably undercounted, it would seem that any real political clout that Indian country will be able to muster in the future might depend on looking to South America, Canada, and pressure from indigenous people worldwide, some type of "rising up," to borrow Silko's phrase from her astounding novel.

There has not been much written in terms of a major study of pantribalism's effects on Indian country, although the subject has been touched on, of course, in many other contexts. For example, Creek writer Tsianina Lomawaima, in her book on the Chilocco boarding school, entitled *They Called It Prairie Light*,[8] has some interesting things to say about cross-tribal bonds in boarding schools, and how such contact between Indian students of many tribes may have strengthened Indian identity, one of the factors that may have caused residential schools to have the opposite of their intended effects. I would like to examine pantribalism in light of one particular tribal writer, discussing ways in which Harjo's Creek grounding strengthens her pan-tribal vision and examining how tribal specificity and pan-tribalism might corroborate each other.

I would like to begin with the poem "New Orleans" from Harjo's book *She Had Some Horses* because it typifies Harjo's later work, particularly her collapse of constructed boundaries that separate time, space, myth, and personal experience. The larger meaning of the poem is also familiar turf in Harjo's poetic landscape — America's legacy of violence and greed, and the lack of consciousness of explorers like de Soto.

What makes the poem interesting for our purposes is the way tribal specificity and pan-tribal experience intersect. Travels in the Southeast, through places important to Creek history, are a catalyst for the speaker's ancestral memory, her ability to empathize, feel, and imagine this legacy of oppression faced by Native people in the Americas. These memories are not a mere romantic subjectivity; her relatives and loved ones, and the poet herself, have been to these places. In a later work, *The Woman Who Fell from the Sky*, Harjo relates that the discomfort she feels in Washington, D.C., relates not only to that city's central role in killing

Indians but to the fact that one of her biological relatives spent time
there on behalf of the tribe:

> One morning I prepared to see a friend off to Washington, D.C., to argue
> a tribe's right to water. The first time I visited there I suffered from
> vertigo and panic attacks. I saw rivers of blood flowing under the
> beautiful white marble monuments that announced power in the
> landscape. I knew of the history embedded in the city. All tribes in this
> country have sharp memories located here. My great-great-grandfather
> Monahwee went there with other tribal members to conduct business on
> behalf of the tribe. Those concerns have never been settled.[9]

Back in New Orleans, specific Creek memories aid Harjo in achieving
pan-tribal vision, as well as the poet's willingness to use her imagination to convert New Orleans to a place of meaning for Creeks: "This is
the south. I look for evidence/of other Creeks, for remnants of voices."[10]
Harjo indicates that it is actually Creek memory itself that determines
the very direction of her travels. Like the migration story, when the
people shoot the arrow and follow the course it leads, Harjo argues that
her travels are not dictated by chance, but by the paths that her ancestors
took. More specifically, she is following a story map, traveling through
Creek narrative:

> I have a memory.
>   It swims deep in blood,
> a delta in the skin. It swims out of Oklahoma,
> deep the Mississippi River. It carries my
> feet to these places . . .[11]

There are two levels to following the ancestor's migration: the way the
Creator, the Maker of Breath, draws one into such a journey beyond
one's own will or control, and the way one creates the journey oneself
by imagining those who journeyed before.

Harjo's time in New Orleans reminds her of one of the tragedies of
removal, Creeks drowned in the Mississippi River.

> There are voices buried in the Mississippi
> mud. There are ancestors and future children
> buried beneath the currents stirred up by
> pleasure boats going up and down.
> There are stories here made of memory.[12]

Michael Green's book *The Creeks* records the observations of one eye-witness to the Creeks being shipped up the Mississippi to Little Rock during removal in the 1830s, and this observer coments on contractors who chartered

> rotten, old, and unseaworthy boats, because they were of a class to be
> procured cheaply; and then to make those increased profits still larger,
> the Indians were packed upon these crazy vessels in such crowds, that
> not the slightest regard seems to have been paid to their safety, comfort,
> or even decency. The crammed condition of the decks and cabins was
> offensive to every sense and feeling, and kept the poor creatures in a
> state unfit for human beings.[13]

Not surprisingly, two of these boats collided: "The *Monmouth*, was being piloted up the wrong side of the river by a drunken crew and collided with another boat, the *Trenton*. There were more than 600 Creeks on the *Monmouth*, and when the boat broke up and sank, more than 300 of them drowned. Most of the survivors were badly scalded by steam after the boat's boilers burst."[14]

Though her ancestors may have drowned near this city, Harjo refuses to allow the submergence of memory. By relying specifically on Creek history for the contents of her poetry, and, most importantly, imagining that history, she fights the temptation to be pulled under the waters of forgetfulness, to bury the pain under a river of denial—Tie-Snake's hypnotic pull comes from the most surprising of water holes. Of equal importance is Harjo's use of pan-tribalism here, her ability to recast Creek history in the larger context of the violence that created America out of the suffering of Indian people, to place herself within the ongoing story of that history, an act that sometimes pains her. As the speaker says in "New Orleans":

> My spirit comes here to drink
> My spirit comes here to drink.
> Blood is the undercurrent.

Empathy and imagination are not always fun when "blood is the undercurrent." This is not the romantic stuff of ancestors calling from hill-sides, but a confrontation of the legacy of colonialism.

Moving on to a later book, *In Mad Love and War*, I would like to examine the poem "Deer Dancer." The Creek specificity of "Deer Dancer" is interesting in light of Harjo's other poetry where deer are recurring and powerful images. Historically, deer were central to Creek food supplies before contact, then important to the Creek economy through trade with the English.[15] In the changing postcontact world thrust upon the Creeks, deer allowed for Creek national survival through trade, so when Harjo refers to the Deer Dancer's fawn as "a blessing of meat," this reflects the historical reality that Creeks are indebted to deer for their livelihood. In this context, deer can also be taken as a symbol of adaptability, survival in the face of change, shifting worlds, and the power to transcend boundaries.

Further, in Southeastern tribal storytelling traditions are variants of the story of the hunter who goes off with a deer, falls asleep in the deer world, is dressed up by the deer's kin in deerskin and antlers, and is transformed into a deer himself. His family's attempts to bring him back to human existence end fatally. The story is similar to the bear transformation stories that will be discussed shortly. This old story is reflected in Harjo's lines "No one knew her, the stranger whose tribe we recognized, her family related to deer, if that's who she was, a people accustomed to hearing songs in pine trees, and making them hearts."[16]

The poem is a transformation poem, about the lure of other worlds, like Leslie Silko's "Story from Bear Country." In Silko's poem, the words work like an incantation—by the time the bear song is over, it is already too late; the listener has been lured into the bear world. At the end of the poem, the reader/listener realizes that the "you" who has been referred to throughout is herself, and the speaker urges her:

Go ahead
turn around
see the shape
of your footprints
in the sand.[17]

Silko's poem is one of the most effective illustrations of the philosophy behind chant in existence, the way that ritual language causes transformation.

Cherokees also have stories of men lured off into the bear world. The bear world is kind of like a candy shop or endless summer vacation—it is a world where the normal responsibilities of human daily life do not apply. The attempts of family to retrieve the bear-men sometimes fail because during the quarantine period, as the former bears become reaccustomed to human society, they die of bear sickness, like someone who succumbs from the bends after surfacing too quickly from deep waters. Memory is a key factor in the bear transformation; once you are pulled off into the bear world, your human existence is a vague blur, and even if you want to go back, you may not remember enough to be able to leave. Ethnographer James Mooney's collection of Cherokee narratives contains a number of stories about the bear world.

Harjo puts a different twist on these other worlds. Rather than worlds of release from responsibility, they become the hope for an improvement in *this world*, the world of human existence. Memory, as we have seen in "New Orleans," is essential to Harjo's Creek philosophy. In addition to the positive aspects of ancestral memory, there are five hundred years of genocide that also haunt Indian memory, making escaping with Deer Woman, going off into the deer world—a world untainted by colonialism, a world where environment and community are restored—a real temptation. Yet this is not a pipe dream, an evasion of human responsibility; this is a belief that the Americas will once again eventually return to some form of indigenous consciousness. This is the world of "Buffalo Woman come back," as Henry Jack the drunk says in "Deer Dancer."

Thus Harjo politicizes the Southeastern transformation idea and brings out the larger meaning for all tribal peoples by making the lure to other worlds the imagining of life without colonialism. This is what makes Harjo's poetry so optimistic—not only does she critique oppressive systems, but she is able to imagine their absence. Harjo first takes up specifically Creek concerns with the deer transformation theme and then opens up the meaning to include other worlds as well. The process of decolonizing one's mind, a first step before one can achieve a political consciouness and engage oneself in activism, has to begin with imagining some alternative. In other words, the pan-tribal meaning of the poem is the belief that tribal consciousness is returning in a new unity that transcends old tribal boundaries.

Harjo and the poets of her generation are key players in the history of this pan-tribalism. Because of a growing urban population in the fifties (when Indians from many tribes were thrown together in large cities by federal relocation programs), the rise of Indian activism in the sixties and seventies, and training centers such as the Institute of American Indian Arts, a new history began to emerge that involved an indigenous awareness that crossed tribal lines. Shifts in thinking about what it meant to be Indian started to occur as early as the late fifties, when the kind of mentality of assimilation and erasing Indianness that was so much a part of federal boarding schools—and programs like relocation and termination—began to be questioned. Robert Warrior and Paul Chaat Smith trace this philosophical shift in the chapter "Fancy Dance Revolution" in *Like a Hurricane*. This kind of conceptual shift, and the pan-tribal contact that fostered it, was necessary before anyone could even conceive of himself or herself as a Native poet or artist, since under the older ideology, any traces of Indianness were to be forgotten. Even the term "Native poet" is pan-tribal in conception.

Pan-tribal awareness becomes especially apparent in the poem "Song for the Deer and Myself to Return On," where the speaker recalls singing a song for hunting deer taught to her by Creek elder Louis Oliver:

> It works, of course, and the deer came into this room
> and wondered at finding themselves
> in a house near downtown Denver.
> Now the deer and I are trying to figure out a song
> to get them back, to get all of us back,
> because if it works I'm going with them.
> And it's too early to call Louis
> and nearly too late to go home. (*Mad*, 30)

"To go home" here is more than heading back to Albuquerque; it is the state of the Native Union where the hoop is no longer broken, lands are returned, people are in control of their own resources; in other words, going home to vibrant Native nationalism, to real self-determination.

Harjo further broadens the Creek images in "Deer Dancer" by relating the woman out of Southeastern tribal motifs to Harjo's ideas about imagination. By the end of the poem, the speaker reveals that she never witnessed the events she is narrating; she is, in fact, "making up" the story. The narrator emphasizes, however, that even though she is inventing her story, it is no less real. This strategy is repeated in many places in Harjo's poetry, a conscious recognition of the imagining, like a person suddenly realizing she is dreaming. The poems build toward this moment, with clues that we are in the dream world, but there is usually an epiphany where this is made clear, such as in "Deer Dancer": "She borrowed a chair for the stairway to heaven and stood on a table of names" (*Mad*, 6). This is a little reminiscent of Dali's juxtaposition of concrete images rooted in reality and abstract ones that defy natural law, and with a similar comic playfulness. What the revelatory moment in Harjo's work involves is the realization that dreaming and waking, natural and supernatural, are deeply intertwined, and moments of grace reveal these intricate relationships.

These revelations involve both power and pain, since experience is recreated during the vision, as in the oral tradition when stories are performed and the events come to pass through the experiential intensity of active telling and listening. Harjo often looks back at her experiences, and sixteen and seventeen, her early teenage years, seem to be critical ones for her. What is significant about this time period, viewed from the vantage point of the poet's adult life, is not only the magic of the retrospective re-creation of events but the fact that the troubled sixteen year old comes alive again, in the artistic moment, through the aesthetic evocation of memory. The poet must once again face the pain of this troubled teenager. Creation and destruction are evoked in the same artistic act. In the poem "Javelina," Harjo says:

> I want to stop the car, and tell her she will find her way out of the soap opera. *The mythic world will enter with the subtlety of a snake the color of earth changing skin. Your wounded spirit is the chrysalis for a renascent butterfly. Your son will graduate from high school. You have a daughter not yet born, and you who thought you could say nothing, write poetry.* (*Mad,* 31)

It is as if this younger woman, weighed down by fear, self-hatred, anger — in other words, the legacy of colonialism — is seen from afar, a blur on a distant shore, the poet no longer burdened in the same way as this young woman; yet the girl's story is a very important part of her history all the same. Maybe the speaker in this poem is one of the bear world exceptions, an example of someone lured off into the bear world, which is difficult, and sometimes impossible, to return from, yet she was able to come back, one of the fortunate ones who found the right medicine to restore consciousness and memory. The last phrase of the poem seems so powerful to me, the speaker surviving racism and the American education system responsible for feeling she "could say nothing" and finding her way toward hearing her own voice, trusting knowledge generated inside her own tribe.

More than just an individual return of voice, the prophecy of the speaker's recovery from speechlessness to authorship stands in as a powerful symbol of the evolution of Indian writers and Native writing itself over the last couple hundred years. This intellectual recovery is no less amazing than the beginnings of physical recovery from genocide we have seen in Native populations this century, which have increased every decade since about 1910. As Harjo says in the poem "Anchorage," this is "the fantastic and terrible story of all of our survival / those who were never meant / to survive."[18]

If we look at the direction of Indian narrative from Christian conversion accounts in the early nineteenth century, to autobiographies written with white collaborators in the second half of that century, to the assimilationist dogma written at the turn of the century by writers like Bonnin, Eastman, and Montezuma closely associated with the Society of American Indians working to bring Indians into the American mainstream, to the novelists of the 1920s and 1930s writing about the tragic mixed-blood and his or her cultural and generational conflicts, to the homecoming novels of the Native American Renaissance of the 1970s and 1980s, to the more radically political and unconventional recent works, we see an incredible movement from the earliest convictions among these writers that they could "say nothing" about tribal experience to an examination of tribal cultures themselves as the means of creating new literary strategies.

In addition to using the personal and tribal to represent broader issues applicable to the history of Native authorship, Harjo continuously broadens her personal experiences of Creek memory, bringing them up to a larger pan-tribal level by arguing that recording the destruction of colonialism is the very responsibility of the tribal poet. In another poem, in regards to the death of Indian men in Oakland, she says, "If I am a poet who is charged with speaking the truth (and I believe the word *poet* is synonomous with truth-teller), what do I have to say about all of this?" (*Woman*, 19). For Harjo, tribal memory does not merely serve as a quick, romantic "ancestral moment." Memory should result in telling and speaking, and, especially, resisting, a combination of imagination, words, and deeds.

In the poem entitled "A Postcolonial Tale," which precedes the commentary just quoted, if one interprets the phrase "rising up" the way Silko uses that phrase in *Almanac of the Dead* (where such language involves a prophecy that Indians will take back the Americas), we have a much darker poem. One of the reasons Silko's novel was so unpopular in comparison to her earlier works was because she refused to divest ancestral memory from the responsibility that such memory implies. If one has racial memory, then one of the primary recollections has to be the fact of genocide and land theft, and the ancestors may have more in mind than quick spiritual highs; perhaps a call to action is being elicited. This darkens the phrase "rising up" in the last line of Harjo's poem considerably:

> No story or song will translate the full impact of falling, or
> the inverse power of rising up.
> Of rising up. (*Woman*, 18)

To return for just a while longer to the Southeastern Indian idea of the deer world, in another poem entitled "Deer Ghost," a poem where the speaker recalls the pain of the loss of a significant relationship, the Creek images illuminate both the personal and the political. The poet begins by telling Creek history:

> I hear a deer outside; her glass voice of the invisible calls my heart to
> stand up and weep in this fragile city. The season changed once more, as
> if my childhood was forced from me, stolen during the dream of the lion
> fleeing the old-style houses my people used to make of mud and straw to
> mother the source of burning . . . (*Mad*, 29)

Harjo's father is Tiger Clan, and references to tigers, lions, and panthers can be found in other places in her work (the Creek clan name refers, of course, to panther). The lion is "fleeing the old-style houses," and it is interesting to contrast the "old-style" Creek life with the poet's urban wanderings, since she seems to be a wanderer like panther. Traditionally, Creeks were decidedly antinomadic, settling along rivers, growing corn individually and communally, and fishing and hunting fairly close to home rather than following buffalo herds over great distances like Northern Plains people. The traditional migration story, seen in light of Creek history, seems like a prophecy that warns "though you may like to settle down, you'll experience many different upheavals." In Harjo's poem here, she faces the reality of displacement, past and present: given the complexity of contemporary Native life and the demographic reality that more than half the Native population in the United States lives in urban cities, in what ways does one maintain a connection to a national homeland and culture? This question is a central concern in evaluating the effects of pan-tribalism.

The answer, given what we have seen thus far in Harjo's poetry, is no surprise. The relationship held in living memory, in hearing and telling stories, in "making things up," is the key to bringing the homeland into urban landscapes. Harjo's vision of pan-tribalism, however, does not endorse Indian genericism, writing that obscures concrete tribal and land relationships, but rather engenders a type of Creek specificity that takes on larger meaning for all tribal peoples because of its very grounding in the poet's own culture, a rootedness that comes out of her willingness to imagine and learn about her own tribe.

In the next poem, the poet emphasizes that her imagining is not merely the result of dreamy yearning, or wistful romanticism, but a survival technique rooted in Creek history:

2.
. . . I am lighting the fire that crawls from my spine to the gods with a coal from my sister's flame. This is what names me in the ways of my people, who have called me back. The deer knows what it is doing wandering the streets of this city; it has never forgotten the songs.

3.
I don't care what you say. The deer is no imaginary tale I have created to fill this house because you left me. There is more to this world than I have ever let on to you, or anyone. (*Mad*, 29)

That the poem is so Muskogee-centric is evident in its images: "Lighting the fire . . . with a coal from my sister's flame" is pregnant with Creek meanings that surround fire, perhaps the most cogent of Creek symbols, given its prominent place at the ceremonial grounds, where fire is ritualistically cleansed, the old fires being cleaned out and the new fires rekindled. There is also the story of Creeks carrying the embers from the square grounds all the way from Alabama to Oklahoma during Indian Removal and rekindling the sacred fire on their arrival in their new home. Then there is the traditional Creek story of Rabbit's theft of fire where a trickster act ultimately results in fire being brought to hearth and home. Fire has an intrinsic relationship to sun, another important aspect of Creek theology. Harjo's poem suggests that one can take up migratory paths if these sacred relationhips are held in active memory, if one remembers these story connections, the act of memory itself a cleansing and rekindling of old fires. As we have seen, the original Creek migration that begins Creek history, according to Louis Oliver's rendering of it, traveled through both the geography of the Southeast and the geography of thought as people speculated about the sun's origins (which are also, in Creek thought, the origins of fire, their most sacred element, the fire being a kind of incarnation of the sun on earth). Memory, for Harjo, is a specifically Creek experience.

Another poem rooted deeply in Oklahoma and Creek experience is "Autobiography." The Creek images here work up, in cumulative fashion, to a cross-tribal identification with a man from Jemez Pueblo in New Mexico who reminds the speaker of her own flesh and blood: "And I talked to him as if he were my father, with that respect, that hunger" (*Mad*, 15). Throughout Harjo's poetry, one often finds encounters with Native street people, with whom Harjo always identifies, sometimes painfully when encountering friends who have fallen on bad times, other times as sources of power, and usually as both.

But first let's examine how the poet arrives at this powerful moment when tribal and familial boundaries collapse. The poem begins with the idea of theft, of Oklahoma as occupied territory, and the battering of Native self-esteem that occurs every day because of the foreign invaders who flaunt their criminal activities so proudly by legitimating them through the lie they call Oklahoma history.

Harjo says, "We lived next door to the bootlegger, and were lucky. The bootlegger reigned. We were a stolen people in a stolen land. Oklahoma meant defeat. But the sacred lands have their own plans, seep through fingers of the alcohol spirit. Nothing can be forgotten, only left behind" (*Mad*, 14). There is a lot going on in these few lines, including the idea that alcohol has been used as chemical warfare on this continent. Students of Creek history know that every land cession that the Creeks made was preceded by the signatories being plied with huge amounts of rum, big-time partying before treaty signing.

As Harjo indicates, however, "the sacred lands have their own plans," and this can be witnessed by comparing Creek geography in Alabama to Oklahoma. As Louis Oliver discusses in his naming of the old Alabama towns, towns in Indian Territory were given their old names, and even the spatial and cultural relationships between upper and lower Creek towns were duplicated, as well as settlement patterns along major rivers; in Oklahoma the new towns were laid out along and between the lower and upper forks of the Oktahutche, the Canadian River. Thus the poet's phrase "Nothing can be forgotten, only left behind" is evident even by a cursory comparison of a map of eastern Oklahoma and Alabama, where many of the town names are replicated by Creek memory reinventing itself in a new landscape. Then there is the larger pan-tribal meaning of the poem — that tribal consciousness has found ways of maintaining itself under the most adverse of circumstances, that so much of indigenous culture remains intact and evolving.

In the next stanza of the prose poem are more references to deer and panther, two animal beings who, as we have seen, wander through Harjo's poetry frequently, deer being central to Creek economy and life, and panther being her father's clan:

> Dreams aren't glass and steel but made from the hearts of deer, the blazing eye of a circling panther. Translating them was to understand the death count from Alabama, the destruction of grandchildren, famine of stories. I didn't think I could stand it. My father couldn't. He searched out his death with the vengeance of a warrior who has been the hunted. It's in our blood. (*Mad,* 14)

The reference is made to the death count in Alabama, which was at least half the tribe, as discussed in the beginning of chapter 1, "The Creek Nation." What is interesting here is that the poet focuses as much on the death of imagination that follows a holocaust as the decimation of population, and the result is not only the "destruction of grandchildren" but a "famine of stories" — physical and imaginative death. Healthy people survive through storytelling, but sometimes the pain is so great that people bury themselves in silence and internalized anger, then pass this fear on to their children; and this, evidently, is the experience of Harjo's father as seen in the last four sentences of the poem.

The midnight encounter with the Jemez man shows how this internalized shame, anger, and fear affects Native people differently: "We had all been cheated. He hid his shame beneath a cold, downy blanket. We hid ours in poems" (*Mad,* 15). In the same poem, we discover the reason for some of Harjo's strong feelings for street people because she indicates that under systems of oppression there is a very thin line between the poet and the homeless; both are responding to stolen lives and cultures, albeit in different ways.

Harjo moves the poem from the Creek and Oklahoma themes to broader issues of tribal consciousness by focusing on the common legacy that Indian people have under colonialism. Though tribal groups have different languages, different ceremonies, different religions, different economies, different histories, different forms of government, they all share a legacy of stolen land, decimated populations, and engineered cultural theft. Sharing one's home with the bootlegger next door culminates in encountering the man from Jemez, a living example of what it means to live in a stolen land. The poet associates the Jemez man's pain with her father, who turned his pain inward: "And I talked to him as if he were my father, with that respect, that hunger" (*Mad*, 15). The idea of hunger is interesting here, especially given the earlier phrase "famine of story," and the narrator seems to long for the connection that language brings, to long for a father figure who can provide meaning for his daughter so that her lot will be a better one, a story to make sense of it all, if in fact five hundred years of genocide can be explained.

There is hope, though, because the poet does in fact survive; the one who thought she could say nothing has discovered that language and memory seem to be her two most potent tools. The poem circles back to Creek concerns and ends with a quintessential Creek line that is hauntingly beautiful, as well as hopeful: "Yesterday there was rain traveling east to home. A hummingbird spoke. She was a shining piece of invisible memory, inside the raw cortex of songs. I knew then this was the Muscogee season of forgiveness, time of new corn, the spiraling dance" (*Mad*, 15).

There are poems in *In Mad Love and War* that foreshadow the extremely dense poetry of Harjo's next book, *The Woman Who Fell from the Sky*. One wonders where to begin in attempting to unravel these poems because an effect of simultaneity is created within their language, where ideas are flying at the reader from every direction. The structure and the style of them reinforce their theme — that physics and love, the ordinary and extraordinary, reality and the supernatural, are not oppositions but close kin, deeply embedded inside each other. That ideas are deeply embedded inside other ideas is readily seen when trying to quote lines from these poems. Often one cannot quote the needed phrase to demonstrate a point without quoting part of another phrase that is connected to the sentence but goes off toward a completely new concept embedded in yet another part of the poem. It is like trying to remove a section of a spiderweb.

"Original Memory," from *In Mad Love and War*, is an early poem that leads to this later dense work, a complicated piece that resists easy analysis yet contains many central Creek, as well as pan-tribal, concerns. In a breathless string of rapid-fire associations, the poet links, among other things, doubt, time's resistance to categories, political torture, the use of time as a colonial construct, contrasts between the Muskogee world and the Western world, lost lovers, relatives, recalling and narrating memory, and chance.

Given this structure, rather than trying to pull out every Creek image or theme, I want to talk about an overriding issue, Rabbit's — that is, Choffee's — presence in the poem. Choffee is the Muskogee trickster. Chippewa writer Gerald Vizenor has given trickster a decidedly postmodern edge, associating trickster's resistance to definition and his shape-shifting abilities with postmodern ideas about the infinite signification of language. I would like simply to point out that trickster is only one figure in Native cosmogony and that he is balanced out by many others. Trickster is not the cultural norm, which is part of the reason people laugh at him. He is goofy, sometimes even dangerous; at other times, his jokes work toward cultural transformation, and often he is a little of all these things. Poised somewhere between Choffee's theft of fire from the stomp grounds, when he runs amok and sets the surrounding woods ablaze, and the other extreme possibility of strict adherence to rules and regulations so that the status quo is always maintained is a delicate world of balance with enough rule breaking to foster cultural change and enough rule abiding to avoid chaos.

In traditional Muskogean thought, there is a balance of oppositions wherein the people seek in ceremony and daily life to keep Upper World from predominating Lower World, Lower World from predominating This World, and so on. It seems to me that Choffee's antics might teach us that it is possible to run off with ideas, too, to allow skepticism to override reverence for language, an emphasis on meaninglessness over possibilities for communication, the failure of the word over the power of the word, postmodern chance over the ordered worlds of Native creation stories, deconstructed Indian identity over cultural cohesion. It is interesting that every time Harjo introduces the chaotic misdoings of Rabbit, a discussion of love as a real force that holds the universe together follows close behind; that is, she strives for a balance between chance and order, following the Muskogean idea of the balance of opposites.

I would like to pause for a moment to examine this Creek philosophy further, since I believe Harjo's poetry is deeply informed by these concepts of purity and balance, analogy and opposition. The Muskogean world is divided into three categories: the Upper World, the Lower World, and This World. The Upper World is the sky world, a looming concern in *The Woman Who Fell from the Sky*. The Lower World is the water and underground realms, and This World is the earth's surface where humans live. These divisions are spiritual as well as geographic and stratospheric. Upper World and Lower World are opposed to each other, and humans are in the middle, in a fragile balance between the three worlds. Creek medicine often involves playing one side off against another to restore things to their proper scheme when someone is sick or events have gone awry. The Upper World is a realm of order and periodicity because of the lunar cycle and planetary orbits. The Lower World is one of chaos, though also of fertility. This World, where humans live, is a less ideal version of the Upper World. Rivers, lakes, and caves are entrance points to the underworld. Hudson discusses these ideas extensively in his book *The Southeastern Indians*,[19] as does Joel Martin in *The Sacred Revolt*.

The Southeastern theory of diseases illustrates the balance of oppositions between the cosmic forces. Hudson says:

> Men must necessarily hunt to live, and as long as they have a properly respectful attitude toward the animals they kill, the animals are not offended. But when men kill animals disrespectfully or carelessly, the animals are offended and exact vengeance on men by causing them to have diseases specific to their offenses. However, when diseases occur, men can use plants, which men seldom offend, as medicine to cure the diseases. (156–57)

The evolution of this relationship can be seen in the Cherokee story about how the animals, angered at man's cruel practice of killing their fellows, met and devised various illnesses as revenge (Hudson, 340). This concept of analogy is called sympathetic medicine by ethnographers. Herbals are prescribed to treat disease because they resemble some feature of an illness or condition. Slippery elm, for instance, might be taken to make things slippery, for pregnant women giving birth, or as an enema, as in a comic and scatological story my grandmother tells about *her* grandmother, who gave the stuff to a man who'd been constipated for days.

As an example of association, Creeks sometimes believe that if a person dreams of fire, it means that she and her family might fall ill with fever. Sleeplessness can be associated with raccoons because of their nocturnal activities. An extensive discussion of how all this works can also be found in Willie Lena, himself Seminole, and James Howard's book *Oklahoma Seminoles: Medicine, Magic, and Religion*.

These associations have to be kept in mind when treating diseases or problems—a counterbalance has to be employed. For example, "fire, the Sun's earthly representative, was also frequently called upon to fight disease. Since fire was a thing of the Upper World, it was used in curing diseases caused by animals of the Under World, including turtles, snakes, and fish. When a medicine had to be drunk, it was often strengthened with the power of fire by dropping four or seven live coals into it" (Hudson, 172).

When one force is out of hand, prevailing over another, the force that is opposed to the inappropriate one is sought for aid (Hudson, 319). One might note that the call-and-response format of Creek stomp dance music could be a structural representation of this worldview that would strive to prevent one force from dominating another: for example, a song leader singing verses echoed by men singers repeating and improvising on his phrases, women shell shakers balanced by men singers, and so on.

Another example, from Southeastern incantations for disease, is to elicit a cure by invoking the spiritual enemies of whatever is causing the disease. If a disease is caused by a fish, a fish hawk might be called to come and seize the invader (Hudson, 346–47). The spiritual balancing forces are called upon. Examples of how this works in Southeastern incantations, which formulate a tremendous body of powerful poetry, can be found in many of the books of the Kilpatricks, a husband-wife team who were both Cherokees fluent in their language.[20]

This belief system is acted out in ceremony where there is the ritual separation of "opposed" categories: birds/four-footeds, fire/water, male/female. During the course of normal human existence there is wear and tear on the categories, which is to say people screw up and do things wrong; there is pollution of the sacred. The purpose of ceremony is to overcome pollution through ritual separation so that the categories can be clarified and cleansed (Hudson, 317). Fire is the ultimate symbol of man's struggle against pollution. The sacred ceremonial fire becomes polluted when people disobey rules; thus the need for a new fire each year (318).

As an example of Harjo's concern for balance, in "Original Memory," Rabbit is critiqued because he doubts the order of creation: "But here is a heart betrayed by childhood catastrophe, or tormented by original memory, memory as old as Rabbit's heart cracking open because he couldn't believe in the perfection of newborn sea perch, or the yawning of the first corn sprout, and let loose doubt into the world in the shape of humans" (*Mad*, 47). Rabbit cannot accept the notion of an ordered and meaningful creation. I wonder if this doubt later took the shape of critical theorists, but that is my own bias. Yet this is not to say that postmodernism's resistance to centers, meaning, coherence, and teleology is entirely antithetical to Native viewpoints, nor that contemporary theory should be abandoned, only that it should be examined critically as to its value in illuminating Native cultures. To my understanding, Harjo, Rabbit, and Creek philosophy suggest that this is to be done with an eye for balance.

Harjo's poem, in fact, concedes the value of a little ambiguity by recognizing Rabbit's insistence on remaining undefined, the power of mystery over definition, the role of the gamble in modern life, the arbitrariness of time as a construct, the need for laughter, not just seriousness. Muskogeans would not abandon the Lower World's chaos in favor of the Upper World's cycles and order; neither does the poet ignore the creative power of shape-shifting in certain contexts. The poem even ends with Rabbit pulling another trick out of his hat: "Rabbit, who invented the saxophone and who must have invented our imaginary lovers, laughs through millennia. And who are we to make sense of this slit of impossible time" (*Mad*, 48).

Further, the Creek cultural trickster, Choffee, provides the context for an important strategic move Harjo makes by using the idea of the Muskogee world to decenter the assumption that things European are normative. If one is always reacting *against* Eurocentrism, then Europe is still the center. If one argues, for example, that Creek warfare in the eighteenth century was not any more barbaric than the Spanish Inquisition, one maintains that Europe is still the moral barometer by which everything is gauged. Harjo rejects such a center (she does not discuss warfare in the poem, this is merely a hypothetical example), and this is the positive side of Rabbit's disruption, his tendency to throw things off balance, to confuse centers and margins, inside and outside: "When I am inside the Muscogee world, which is not a flip side of the Western time chain but a form of music staggered in the ongoing event of earth calisthenics, the past and the future are the same tug-of-war" (*Mad*, 47).

In other words, the Muskogee world is not the opposite of the Western world, *it is a world that must be judged by its own merits, in its own terms.* This is the argument of this study, that Native literatures deserve to be judged by their own criteria, in their own terms, not merely in agreement with, or reaction against, European literature and theory. The Native Americanist does not bury her head in the sand and pretend that European history and thought do not affect Native literature, nor does she ignore the fact that Native literature has quite distinctive features of its own that call for new forms of analyses. On another political level, Native Americans have the right, for whatever reasons they choose, to decide how to evaluate their literatures, just as white critics, for decades, have formulated schools of thoughts according to their own dictates.

Harjo's latest book, *The Woman Who Fell from the Sky*, not only falls in line with Hobson's aforementioned prediction that her work will ever increasingly deal with Oklahoma but marks an even more radical evolution from her earlier poems than does the change between the first two chapbooks and *She Had Some Horses*. As the title indicates, the major theme holding the poetry together in this new book is sky world concerns; more specifically, physics, stars, overlapping universes, space, motion, whirling orbitals, the speed of light. These highly conceptual poems are sophisticated and resist easy analysis.

Whereas the first shift in Harjo's poetry was characterized by a deep interiorization, the poet's delving far into the space of the subconscious, especially in its relation to myth, these new poems are deeply exteriorized, pointing to overlapping energies throughout the universe, the interconnectedness of all things, and, like the earlier poems, tying these forces together with myth, a uniting factor that causes both interior and exterior worlds to cohere.

Harjo sees myth as an ongoing, relevant expression, the deepest part of human consciousness, as well as a fundamental reality. Regarding the Creek water monster Tie-Snake, she says, "*He is still present today in the lakes and rivers of Oklahoma and Alabama, a force we reckon with despite the proliferation of inventions that keep us from ourselves*" (*Woman*, 17; italics in the original). This story, entitled "The Flood," recounts a woman who has encountered Tie-Snake at various times in past lives. The woman may be symbolic, in some ways, of all sixteen-year-old girls choosing between filial obedience and independence and exploring incipient sexuality, but Tie-Snake is real. In other poems, Harjo does this also, looks back at the young girl who she used to be with distance, irony, sometimes humor, and other times with amazement at her former pain and confusion. In "The Flood" Harjo argues that part of the dilemma of modern identity, which creates this kind of confusion, is the way in which contemporary culture generates its own metamyth in order to distance itself from the true role of myth as a function of humans understanding themselves.

Further, in Creek cosmogony, Tie-Snake is an anomalous creature combining features of the Lower World and This World; not only does he appear to be a fish and serpent, but he has horns. This demonstrates a distinctively Southeastern tribal philosophy, an acceptance of "queerness," if you will, incorporating into the belief system beings who go against what is normal, who defy explanation through the usual status quo definitions, what Hudson calls "anomalies." Rather than disrupting society, anomalies actually reify the existing social order. Anomalous beings can also be powerful; queerness has an important place. Phenomena that do not fit "normal" categories are ascribed special powers. For instance, the Lower World is a world of monsters but also of water, fertility, and a means of coping with evil. That which is anomalous is also an important source of power. The Southeastern belief system is not an oppositional world of good and evil.

Anomalies actually reinforce the categorization process of Upper World, Lower World, and This World because the categories do not have to be thrown away when the unexplainable occurs; the anomalies can be attributed to special powers (Hudson, 148). Queerness actually reinforces straightness in this way because it can be explained as extraordinary exceptions with special powers that do not cancel out the belief in the categories. Hudson explains Southeastern beliefs thus:

> Because of our ability to store information in written form and on magnetic tapes, we have an incredibly large number of categories with which to classify the things in the world around us. If we encounter something which does not neatly fit into a preexisting category, then we simply create a new one.
>
> But among the preliterate people like the Southeastern Indians, who had to carry all their categories in their heads, the case was quite different. Lacking writing, the number of categories at their disposal was tiny as compared to ours. And given such a small number of categories, they necessarily encountered things which did not neatly fit, things which fell into two or more categories. Thus anomalies and abominations were inevitable. But instead of throwing their classification system asunder, the Southeastern Indians held up the bear, the owl, the cougar, and so on, as special animals, investing them with

special meaning in their world view. Moreover, they created the Uktena and the Water Cougar, creatures even more anomalous than the bear, the owl, and the cougar, making them at the same time objects of fear and power. And so by deliberately holding these anomalies up to public view, they shored up the integrity of their classification system. (Hudson, 148)

Harjo probably does not necessarily endorse this ultrarational anthropological explanation about the "creation" of categories, as if they are arbitrary ex post facto explanations for primitive people to explain the things they do not understand; she simply insists on the primacy of myth for Muskogeans, past and present. Tie-Snake's anomalous nature, however, does relate to Harjo's poem. One of the superlative qualities of "The Flood" is the deftness and fluidity with which the story moves between past and present, so that ultimately the life of the contemporary Muskogee young woman drowned in a drinking-related incident and her Creek kinswoman who is visited by Tie-Snake cannot be distinguished as separate story strands. The poem is about the complexity of memory—memory itself being anomalous. The very structure of the story's sentences are modeled after the notion of anomaly, the disruption of the boundaries between worlds, as the poet moves between water and land, present and past, myth and "hard reality," like the amphibian that she is. In both the poem and Muskogean philosophy, boundaries between "queer" and "normal" are challenged. The queer world is as necessary toward the all-important function of balance as the normal world. A Muskogean world opens up a circle of inclusion that lets queerness in rather than driving it out.

Any tribal poet, himself or herself, is a queer, anomalous creature. The tribal poet finds himself or herself writing stuff read by non-Indians yet trying to write for his or her tribe, having to engage in the business of selling books through agents and publishers yet striving for cultural integrity, often living away from home yet retaining one's primary landscape in imagination and memory and transforming it into art, preserving one's culture for future generations yet trying not to give away anything one's community believes should not be shared, and on and on it goes. In Louis Oliver's case, we saw how his education put him in an awkward relationship to his community that reminded him of Tie-Snake's betweenness. Tie-Snake is almost like the person who goes off to the bear world or the deer world, as if when he is brought back to human society, he only makes it halfway, forever stuck between worlds and bearing in his body signs of both. I think many Native writers feel that way, too.

Ray Young Bear, in *Black Eagle Child: The Facepaint Narratives,*[21] writes about the "wall of words" that begins to distance Edgar from his best friend, Ted, as Edgar takes up the road of the literary artist, and the way such a role even distances him from the rest of the Mesquakie community where he lives. The author's most dramatic symbol of this is when Edgar is imprisoned inside a cocoon of paper, and he writes his stories on the inside of this cocoon that has entombed him, another example of suspension between worlds. The Native literary artist's writing affects her relationship to her tribal community, which is her home, making narration not entirely unlike the watery Tie-Snake hole, the threshold between Upper and Lower Worlds. There is both a magnetic pull that surrounds such places and the danger of being sucked under. Ultimately, most tribal writers decide that the role of truth telling and contributing to their cultures is worth the risks involved. Harjo certainly dives into these waters, mustering as much integrity and honesty as she can in the process.

Harjo's Science of Love

In *The Woman Who Fell from the Sky,* Harjo unites story and science. Harjo's universe is held together by stories as much as gravity. It is myth that allows Harjo to explore the world of physics without ever abandoning the personal. Harjo's science is a wholistic one informed by love that keeps inquiry, discovery, and exploration in check, given the history of the employment of the scientific method as a tool of colonization. In fact, Harjo's brand of physics, or metaphysics, claims that love *is* relativity:

> You can manipulate words to turn departure into aperture, but you cannot figure the velocity of love and how it enters every equation. It's related to the calculation of the speed of light, and how light prevails. (*Woman*, 62)

Lack of love, the poet claims, is the loss of relativity: "Being in love can make the connections between all life apparent—whereas lovelessness emphasizes the absence of relativity" (30). The possibility of the role of imagination and language in transforming hatred to love has always been a theme in Harjo's work, but here it is related to the very energy that holds the universe together, to coin Dylan Thomas's phrase, "the force that through the green fuse drives": "I understood love to be the very gravity holding each leaf, each cell, this earthy star together" (10).

In "Promise of Blue Horses," Harjo relates the idea that the human body itself is constructed of physics: "The heart is constructed of a promise to love. As it distributes the blood of memory and need through the body its song reminds us of the promise—a promise that is electrical in impulse and radiation" (48). As Harjo's poetry *In Mad Love and War* deals with both the possibilities and limitations of language, so the poems in *The Woman Who Fell from the Sky* deal with the possibilities and limitations of physics.

The structure of the poems is marked most dramatically by Harjo's use of prose forms. Harjo's earlier work in *Secrets from the Center of the World* prefigures this abandonment of poetic line breaks, but *Secrets* does not make the radical departure that *The Woman Who Fell from the Sky* does in that the latter work contains stories with character and plot development. In fact, two of the poems, "The Flood" and "Northern Lights," were published previously as short stories in Craig Lesley's anthology *Talking Leaves*. The typography of most of *The Woman Who Fell from the Sky* is simply right justified on the page, so that the line breaks occur wherever there is no more room, like regular prose formats. Accordingly, in my representation of Harjo's poetry, I have quoted the lines as prose rather than with indications of line endings.

The beauty of Harjo's technique is that it is concrete and highly visual and at the same time surreal and abstract. She not only negotiates so many worlds thematically between myth, daily experiences, dreams, and the subconcious but also negotiates between many techniques. She is a poet with a great deal of range. Take, for instance, the following palette in the poem "Petroglyph," which is stunning not only in terms of images but for its parallelism, which causes each line to build cumulatively on the previous ones, and on its sounds (especially its repetition of *s* sounds):

> As she stands outside the kitchen door, drawn by the whirling pattern of the electric stars, she can see herself painting the dawn as it elopes over the Sangre de Cristos, the crisp nostrils of Sally the horse snorting cool breaths into clouds, Rudy the collie dog brushing the ground with her tail as she anticipates the presence of the human she has chosen,

forgetful chickens scratching for seed and the grandparents on horses
with grandchildren in front of them, forming the border of ongoing
composition. (*Woman*, 59)

After each poem, Harjo gives a first-person autobiographical commentary, a little reminiscent of N. Scott Momaday's arrangement of the triadic voices in *The Way to Rainy Mountain*, except that Harjo has two storytelling strands instead of three. The personal retrospection is no less poetic than the poem proper, and many of them equal or surpass the poetic statement on the opposite page. This, too, is an influence of the oral tradition, where conversation gives birth to story, and where both are equally important. One of many moving examples is on the opposing page to the poem "The Naming" where Harjo discusses her maternal Cherokee grandmother, whom she never much cared for, and how she learned, after hearing some of her mother's stories, to see this woman's suffering in a new light. The commentary is interactive with the poem that precedes it, woven together with poetic storytelling threads.

"The Naming" concerns the birth of a granddaughter and all the factors that are significant to her name. The commentary that follows shows this finely nuanced linking strategy of Harjo's, which discusses naming, that is, naming a story correctly. Even the ugliness of a mean old woman's life deserves to be told, named honestly for everything it was. The surprise is the power of empathy that is created in this process of telling the woman's story, the identification that happens through the act of narrating, so that the poet even recognizes this grandmother's presence in the birth of her granddaughter, and the possibility that in the next world the grandmother had peace, enabling her to bless her great-great-granddaughter.

Harjo's combination of commentary and poetry suggests an inherent argument against the formalist "text-only" approaches that separate literature and criticism. In Harjo's poetry, the life of the artist intersects with the work of the artist, political discussion complements the aesthetics of the poem, and there is no attempt at a schizophrenic split between the political and the personal. Harjo engages in a powerful synthesis, combining metaphor in the prose poems with direct political statement in the commentary. Many times, the political statement is as artfully evocative as the poem, creating complementary forms between the two expressions rather than oppositional ones. Harjo's poetry uses traditional models in that, in a tribal worldview, the life of the community is not separate from the art of the community, and in bringing this notion to her poetry, Harjo makes the poem a vehicle of political discussion, which it has always been in many cultures and should continue to be. Harjo provides an important model for Native writers looking to merge personal and political concerns in their art.

If one looks at the issue of persona in Native American poetry, an interesting aspect is that the vast majority of the work is what, in modernism, is referred to as "confessional poetry." Many times, the poems are autobiographical, and there is not as great a fictive distance between the speaker of the poem and the author of the poem as there is in poetry at large. This is not a derivation of the Plath and Sexton school but a natural evolution from the oral tradition where a performed story is very close to the person who tells it. First of all, in the oral tradition, the story literally emanates from the speaker's body. The story is never performed as a fixed entity but is personalized through the speaker's voice and movements. And the story, passed down from generation to generation, is communal property, the history of the people, so that the story explains the teller's place in the scheme of things; it incorporates both "I" and "we." Because of the performative dimension and the passed-down dimension of the stories in an oral community, all stories are autobiographical to varying degrees. Autobiography is not as foreign to tribal societies as has been assumed, though certainly written, published accounts of one person's life story are different from the relationship to oral narration just described. Oral stories tell the history of individuals and their communities. As we saw earlier with the Creek migration story, it explains both Creek history and Louis Oliver's history, since he has a place in the community whose history he is recounting. The story continues to serve the nation well because it also explains the lives of contemporary Creeks who continue to live out the migration account. That Harjo should choose to accompany her poems with autobiographical statements is consistent with tribal tradition.

One of Harjo's greatest technical strengths is her use of overlapping time frames, an effect of simultaneity that she achieves in a way that is as sophisticated as any American poet writing today. She creates a deeply embedded effect because the time frame of one story is always revealed in terms of its place within another story, which is in turn shown to be inside yet another story, almost infinite regress, although "regress" seems the wrong word choice here. Harjo can work back and forth between these time frames, often within the same line and with minimal verbiage.

Fiction writers can approach this effect only by subverting chronology; one might compare Louise Erdrich's *Love Medicine*, where the stories skip generations, for instance. The effect of such a novel is an emphasis on what links events rather than the order in which events occur. Fiction has its limitation in this area, however, in that writers are usually obliged to complete one story and move on, or at least give enough of the story to develop a vignette or episodic fragment, regardless of what order they are arranged in. The dense, extremely pared-down language of poetry allows for more of an overlap and simultaneity, rather than a mere rearranging; it makes possible movement across boundaries within the same line, for instance. Many of Harjo's poems deal with the poet's recognition, and awe even, of these time mergings.

This concept of the collapse of boundaries is demonstrated by an important word in the Harjo lexicon: "spiral." This word has deep Muskogean significance because of the spiraling circles of shuffling dancers and women shaking shells in a counterclockwise direction around the fire (something like the coil of a snake), a very striking sight, given that the outer rings of dancers, because of the greater perimeter, are moving faster than the inner ring, which is composed of leaders, turning toward the fire and waving their hands at the flames at certain song cues. To be in such a spiral is beyond description, and the best attempt is Louis Oliver's, quoted in an earlier chapter. Here are a few instances of Harjo's use of the word "spiral," or instances where a spiral is implied:

> When the mythic spiral of time turned its beaded head and understood what was going on, it snapped. (*Mad*, 54)

> I embrace these spirits of relatives who always return to the place of beauty, whatever the outcome in the spiral of power. (*Woman*, 29)

> I think about him at the stompdance when I see the fire climb, turn to the stars. (53)

> And the day after tomorrow, building the spiral called eternity out of each sun, the dance of butterflies evoking the emerging. (64)

A spiral is three-dimensional (imagine the spiral of smoke rising from a fire, its embers slithering up the night sky during a summer evening at the grounds), but beyond that even, it resists fixed shape or definition because it is fluid, moving. One might note the beauty of the stomp dance spiral in terms of Muskogean philosophy, its three-dimensional quality's correspondence to the interaction of This World, Upper World, and Lower World in both its shape and its movement from earth to sky. Further, for a poet such as Harjo—whose concern is imagining the many worlds that surround us, with collapsing spatial and temporal boundaries, with interweaving mythical, personal, and political consciousness and relating physics to love and matters of the spirit—the spiral seems the perfect metaphor.

The concept of the spiral is essential to Harjo's work as a whole, as well as to her tribute to Louis Oliver in the poem "Fishing." The poet recalls here a promise she made to Creek writer and elder Louis Oliver to go fishing with him, and he died before she could keep the promise, so she keeps her word by inventing a story, by telling a fish story. The poem is poignant because "the one that got away," this time, was Oliver himself, a very dear man whom Harjo, and many other Native writers, loved.

The poem has to do with lying and cheating, telling fish stories and fooling death, breaking promises and keeping them, exchanging the world of hard reality for greater possibilities of imagination. Throughout is a comic sensibility not unlike Louis Oliver's talents for teasing an audience. In the fishing poem, air is exchanged for water, and the greatest warriors, we learn, can transcend boundaries between This World and Lower World, can formulate new ways of seeing and imagining, as important a part of resistance to genocide as physical struggle, these strategies for dodging the hook through imaginative and intellectual vision.

Tie-Snake's dimension, where fish hang out, is a world unknown to most humans, though certain extraordinary travelers, like the sixteen-year-old girl in Harjo's prose poem "The Flood," a young woman floating between the contemporary realities of modern Muskogean life and her ancient kinswoman who visited Tie-Snake below the waters, have been there. Harjo visits the Lower World by dreaming; she compares her poetry to Jaune Quick-To-See Smith's paintings, which are "rich with levels of dream stuff intermixed with hard reality" (*Woman,* 59).

"Let's take time to hear what the fish have to say," this poet seems to suggest, "it's important to imagine this, to look at the matter from below the surface, from another world." From that vantage point, we find out that the fish, all along, have been fishing humans, not vice versa, and that what they have to say is, "When is that old Creek coming back? He was the one we loved to tease most, we liked his songs and once in a while he gave us a good run" (*Woman*, 60). This is high praise for Mr. Oliver, to be thought so well of by fish — praise, I reckon, that he would have deeply appreciated.

But back on the shore, the poet has the answer to the fish's inquiry: the old Creek is always coming back "where the wisest and fattest fish laze. I'll meet him there," she says. Death is the ultimate trick, the biggest fish story of all, and the poem is a moving one because of its insistence on resisting forgetfulness. In "New Orleans" and other poems, we have seen Harjo's commitment to Creek national memory in the landscapes she traverses, and here we see her determination to remember a personal friend, a fellow Creek writer, and a colleague. As Leslie Silko says in her correspondence with James Wright, "At Laguna when someone dies you don't 'get over it' by forgetting; you 'get over it' by *remembering*, and by remembering you are aware that no person is ever truly lost or gone once they have been in our lives and loved us, as we have loved them."[22] Harjo's invented fish story is essential to her relationship to Louis Oliver, who has passed on to the next world, and is part of the love she is trying to write about throughout *The Woman Who Fell from the Sky*.

To follow through with Harjo's physics of the spirit, death is part of the spiral of life where energy simply changes forms but does not dissipate. In response to a comical experience where Harjo dreams she goes off to die, but even death will not cooperate, she says, "I guess it wasn't my time, I explained, and went fishing anyway as a liar and I know most fishers to be liars most of the time. Even Louis when it came to fishing, or even dying" (*Woman*, 60).

Now, relating this concept of the spiral to Harjo's pan-tribalism, and the power of indigenous movements worldwide, I believe this idea, of energy changing shape and form but not dissipating, is vital. Here, once again, I return to one of the most important books of this century, Leslie Silko's monumental opus *Almanac of the Dead*. One might compare *Almanac* to another big-ass, encyclopedic work, Thomas Pynchon's *Gravity's Rainbow*,[23] the book that everybody talked about and nobody finished reading in the early seventies. Pynchon's depictions of oppressive governmental groups and global conspiracies are not unlike Silko's black comedy toward the end of *Almanac*, when one of the most motley groups of tribalists in human history is assembled to take back the land (to say that the ending is comedic is not to say that it is not serious; humor is an important aspect of the sacred).

There is also an important contrast between the two works, between Pynchon's and Silko's, one that a graduate student, Jim Nicklin, pointed out to me outside of class one day at the University of Nebraska at Omaha. Pynchon's central metaphor is entropy, but Silko has different ideas altogether. As the European order dies off because of its moral and spiritual bankruptcy and capitalism's inability to sustain itself, this is *not* the end of the world as we know it, to quote REM. Silko's metaphor is not entropy but a redistribution of energy. As things European fall back to earth, indigenous consciousness takes over. Ancestor spirits spiral and swirl around the world's indigenous populations, urging them to rise up, and the continent begins a return to more communal ways of being. From this comparative framework, given Pynchon's entropic novel, Silko's work is quite optimistic rather than the dark vision that has been described by the critics in regards to *Almanac.*

Returning to Harjo's sky-world concerns, her notions of physics, and particularly her Muskogean notion of the spiral, she also follows this idea of redistribution of energy rather than decay. We have already discussed poems such as "The Naming" and "Letter from the End of the Twentieth Century," for example, that argue that hatred can be transformed into another type of energy, but this philosophy can be found everywhere in myriad forms in the poems, this transfer of energies:

> See the children who became our grandparents, the old women whose bones fertilized the corn. They form us in our sleep of exhaustion as we make our way through this world of skewed justice, of songs without singers. (*Woman,* 29)

Another instance is the way in which, in a very few lines, Harjo deals with a Plains dance group she watches performing at the university where she teaches, the associated memory of a Bear Dance in Reno, and a recollection of a lapse into mythic timelessness where bear dancers join human dancers and then, later, the same event reoccurring as the poet watches the Plains group where "we joined the bear world as they danced for us [in Reno], the same as we join the dancers *spiraling* [italics mine] from this lawn [at the university]" (*Woman,* 49). These worlds are further embedded in the story of her son's phone call and a mother's concern in a different time and place:

I hear the opening of the Bear Dance I saw performed at the Holiday Inn in Reno. Suddenly bears converged in that conference room as slot machines rang up pitiful gains and losses.

We joined the bear world as they danced for us, the same as we join the dancers spiraling from this lawn.

We have always been together. (*Woman*, 49)

The last line is a reference to the son's troubled phone call and may be an allusion to the ending lines of Leslie Silko's beautiful short story "Lullabye," where another mother faces a different kind of parental pain, the loss of children taken out of her home by BIA officials, and thus she sings a song of remembrance in her children's absence:

We are together always
We are together always
There never was a time
when this
was not so.[24]

The lines in Harjo's poem, like the woman's yearning in Silko's "Lullabye," show a collapse of time and spatial boundaries between mother, son, and dancers and a redistribution of energy from grief to memory. In *Almanac of the Dead*, Silko treats the idea of energy transfer in a very large, expansive way, tracing the way such a phenomenon occurs in events around the world and throughout history, and how ultimately such a phenomenon will be the future of the Americas as the continent reverts to its former self. Harjo deals with the same theme but through the extremely pared-down language of poetry:

I see the moon as I have never seen the moon, a half-shell, just large enough for a cradleboard and the child who takes part in the dance of evolution as seen in the procession of tadpoles to humans painting the wall with wishes. (*Woman*, 62)

If one were to draw a Venn diagram here, one would find at least four different time frames within these few lines: the speaker's as she looks at the moon, the timelessness of mythical expression where the moon resembles a child in a cradle board, the whole expanse of human evolution, and early tribal history when people painted pictographs, all the images dealing with transformation and movement from one state to another.

Silko predicts the future of the Americas; Harjo, in *The Woman Who Fell from the Sky*, reflects on where America has been in this retrospective moment the approaching year 2000 suggests. The poems in *The Woman Who Fell from the Sky* are very much end-of-the-century retrospective poems that examine the ongoing effects of colonialism and its history. The title of one of the poems, "Letter from the End of the Twentieth Century," confirms this millennialist theme. Further, the poet conveys urgent messages in this book, calling America to wake up before it is too late. In a poem about wolves delivering a message to a man and his dogs, the poet says that the role of prophetic visionary statement is not simply to proclaim disaster but to name possibilities for change so that destruction may be averted:

The world as all life on earth knew it would end and there was still time in the circle of hope to turn back the destruction.

That's why they had waited for him, called him here from the town a day away over the rolling hills, from his job constructing offices for the immigrants. (*Woman*, 46)

The poem is not fatalistic. Language and responsibility are key factors in turning back the prophecy. In her commentary, Harjo argues, "I believe in the power of words to create the world, as did the wolves who told that story to the young man, as did Bob Thomas who told me the story, and my friend who took this story with her and the tribe to Washington, D.C." (*Woman*, 47).

The reader, once exposed to the prophetic warning, has a role in turning back the destruction: "The story now belongs to you too, and much as pollen on the leg of a butterfly is nourishment carried by the butterfly from one flowing to another, this is an ongoing prayer for strength for us all." This is consistent with the oral tradition, where didacticism is not a nasty word, literature often being intended to embody a message for community.

And again we are brought back to the huge concerns expressed in *Almanac of the Dead*. Silko does not flinch from one thing — Indians will get their land back. The novel moves inexorably toward such a conclusion. The novel is less certain in terms of spelling out just *how* this land transfer will take place — whether through the bloody revolution that some of its most radical characters espouse or by the land and its cultures simply reverting to an indigenous consciousness as capitalism inevitably burns itself out. By using Harjo as a gloss of Silko, where humans are given the opportunity to heed the prophecy and amend their lifestyles, we might hold out some hope that as a culture we are on the brink of a singular moment in history when we can choose to do the right thing by indigenous people worldwide and at home and avoid a lot of pain and bloodshed, instead of making disastrous choices that will be the ruin of American culture as we know it. Throwing Silko back into the mix here, her argument in *Almanac* seems to go that either way, voluntarily or by force, the land will regain its indigenous integrity. Unfortunately, the importance of Silko's novel is so glaringly obvious that no one can see it, and whether American consciousness is voluntarily altered by choice rather than involuntarily by disaster is a frightening question that no one wishes to face. This is why I say that Silko's novel may be one of the most important works of this century.

In the first poem, "Reconciliation," in *The Woman Who Fell from the Sky,* the speaker's America is a "land of nightmares which is also the land of miracles."[25] The poems are amazingly optimistic, in spite of the ways in which they record the horrors of the twentieth century; the poet, over and over again, posits that hatred can be transformed and that "all acts of kindness are lights in the war for justice." I like what a graduate student in one of my classes, Jim Nicklin, said about the book's opening poem:

> It is interesting that Harjo starts this collection off with "Reconciliation: A Prayer." The act of prayer imposes its own order on the world through the magical power of language. Words can change the cosmic flow, as it were. That Harjo prefaces *The Woman Who Fell from the Sky* with a prayer invites an analysis that describes her poetry as action-oriented and not just the lyrical musings of someone of Native blood. Harjo intends to *do* something with her poetry. Various poems in this collection are *acts* in the form of poems: "Wolf Warrior" prophesies; "A Postcolonial Tale" reminds; "Letter from the End of the Twentieth Century" heals.[26]

I like Nicklin's suggestion that Harjo seeks poetic expression that will have some physical effect on the world of tribal people. Another early poem in the book, "The Creation Story," backs up this idea by relating the creation of the universe through language, when the stars are spoken into existence, to the role of the poet, struggling to find language that will actually benefit her tribal community. Here the poet laments that she has not always been completely successful at such an effort, as none of us have been:

> I am ashamed
> I never had the words
> to carry a friend from her death
> to the stars
> correctly.
>
> Or the words to keep
> my people safe
> from drought
> or gunshot. (*Woman,* 3)

Although here, and throughout her work, Harjo discusses the limitations of language, she nonetheless seeks ways to make words a blessing, a gift, that returns to the community she is writing about.

After the poem, "The Creation Story," the commentary that follows deals with Creek emergence and the beginning of clans. The purpose of clans is to establish social and ceremonial relationships such as who will teach you (in the case of Creeks, traditionally, this would be your clan uncle, your mother's oldest brother, who would instruct you about what to do at the stomp grounds as well as in other matters of Creek social life). Clans are also an important part of an intricate system of societal balances, of which there are many in Creek life — red towns and white towns, rival towns and towns of the same "fire," the House of Kings and the House of Warriors in Creek government, men's roles and women's roles, the Upper World, the Lower World, and so on. Further, there are all the spiritual dimensions of clan membership and relationship to one's clan entity. These clan relationships, no matter how modified they may be in contemporary life, are still ongoing, according to Harjo: "The creation story lives within me and is probably the most dynamic point in the structure of my family's DNA" (*Woman,* 4).

Clans are thus a part of Creek societal balance. It seems to me that the idea of Creek balance applies to writing as well. There is a particular kind of truth that poets and novelists attempt to tell — they try to write honestly about the way they see the world around them. Yet for the tribal writer, there is a struggle for balance between individual expression and writing on behalf of the tribe. There are important differences here from the Western notion of the alienated artist on the fringe of society expressing his or her highly individualized version of the truth of that society. Rather than simply exposing the ills of the society, certainly part of the role of a truth teller, the tribal writer also has the moral responsibility to use writing in whatever ways possible to build that society, to strengthen the tribal nation. This is a communal function of writing foreign to mainstream notions concerning art and society, an act of love of one's nation and its people.

Harjo herself develops love into a theme that ties together *The Woman Who Fell from the Sky*. The word "love" appears in almost all of the poems in the book. Another interesting word in Harjo's corpus is "grace," and both these words have meanings in terms of the Christian virtues, but these are not the meanings with which Harjo chooses to invest them. "Grace," in the Harjo lexicon, is most often associated with those moments of vision when boundaries collapse between mythical spaces, personal spaces, the invisible world, and the physical world so that blinders fall off and one sees into these other dimensions. This vision, this world of imagination, is even more real than what is more easily seen with natural vision in ordinary day-to-day living, and "grace" has to do with those gifted moments when one is sensitive enough to see these things:

> Like Coyote, like Rabbit, we could not contain our terror and clowned our way through a season of false midnights. We had to swallow that town with laughter, so it would go down easy as honey. And one morning as the sun struggled to break ice, and our dreams had found us with coffee and pancakes in a truck stop along Highway 80, we found grace.
>
> I could say grace was a woman with time on her hands, or a white buffalo escaped from memory. But in that dingy light it was a promise of balance. We once again understood the talk of animals, and spring was lean and hungry with the hope of children and corn. (*Mad,* 1)

Love, in Harjo's poems, is a more tangible concept than grace, not simply an emotion but an action, a deed done for justice. In the poem "Letter from the End of the Twentieth Century," Harjo advocates love over violence, but this does not equate with a refusal to fight against injustice. It has to do with a transformation of hatred to love that, in this particular poem, reminds me of Leslie Silko's character Tayo in the novel *Ceremony,* who resists driving the screwdriver into Emo's head because that is what the witchery wants him to do.[27] The Harjo poem is about the

ghost of a murdered man resisting revenge, a taxicab driver killed for
money whom Harjo heard about in a taxi on the way to O'Hare:

> He searches for his murderer in the bowels of Chicago and finds him
> shivering in a cramped jail cell. He could hang him or knife him — and
> it would be called suicide. It would be the easiest thing.
>
> But his mother's grief moves his heart. He hears the prayers of the
> young man's mother. There is always a choice, even after death.
>
> He gives the young man his favorite name and calls him brother. The
> young killer is then no longer shamed but filled with remorse and cries
> all the cries he has stored for a thousand years. He learns to love himself
> as he never could, because his enemy, who has every reason to destroy
> him, loves him. (*Woman*, 36)

The story follows Harjo around, including when she is inside the Creek
Nation and away: "That's the story that follows me everywhere and won't
let me sleep: from Tallahassee Grounds to Chicago, to my home near the
Rio Grande" (*Woman*, 37). Tallahassee is the stomp grounds just outside of Eufaula, Oklahoma. The story, then, has meaning inside Creek
country, and also in terms of worldwide alliances that Native people have
with other indigenous peoples: "As an Indian woman in this country
I often find I have much in common with many of the immigrants from
other colonized lands who come here to make a living, often as taxi dri-
vers" (38).

When Harjo talks about love, then, it is not trivially universalizing
but fully contextualized with an awareness of the colonization process.
Love, in Harjo's work, is also an act of resistance. It not only means avoiding acts of gratuitous violence but can also be proactive, part of the
spirit of resistance that has kept Indian people alive these last five hundred years as they have stood against the forces of colonization. Harjo's
poetry reminds us that we are not a defeated people, that we have often
resisted successfully, and that we continue to do so. There is still much
to be resisted: "The children were in school learning subtraction with
guns, although they appeared to be in classes" (*Woman*, 18).

In comparison to other Native poets, Harjo has one of the strongest
voices, if not the strongest. Harjo's poetry is at least as good as the best
of Native poets such as Duane Niatum, Louise Erdrich, Adrian Louis,
Linda Hogan, and Simon Ortiz. There is a large and rich body of Na-

tive American poetry; at the Returning the Gift writers festival held in Norman, Oklahoma, in the summer of 1992, there were more than three hundred published Native writers in attendance, many of them poets. Harjo has very recently (spring 1995) been conferred the Lifetime Achievement Award that is given by the Native Writers Circle of the Americas, an award given *by* Native writers *to* Native writers, the only of its kind.

Native poets range widely from the more formalist writers, influenced by European forms such as meter and rhyme, to those poets trying to adapt the oral tradition to modern poetry. An example of the formalist end of the spectrum would be some of the poetry of N. Scott Momaday, and on the oral-tradition end are such poets as Simon Ortiz and Luci Tapahonso, whose poetry relies heavily on spoken conversations and oral stories. By and large, the works of Native poets lean more toward the oral-tradition influence than the formalist one. Harjo's work is no exception here, though she relies a little less on representing spoken voices and a little more on the use of surrealism and imagism than Ortiz or Tapahonso. It should be noted that from a tribal perspective, where visionary experience is a reality, such an adaptation may flow more out of a natural connection to tribal culture than an adherence to European poetic techniques.

I hope that I have demonstrated that Harjo's work is deeply Muskogean. This is not to detract from her other influences but to name what I feel is the very foundation of her work, the cornerstone on which she builds her pan-tribalism. Reading her poems without some attention to their Creek content diminishes their power. Further, the power of Harjo's pan-tribalism cannot be dismissed, either.

Placed in a historical context, it is interesting to note that Creeks have always experienced powerful cultural growth as a result of pan-tribal influence. Unlike the coastal tribes, who, at the time of contact, immediately faced settlers, disease epidemics, and changing economies simultaneously, the Creeks, as an interior nation, had a little time to adjust before the onslaught of the English.[28] Creek country became a place of refuge for coastal groups devastated by contact. This contact caused Muskogeans both to shore up the strength of their own culture and to adopt songs, dances, and linguistic features of the Indian refugees. They were able to both incorporate weaker groups and bolster their own strength at the same time (Martin, 49). To maintain Creek nationhood and identity, for instance, the clan system became very strong, so that Creek matrilineal culture was still continued even with the influx of newcomers (49). Clan members could not marry those of their own clan, and "because the system required exogamy, it encouraged the assimilation of strangers" (50). Tuckabatchee town is a prime example of this pan-tribal ethnic diversity, a town that remained very strongly traditionally Creek, "one of Muskogee's largest and most important, [yet it] cannot be easily classified ethnically. Rather than representing any single group, it consisted of many peoples involved in a dynamic process of coalescence" (50).

Later, a similar process of cultural contact would occur with runaway slaves, given Creek country's central southern location. Harjo, in her wonderful poem about the musician Jim Pepper, a poem replete with images of fire and sounds from the stomp dance, makes a convincing argument that Creeks, because of this contact, probably contributed to the evolution of jazz:

> I've always believed us Creeks ("Creek" is the more common name for
> the Muscogee people) had something to do with the origins of jazz.
> After all, when the African peoples were forced here for slavery they were
> brought to the traditional lands of the Muscogee peoples. Of course
> there was interaction between Africans and Muscogees! (*Woman*, 52)

Harjo's use of Creek history, then, to illuminate larger tribal concerns and even global indigenous issues, is an old song indeed.

Dear Hotgun:

Well, so Stijaati and Big Man and Rabbit was took a trip to Washington, D.C.

Big Man was had occupy a National Creek Council seat and represent Okfuskee District, and when I say occupy a seat I mean take up the whole saddle. Every now and then he go to D.C. on tribal bidness. Rabbit and Stijaati come along this time just to hang around like two ole curs around a *sofki* pot, but they had to pay for their own room. Big Man was need to remind them they never knowed how much work it was being a Creek representative what with all the legal documents to read and meetings to attend. During the day they was sightsee on Capitol Mall and wait for Big Man to get done official bidness, so they can find a cheap place to drink Budweisers. The three of them was invited to a big cultural event at the Kennedy Center and had to figger out how to match the right slacks to they bullhide boots without their wives to hep them.

They found out the tickets waddn't free but eighty dollars cash on the barrelhead for a show called *Les Miserables*. Big Man asked Stijaati what was that supposed to mean on account of Stijaati most educated and had one semester at Bacone.

Stijaati was say, "The miserables."

Rabbit was said, "We can see our relatives back in Weleetka."

Big Man was say, "We get free HBO here at the hotel and room service send up cold Budweisers."

Stijaati was ask, "What's playing?"

Big Man was answer, "*Strangers on a Train*, the old Alfred Switchcock classic."

Stijaati was say, "You mean Hitchcock."

Rabbit was say, "Wait until you see the movie: Criss-cross, Guy and Bruno, switching murders."

So they called down to room service and ordered fried mozzarella cheese sticks, marinarey sauce to dip them in, three handburglers with cheese, and frosty dogs dipped in chocolate for desert. Rabbit run down to the bar and brung up a pitcher of Budweisers before the movie was start.

The credits was begun to roll: Screenplay by Raymond Carver, Directed by Alfred Hitchcock, Starring Josh Henneha as Bruno and Jimmy Alexander as Guy Hamilton.

Big Man and Rabbit and Stijaati was all look at each other and then look at empty pitcher of Budweiser. Stijaati was say, "That's some strong stuff mebeso brewed downstream from bear pissing hole. What was had happened to Farley Granger and Robert Walker?"

Rabbit was say, "Stijaati, your kin get to be in everything." Then he stop whining and say, "Let's go get another pitcher," so he did.

Big Man got off easy chair and walloped the TV upside the head.

Rabbit come back in with 'nuther pitcher stronger bear piss and say, "These TVs was a lot more reliable in old Indian days when they had rabbit ears you could adjust."

They get to watching the movie again and the scene was opened with two men boarding a city bus at the downtown station across the street from the Myriad Convention Center in Oklahoma City.

Rabbit was say, "What happened to the train?"

Big Man was say, "Hit tracking."

Stijaati was say, "Tracking is for the VCR, not the TV."

Big Man was go on and say, "Tracking is for trains."

The camera focuses only on two men's shoes as they get on the bus. A very large third man, could be Osage, boards the city bus carrying a big bass fiddle in a cloth case. The camera shot returns to the first two men's shoes; we still haven't seen their faces or bodies. One man is wearing very mod black leather half-boots with silver metal buckles on the sides, the other plain calfskin Justin Roper cowboy boots, his boot tops covered snugly by his Wrangler jeans. The camera moves away from their feet and pans on their surroundings, and the men are no longer on a bus but transformed to an earlier era, evident by an art deco interior and the black porter walking by. They are in the dining car of a train.

Guy Hamilton, the one with the mod shoes, is sitting alone, reading the newspaper. Bruno enters the posh dining car, looks around, and approaches Guy's table.

"Car rather full. Mind if I sit here?" Bruno asks, smiling.

"Uh, sure," Guy says hesitantly, indicating the empty seat next to him. As Bruno sits down next to Guy, their feet collide under the table as they cross their legs. Guy recovers and pulls out a cigarette from an elegant gold case monographed "from J to J." Bruno hurries to help him, quickly offering a light while Guy fumbles in his suit pocket. Bruno leans over, in close enough proximity to make Guy uncomfortable, and gazes intently at Guy's face as he lights up.

Bruno says, "I recognize you; we were in that novel together. You're..."

"Shhhhhh..." Guy whispers, "it's not traditional to say our real-life names."

"Oh, Guy, those are our story names, relax. Do you want to get together after the movie?"

Guy seems unsure, as if he doesn't know what Bruno is after. Bruno realizes he has pushed himself too suddenly on Guy, and he makes casual conversation to ease the tension. Only the more Bruno talks, the crazier his stories get until Guy excuses himself and stands up, saying he wants to get back to his sleeping car and rest. Bruno grabs Guy's arm, a little forcefully. "Don't go," he begs, "I have a plan for the perfect poem!"

"What?!" Guy asks incredulously, pulling his arm away. But Bruno has Guy hooked, and he doesn't leave. He sits back down at the table.

"Oh, yes," Bruno says, "I've laid awake many a night dreaming of it," looking almost beatific now. "Two strangers meet on a train. They've never seen each other; they've never spoken to one another."

"But we're only strangers in this movie," Guy says skeptically.

"But don't you see? That's the beauty of it!" Bruno bums a smoke from Guy and lights up hurriedly, wanting to finish explaining.

"What does this have to do with poetry?" Guy asks.

"Well, if you come back to my sleeping car, I could show you," Bruno says. He recognizes his overweening enthusiasm and holds himself in check. "*Tell you*, I should say," he adds coyly.

"Only if you tell me what this has to do with writing the perfect poem."

"Really, Guy, you're a hard sell. OK, I'll tell you. Criss-cross. You do my poem, and I'll do yours. You see, two strangers meet on a train, as I was saying. They write each other's poem. What is the one thing that trips up everyone committing the act of poetry?"

"What on earth are you talking about?" Guy says in exasperation, tamping down another smoke on the tabletop.

"The motive, Guy, the motive," Bruno says.

"But I don't write poetry," Guy protests.

"Oh, Guy, please try. Be a sport."

"Well," Guy says, thinking. "One time I heard Joy Harjo read her stunning poem 'She Had Some Horses' at Oklahoma State at Stillwater. Once I heard Joy calling forth those horses, I was never the same."

"That's the spirit," Bruno exclaimed. "Oh, Guy, I knew you'd get into it. Well, I read the collected works of Alexander Posey's poems in order to audition for that character I played in the novel we were in. This is perfect. Just like I dreamed it!"

The two men retire to Bruno's sleeper. The camera pans on the hands of the dining car clock spinning rapidly around the hours until 4 P.M. has turned to midnight. The camera then moves from the dining room and down the narrow corridor of the train into Bruno's sleeper, where the two men are disheveled, their hair wildly mussed, their ties loose, and their white shirts wrinkled. They are surrounded by crumpled-up wads of paper.

"Well?" Bruno asks anxiously, looking at his two sheets, beside which he has laid his pen.

"Criss-cross, right?" Guy says, grinning, obviously won over by Bruno.

"Yeah, Guy, Criss-cross. That means I'll do the Joy Harjo poem I wrote for you," Bruno says. "Then you can do the Alex Posey poem you wrote for me." Bruno picks up the poem he wrote for Guy and starts to read:

She Heard Some Whippoorwills

She heard whippoorwills who called themselves Lucille
She heard a whippoorwill name herself Lucille inside her head,
  then crawl out her ear at dawn, flying from her window toward the
  direction of the sun
She heard a whippoorwill crying from the cornstalks, her shorn tongue
  silenced
She heard a whippoorwill send her from her father's house with a
  blessing, a curse

She heard some whippoorwills

She heard a whippoorwill shaking shells with poems
She heard a whippoorwill shaking shells with a saxophone, blowing
  words from Tallahassee stomp grounds all over the Americas
She heard this whippoorwill tending fire with half-diminished jazz
  scales, slithering sixteenth notes up the night sky backwards and
  forwards in time, sparking the darkness with the last song she'd ever
  sing
She heard whippoorwills who listened in silence and flashed their own
  words like lightning bugs on hot wet Oklahoma nights

She heard some whippoorwills

She heard whippoorwills tell her she was crazy

She heard the ping of a whippoorwill spitting snuff in an empty planter's peanut can, then putting the plastic lid back on and hacking from inside a sanatorium

She heard a whippoorwill with a bad blonde dye job singing "Lover Man" one night at the Horse, corner of 10th and May, Oklahoma City

She heard a whippoorwill telling stories as he cruised for white men on 39th Street; he'd entered a pretty-boy bar only to find himself diving down into Canadian river sinkholes riding behind the sharp spines of a channel catfish

She heard some whippoorwills

She heard whippoorwills talking to the Little People in their homes in trees

She heard whippoorwills whispering hope, the cruelest dickster of them all, taunting, "yesterday's sweet skin might stay until tomorrow"

She heard a whippoorwill who'd fallen dead among the cotton rows, her tow-sack dropped behind her in exhaustion

She heard whippoorwills talking in lawn chairs between dances, then rising up and walking toward the fire as pebbles rattled in their shells and men called "*Loca, loca*"

She heard some whippoorwills

She heard whippoorwills sharing recipes for homemade sheepshire wine

She heard whippoorwills teaching young girls to lay out turtle shells on ant hills

She heard a whippoorwill say that one winter it was so cold she had to wrap burlap around her feet to go out and get the horses

She heard whippoorwill songs turn into words of her own choosing

She heard some whippoorwills

She heard a whippoorwill dreaming the devil's shadow, a burning weight that pressed her down

She heard the whippoorwill tell the devil quoting her scriptures, "You might try to bury me, but it would take a right smart of dirt to hold me down."

These were her whippoorwills.

Bruno is beaming, beside himself with his poetic achievement. Guy whistles between his teeth, amazed.

"Bruno, I'm ... astonished."

"Do you really like it, Guy?" Bruno asks. "I so hoped you'd like it."

"Sure, Bruno. But I'm afraid what I've written is not quite..."

"Oh, Guy, I knew you'd be the only one to understand!" Guy picks up his poem and waits for the courage to start, then begins reading, hesitantly, picking up momentum as he gets into character:

Hotgun on the Art of Creek Writing and Criticism

"Well, so," Hotgun he was say,
"Creek writer training got to have
Pick green onion by the brook
Spend time on Oktahutche and in Creek woods
And carry with him Alex Posey book."

"Like I do sit under post oak, me
Mebeso all kind of Creek letters write
Put in there old guys for grunt and spit
And send him out to all my kin."

"Go to stomp ground when he could
If water not way high over bridge
Stay out there don't fall asleep
Dance all night and feel sho' good
And only her write about what he should."

"Got to other Creek writers read and talk
And to Creek story listen up real good
Like woman who give corn from her side
Tar-baby and mebeso *Choffee* too
Buzzard doctor rabbit by gouge hole in his hide
And cockroach who teach high school class."

"When young writer all her training got
With other Creek writers she throw her lot."

Tookpafka Micco and Kono Harjo listen in front yard
And tilt they chair ag'in' the tree
When Hotgun finish Creek writer talk
They spit and say, "That Creek writing bidness sound for me too hard."

In the final scene of the film, Guy and Bruno are stepping off the train, and Bruno is behind Guy with his hand on Guy's shoulder. They step down only to find themselves once more at the downtown bus station across the street from the Myriad Convention Center in Oklahoma City.

"The end" was had flash on the screen and Stijaati kind of look shell-shock and say to his friends, "Mebeso we better stop drinking Budweisers and go to more hymn sings with the missus."

Big Man was swore to fish with both hands on the pole instead of one on the beer can, and Rabbit say he don't care nohows seen stranger stories than that and runs downstairs to refill pitcher don't need no reformation.

Stijaati he was try to make meaning out of it all and says, "What we seen is how Creek writing becomes a passed-on tradition. Creek writers read other Creek writers and mebeso feel the influences of their styles on their own work; the older writers was teach the younger ones. So we was had Thomas Moore under the pen name William Harjo imitating Alex Posey's letters in the 1930s in the Okie City rag two decades after Posey's death; then Louis Oliver writing about Posey in the 1980s; then Joy Harjo was write a fishing poem about Louis Oliver in the 1990s; and now young Creek writers study Joy Harjo. Jimmy and Josh bust into our movie and write about these Creek authors too. To have writers like Harjo, Oliver, and Posey, come out of our own nation, all with an understanding of what it means to write as a Creek, should make us right proud. This chain of authors is part of our tradition, and they work constitutes a body of literature unto itself, part of what it means to be a Creek Nation, I reckon."

That was all the news I dare put in this time. To tell of such an episode clean wears you out.

Sincerely,
Jim Chibbo

CHAPTER EIGHT

Lynn Riggs as Code Talker: Toward a Queer Oklahomo Theory and the Radicalization of Native American Studies

Although I have mainly focused on writers of the Creek Nation, I would like to turn now to a Cherokee writer whose work is provocative, in terms of this study, because of the the way in which he seeks to formulate a theory regarding Oklahoma. Lynn Rollie Riggs, Oklahoma Cherokee, born and raised at Claremore, Oklahoma, is best known as author of *Green Grow the Lilacs,* later turned into one of the most popular musicals of all time — Rodgers and Hammersteins' *Oklahoma!* Riggs, a prolific playwright, wrote thirty plays, two books of poems, short stories, and an unfinished novel. Although Riggs never received the critical acclaim of Tennessee Williams, Arthur Miller, or Eugene O'Neill, he nonetheless wrote important work that fully used American settings and dialect and that was experimental in quality, breaking with the structure of Ibsenian drama so familar to the majority of theatergoers in the 1930s.

Two aspects of Riggs's life and work that have gone largely uncommented on are his Indian identity and his gay identity. A reading of Phyliss Braunlich's compelling autobiography of Riggs, *Haunted by Home*,[1] as good as the book is, reveals two glaring omissions — no analysis whatsoever of what Riggs and many others considered to be his most important play, *The Cherokee Night*,[2] or its relation to Riggs's Cherokee identity; nor any discussion of the meaning of Riggs's homosexuality in terms of its impact on his life and work. Throughout his entire life, Riggs referred to himself as a Cherokee and, being born in 1899 in Indian Territory several years before statehood, received a land allotment and was enrolled in the Cherokee Nation.

In addition to the silence about Riggs's relationship to things Cherokee is the lack of discussion of Riggs's life as a gay man. Braunlich teases her readers with tantalizing information but immediately pulls back. For instance, in her opening chapter concerning Riggs's nervous breakdown at the University of Oklahoma and recovery in Santa Fe under the auspices of the publicly gay writer and former OU prof Witter Bynner, Braunlich says:

> Warmed by Bynner's geniality, Lynn Riggs used him as a role model in many ways; but although he shared most of Bynner's views, Riggs preferred privacy. Newly freed by the recognition of his own homosexual orientation, he nevertheless was constantly wary of Oklahoma's judgments, and never quite so full of self-esteem as Bynner was. Like Bynner, after success came, Riggs seized every opportunity to promote the careers of young writers and artists. (13)

End of subject, but this reader wants more. What was the nature of this homosexual epiphany of Riggs's when he becomes "newly freed"? How does Braunlich know about it? Did she find out through interviews with those who knew him? How was this new understanding different from the one he had before, especially since he remained closeted all his life? How did this newly found freedom affect his work? What are some of these views she alludes to that Riggs shared with Bynner? These brief teasing glimpses, followed by silence, set the stage for the rest of Braunlich's treatment of Riggs's gay life and identity.

Riggs's gay lovers were artists and playwrights whom he collaborated with; in the case of Enrique Gasqué-Molina, they wrote a play together, and Riggs includes Enrique's ideas in his elaboration of his theater manifesto, his theory of what drama should do, which Riggs called "The Vine." Arguing, then, that attention to Riggs's homosexuality is central to an understanding of his work does not seem like much of a stretch. An obvious tactic might have been to interview some of these lovers if still living or willing to talk (many were younger than Riggs) or to have at least asked the friends of Riggs who were interviewed about these gay relationships. If this information was unavailable, it would be interesting to know why.

And the same holds true of Riggs's Cherokee identity. Although his Cherokee mother died in Riggs's first year of infancy, and his Cherokee stepmother was given to a foul temper, causing Riggs's father to rely on the white side of the family to take up the slack in raising his children on the occasions that his wife lost her temper, still, Riggs grew up in Claremore around Cherokees and in a Cherokee home. There are a lot of Cherokees in and around Claremore. Riggs had to have been around Indian people to some degree, and his one play that deals with Indian identity certainly confirms this.

When I think of my own family's mixed-blood experience, I recall stories my paternal grandmother tells (three of my grandparents are Indian) — her dad wouldn't let her date full-bloods, so to some degree she suffered alienation from the larger Indian community. Yet grandma was around full-bloods, attended stomp dances occasionally, knew some language, and related incidents about Creek and Cherokee culture, as well as everyday experiences of Indian people. Although some of Riggs's depictions of Cherokees in *The Cherokee Night* are stereotypical (a mystical Cherokee in a warbonnet who inhabits Claremore Mound comes immediately to mind as one of the characters who is more of a type than a fully developed personality), there are also specific Cherokee cultural references that show, for example, some degree of familiarity with Cherokee incantations.

Riggs's Indian identity seems an obvious point of discussion in a biography, even if only to address why he never dealt with it in any of his plays except *The Cherokee Night*. It is surprising that no Cherokees from Claremore were queried as to what they might be able to tell about Riggs — just as mysterious as why no gay friends or former lovers or straight people whom Riggs trusted were asked to contribute.

I would like to argue that Riggs's Indian identity and gay identity are the two most relevant aspects of his life and work, but owing to the constraints of his time, he was forced to deal with these issues through coded statement. Most important, since Riggs's life brings together gay and Native concerns, I would like to use his ideas, and particularly his play *The Cherokee Night*, to explore ways in which gay sexual orientation is relevant to the larger category of Native studies. Just what might a Queer Oklahomo Indian theory provide that would enrich the study of Native literature and culture, and how does such a theory relate to the nationalistic literary approach I advocate in this book?

What makes a study of Riggs so useful in these regards is that he actually articulated a theory of Oklahoma and Oklahomans, as well as a theory of literature — or, more specifically, of the theater. I want to begin by summarizing these ideas of Riggs's, and then relating them to the aforementioned larger theoretical frameworks.

Riggs saw Oklahomans as a distinctive group of people. While Riggs was on a Guggenheim Fellowship, writing in Paris and studying European theater, he responded to a review of his plays, and this response contains a statement concerning Riggs's theory of Oklahomans. I include this rather long quotation from Riggs's letter to his friend Barrett Clark because of its direct relevance:

> And I know that what makes them [Oklahomans] a little special, a little
> distinct in the Middle West is the quality of their taciturnity. They are
> voiceless, tongueless; they answer the challenging "Who goes there?"
> only by a flash of a lantern so quick, so momentary, that none but the
> acute guard sees more than a shadowy figure retreating into the
> darkness. There are two reasons for this: one — faulty education (or
> none at all); the other, the people who settled Oklahoma were a suspect
> fraternity, as fearful of being recognized by others as they were by
> themselves. Gamblers, traders, vagabonds, adventurers, daredevils, fools.
> Men with a sickness, men with a distemper. Men disdainful of the
> settled, the admired, the regular ways of life. Men on the move. Men
> fleeing from a critical world and their own eyes. Pioneers, eaten people.
> And their descendants have the same things in them, changed a little,
> grown out of a bit, but there, just the same. And so they don't speak.
> Speech reveals one. It is better to say nothing. And so these people, who
> had been much admired and much maligned, have been *not quite*
> *known* — a shifting fringe of dark around the camp-fire, where wolves,
> perhaps, and unnamable things lurked.
>
> I happened to be born myself just outside the rush of light. And I
> know how it feels, and I think, how those others felt. And it seems to me
> that if there was much ignorance in these people, there was also a minor
> wisdom; if there was much cruelty and darkness, there was also
> gentleness, and the singing of old songs. These people, human, were
> victims of a special and touching disinclination, and even inability, to
> publish their humanity. That's what I'm trying to do for them, and for
> their descendants, falteringly, imperfectly, incompletely, in the plays.
>
> And now that I've said this, it all sounds pretentious and wrong. It's
> better for me to say nothing, I'm coming to believe, except in poetry or
> drama. (Braunlich, 71–72)

In summary, in these "pioneers," we have the qualities of voicelessness, haunting presences outside acceptable places of refuge such as home and campfire, fear of recognition by others and by oneself, sickness, disdain of socially acceptable behavior, cannibalism, anonymity, and life on the margin outside the campfire with wolves and the unnamable. Then we have a shift in the theory, Riggs relating the ideas to his own autobiography, where he says he too was born outside the light, like one of these mysterious Okies lurking in the shadows. Given that the Okies cannot understand their essential humanity, Riggs must speak on their behalf. He says he believes it is better for himself to say nothing except through poetry and drama, and in fact, he remained committed to apoliticism throughout his entire life. Immediately apparent in his description of Oklahomans is Riggs's complete neglect of the role of Indian people, since he focuses his theory only on the white boomers and sooners who invaded Indian Territory.

Here is what I make of all this. I wish to argue that Riggs's Oklahoma theory is better understood as the internal terrain of a closeted gay man than as an actual literal rendering of Oklahoma and its people. The characterization of these pioneers, in other words, actually describes a sexual frontier that in the 1930s could certainly be described as a state of silence, of hanging out in secret places, of fear of being found out as well as fear of self-recognition, of self-hatred and viewing oneself as sick, of social restrictions on the possibilities of meeting places for gay men, and a sense of cannibalism even, of being devoured by a dark other, and being such a devourer oneself, secretly feeding on one's own. (Here we might note briefly that Anne Rice's enormously popular vampire books have picked up on the similarity between the life of the coffin and the life of the closet in earlier periods in the South: the vampire who must hide by day from society at large but who is recognized by his own when he "comes out" at night for a brief period before shrinking from the light of day at dawn.)

Riggs goes on to describe Oklahoma in terms of the limitations concerning what he can say about it. He indicates a frustration with his lack of ability as an artist, as well as the limits of language to represent experience:

> When I get like this — and I do often — there's nothing to do but bear it. Or forget it. Or pick on some kind person who will listen — and not hold it against me. It's this — I'm deep, deep down on account of the things I can't do in any way.

I can't make—in drama or poetry—the quality of a night of storm, for instance, in Oklahoma, with a frightened farmer and his family fleeing across a muddy yard (chips there, pieces of iron, horseshoes, chicken feathers)—to the cellar, where a fat bull snake coils among the jars of peaches and plums.

I can't begin to say what it is in the woods of Dog Creek that makes every tree alive, haunted, fretful. I can't tell you what dreadful thing happened last Christmas—when a son and his wife stumbled drunkenly into his mother's house; the words that came out of brazen tortured throats, the murderous hints, threats—and all the time a little sick child, radiant, great-eyed, sat up in her bed and saw and heard and wept at something foul in her presence for the first time, life with venoms beyond her comprehension. And most of all—after sorrow, fear, hate, love—I can't even begin to suggest something in Oklahoma I shall never be free of: that heavy unbroken, unyielding crusted day—morning bound to night—like a stretched tympanum overhead, under which one hungers dully, is lonely, weakly, rebellious, and can think only clearly about the grave, and the slope to the grave.

It seems to me more and more that I am haunted and driven by pictures and pictures—ominous, gray, violent, unserene—and this in spite of the fact that I become more and more sane, more and more free of hysteria. So it begins to grow on me that only in that borderland of life, that disjointed, slightly unfocussed arena can we touch the pains of truth. And wouldn't it be good to be felled by those feet, to be a good Christian in those unholy playful jaws?

I wish I were writing a play about *Twilight,* or *Yellow Radiance after Rain,* or even *More Sky.* There's verity in little else. (Braunlich, 75–76)

Rather than Riggs's somewhat unconvincing claim that he is dealing with the limits of art and the artist, might he actually be trying to express less ethereal concerns—those of a closeted gay man dealing with an incredibly oppressive societal realm that sanctions what a gay man can say, sanctions what an Indian can say, and contributes to the silence and voicelessness that Riggs attributes to Oklahomans and to the Oklahoma artist trying to describe them?

Riggs has some very interesting contradictory impulses. In addition to the grim Oklahoma realities that Riggs claimed he wanted to represent realistically, portraying truth rather than merely entertaining his audience, Riggs nonetheless believed that a golden era preceded the grim one, a happy bucolic romp where Okies spoke naturally poetic language and lived in innocence, rather an Okie version of noble savages. White folks, to be sure, started to invade Indian Territory fairly early on after removal, but they did not begin arriving in really large numbers until the early 1880s, after tribes begin losing the battle to the railroad interests and white towns began springing up within tribal nations—Muskogee within the Creek Nation is one such example. So the transition period between Riggs's bucolic Oklahoma and Riggs's bleak Oklahoma had to be short indeed, since his plays take place immediately before and after statehood. Posey's golden age for Creeks, as we have seen earlier, can at least be traced to several decades when it could have occurred during relative peace within the nation. In Riggs's case, it is almost as if the two Oklahomas, the bucolic one and the horrific one, represent two sides of Riggs; and this split personality can also be seen in his characters, a dimension of his play *The Cherokee Night* we will examine presently. Riggs never addresses what caused the expulsion from Okie Eden. Nor does he deal with the disastrous effects of this putative white paradise on tribal nations. What I want to argue is that these two time periods, and the transition between them, occurs in Riggs, not in Oklahoma. Again, this is an Oklahomo's interior landscape rather than Oklahoma physical geography.

This golden age, Riggs believed, contrasts with the grim Oklahoma reality he was born into, and *Green Grow the Lilacs* reflects this earlier epoch. Commenting on the progress of the play while writing it, Riggs said to Henry Moe of the Guggenheim Foundation:

> It's a play about a vanished era in the Middle West—an era a little more golden than the present one; a time when people were easier, warmer, happier in the environment they had created. Song flourished. There were the usual human anguishes, of course. But there was *wholeness* in the people, there was great endurance. And in spite of ignorances and darknesses, there was a cool wisdom our radios and autos have banished forever. Even the speech of the people, backwoods though it was, was rich, flavorous, lustrous, and wise. And the songs are now forgotten, except for a few which have gotten into anthologies. (Braunlich, 77)

If Riggs experienced, as he must have, and as his coded letters to gay friends Bynner and others indicate, an extremely hostile and oppressive society from which he had to hide most of his life, erasing his gay identity from his public identity in order to survive, might it be psychically necessary for him to believe in a previous age when things could not have been so bad? The idea that Riggs is born haunted, cursed by queerness, probably contributes to this oppositional thinking—a present-day grim Oklahoma versus a previous golden epoch.

The golden speech of the golden age, according to Riggs, was a response to poverty and monotony, which create noble thoughts and speech. As an Indian man, one might assume that Riggs was well aware that the real legacy of poverty is not nobility but alcoholism and violence. What caused, one wonders, the transition from the golden era, to the grim one, to the people who need to hide outside the camp? Riggs never explains this, but I suspect that this transition occurs in Riggs's internal landscape, the bleak terrain of the closet, in his own need to hide. As Riggs came of age sexually, the problems seem to begin for him—it was Riggs himself who moved from the golden to the grim age. It was after his brief attempt at heterosexual dating, when a college woman at OU spurned him, that Riggs had his nervous breakdown and fled to Santa Fe for recovery. After his hopeless attempt at heterosexual passing, which put an end to the possibility of life "inside the camp," he moved into the shadowy world for which he had no language to describe. The young Indian artist of the golden age became the inarticulate outsider of the grim age as he was forced into the silence of the closet, again a landscape seen through gay lenses. Even now, how many Oklahoma Indian guys do I know who, like Riggs, have fled to New York City and San Francisco in hopes of not having to erase themselves any longer?

For Riggs, as the title of Braunlich's autobiography *Haunted by Home* indicates, Oklahoma always meant pain, a place he cared about deeply, wrote about all his life, measured his identity in relation to, yet felt he must leave for less restrictive environs. This began with his first trip to New York City as a very young man, then his return to Oklahoma, where he had the nervous breakdown at OU and, under the direction of Witter Bynner, moved to Santa Fe. Throughout his life, Riggs could only stand Oklahoma for very short stints, yet he returned there often. In a moving poem written in a letter to Bynner, Riggs described the pain of his relationship to Oklahoma, which forced him to hide, cover up, erase himself:

And we who part must do so casually
Lest we betray
Too much of what it means renouncng home
To go away. (Braunlich, 39)

Riggs did not even attend his own father's funeral in 1951 in Claremore (Braunlich, 191); nor did he show up for any of the celebrations Claremore threw in his honor, though he never expressed any enmity toward the community and responded warmly to the awards (146–47). He never had friends in Claremore, though he had lots of friends everywhere else, especially in Santa Fe, Greenwich Village, and Hollywood.

Riggs's Oklahoma theories, interestingly, completely ignore the pre-existence of tribes in Oklahoma. The oppressed pioneers do not consider their own role as oppressors; nor does their creator mention this. Riggs's mission, as he sees it, is to give voice to these voiceless, oppressed Okies. Might he really be searching for a voice within himself? For words, for language, for stories — an emergence story for an Indian gay man wanting to come from the darkness out into the light of the broader landscape, yet knowing that the journey requires finding the right words in a time when those words cannot, must not be spoken? No wonder Riggs wants to believe in a golden era when things were kinder and gentler. And might his complete denial of an Indian presence in Oklahoma be part of this psychic pain? Perhaps Riggs simply does not have the imaginative capacity to deal with a queer Indian presence in his work, though in all other matters, he creates a haunting realism to depict his places and people.

The queer Indian, after all, fits neither the noble nor barbaric savage stereotypes so popular in Riggs's time, whereas the happy Okies and the grimly realistic Okies fit nicely into both realms, not to mention the white mythology of the impoverished pioneer whose destitution builds character out of hard times. There simply was *no* available framework to provide a context for imagining the queer Indian, and perhaps Riggs, then, applies his own inner queer experience to Indians as a whole and gives up trying to talk about them.

Things may not be that different today for Native gay and lesbian writers. One of the reasons they may be less out than their white counterparts may have to do with the way that the queer Indian, even more than contemporary Indian culture generally, defies the stereotypes of the stoic warrior, the nature-loving mystic, the vanishing American. Contemporary Indian writing, especially if it is fiction, can be palatable enough for public consumption; at least book sales seem to indicate this. This may be due to the fact that contemporary works, and their occasional nostalgia for the past, may unintentionally reinforce some of these romantic stereotypes. Americans refuse to let go of their most cherished beliefs about Native people because their imaginings of Indians define who *they* are themselves; the whole system of America justifying what it means to be American depends on certain beliefs about Indians. The public will not let go of these images. Indian fiction, for example, to a great degree, has not yet dealt with the issue of land redress, and when it did, in the case of *Almanac of the Dead,* the book was panned by the critics and largely ignored by even those friendly to Native literature. I would speculate that a queer Indian presence (as did *Almanac,* albeit in a different way) *fundamentally* challenges the American mythos about Indians in a manner the public will not accept. Deeply embedded in the romanticism about Indians are ideas regarding gender, specifically the brave warrior willing to stake himself down while crying out, "It's a good day to die," and his woman or women back at the camp whose idea of a good day is scraping on a buffalo hide all day long. The queer Indian fits none of these popular imaginings. Further, identifying an Indian as lesbian or gay makes the Native radically resistant to the popular tendency to make Indians artifacts from the past, since no one associates such terms with the warrior days when men were men and buffalo were scared.

Riggs, even more confused in his own earlier era by his inability to link Native and gay identity together, to recognize that both were an inextricable part of his makeup, pulls back into a golden (literally blond and white) Oklahoma. Winsor Josselyn summarized an interview in which Riggs commented further about his theories regarding the prior innocent era:

> Then he was telling how he thought that release was a strong factor in his plays. Yes, and homesickness. Homesickness for an era lost, for a frontier vanished; homesickness for something that people might not have known, but, now knowing, they miss — almost as if it were a magic land, the key to whose gate they cannot have. Release and homesickness, admixed with a fantastic quality, an underlying rhythm and even the use of ancient forms, such as the Greek chorus as represented in *Roadside* by the lovable louts Red Ike and Black Ike.
>
> "And yet so far as personal release goes for me," mused Riggs, lighting a cigarette with a tiny square silver pillar, "playwrighting never gives me the freedom that writing verse does, and in a little book called 'The Iron Dish' I had more complete outlet than through any of my plays."
> (Braunlich, 131–32)

Riggs's work as a screenwriter and his close friendships with actresses Bette Davis and Joan Crawford removed him as far as possible from his painful Oklahoma beginnings. These women provided a cover for his homosexuality, and their husbands knew their wives were safe in the arms of Riggs, who played the role of gay courtier with a good deal of skill — dancing, dining, and courting these famous women. This Hollywood fantasyland may have been a kind wish fulfillment of his golden-age yearnings, what with the protection of the womenfolk by their gay knight and the complicity of noble husbands. Hollywood was probably the closest reality to the safe world he yearned for in his imagining of the golden epoch. Yet even this world demanded silence. And, sadly, it was far from Riggs's Cherokee world.

Riggs's golden-age nostalgia fails to account for what happened to Indian people as a result of his hardy settlers. In fact, his grim/golden age opposition ignores Indian people altogether. The golden-era theme, however, appealed greatly to the war-weary public, tired of World War II. In a review of *Oklahoma!,* the phrase "racial memory" is used in an interesting way:

> Throughout the performance [of Oklahoma], there is a certain tidal pull of nostalgia. The show presents an era that, like the Wild West of the films, has become a racial memory in the American mind; a mythical period before world wars, before the idea of One World was neatly counter-balanced by the idea of One Bomb. An era of incredible peace, all of 40 years ago. My, my — we have come a long way since then! (Braunlich, 185)

One of Riggs's other theories is his theater manifesto, formulated with his lover Enrique Gasqué-Molina (Ramon Naya), entitled "The Vine" (Braunlich, 154–155). In keeping with the high modernism of Riggs's time, the theory asserts that politics should be intrinsic in art, not extrinsic. It might be noted that although Riggs was consistent with the rising New Critical ethos applied to fiction and poetry, within the depression-era theater of the 1930s, nonetheless, there were still very strong elements of social criticism, especially in the WPA-sponsored plays, an important source of government funding for the arts. When the red scares began in the next decade, the political consciousness of theater would change, but the idea of a play containing overt political statement would not have been a foreign one to Riggs. He argued, instead, for happy plays — by making plays affirmative, people will gravitate toward justice naturally, according to his claims, making direct political statement unnecessary. Plays should not take up direct attacks or exposures of social issues, according to Riggs, whose area of interest was personal conflicts, dramatized in his plays, and not politics. Of course, one social issue that affected Riggs every day — the treatment of gay men in the thirties — could not be written about or even spoken. No wonder Riggs gave up on a more politically engaged theater.

In his argument that plays should be affirmative, one is reminded of Riggs's gay golden era in that his theater manifesto also advocates pulling back inside a safe, insulated place for a rather happy romp. Yet at the same time, Riggs felt a contradictory impulse toward gritty realism, as long as the realism involved personal, not political, conflict (as if the two are separable). Riggs's version of realism refused to ask the bigger questions: How is personal conflict related to political oppression? Why were whites pouring into Oklahoma? What kinds of displacements occurred for Indian nations who were already living in Riggs's Eden? Where do white-red relations come into play? Riggs, however, wanted to deal only with psychological motivations, not surprising from a man who could only puzzle about his inner turmoil but never speak out loud about it.

Riggs's theater manifesto, like his Oklahoma theories, is as much the response of a closeted gay man to an oppressive society as an aesthetic ideal about the state of the theater world. Homosexuality, when it was named at all, was considered a personal psychological aberration during Riggs's time. Never taken into consideration was the notion of homophobia as a social disease, the notion that the culture might be sick, not the individual. Thus Riggs, a product of this thinking, had learned well to locate everything on the level of the individual rather than the larger society.

This tendency to locate everything on a personal level can even be seen in Riggs's depictions of Cherokees, I believe, where he makes everything a personal conflict rather than historicizing Cherokees in terms of their suffering under an oppressive U.S. government. If Riggs's Cherokees are absorbed and doomed, as he argues they are in *The Cherokee Night*, they had to go through some process to reach this state of malaise; there has to be a history of oppression or, at the very least, something that went wrong. Riggs, however, fails to articulate any reasons for this supposed cultural disintegration. I would argue that his gay orientation, which has taught him not to critique dominant culture for fear of being found out himself in terms of his homosexuality, causes him to deal with Indian issues in a similar manner wherein he fails to look to the larger causes of oppression and focuses on individual conflicts instead.

Many others besides Riggs, to be sure, endorsed the vanishing mentality during Riggs's lifetime. The most popular book on Creeks, written by Angie Debo and published by the University of Oklahoma Press, is entitled *The Road to Disappearance*,[3] the title reflecting pretty common thinking about the fate of Indians during this time period — the book was a reflective look back on a bygone era. Yet even white authors like Debo (and many others who end their works on Indian people in 1907, when Oklahoma became a state, as if Indian history ended that same year) are relentless in their discussions of the land theft and injustices committed against tribes in Indian Territory. Riggs's work completely ignores this history of mind-boggling acts of criminality.

Today, in Oklahoma, Cherokee language and culture is alive and well — although there is a large assimilated portion of the tribe, there are also about ten thousand Cherokees who speak the language and closely follow Cherokee traditionalism. This group of traditionalists is larger than many entire tribes. During Riggs's time there would have been a similar number of Cherokee traditionalists, and in rural areas like Claremore and its surroundings, they were, and are, a significant presence. Riggs's play *The Cherokee Night* fails to articulate any explanations for the mysterious end of Cherokee people and culture. Riggs's end of the trail is truly queer and, like his Oklahoma theories, is more of a reflection of Riggs's inner gay life, which he was allowed to examine only through coded statement in his work as well as with his gay fraternity of friends, issues that I will take up later.

Riggs's life contained other contradictory impulses driven by queerness. Riggs's lover Enrique Gasqué-Molina, unlike Riggs, was interested in socially activist plays (Braunlich, 156), so Riggs was not entirely separated from influences that would link art with politics; but his gay life, I believe, made him more susceptible to hiding his light under a bushel. The very metaphor of the closet, after all, involves keeping things hidden and locked away, and formalism similarly demands keeping political concerns submerged beneath metaphor and locked inside the autonomous text rather than advanced through direct statement. Riggs, as a gay man, becomes just such a code talker; however, he does so most likely to pass as straight rather than out of any real commitment to a formalist aesthetic.

Riggs demonstrated a subconscious need to hide from the light in many ways. Riggs was averse to autobiography and when asked about his life would stick to a bare minimal recitation of facts, more like a résumé, and a very brief one at that, than any kind of personal statement or analysis of his life. Braunlich says, "On June 28, Riggs wrote a brief and, to him, painful autobiography for Barret Clark: 'I've made three (this is the fourth) attempts to do this biography stuff. Won't just the exterior facts do?'" (Braunlich, 63). He taught a class at Baylor University on basing writing on personal experience, ironic given that he did not want to discuss his own experience outside his plays and poetry, not to mention his life as a gay man. Of course, a guy like Riggs is going to hate autobiography—his very existence depends on keeping his life hidden! Perhaps he should have taught a course on code talking. His apolitical stance, I would argue, is directly related to this taciturnity, which, in turn, is related to the life of the closet. Riggs himself wrote that he hated his life, wanted to avoid inquiry about it, and would have liked to separate his plays from any personal associations:

> And while I think of it, I wish you'd throw away that chronology of my life. I don't like my life very well, after all, and there's no point in its being made public. I suppose I'm getting morbid about it—if any of my plays ever merited any public attention, I'd be terribly pleased if no one ever thought of the play except as a play, and forgot to inquire who wrote it. (Braunlich, 89)

In discussing Riggs's interior terrain, I should also say that the sanctions that caused him to pull back inside his shell were very real, not imaginary ones. Although Riggs had a fear of rejection all his life, a sensitive self-esteem, and the feelings of a homeless person who nonetheless loves home, for a gay man in the thirties, fear of alienation and rejection was not a neurosis but a reality. Bynner was more open, but Bynner was not from Oklahoma. If Riggs had been found out, he would be literally rejected back home, and his work, most of which was set in the state, showed that he measured his identity in relation to Oklahoma. Bynner did not have this same kind of communal sense, or a commitment in his work to discussing a single geography.

Riggs's insecurities caused possessiveness and isolation in his relationships with lovers, with whom he tended to hide away and withdraw from social life when he found a man he really cared about. He had good reasons for this. Even in the much more liberal atmosphere at Santa Fe, he had a falling out with socialite Mabel Dodge Luhan, probably over a homosexual encounter of his. In an interview, one of Riggs's friends, Willard "Spud" Johnson, said:

> Mabel asked him to stay there and they had a cozy time together. Then Lynn had a friend joining him, a boy from the University of Denver, who came to stay with Lynn for a while. Mabel took instant dislike to this boy and from that moment on, although Lynn stayed on in Taos and had a house, she wouldn't even speak to him. (Braunlich, 114)

Riggs himself addressed these issues, very cautiously, by pleading to others not to let such matters find their way to the folks back home. In a letter to Walter Campbell advising caution concerning any autobiographical statements about his life, there is a hint that Riggs had an affair with Bynner, or at least something that might be interpreted as an affair and cause him to be rejected in Oklahoma:

> And while I think of it, will you please leave Witter Bynner out of the story. For years that poor man has been getting clippings about me, which somehow hoping to improve the story of me have dragged him in. And especially in Oklahoma, it's done to death — of course there are implications back of it which are slightly embarrassing, as you'll know. So do you mind killing this fictitious overtone by ignoring it. (Braunlich, 90)

The result of all of this is an author deeply afraid, able to talk about the things that are really most important to him only through code, and completely ignoring the oppression of his own people, the Cherokees, or that of other tribes. It is no wonder that John Joseph Matthews could not persuade Ponca singers or Osage dancers to come to the premiere of *Oklahoma!* in Tulsa, as Braunlich recounts in her book. Why would they? Matthews, certainly, must have understood the irony fully (it is interesting to note that Matthews and Riggs were in the same writers' group at the University of Oklahoma, but Matthews's life took a divergent path; though a mixed-blood like Riggs, his work is immersed in things Osage). *Oklahoma!*, after all, celebrates one of the biggest land rip-offs in U.S. history. Pawnee dancers did end up coming. Interestingly, no Cherokees were invited, and Riggs himself did not attend.

Riggs's endorsement of manifest destiny, though perhaps more understandable by examining it in light of the life of the closet, nonethe-

less is not innocent. He wrote a number of outdoor dramas that celebrate America's worst impulses. The danger of Riggs's apoliticism, then,
is that it ended up being political as all hell, and he turned physical and
cultural genocide into song-and-dance numbers. An examination of
the titles of some of Riggs's commissioned outdoor dramas almost looks
like a top-ten list for colonialism's greatest hits:

> He used music, dance, and visual arts with broad strokes in these dramas
> to dramatize the history of a place or the biography of an important
> historical figure. Among his annually recurring outdoor dramas are *The
> Stephen Foster Story*, in Bardstown, Kentucky; *Cross and Sword*, in St.
> Augustine, Forida; *Texas*, in Palo Duro Canyon, Texas [note ironies for
> Kiowa people here]; *The Lone Star*, in Galveston, Texas [Texas has one of
> the worst records of genocide against Indian people of any state in the
> union]; *Trumpet in the Land*, in New Philadelphia, Ohio; and *Wilderness
> Road*, in Berea, Kentucky [originally Cherokee country before a forced
> land cession]. (Braunlich, 190–91)

This commitment to endorsing status quo interpretations of manifest
destiny had poignant consequences in Riggs's life. Although in his letters he often spoke enthusiastically about his work, he also grieved over
what he had kept hidden. He makes this statement in response to an
award for promoting the state of Oklahoma: "Actually, I have done little in life except try to discover who I am and what my relation to the
world I know consists of. In the world itself I have never really felt at
home.... [My achievement is] pitiable and it's puny—and it's all I know"
(Braunlich, 174). The statement is especially moving because it is true—
no feigned humility here—as it must have been taken. A huge part of
Riggs's life as an Indian man and as a gay man was either left unexplored,
coded, or, worse, rejected in favor of endorsement of dominant white
history.

In fact, denial ran so deep and was such a norm in Riggs's life that he
never even acknowledged the seriousness of his final illness. Up to the
very end, he would not admit that he was dying of cancer even though
the doctors had told him, and this pervasive hiding of the truth, originating in the life of the closet, affected every aspect of Riggs's life—the
way he thought, viewed history, conceived of Oklahoma, understood the
theater, and, finally, refused to speak of his very death. Even Willard Johnson, Riggs's lifetime friend, participated in the charade. Braunlich, in
one of her characteristically frustrating minimalistic statements, says that

Johnson had been Bynner's secretary and "companion" (Braunlich, 9). He is also the one who told of Riggs's falling out with Mabel Luhan over the homosexual encounter. The letters between the two certainly indicate a campy insider gay speech and humor, as when Riggs writes, "The lamp is a knock-out. I'm sure you outdid yourself. It certainly made quite a sensation with La Davis [Bette Davis]" (132). Riggs even jokes with Johnson about hiring a young male "secretary" who cannot even type or take dictation: "I've hired — at last — a permanent secretary, Marvin Clarke. I've known him for years. Used to be on switchboard at Chateau Elysee. Has to brush up on shorthand and typing — so tell Henri I still need him for *Big Lake* while Marvin straightens out my complicated mass of papers, organizes the house running a little, etc." (143).

At any rate, at Riggs's deathbed, Johnson was met by Riggs's sister and "a young actor, a friend of Riggs's" (Braunlich, 200). Johnson played along with Riggs's denial, sort of a tag team for denial, and, by his own admission, made up a completely fictitious story about finding a house for Riggs in Santa Fe, completely refusing, as did Riggs, to say anything about the state of Riggs's health (he died the next day). Johnson's recollection of these closing events in Riggs's life is such a powerful metaphor for Riggs's code talking that I quote it here:

> He was very pleased and said it sounded just about what he would like and he *staggered* me by saying well, how much was it [the house Johnson was supposed to find for Riggs]? Why, I had never got that far at home and so I had no idea. So I simply pulled out of the air $10,000. He said, "That sounds reasonable," and I promised I'd come the next day and I would sort of make a drawing of exactly where it was . . . and of course I had to leave just exhausted, pretending that nothing was the matter and, if possible, not giving him any hint that it was a final goodbye or anything like that. . . .
>
> I went out of the hospital, and it was raining. I luckily had a raincoat and walked all the way from wherever it was to the hotel, crying in the rain. Of course, nobody would have known it because I was dripping rain all over.
>
> And the next morning someone phoned that he had died. . . . I probably was the last to see him of his old friends. . . .
>
> It was a long walk, in the rain. (Braunlich, 200)

This tragic statement needs little commentary as a poem for passing, hiding, covering up, and, finally, one's pain going unnoticed, tears hidden by the rain. That Riggs's closeted life, his apoliticism, and his endorsement of dominant culture versions of white history had powerful consequences seems evident to me in this final rendition of Riggs's life.

I would like to move on to an analysis of Riggs's Indian play, *The Cherokee Night,* since I believe that this particular work brings together Indian and queer concerns, though through the code that is deeply embedded in Riggs's philosophies. Although I have argued that Riggs's Oklahoma and theater theories, as well as the majority of his plays, seem to take an apolitical stance that actually endorsed the status quo, in *The Cherokee Night* there is some attention given to the loss of Indian lands after the Dawes Act, and it is interesting to note that Riggs refers to "the town of Tahlequah, seat of the Cherokee *Nation,*"[4] in a scene that takes place in 1913, six years after Oklahoma statehood. Because Oklahoma argued that the dissolution of tribal governments occurred after allotments at the time of statehood, this phrasing is an inherently political counterargument. One of the best lines in the play is when one of the posse members breaking into the full-blood John Gray-Wolf's house proclaims, "You Indians must think you own things out here" (*Cherokee Night,* 260).

These statements suggest some amount of ambivalence toward Riggs's seeming endorsement of the vanishing notion, which he seems to present throughout the play with his doomed Cherokees, leading me to believe that all the talk of cultural disintegration may be a subterfuge for something else entirely. I am saying that all the talk of doomed Cherokees is coded statement that reflects Riggs's own suffering as a result of the closet, a link between his Indian and gay life, albeit a bleak one.

We have seen the evidence for such an argument in terms of Riggs's gay life. But what evidence exists for a merging of gay and Native American concerns in Riggs's play? I believe that four elements in the play suggest just such a reading: (1) the sequences of hauntings, (2) the many doubled and conflicted characters that recur throughout the work, (3) an autobiographical character named Gar, and (4) an emblematic cult scene. The ways that these themes demonstrate merged queer and Cherokee concerns will be the focus of my examination of *The Cherokee Night.*

The play begins with a haunted landscape, Claremore Mound, a place connected to narrative. This is where the Osages and Cherokees, according to local legend, fought their last battle, and strange doings abound here. Gar, the character with the highest Cherokee blood quantum (and, consequently, the one most in tune with things Cherokee according to the play's endorsement of racial purity), senses the haunted spirits more than the other characters. Claremore Mound is larger than life; the mound is absolute and undiminished (unlike the washed-out mixed-bloods in the play). Like a beacon, "Claremore Mound looms in the darkness, dim and silent, dwarfing the scene" (157). The young breeds encounter Jim Talbert, who is haunted by the ghost of one of the warriors of the Cherokee-Osage battle. Here the play gets a little hokey with its Cherokee "brave" in a warbonnet who visits Talbert.

Another haunting occurs when Art, Hutch, and Gar, as ten-year-old boys, find the place where a black man was murdered. The play is non-chronological and ahead of its time in terms of structure, and Riggs took a lot of flak for trying to do something different that later became a common dramatic device. At any rate, in actual chronology, Art will later become a murderer himself and will be tricked into believing his murdered wife is haunting him.

In the discovery of the murder scene where the black man was killed, Art already demonstrates a capacity for violence (200–201), which he will later act out as an adult when he murders his wife. Art is turned on by the blood on his hands when he touches the place of the killing, as well as horrified by it. In the discovery of the blood, Claremore Mound, and its nonstop drumming, is actually dictating some of the boys' actions: "The three back away, side by side, in a line, staring fearfully at the place, stepping together with the beat of the drum" (201).

The haunting theme is rendered homoerotically as the murdered black man rises from his grave:

Then slowly, rising from the warmed and fertile earth, a giant NEGRO, naked to the waist, lifts himself into the sun from behind the thick underbrush. His black body glistens. He stares off toward the fleeing boys, stretches himself, comes forward a step from sun into shadow, in a movement real and ghostly, as if he were two presences: the murderer undismayed by his crime, and the very emanation of the dead man himself. He stands a moment in the gloom, his dark hulk tremendous against the sun. His eyes follow the boys; one hand moves itself forward to a blackberry spray, in an uncalculated reflex, gathers two berries and lifts them idly to his mouth. Then he yawns. Then the sun dies. All below becomes dark. (201)

It is interesting that the most homoerotic passage in the play is a depiction of a black man, so that gayness—given the time of the play, 1936—

is rendered as totally Other, as blackness, as night, yet eroticized at the same time, turned into a strong love-hate relationship. The doom of Cherokees is described throughout the play as night descending on the people, and homosexuality, in the form of blackness here, is subtly and poetically linked with the vanishing Indian theory. At the same time that the black man rises up, an Indian man rises on top of the mound, strengthening this association. All this rising, the rhythmic drumming, and the presence of the mound itself, is a little too phallic and sexualized to ignore: "A light goes up, glows on the summit of Claremore Mound. An Indian, slim, aristocratic, minute in the distance, stands up against the sky. A drum is beating—harsh and troubled. It is like a fevered and aching disquiet in the pit of the world" (201–2).

It is interesting to note the difference between the earthy black man and the slim aristocratic Indian, the darker one being rendered more sexually. Although blackness is rendered as Other, there is a simultaneous attraction. Riggs was a light-skinned mixed-blood, and throughout his life his lovers were often Mexican and Hispanic men; he seemed to be attracted to darkness. The vanishing Indian on Claremore Mound becomes linked to dark sexual attraction, which the play depicts as doomed blackness.

I believe that the gothic quality of the play, the themes of the vengeful spirits of the murdered dead, reflects the secret and hidden life of the closet, just as Riggs's Oklahoma and theater theories do. What is the gothic about anyway, if not hidden secrets? It is interesting to note that Braunlich may pick up on this theme as well by titling her autobiography *Haunted by Home*. The idea of secrets and the hidden life especially come through in split and doubled characters.

Doubling of characters, like the sampling just discussed of the many hauntings, is pervasive in *The Cherokee Night*. The doubling occurs in two forms: single characters who suffer extreme schisms, and characters who occur in pairs. The characters are almost always conflicted with few exceptions. One such exception might be the Cherokee full-blood John Gray-Wolf, who is still culturally, morally, and spiritually intact, though he claims that his kids are dead to their own culture because of their mixed blood. Gray-Wolf's integrity comes merely from being of a different generation and having a higher blood quantum. Change and dynamism are enemies in this play. Gray-Wolf tells a story about a warrior who separates his life from his body for protection:

The big fighter of the Cherokee Tribe, when he was in a battle didn't want to be killed. So he found out how he could put his life up in the top of a sycamore tree while his body went on fightin' in the front row of the battle. Then his enemies would shoot at his body but couldn't hurt him a-tall. His life was safe—way up high in the tree out of sight. Once his enemies found out about it. At the next battle, they quit shootin' at his body, and shot all their arrows up in the top of the sycamore. So the warrior fell down dead. (*Cherokee Night*, 249)

I realize that my modus operandi here requires "reading into" passages, a technique that, to some, may seem like a stretch, but in the beginning of the chapter, I presented an extensive argument for why Riggs is sending us these messages in code that calls for just such readings. I cannot help but be struck by this passage as a possible metaphor for hiding away one's real life from public scrutiny. This passage underscores the terrible desperation of the schisms of the closet, the necessity of presenting a heterosexual act on one front, and keeping one's true nature hidden someplace else, trying to separate body and soul, like the warrior, a ploy that results in death. Unlike the actors in Riggs's plays, Riggs himself had to remain on the stage twenty-four hours a day for his entire life, forever playing the straight man, with the exception of a few relaxed moments in the sanctity of his home with his lovers. No wonder that when he fell in love, he would isolate himself from the rest of his friends and acquaintances. Further, the story of the deeply divided warrior describes almost every character in the play.

Art is one of these strongly conflicted characters. After the murder of his wife, Art tells two completely different versions of the killing to the prostitute Bee, whom the sheriff has placed in an adjacent cell in order to trick a confession out of Art. Art tells two contradictory stories, back to back, of the killing. Because Art believes he is speaking confidentially, there is no motivation for the radically different versions in terms of protecting his alibi. In the first version Art tells, he explains how his daughter Clara has a premonition and begs her mother not to go upstream with Art to purchase a cow pony. Art's wife stands up crazily in the boat and jumps into the water headfirst, hitting her head on sharp rocks. In the second version, told immediately after the first, Art describes his overwhelming hatred for his wife, which culminates in her murder: "I hated her, that's why, hated *her,* hated everybody—!" (167). What perhaps is implied is that along with everybody else he hates, Art also hates himself. Here, as with every instance in the play, heterosexual relationships are extremely problematic. Bee, the prostitute, listening to Art's account, relates to his story because she feels hatred toward men:

BEE: [*With savage joy, topping him in volume.*] Hate! Everybody! Me, too! Like me! [*Almost hysterically.*] I won't — that's all right — I'll never tell — I won't give you away — I thought it was money — I thought — [*Darkly, terribly.*] Anh, that's different! I never had the nerve! Listen, that's the way I feel — All the men I'd kill! I can see how you felt. [*Hypnotized.*] I can see her there in the boat — grinnin' up at you — her hair stringy, her eyes all bloodshot! Kill her! [*Startled.*] (167)

Each seems interested in killing off heterosexual partners. Art, it seems, acts out the dark impulses that Bee has restrained. Art's deep schisms are acted out violently; Bee's remain pent up. It seems to me that these deep splits are related to the "night" that has come to the Cherokees, spoken of in the opening epigraph of the play. This darkness, I'm speculating, is not simply the assimilation of Cherokees.

The startling personality splits continue in rapid-fire succession. Bee's hate speech (167), amazingly, is followed by a love speech (171). Although she changes her tune when she learns the sheriff has been listening in, the reader of the play might wonder why she needs to take back her outraged outburst about wanting to kill men. She is not being accused of murder; that is not why she is in jail. There is no real reason for the complete turnabout:

BEE: God, did that thing hear ever' word *I* said, *too?* [*With desperate irony, her voice harsh and troubled.*] It's a lie, Big Boy! I wouldn't hurt a fly! I go to church. I'm a good girl — I'm happy as hell. I love everybody. You'll see. You'll find out. When I was born, they wondered why I looked so sweet. Now they *know* why. I *am* sweet, that's the trouble with me. I cain't help it. I was born that way — . (171)

Particularly interesting are her last two lines: "I cain't help it. I was born that way." Bee is Gar's sister; both were fathered by the full-blood outlaw Spence. Spence, on the margins of society, seems to pass his outcast status on to his children. At the end of the play, which actually occurs before the aforementioned scene in terms of chronology, the character named Marthy presents the dying outlaw Spence with his own son, proclaiming prophetically that the internal misery, the deep schisms, and the self-hatred will continue, passed on to Bee and Gar from their no-good father (261). Stepping forward with their son Gar, Marthy tells

Spence: "But here's your son. In him your trouble. It goes on. In him. It ain't finished" (261).

Though the play throws up a smoke screen, arguing that the trouble referenced here is blood quantum troubles that will eventually disappear in future generations when the offspring will have so little Cherokee blood that they will not be "troubled" by their Indian heritage, such an argument makes no sense. Many of the characters in the play have minimal blood quantums, yet they still suffer the same cultural pain; they have not been "blessed" yet with this magic forgetfulness. So when Marthy says, "In our children, yes. [the continued trouble] In our children's children, maybe no" (262), this argument is not consistent. The characters in the play with the lesser blood quantums, the same blood quantums that Bee and Gar's children will have, are still problematized.

In the opening scene of the play, Talbert tells the whole mixed-blood gang of friends gathered at Claremore Mound that they are doomed because they have no connections to Cherokee culture. Riggs, most likely, is referring to something other than mere blood quantum and Cherokee cultural decay because he contradicts these arguments elsewhere. Gray-Wolf says that Spence, even though he is a full-blood, is "not enough Indian," indicating that his bad blood comes from abandoning a Cherokee worldview toward balance and appropriate living that is not directly correlated to Spence's degree of Indian blood (258). Spence is a man on the margins of society, an outlaw, acting out dark impulses. This "queer" behavior is passed on to Gar and Bee.

Another pairing involving siblings is the sisters Sarah and Viney. Though they share the same parents, Sarah and Viney are different as night and day, so to speak. Sarah, extremely impoverished, like Riggs himself did during his lean years, had to mortgage off her Cherokee land allotment, as did Sarah's son, reflecting the reality that within a few years after Oklahoma statehood the majority of Indian land was in white hands — as much through theft, however, as through Indians selling it. Sarah, though poor, maintains a sense of Cherokee identity, whereas Viney, who has prospered and married the mayor of Quapaw, Oklahoma, negates any connection to Cherokee culture. The passage bears a striking resemblance to issues of passing for gay men:

SARAH: And what about you, Viney?
VINEY: What about me?

SARAH: You're more Cherokee than Hutch.

VINEY: Well, I'm thankful to say it doesn't show.

SARAH: [*Strangely.*] Every word you say shows. Everything you say shames you. You try too hard to deny what you are. It tells on you. [*Harshly.*] You say Hutch didn't have any *change* in him. They's nuthin' else in you *but* change. You've turned your back on what you ought to a-been proud of. (182–83)

The play refuses to acknowledge the possibility that change does not by necessity equal cultural decay; that change, in fact, is often the sign of a living culture rather than a dead one; that in the face of change cultures often continue to maintain their worldviews, value systems, and language. In these regards, Riggs is consistent with the Indian novelists of the 1920s and 1930s whose works reflect uncertainty as to whether cultural survival was possible. I see more here, however, than the usual assimilationist ideology of Indians moving into the mainstream and disappearing.

How do we get a queer reading here, given that Riggs's passage reflects common attitudes regarding Indian people, an endorsement of the rather typical end-of-the-trail icon? If we continue to read to the very next page of the play, Sarah proclaims, like an oracle, an incantation that curses Viney and prophesies her destruction. Like Cherokee incantations, the chant employs language that states that the prophecy is being set into motion as it is spoken. The will of the incantator is set toward the accomplishment of what she is speaking. But does Sarah curse Viney for taking up the white man's road, for forgetting Cherokee culture, for trying to pass as a prominent white citizen of Quapaw, Oklahoma? No, instead, Sarah predicts Viney will self-destruct because of her unnatural predilections:

One thing you can't do, you with your table full of meat and furs around your neck:
You can't take a path you ain't meant to.
It'll take you to the jaws of wild animals,
It'll take you west, to the rivers of quicksand,
It'll take you to jagged cliffs,
It'll lead you to death! (184)

If, as the play argues, the "absorption," to use Riggs's term, of the Cherokees is inevitable, how can Viney's efforts to become white mean "tak[ing] a path [she] ain't meant to"? Over and over again, Riggs undermines his own arguments, leading me to believe that he uses the doom-and-gloom vanishing-culture arguments as a subterfuge for his own queer struggle. The potency of the lines comes from the way they cover multiple possibilities—both self-hatred (queerness is unnatural, in that way lies madness) and a healthier view of gay life (if you try to cover up your sexual orientation, you will make yourself crazy). The ambivalence points toward an author, I believe, who is incredibly tormented—on the one hand, closely allied with a man like Bynner who dared public exposure, very "out" for his time; yet, on the other, unable to follow Bynner's example and emulating more closely his friends who lived, like Riggs's Okies, completely in the shadows, daring not to speak or emerge into the light.

And I am haunted by the land allotment Sarah mortgages. Especially because Sarah's and Riggs's experiences exactly parallel here. The land, more than a matter of ownership (which was inimical to a traditional Cherokee worldview anyway), is an identity marker, literally an indicator of Cherokee national citizenship. But before allotment, land was held communally, and a traditional understanding of being a citizen of the Cherokee Nation involved a communal view marked by family and clan relationships and membership at a particular ceremonial grounds determined matrilineally rather than by the ownership of 160 acres.

Riggs, torn between Bynner and more closeted friends, also seems to be torn between the possibilities Sarah and Viney represent. What are these possibilities? There seems to me a powerful merging of queer and Indian interests here. The question is, can a cohesive tribal communal worldview be brought forward into contemporary circumstances? The play, on the surface, seems to say no. Tribalism, seen by Riggs, is outmoded; queerness, even worse, is anathema. Riggs hungers for this Indian and queer community, but one is doomed and the other cursed. Even more impossible—if you can get any more impossible here—is the idea of bringing the two together somehow.

These powerful ambivalences are demonstrated by the fact that Sarah—like Bee, who has a hate speech and a love speech, and like Art, who has two completely different renditions of his wife's death—has a curse chant and a blessing chant. After predicting Viney's destruction, Sarah immediately turns around and quotes her mother's chant that predicts the prosperity and cultural survival of the Cherokee Nation, another strong example of Riggs subverting his own vanishing argument. But then Sarah, in another complete turnaround, cries out in dismay that she is cut off from this communalism, that the way is not plain any more, that she can no longer follow (185).

A special case, a character who stands out from these doubled and conflicted mixed-bloods, is Gar. Gar is not only the most Indian character in the play, given the play's argument that because of his higher blood quantum he can sense things Cherokee (as if ancestral memory can be measured by the fractions on the Dawes Commission field records); he is also the queerest character. When Gar is first introduced in the opening scene, he is a little stereotypically stoic and found "relapsing into his customary uncommunicativeness" (140). Calling to mind Riggs's inarticulate Okies and his own coded frustrations about the limits of what his craft will let him say, as well as his resistance to autobiography, we might notice some parallels with the author's life. Gar, among his friends, is always on the margins of conversation, but when he does speak, his words are potent, prophetic, and connected to the invisible world. Paul Baker, a professor at Baylor, where Riggs taught for a while, described Riggs in an interview. Braunlich summarizes the interview thus:

> He often talked with students, even though he was "rather reclusive, since he was writing at the time also." Students came and brought food for Sunday evening dinners at Baker's house, where Riggs would sit on the rug, smoke his pipe, and talk for hours in his slow, thoughtful way. "An intelligent speaker, he never forced his ideas on anyone.". . .
> One of Riggs's students, Gene McKinney, later of the drama department of Trinity University in San Antonio, said in October, 1979, that Riggs seemed rather shy and that he spoke in anecdotal ways, using no prepared notes, telling stories about early days in Oklahoma. (Braunlich, 165)

In the play, predictably, Gar's mixed-blood friends have a capacity for sensing the supernatural Indian presences at Claremore Mound to a greatly diminished degree, their intuition only showing up faintly during times of distress, "something forgotten coming to life in them" (*Cherokee Night*, 139).

One of the most memorable—as well as bizarre—scenes in the play occurs when Gar, who has run off to Tahlequah on a quest to find out if anyone still remembers how to be Cherokee, ends up on the moun-

taintop religious commune of a cult that calls itself "the Tribe," based
on the notion that they are the lost tribe of Israel (an actual eighteenth-
century idea argued by the ethnographer James Adair, and many others
after him, that Indians are descended from one of the Jewish lost
tribes).

The play, which — except for its achronological sequencing and tendencies toward sensational violence — has been somewhat conventional
up to this point, gets really wild and whacky, taking a radically different
narrative turn. Gar has fallen into truly queer hands when cult members capture him. Afraid that Gar has been sent to spy on them, the
cult members wait for Jonas, their leader, to arrive and instruct them.
Two women tell a story about a man who will not admit his effeminate
reaction when he shows fear of a copperhead snake (208). One of the
women comments on the man's fear: "Women folks won't lie to *their*
selves" (209).

Why or how Gar ends up wandering to the mountain is never explained. According to the play, Gar is already culturally Cherokee, one
of the few real Indians, so his claim to have gone to Tahlequah to learn
how to be Cherokee makes no sense, another one of Riggs's contradictory arguments. I suspect it is as much an attraction to the queer cult
as anything else that draws Gar up the mountain, like an innocent Oklahoma gay Indian guy who flees to San Francisco or New York as much
by intuition as by foresight, like Riggs himself, for that matter, establishing homes in Santa Fe and Greenwich Village.

At any rate, when the crazy and sadistic preacher, Jonas, arrives on
the scene after Gar has been captured by the other cult members, Gar
reveals that he has a pent-up secret, saying to Jonas, "Listen! It's all shut
up in me, it's drivin' me crazy!" (221). Obviously, he is not talking about
being Cherokee here; because he is physically recognizable as a Cherokee, his Indian identity cannot be "all shut up" in him. Further, Gar's
trip to Tahlequah was a bust. He seems to be looking for more than
Cherokee lessons, since he determines that the old men in the town
square can't teach him anything anyway, and these are the same old men
who Riggs would argue are still culturally intact. Gar says:

> They's no place for me anywhere, see! Mr. Ferber wanted me to be
> educated, like him. He's my guardeen. He sent me to A. and M. I played
> football, made the track team. Didn't study. Didn't want to study. I got
> kicked out. I didn't belong there. Don't belong in Claremore. No place

for me anywhere! Come down to Tahlequah yesterday to see if—to
see—I thought this being the head of—Listen, I'm half Cherokee. I
thought they could help me out here. I thought they—Old men sittin'
in the square! No Tribe to go to, no Council to help me out of the kind
of trouble I'm in. Nuthin' to count on—! (222–23)

What kind of trouble is Gar actually in? Why did they kick him out of
school; was it only for poor study skills? The close parallels to Riggs's
own autobiography, with his aborted attempt at the University of
Oklahoma and his lifelong sense of not belonging in Claremore, are
apparent.

The whole passage is really bizarre, and even if my queer reading is
totally misplaced, nonetheless it is pretty obvious that this part of the
play calls for an interpretation beyond what is immediately obvious, so
I am trying to offer these possibilities that, to me, make a lot of sense.
While Jonas's congregation of sadistic rabble-rousers is clamoring for
Gar's torture and death, Jonas, a very queer preacher indeed, counsels
Gar on the grim realities. From Jonas's perspective, Cherokee culture is
dead, and queer identity, he hints, is unspeakable. The only thing that
remains is manipulation of the dim-witted members of "the Tribe":
"Their [Cherokee] ways are going. Their customs change. That part of
you can never be fulfilled. What's left? You must look to heaven! Like
us!" (223). For the first, last, and only time in the play, Claremore Mound
fades. This is a low point, an abandonment of hope for both Indian and
queer viability: "Claremore Mound's faint outline no longer stands up
on the horizon" (223). The stage directions say: "Somewhere in the
speech, JONAS crosses, mounts the rostrum, hypnotic, queer, powerful"
(224).

Part of Jonas's and the cult's queerness is a rejection of Christianity:
"We had seen the ways men called Christian. And that is why we pre-
ferred the peace of this high mountain" (224). The cult is communal
and naturalistic. Jonas never quite articulates the larger issue—respecting the natural tendencies of humans regarding sexual orientation—
yet Jonas tries to recruit Gar to take his place as leader of the Tribe,
since Jonas is looking for a queer replacement for his queer leadership
of a queer group.

Jonas is the more intelligent queer; his congregation is ignorant and
simple. The life he promises Gar is simply controlling and lording it over
these morons, the sterile joy of the oppressed becoming one of the op-

pressors. This grim possibility corresponds with what gay men often faced during Riggs's lifetime—turning on your own kind to cover up your own orientation, disguising that you are one of the cursed ones yourself; internalizing hatred, directing it against yourself and others.

Gar rejects queerness in any form, though he is starving for it. Jonas says to him, "You scorn our religion! You mock our way of life! You refuse bread offered you when you're starving" (226). Jonas indicates his sadistic attraction to Gar: "We wouldn't want God to kill you, too— you *so young*—!" (226).

The symbolic end of the scene closes with Gar being chained to a post in the sanctuary—not subtle, exactly—where presumably he will be tortured and killed, as was a sheriff who wandered up the mountain by accident from Tahlequah. Gar does not bare his chest to reveal his scarlet *Q*, quite the opposite. From the chaining posts, Gar swears loyalty to an epic quest to search and destroy all semblances of queerness within himself:

> I won't die this way! I'm tied up here, yes. But some day I'll get loose.
> You won't kill me! You won't kill me! You can't kill me! I'm going to live.
> Live! And I'll burn down your God damned tabernacle to the ground!
> Do you hear me? Your God damned tabernacle to the ground! (229–30)

Like the young Gar, Riggs, too, remained divided and, tragically, probably remained so throughout his life. One of the more bizarre incidents Braunlich writes of is Riggs's childhood visiti to see Bosco the Snake Eater in Claremore; after the performance, the boy sat on the curb and vomited. The scene does not exactly beg for a Freudian reading. In a letter to Bynner after the nervous breakdown at OU over an incident when a girlfriend (hope for salvation from queerness, perhaps?) spurned him, Riggs said, "It will take several decades to overcome wrong habits of thought, won't it?" (Braunlich, 7). At the same time, he was a very generous man throughout his life, especially in terms of discreetly promoting the careers of young gay male writers.

One of Riggs's themes is innocent youths in conflict with oppressive adults and restrictive social institutions that hold back natural and free impulses. Idealism, especially in youth, succumbs to convention. In each play there is an individual who resists subjection, but in Gar's case, the end result is his torture. The plays also depict love as a source of pain and pleasure. In an autobiographical short story, Riggs, a dog lover who kept dogs all his life, has an interesting interpretation of what it means to be an animal lover:

> Mutilated by love. Shucked and tortured, desolated and gone dry with pain and desertion — how many times? . . . And yet such love was in him ready to spring and burgeon (and envelop if not watched) and there is no real stopping a man who has in him such a tenderness and desire and capacity for giving and receiving joy and hurt. But at this stage, a dog would help, he knew that, he had known it before, and survived darkness thereby. (Braunlich, 194)

The tragicomic last line underscores the difficulty of maintaining gay relationships in the thirties and forties, which must be compensated by whatever feeble means available to Riggs, including pet ownership.

Without the double reading — that is, linking the play's Indian and gay concerns — *The Cherokee Night* is powerful but puzzling. It is as if the play never gets to wherever it is trying to go, that final destination, in fact, remaining a mystery. The lines are lyrical, but their significance is hard to ascertain. Under a gay reading, the play's poetic power, its ability to take on richly nuanced layers of significance, amplifies considerably. A queer reading of *The Cherokee Night*, I would argue, enriches the play and points to Riggs's artistry as a man advancing controversial themes under very difficult circumstances that, as in other uses of code, require avoiding detection by the enemy. As an Indian work, *The Cherokee Night* is a good play. As a queer Indian work, *The Cherokee Night* is a fabulous play; haunting, poetic, layered in meanings.

I would like to explain my use of the word "queer" throughout this chapter. Behind the use of the term is the argument that gay people are not the same as straight people, that a queer frame of reference causes one to see the world differently than a straight frame of reference does, and that queerness, those things that make gays and lesbians unique, should be celebrated rather than assimilated. This could be related somewhat to Harry Hays's famous statement that the one thing gays and straights *do* have in common is what they do in bed. Hays, in other words, was arguing that a queer sensibility exists that is significantly different from a straight one. When liberals argue, "It doesn't matter whether someone is gay or straight, we are all the same," the queer argument would be, "No, it *does*, in fact, matter; we're *not* all the same." Behind the liberal "why can't we all just get along?" line of reasoning, often applied to race as well, is an underlying supremacism, a demand that everybody be white and heterosexual, that cultural identities be sacrificed so that dominant culture can rest safely. It is a continuance of the melting-pot mentality, placing whiteness at the center and demanding that all other identities be subsumed by it.

The term "queer" works for me because it acknowledges the importance of cultural differences and the usefulness of maintaining those differences rather than simply submitting to dominant-culture norms. In other words, it is an anti-assimilationist term and bears a relationship to the kind of radical possibilities I wish to discuss. Also, the thinking behind the term "queer," which seems to celebrate deviance rather than apologize for it, seems embodied with trickster's energy to push social boundaries. Such a celebration, obviously, was not available to Lynn Riggs, whose only association with trickster was donning disguises, and those not for the purpose of liberation.

One of trickster's primary modi operandi, shape-shifting, the power to move fluidly beyond static definitions of cultural boundaries and taboos, is an impulse with both positive and destructive possibilities. Celebrating tricksters, it seems to me, should be done with caution. It is important to remember that shape-shifting can also be a form of witchery and that tricksters can be oppressive assholes as often as liberators — just check out the stories. Riggs's life demonstrates a form of shape-shifting that employs disguises that cause a split between one's inner nature and one's social behavior, not unlike the warrior in *The Cherokee Night* who separates spirit from body, hiding his true self up in the top of a tree. This form of shape-shifting causes schisms, self-hatred, and ultimately death, rather than creative life-giving forms of transforming static social boundaries. It is a form of shape-shifting that endorses, rather than resists, the spirit/flesh, mind/body, head/heart splits that Western thinking has labored under for so long.

Yet trickster strategies, a little creative wordplay, some attention to shape-shifting and multiple possibilities for meaning, can go a long ways toward opening up understanding. I offer the following positive example. Many Native gays and lesbians have begun to use the term "two-spirit" to describe themselves. Although the term is pan-tribal, because each nation has its own word for homosexuals in its tribal language, "two-spirited" is a metaphor, a trope, that reflects the fact that many traditional cultures see gays as between genders, doubly empowered because they can see from both male and female perspectives. Trickster energy empowers the term because many Indian gay guys have decided they do not want to be called by the degrading, offensive, and racist term "berdache" that is used in white anthropological literature about Indians.[5]

So Native gays and lesbians made up their own word, and especially significant is the idea behind the word that gayness is a blessing, as well as that the choice of the term is an act of self-definition. This metaphor has been transformative to many Native gays and lesbians, who for the first time have a new way of imagining themselves that has to do with giftedness rather than as grotesques or sinners. If Lynn Rollie Riggs had this one term at his disposal, or better yet, if he had ever been able to accept the legitimacy of a more Cherokee view of the world, his life might have been a very different story, who knows? Instead, he ended up like his character Gar with no place to flee inside or outside Tahlequah.

Have I strayed far afield from Lynn Rollie Riggs? I do not think so. Riggs's theories of Oklahoma and Oklahomans, of the Oklahoma artist representing Oklahomans, of the grim and golden ages of Oklahoma, and the end of Cherokee culture, all coded statements for the despair of the closet, suggest possibilities for examining the state of Native studies. Some key issues in Native studies include the application of theoretical frameworks from within Native cultures, allowing the cultures to generate a theory of themselves; exploring issues of identity and authenticity; allowing Native people to explicate their own texts and cultures, even when the interpretations differ from those of dominant culture; bringing hitherto silent histories to light; developing aesthetic criteria that emphasize tribal viewpoints; engaging in social activism; connecting Indian literatures to Indian communities who might find such literatures useful in passing on cultural information or political viewpoints; and examining social issues like poverty, alcoholism, activism, protest movements, protection of treaty rights, and the role of outsiders writing and speaking about Indian people, just to name a few areas. The aforementioned issues, as well as Riggs's life and work, deal with interiority and exteriority, insider status and outsider status, being silenced and speaking for oneself.

Code involves avoiding detection by the enemy. Its power lies in communicating messages only understood by a select few. Those few who have ears to hear find comfort in a coterie of those who are like them in shared knowledge and experience. This may be the only means available for communication, the only opportunity to show their true face among others who understand and will not reject them. Signals, signs, and tropes develop so that they can recognize who is safe, who is not. Messages have to be interpreted as much for what they do not say as what they do say. In some cases, perhaps in Riggs's, this ambiguity of language is oppressive rather than liberating, though better than no form of expression at all. Unfortunately, however, it would seem that the enemy from whom Riggs is avoiding detection is not only others but himself, and the code functions as a deep denial, a way of writing about everything except what he really wanted to write about—being Indian and gay.

Riggs's use of code reinforces the assumption that dominant culture is always right, that inside the camp is the best place to be. It leaves both Indian and queer identities on the margin, the status quo at the center. I believe that the future direction of Native studies will be to break down this hierarchy, to challenge the nature of what we have inherited in the discipline. Rather than revising dominant-culture literary and critical aesthetics and "fitting" Native texts and cultures to such criteria, the criteria themselves will be questioned as to their applicability, and more radical approaches will be posited as possibilities. Integration, acceptance, and assimilation to literary norms will no longer be our highest goal. Native critics will turn toward more disruptive tactics, and this new group might be closer kin to Rabbit, leaping away with the very flames themselves, rather than victims outside the campfire waiting for someone to invite them over for a little warming up.

Dear Hotgun:

Well, so Stijaati Thlaako, Big Man, and Rabbit was decided to go fishing at Lake Oologah. Big Man pack cane pole and bobber. Rabbit tighten down the screws on reel of old open-face baitcaster. Stijaati go for challenge and bring fly rod on account of just watched *A River Runs through It* and claims fly casting is pure poetry mebeso wants to be young hunk like Brad Pitt, quien sabe?

They was go through MacWhopper drive-thru at Henryetta and order french fries with gravy; they was stop at Creek National Council House at Okmulgee and take pitcher on council square with Japanese instant throwaway camera; they was stop off at Sapulpa for free supper at kinfolks; they was go to Johnny Lee Wills music shop in Tulsey town to pick up old Bob Wills tapes to listen to on the way; then they was pick up Highway 169 and leave Creek Nation after nice little tour good thing summertime too so they still was had daylight to see by before they cross border into foreign country.

After the border crossing they seen Cherokee country sho nuff, and Stijaati make commentation on ever little detail. Stijaati was say, "Instead of Oktahutche, we got scrub size Caney River; instead of steep hill and post oak, we got rolling pasture and farm pond more like Kansas; instead of Eufaula Lake, we got Oologah Lake; instead of Indian Turnpike, we got Highway 169; instead of Creek Nation Bingo Parlor we got billboard him say apply for Cherokee Nation Visa Card; instead of pass through Creek writer country, Bald Hill, home of Alex Posey, Coweta, home of Louis Oliver, Tulsa, home of Joy Harjo, we got Cherokee writing landscape, Claremore and Oologah, home of Lynn Riggs and Will Rogers."

Stijaati was had not finish his lecture and has captive audience unless they jump out in roadside ditch, so he go on and say, "Chalakees has a whole set of writers of they own with a different set of national problems that surround they work. For instance they got Elias Boudinot who wrote a novel in the Cherokee syllabary way back before Indian Removal called *Poor Sarah,* but Boudinots and Ridges was members of the Treaty Party who signed away Cherokee lands illegally. Then they was got John Rollins Ridge whose father was executed for treason in Indian Territory the same night in 1839 as Elias Boudinot was killed also for treason. Now this here boy Ridge ended up shooting a member of the Ross faction in revenge and fleeing to California. Out there he was write *The Adventures of Joaquin Murieta.* Problem is the novel don't deal with Cherokees but a legendary Mexican bandito. Then there is John Oskison, from Vinita, a buddy of Will Rogers all they lives, who wrote three novels in the 1920s about Oklahoma life in the 1880s but his books is mostly about white cowboys and cattle ranching. Then there is Lynn Riggs, who came up with a play that turned into the most popular musical in American history, but Riggs waddn't able to express his truest subject matter. Cherokees writing today come from this history to where they are now, just as Creek writers is descended from those Creeks writing before them. Each group faced its own history of problems that they was to overcome in order to write about tribal life."

Rabbit he was grab co-cola from ice chest and say, "Not to mention they sing Creek songs at Cherokee stomp grounds."

Well, so they was pass through Oologah and stop and get groceries but Rabbit say he got headache and set out in the car so he don't have to hep pay when they go through checkout line. He done wore out his "I forgot my wallet." They got the groceries loaded and drove on until they come upon a nice little campground near the big bridge outside of town. Stijaati was pulled in and asked the lady how much for a spot, and him was said five dollars for a night. Big Man and Rabbit had they hopes up on account of the place looked right civilized with its whitewashed stone tables and shade trees and mowed grass and even laundromat with sody-pop and candy machine. But it was a mile from the lake, and Stijaati wanted to pull up longside his fishing hole and set up camp.

Stijaati was say, "I know a better spot right next to the water." Well, so they drove way round the lake until Rabbit thought he could see Kansas, then Stijaati got them off in the woods down a dirt road that dead-ended at a rock pile. But like he said it was next to a cove of water.

Rabbit got out in the middle of the rock pile and was say, "This ought to get us ready to rent that new Fred Flintstone movie." They was another truck parked there with a Confederate flag in the back window and white fellas with ZZ Top beards clean down to they knees smoking dope in lawn chairs in the back and listening to Lynrd Skynrd belt out "Sweet Home Alabama" before the tragic plane crash that took their lives. They glared at Stijaati and Big Man as they unpacked, and Rabbit snickered in Creek, "Must be Cherokees."

Stijaati was laugh and say, "The one with the white beard looks a little like G. W. Grayson." But they was get their tent set up under the watchful eyes of the Confederate faction and then they got to light Coleman lantern because if they is to get their poles wet it's gonna have to be night fishing.

But they build up a fire instead and heat up a can of Bush's baked beans. Rabbit tells them he got a secret family recipe that knocks the fart out of them while they cooking. They sit around the campfire, and like Indians must do, they gotta scare the beejesus out of one another with story of *stikini,* and, *lokha,* and sleep maker except unlike white people they know these stories to be true. The scariest thing is not believing. One thing they do learn for sure is Rabbit's family recipe don't work, and Stijaati say to Rabbit, "Good god-a-mighty what was had crawled up your ass and died?" Stijaati and Big Man make Rabbit go stand off a distance downwind except Rabbit scared from too many ghost stories to get out of the light of the fire. Big Man and Stijaati hold they noses shut, and wave the air in front of they faces and say "fumbee" too much.

Then Stijaati tell the story of his hunting buddy Derek Stiff Rabbit and how Derek got his Indian name. Stijaati and Derek was go on big duck hunt on Sac and Fox land down by Stroud where Derek's kin live. Stijaati wanna get in last minute duck shoot before drive off to Californey next day and see grandchildrens in Fresno. Him and Derek laid out all day long on farm pond and wait on pintail or mallard to show up. They didn't had no luck and pulled up decoys, packed her in. On the way back to the truck, they scared up a jackrabbit come running out of a bush and acrost a muddy cow field. Derek shot at it with his twelve gauge since no dang duck luck mebeso last hope is rabbit stew which is almost as good as duck nohows even if you haveta spit out a piece of shot ever now and again but not near as good as squirrel with dumplings.

Rabbit was cover his ears with his paws during this part of the story and say, "I can't look" like at scary drive-in pitcher show with Creek girlfriend.

Stijaati go on and say, "Derek went and picked up the rabbit. He was always real lazy about cleaning whatever he killed or caught and would put it off until he get home and mebe someone else do it for him. We got back to the truck and Derek put the rabbit in a paper sack and stick him behind the seat of my pickup."

Stijaati was say, "We drove out on a country road back to Stroud and poured out our last cup of coffee from the thermos we'd been drinking out of all day long. It was starting to get kind of dusky out, but we was enjoying our coffee, wrapping our hands around the hot cups, and got the heater cranked up real good when I mean out of nowheres in the middle of the road rose up a big ole horned owl in front of the pickup. I slammed on the brakes but too late and we heard that owl thump under both the front and back tires. Naturally, me and Derek was to turn around and look behind us, and we both seen that owl just get up and fly into an oak tree on the side of the road like nothing ever happened. Just sitting there and looking at us. We was drove off, and he boomed a couple times, then we didn't hear nothing.

"I left Derek off in Stroud, and I was anxious to get on the road for Fresno, wanted an early start to see my grandkids. Went to bed early in Weleetka, then was got up before daybreak and headed myself out. Didn't notice nothing unusual until around Flagstaff after a hard day of driving. Something in the cab of the truck smelt, but it waddn't like one of Rabbit's farts make you jump clean out of the cab, just a faint odor of something rotten. I'd had the heater blasted wide open just about the whole time since I'd left Weleetka cause it had been plumb cold out. Then I crossed that terrible stretch after you leave Needles, California, worst long distance between a gas station I ever seen, when that smell come on full bore. I'd eaten Chinese food way back in Gallup, and I'd been kind of nervous at the idea of Yazzies and Begays cooking up lemon chicken, but it's my favorite and I ate him nohow. I got to thinking, 'Good god, is that smell coming out of me?' I finally reached the station at Ludlow and gassed up. I pulled the bench seat forward to get a can of Pennzoil back there and that's when I seen that paper bag. I was said, 'Derek you sorry son-of-a-bitch.' "

Big Man was say, "Now that's some ghost story."

Rabbit was say, "I thought it was a story about how Derek got his Indian name?" Rabbit has worked Bush baked beans out of his system and moved back to the fire. "I got a ghost story," he says. "It's a Cherokee ghost story. It's about how Lynn Riggs haunts these parts around Claremore. It's a story about how Claremore haunts Lynn Riggs. It's a story about how an Indian gay guy in the 1930s is himself haunted."

Stijaati was waiting for break to jump in and tell joke and says, "Did I already tell the one about the difference between the white ghost and the Indian ghost?"

Rabbit was say, "Riggs was afraid of the light and only come out at night. Only other ghosts would have recognized him. He must had wandered the earth, restless, waiting for his pain to go away, one of the living dead. He can't come home until a ritual is performed that allows him to rest in peace. He scares people. He's frightened of himself."

Big Man was say, "That sounds like hell."

Stijaati was say, "That sounds like the closet."

Rabbit was say, "This ghost story is important even though it's so scary. We was talk about Creek writers and how far they have come from their beginnings. Lynn Riggs just tried to survive and hope for a better day when someone come along and read his work and crack the code, set him free so he could rest in peace.

"One question we still gotta consider before we put this book to bed — what happens to the Indian gay guy or gal writing today? Will they speak the truth about their lives and places in their tribes? More important than that, even: What's the future for Indian gay and lesbian readers wanting to read something honest about theyselves? Without no help and no stories, maybe they will become haunted like Lynn Riggs. Mebeso if writers don't write about things, they is partly responsible for turning kids into ghosts. If Indian writers write only about straight Indians and not all kinda Indians, what sets them apart from white writers making up Indian romances?"

Big Man was say, "Mebeso it's not traditional to talk about sex."

Stijaati was say, "Good god, man, did you ever listen to oral tradition? Did you ever hear old women and old men teasing one another? Where does this 'Indians don't talk about sex business' come from anyway? I thought that's all we ever talk about. They useta say Indians don't protest; now they say they don't talk about sex."

Rabbit was say, "Well, there's hope. We have to give credit to the women writers, especially Chrystos, Beth Brant, and Janice Gould."

Stijaati was say, "And now the guys gotta be next. They's a couple young ones that don't give a saltine cracker about acceptance, just doing they thing making art and stories about as Indian and queer and hilarious as they can."

Well, so I would put in more news, but that was the end of the ghost stories, and Stijaati, Big Man, and Rabbit was to lay down in the tent until a big storm blowed in around 3 A.M. and the canvas walls sucked in and out like a bellows and the rain took to running down the sides in small streams. They knowed if they waited a minute too long they'd never get out on the dirt road they come in on, so they pulled up tent stakes and throwed everything in back—never even took they fishpoles out of the truck— and headed back home in the dark. They stopped off again at Sapulpa at 6 A.M., woke their kin up, warmed up the left-over beans, and made hot dogs for breakfast with the package of wieners they hadn't opened yet.

They was tired and wanted to end the book nohows; those last two chapters was especially long and tiresome.

Sincerely,
Jim Chibbo

Notes

Introduction

1. Durango Mendoza's short story "Summer Water and Shirley" is analyzed in the original dissertation version of this book, as is the work of Thomas E. Moore (William Harjo) and Susanna Factor. "Summer Water and Shirley" is anthologized in Natachee Scott Momaday's book *American Indian Authors* (Boston: Houghton Mifflin, 1971). Thomas Moore's work *Sour Sofke* was published in Muskogee, Oklahoma, by Hoffman Pringing Company and can sometimes be found in places like the Creek National Council House Museum in Okmulgee. Vincent Mendoza has an interesting autobiography about growing up Mexican American and Creek entitled *Son of Two Bloods* (Lincoln: University of Nebraska Press, 1996). Eddie Chuculate is a budding Creek creative writer published in various anthologies. Susanna Factor has written bilingual children's books used in schools in the Creek Nation. Helen Chalakee Burgess is a Creek writer, essayist, and journalist who has worked for the Creek Nation. Jim Pepper was an outstanding jazz saxophonist interested in syntheses of tribal music and jazz.

2. See Daniel F. Littlefield for many of Gibson's letters, as well as other early Creek writers who appeared in print in *Native American Writing in the Southeast: An Anthology, 1875–1935* (Jackson: University Press of Mississippi, 1995).

3. G. W. Grayson, *A Creek Warrior for the Confederacy: The Autobiography of Chief G. W. Grayson*, ed. David W. Baird (Norman: University of Oklahoma Press, 1988).

4. Howard Adams, *A Tortured People: The Politics of Colonization* (Penticton, B.C.: Theytus Books, 1995), 38.

5. Ibid., 45.

6. Anna Lee Walters, *Talking Indian: Reflections on Survival and Writing* (Ithaca, N.Y.: Firebrand Books, 1992), 86.

7. The genesis of this idea began for me in a conversation with historian Tony Hall, who was commenting on the way in which Native issues in Canada are so much more prominent in public discourse than they are in the United States. Hall observed that perhaps Indians are allowed to exist only as fiction in the States.

8. Joel W. Martin, *Sacred Revolt* (Boston: Beacon Press, 1991), 179.

9. Elizabeth Cook-Lynn, *Why I Can't Read Wallace Stegner and Other Essays: A Tribal Voice* (Madison: University of Wisconsin Press, 1996), 84–85.

10. I am indebted to Morgan for allowing me to read and cite her dissertation in progress for the Ph.D. at the University of Oklahoma on the subject of Lakota women writers. Morgan has since successfully defended her dissertation and earned the Ph.D. in the spring semester 1997.

11. See, for example, Leon Portilla's essay "Have We Really Translated the Meso-American Word," in *On the Translation of Native American Literatures,* ed. Brian Swann (Washington: Smithsonian Institution Press, 1992).

12. Kirk H. Zebolksky, "Recent Works of Louis, Harjo, and Silko: Emphasizing Land Rights, Subsuming Native Culture," student paper for Native American literature class at the University of Nebraska at Omaha.

13. Beth Brant, *Writing as Witness: Essay and Talk* (Toronto: Women's Press, 1994), 45.

1. The Creek Nation

1. These figures were obtained via a telephone conversation with Creek tribal headquarters in 1994.

2. Grant Foreman, *Indian Removal: The Emigration of the Five Civilized Tribes of Indians* (Norman: University of Oklahoma Press, 1953), 107.

3. Basil Johnston's work seems amazingly useful in this area, particularly his artfully written account of Ojibway oral tradition entitled *The Manitous: The Spiritual World of the Ojibway* (New York: HarperCollins, 1995), as well as many of his other books.

4. Susan Scarberry-Garcia's work *Landmarks of Healing* (Albuquerque: University of New Mexico Press, 1990) closely explicates the Navajo and Jemez material in *House Made of Dawn.*

5. Louis Littlecoon Oliver, *Chasers of the Sun: Creek Indian Thoughts* (Greenfield Center, N.Y.: Greenfield Review Press, 1990), 3.

6. See the prologue in N. Scott Momaday, *The Way to Rainy Mountain* (Albuquerque: University of New Mexico Press, 1969).

7. Oliver, *Chasers of the Sun,* 9.

8. David H. Corkran, *The Creek Frontier: 1540–1783* (Norman: University of Oklahoma Press, 1967), 3–4.

9. Angie Debo, *The Road to Disappearance* (Norman: University of Oklahoma Press, 1941), 3.

10. Ibid., 4–5.

11. Charles M. Hudson, *The Southeastern Indians* (Knoxville: University of Tennessee Press, 1976), 34–119.

12. George Lankford, "Red and White: Some Reflections on Southeastern Symbolism," *Southern Folklore* 50, no. 1 (1993): 56. Hereafter cited in the text.

13. Corkran, *The Creek Frontier,* 41.

14. Sharon O'Brien, *American Indian Tribal Governments* (Norman: University of Oklahoma Press, 1989), 121. Hereafter cited in the text.

15. Foreman, *Indian Removal,* 107.

16. Angie Debo, *And Still the Waters Run: The Betrayal of the Five Civilized Tribes* (Princeton, N.J.: Princeton University Press, 1940).

17. Alexander Posey, *The Fus Fixico Letters*, ed. Daniel F. Littlefield Jr. (Lincoln: University of Nebraska Press, 1993), 227.

18. *Nations Remembered: An Oral History of the Cherokees, Chickasaws, Choctaws, and Seminoles in Oklahoma, 1865–1907*, ed. Theda Perdue (Norman: University of Oklahoma Press, 1993), 184.

19. Ibid., 184–85.

20. G. W. Grayson, *A Creek Warrior for the Confederacy: The Autobiography of Chief G. W. Grayson*, ed. W. David Baird (Norman: University of Oklahoma Press, 1988), 163–64.

21. Debo, *Road to Disappearance*, 7.

22. Hudson, *The Southeastern Indians*, 234–39.

23. Willie Lena and James H. Howard, *Oklahoma Seminoles: Medicine, Magic, and Religion* (Norman: University of Oklahoma Press, 1984). Hereafter cited in the text.

24. Harry A. Kersey Jr., *The Seminole and Miccosukee Tribes: A Critical Bibliography* (Bloomington: Indiana University Press, 1987), 1–70. There are also Florida Miccosukees who separated from Florida Seminoles in the early 1960s and speak Hitchiti, a dialect that, though part of the Muskhogean language group, is by now virtually a distinctly separate language from Creek.

25. A Creek favorite made from hominy that is allowed to sour slightly. A fairly complicated process involving filtering water through ashes, and so on, is required to make *sofki*.

26. For the full account of the Creek busk on which the preceding summary is based, see the chapter "Ceremonialism: The Green Corn Ceremony," in Lena and Howard.

2. Reading the Oral Tradition for Nationalist Themes

1. Charles M. Hudson, *The Southeastern Indians* (Knoxville: University of Tennessee Press, 1976), 34–119.

2. David H. Corkran, *The Creek Frontier: 1540–1783* (Norman: University of Oklahoma Press, 1967), 23.

3. Joel W. Martin, *Sacred Revolt: The Muskogees' Struggle for a New World* (Boston: Beacon Press, 1991), 128–29.

4. Ibid., 121.

5. Ibid., 127–28.

6. Ibid., 132.

7. Corkran, *The Creek Frontier*, 16.

8. George E. Lankford, "Red and White: Some Reflections on Southeastern Symbolism," *Southern Folklore* 50, no. 1 (1993): 56.

9. David Michael Lambeth, *The World and Way of the Creek People*. I purchased Lambeth's book at the Creek National Council House. Evidently it was self-published in the early eighties. The project was completed with money from the State Arts Council of Oklahoma, according to information in the book, and there is a statement on the inside cover that says copies may be obtained from David Mike Lambeth, 219 South 5th, Okemah, OK 74859. I have not seen the book anywhere other than the National Council House, though it may very well be in other places. Lambeth's collection of transcribed oral stories from Creek elders has no page numbers; thus I have no citations for pages, either.

10. Ibid. Deere's account transcribed in Lambeth's book.

11. Ibid.

12. Ibid.

13. Theda Perdue, *Nations Remembered: An Oral History of the Cherokees, Chickasawas, Choctaws, Creeks, and Seminoles in Oklahoma, 1865–1907* (Westport, Conn.: Greenwood Press, 1980), xix.

14. *The Shadow of Sequoyah: Social Documents of the Cherokees, 1862–1964*, ed. Jack Frederick and Anna Gritts Kilpatrick (Norman: University of Oklahoma Press, 1965).

15. Lambeth, *The World and Way of the Creek People*. Factor's account transcribed in Lambeth's book.

16. Howard Adams, *A Tortured People: The Politics of Colonization* (Penticton, B.C.: 1995), 143–54.

17. Adams, *A Tortured People*, 135.

18. Percy Bullchild, *The Sun Came Down* (San Francisco: Harper and Row, 1985). Unfortunately, this book has gone out of print, though it is still widely available in libraries.

19. Basil Johnston, *The Manitous: The Spiritual World of the Ojibway* (New York: HarperCollins, 1995).

20. Jack Kilpatrick and Anna Gritts Kilpatrick, *Friends of Thunder: Folktales of the Oklahoma Cherokees* (Dallas: Southern Methodist University Press, 1964), and *Walk in Your Soul: Love Incantations of the Oklahoma Cherokees* (Dallas: Southern Methodist University Press, 1965), are exceptional works of Cherokee literature translated by Cherokees fluent in their language.

3. In the Storyway

1. Paul Radin, *The Trickster* (New York: Schocken Books, 1956).

2. N. Scott Momaday, *House Made of Dawn* (New York: Harper and Row, 1968), 58–59.

3. The dissertation version of this book took up this subject in the chapter entitled "Within and without the Storytelling Circle: Native and Ethnographers' Versions of Oral stories."

4. John Swanton, *Myths and Tales of the Southeastern Indians* (Washington, D.C.: Bureau of American Ethnology Bulletin 88, 1929). This was also reprinted, under the same title, by the University of Oklahoma Press in 1995. References are to page numbers in the BAE bulletin.

5. Ibid., 40.

6. Ibid.

7. This too was taken up in my original dissertation in the chapter entitled "Within and without the Storytelling Circle: Native and Ethnographers' Versions of Oral stories."

8. Swanton, *Myths and Tales of the Southeastern Indians*, 41.

9. Ibid.

10. Ibid.

11. Ibid.

4. Alice Callahan's *Wynema*

1. Alice S. Callahan, *Wynema: A Child of the Forest,* ed. A. LaVonne Brown Ruoff (Lincoln: University of Nebraska Press, 1997). Hereafter cited in the text.

2. Ibid., xvi–xviii. This information is from Ruoff's introduction.

3. Michael D. Green, *The Creeks* (New York: Chelsea House Publishers, 1990), 87.

4. Ibid., 88.

5. Ibid., 89.

6. Callahan, *Wynema,* xiv. From information in Ruoff's introduction.

7. Homer Noley, *First White Frost: Native Americans and United Methodism* (Nashville, Tenn.: Abingdon Press, 1991).

8. Callahan, *Wynema,* xiv–xv. From information in Ruoff's introduction.

9. See Daniel F. Littlefield's introduction to *The Fus Fixico Letters* (Lincoln: University of Nebraska Press, 1993), the biography *Alex Posey: Creek Poet, Journalist, and Humorist* (Lincoln: University of Nebraska Press, 1992), or *Native American Writing in the Southeast: An Anthology, 1875–1935* (Jackson: University Press of Mississippi, 1995).

5. Fus Fixico

1. Daniel F. Littlefield Jr., *Alex Posey: Creek Poet, Journalist, and Humorist* (Lincoln: University of Nebraska Press, 1992), and Alexander Posey, *The Fus Fixico Letters,* ed. Daniel F. Littlefield Jr. and Carol A. Petty Hunter (Lincoln: University of Nebraska Press, 1993); hereafter cited in the text.

2. Louis Littlecoon Oliver, *Estiyut Omayat: Creek Writings* (Muskogee, Okla.: Indian University Press, 1985), 17.

3. Ibid., 17.

4. Alexia Kosmider, "Tricky Tribal Discourse" (Ph.D. diss., University of Rhode Island, 1994), 55–56. Hereafter cited in the text.

5. Beth Brant, *Writing as Witness: Essay and Talk* (Toronto: Women's Press, 1994), 92.

6. Littlefield, *Alex Posey,* 167.

7. John R. Swanton, *Myths and Tales of the Southeastern Indians* (Norman: University of Oklahoma Press, 1995).

8. Walter J. Ong, "The Writer's Audience Is Always a Fiction," *PMLA* (January 1975): 9–21.

6. Louis Oliver

1. This is my paraphrase of remarks Joseph Bruchac made before presenting the Louis Littlecoon Oliver Memorial Award at the Returning the Gift Festival held in Norman, Oklahoma, July 1992.

2. I should extend my thanks at this point to Creek writer Helen Chalakee Burgess for allowing me to quote her unpublished essay here.

3. Here I borrow the phrasing from the title of Joy Harjo and Gloria Bird's anthology *Reinventing the Enemy's Language: Contemporary Native Women's Writing of North America* (New York: W. W. Norton, 1997).

4. Louis Littlecoon Oliver, *Chasers of the Sun: Creek Indian Thoughts* (Greenfield Center, N.Y.: Greenfield Review Press, 1990). Hereafter cited in the tet as *Chasers*.

5. Louis Littlecoon Oliver, *Estiyut Omayat* (Muskogee, Okla.: Indian University Press, 1985). Hereafter cited in the text.

6. Louis Littlecoon Oliver, *The Horned Snake* (Merrick, N.Y.: Cross-Cultural Communications, 1982).

7. Louis Littlecoon Oliver, *Caught in a Willow Net: Poems and Stories* (Greenfield Center, N.Y.: Greenfield Review Press, 1983). Hereafter cited in the tet as *Willow Net*.

8. In the process of reading the rough draft of my dissertation, my adviser, Professor Geary Hobson, observed the similarity between Mr. Oliver's account of Creek migration and the way N. Scott Momaday describes the Kiowa's emergence from below the earth through the hollow log in his book *The Way to Rainy Mountain* (Albuquerque: University of New Mexico Press, 1969). The similarity is in the way the two authors understand ancestral memory; Momaday recalls that his living, and passed-on, relatives had undertaken the Kiowa migration from the headwaters of the Yellowstone through the terrain of oral tradition, even though the physical migration occurred in the 1700s, before their lifetimes.

9. Leslie Marmon Silko, *Storyteller* (New York: Seaver Books, 1981), 130–37.

10. Joy Harjo, *The Woman Who Fell from the Sky* (New York: W. W. Norton, 1994). Hereafter cited in the text.

11. Tsianina K. Lomawaima, *They Called It Prairie Light: The Story of Chilocco Indian School* (Lincoln: University of Nebraska Press, 1994). Hereafter cited in the text.

12. Elizabeth Cook-Lynn, "American Indian Intellectualism and the New Indian Story," *American Indian Quarterly* 20, no. 1 (winter 1996): 57–76.

7. Joy Harjo

1. Joy Harjo, *The Last Song* (Las Cruces, N.Mex.: Puerto Del Sol, 1975), *What Moon Drove Me to This* (New York: I. Reed Books, 1980), *She Had Some Horses* (New York: Thunder's Mouth Press, 1983), *Secrets from the Center of the World* (Tuscon: University of Arizona Press, 1989), *In Mad Love and War* (Middletown, Conn: Wesleyan University Press, 1990), *The Woman Who Fell from the Sky* (New York: W. W. Norton, 1995).

2. John Scarry, "Representing Real Worlds: The Evolving Poetry of Joy Harjo," *World Literature Today* (spring 1992): 286–91.

3. Ibid., 290.

4. Geary Hobson, "The Literature of Indian Oklahoma: A Brief History," *World Literature Today* 64, no. 3 (summer 1990). Professor Hobson also made these comments when presenting Harjo with the Lifetime Achievement Award at the Returning the Gift Festival in July 1995 at Norman, Oklahoma.

5. The back cover of either *The Last Song* or *What Moon Drove Me to This?*

6. Howard Adams, *A Tortured People: The Politics of Colonization* (Penticton, B.C.: 1995), 12.

7. Leslie Marmon Silko, *Almanac of the Dead* (New York: Simon and Schuster, 1991).

8. Tsianina K. Lomawaima, *They Called It Prairie Light* (Lincoln: University of Nebraska Press, 1994).

9. Harjo, *The Woman Who Fell from the Sky*, 47. Hereafter cited in the text as *Woman*.

10. Duane Niatum, *Harper's Anthology of Twentieth Century Native American Poetry* (San Francisco: Harper and Row, 1988), 286. I am going to cite the pages for the poem "New Orleans" from Niatum's anthology. This collection is quite a bit easier to find these days than the small-press publication of *She Had Some Horses*. In *Horses*, the poem can be found on pp. 42–44.

11. Niatum, *Harper's Anthology*, 287.

12. Ibid.

13. Michael D. Green, *The Creeks* (New York: Chelsea House Publishers, 1990), 82.

14. Ibid., 83.

15. See the chapter "Muskogee and the English Trade in Slaves and Skins," in Joel Martin's *Sacred Revolt: The Muskogees' Struggle for a New World* (Boston: Beacon Press, 1981), 46–69.

16. Harjo, *In Mad Love and War*, 5. Hereafter cited in the text as *Mad*.

17. Leslie Marmon Silko, *Storyteller* (New York: Seaver Books, 1981), 207.

18. Niatum, *Harper's Anthology*, 294. Harjo's poem also quoted here from Niatum rather than *She Had Some Horses*. The poem is on pp. 14–15 in *Horses*.

19. Charles M. Hudson, *The Southeastern Indians* (Knoxville: University of Tennessee Press, 1976). Hereafter cited in the text.

20. Jack Frederick Kilpatrick and Anna Gritts Kilpatrick, *Muskogean Charm Songs among the Oklahoma Cherokee* (Washington, D.C.: Smithsonian Press, 1967), *Notebook of a Cherokee Shaman* (Washington, D.C.: Smithsonian Press, 1970), *Run toward the Nightland: Magic of the Oklahoma Cherokee* (Dallas, Tex.: Southern Methodist University Press, 1967), *Walk in Your Soul: Love Incantations of the Oklahoma Cherokees* (Dallas, Tex.: Southern Methodist University Press, 1965).

21. Ray A. Young Bear, *Black Eagle Child: The Facepaint Narratives* (Iowa City: University of Iowa Press, 1992).

22. Leslie Marmon Silko, *The Delicacy and Strength of Lace: Letters between Leslie Marmon Silko and James Wright* (Saint Paul, Minn.: Graywolf Press, 1986), 29.

23. Thomas Pynchon, *Gravity's Rainbow* (New York: Viking Press, 1973).

24. Silko, *Storyteller*, 51.

25. This is the first poem in the book immediately after the acknowledgments and before the title page. There is no page number.

26. Jim Nicklin, "Where We're Going Is like This: Harjo's Recreation of the World," student paper for Native lit class at the University of Nebraska at Omaha.

27. Leslie Marmon Silko, *Ceremony* (New York: Viking Press, 1977). See pp. 238–54, esp. 253–54.

28. Martin, *Sacred Revolt*, 48. Hereafter cited in the text.

8. Lynn Riggs as Code Talker

1. Phyliss Cole Braunlich, *Haunted by Home: The Life and Letters of Lynn Riggs* (Norman: University of Oklahoma Press, 1988). Hereafter cited in the text.

2. Lynn Rollie Riggs, *"Russet Mantle" and "The Cherokee Night": Two Plays* (New York: S. French, 1936).

3. Angie Debo, *The Road to Disappearance* (Norman: University of Oklahoma Press, 1941).

4. Riggs, *The Cherokee Night,* 205. Italics mine. Hereafter cited in the text.

5. See, for example, Navajo writer Wesley Thomas's discussion of the origins of this term in the article on Native gay men in the 26 June 1996 issue of the *Village Voice,* in which Thomas recounts the word's derogatory etymology having to do with male prostitution.

Permissions

The University of Minnesota Press gratefully acknowledges permission to reprint the following.

"Alexander Posey," by Louis Littlecoon Oliver, from his book *Estiyut Omayat: Creek Writings* (Muskogee, Okla.: Indian University Press, 1985); permission to reprint granted by Indian University Press, Bacone College, Muskogee, Oklahoma 74403.

Lines from "In Honor of Ya'ha" and "Powers to Be Had," by Louis Littlecoon Oliver, from his book *Chasers of the Sun: Creek Indian Thoughts* (Greenfield Center, N.Y.: Greenfield Review Press, 1990); reprinted by permission of the Greenfield Review Press.

Lines from poems in *The Woman Who Fell from the Sky*, by Joy Harjo (New York: W. W. Norton, 1994); copyright 1994 by Joy Harjo. Reprinted by permission of W. W. Norton & Company, Inc.

"Indian Macho," by Louis Littlecoon Oliver, from his book *Caught in a Willow Net* (Greenfield Center, N.Y.: Greenfield Review Press, 1983); reprinted by permission of the Greenfield Review Press.

Lines from "Deer Dancer," "Song for the Deer," "Javeleina," "Deer Ghost," "Autobiography," "Original Memory," and from pages 1 and 54 of *In Mad Love and War*, by Joy Harjo (Middletown, Conn.: Wesleyan University

Index

Craig S. Womack (Oklahoma Creek–Cherokee) teaches in the Native American Studies department at the University of Lethbridge, Alberta, Canada.